WRITTEN THAT YOU MAY BELIEVE

WRITTEN THAT YOU MAY BELIEVE

Encountering Jesus in the Fourth Gospel

NEW AND EXPANDED EDITION

SANDRA M. SCHNEIDERS

with a Study Guide by
John C. Wronski, S.J.

A Herder & Herder Book
The Crossroad Publishing Company
New York

The Crossroad Publishing Company
481 Eighth Avenue, Suite 1550, New York, NY 10001

Printed in the United States of America

Library of Congress Cataloging-in-Publication Data

Schneiders, Sandra Marie.
    Written that you may believe : encountering Jesus in the fourth Gospel
 / Sandra M. Schneiders. — 2nd ed.
        p. cm.
    Includes bibliographical references and index.
    ISBN 0-8245-1926-4 (alk. paper)
    1. Bible. N.T. John—Criticism, interpretation, etc. 2. Bible. N.T.
John—Feminist criticism. I. Title.
BS2615.52S36 2003
226.5'06—dc21

                                            2003012925

In grateful and loving memory of
my teachers and friends

RAYMOND E. BROWN, S.S.
(1928–1998)

and

EDWARD J. MALATESTA, S.J.
(1932–1998)

... these are written that you may believe that Jesus is the Christ, the Son of God, and that believing you may have life in his name.

—John 20:30

Contents

PART 3
A FEMINIST REEXAMINATION
OF THE AUTHORSHIP OF THE FOURTH GOSPEL

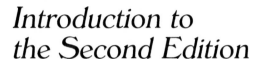

Introduction to
the Second Edition

Since the appearance of the first edition of this work I have been gratified by its enthusiastic reception by the very audience to whom it was primarily addressed, namely, students and educated lay readers seeking an understanding of the mysterious and beautiful Gospel according to John as enrichment for their own spirituality and as a resource for their ministry. Although the text of *Written That You May Believe* has proved challenging for many of its readers, most, apparently, have found it manageable. However, this revised edition now offers readers an excellent support for their study, a detailed study guide prepared by my student and colleague, Mr. John Wronski, S.J., who developed it while taking a course on the Johannine Gospel with me in the fall semester of 2002. His grasp of the material, his pedagogical skill, and his clear written style came together in the creation of a genuinely helpful aid for the reading and appropriation of the text that will help students, Bible study groups, and individual readers working alone on the text. His collaboration has been a pleasure for me as well as a wonderful contribution to the usefulness of the volume.

The other major addition to this new edition is a new chapter on the story of the man born blind in John 9 in relation to the story of the paralyzed man in John 5. The addition of this chapter completes the treatment of the three major texts used by the church in its Lenten preparation of catechumens for the sacraments of initiation, namely, the Samaritan woman, the healing of the blind man, and the raising of Lazarus. Consequently, I hope this new chapter will make the volume more useful for people engaged in ministry, especially in the ministry of sacramental preparation of adults. But John 9 has another important contribution to make to the understanding of the Fourth Gospel. As the new chapter will make clear, the story of the man born blind is a kind of synthesis of the Fourth Gospel's approach to the important religious issue of believing which is at the core of Johannine theology and spirituality. And it supplies resources for reflection on the contemporary issue of how divine initiative and human freedom interact in the journey to discipleship.

I wish to express my sincere appreciation to the many students with whom I have studied this Gospel over the years and whose questions and insights have deepened my appreciation of the Fourth Gospel and helped me see its relevance for Christian faith and life; to my colleagues at the Jesuit School of Theology who discussed the new chapter with me in a faculty colloquium and improved it considerably; to Mr. John Wronski, S.J., already mentioned, who prepared the study guide; to Sister Ray Maria McNamara, RSM, my invaluable research assistant; and to my editor, Mr. John Jones of Crossroad, whose enthusiastic encouragement and careful attention to detail have brought this new edition to completion. My hope is that it will make some contribution to Johannine scholarship, nourish the faith of its readers, and serve as an aid in ministry.

Berkeley, CA
Easter 2003

Acknowledgments

Although we distinguish authorship in the biblical world in which a tradition is shaped by schools or communities and reshaped by successive redactors from modern authorship attributable to a single scholar, all writers know that the actual process of composition, even today, is much closer to the ancient model. One person actually puts fingers to keyboard, but a host of people play a role in the conception of the project and in its actual execution. This book is no exception.

The idea of collecting the articles, essays, and book chapters on the Fourth Gospel that I have written over the past two decades was suggested to me by Michael Leach, then of Crossroad and now at Orbis. I was less than enthusiastic, being instinctively suspicious of republication projects. But when my esteemed colleagues John Donahue, whose judgment is singularly sound on such matters, and Gina Hens-Piazza, who is no friend of the pedestrian, concurred, I had to reconsider the suggestion, and to these three encouraging friends I owe a debt of gratitude as this volume, much expanded in relation to the original idea, goes to press.

In the background of this book stand the two scholars to whom it is dedicated. To Edward Malatesta, who directed my doctoral dissertation on the Fourth Gospel, and to Raymond Brown, who taught me in so many formal and informal ways, I owe far more than I can say. Both of these scholars helped inspire and shape my love of the Johannine Gospel; both modeled for me not only rigorous scholarship but the kind of faith-filled ecclesial commitment that makes such scholarship meaningful; and both became not only mentors but colleagues and friends in the succeeding years. This volume is a small expression of my loving appreciation of their remarkable lives and gratitude for their place in mine.

In a special way this book is a tribute of thanks to my students. In the classrooms of my own institution, the Jesuit School of Theology in the Graduate Theological Union in Berkeley, as well as of numerous colleges and universities at which I have taught the Fourth Gospel during summer schools and as a visiting professor, I have experienced the stimulating interchange around the Gospel text that has made it ever more meaningful to me as I have tried to make it accessible to my students. This scholarly stimulation from full-time students has been augmented by the enthusiasm of thousands of people, ministers of many denominations, women and men religious, and lay believers from many walks of life and various countries who have participated in retreats, workshops, study weeks, and lectures around the text of the Fourth Gospel. To all of these people who have shared with me not only their ideas but their faith I am profoundly grateful.

My work in general, but especially that in Scripture, has been supported both materially and personally by my religious congregation, the Sisters, Servants of the Immaculate Heart of Mary of Monroe, Michigan. I am deeply grateful for that support and for the life we share.

The present historical moment is not the easiest in which to be a Catholic scholar in the sacred sciences, and I am ever aware of the respectful support of Bishop John S. Cummins of the Diocese of Oakland for theological work in general and for mine in particular. His warm friendship, intelligent conversation, and unfailing encouragement are a source of strength and an incentive to service.

Outside the academic arena I have benefited immensely from the support and interest, the encouragement, as well as the informed conversation of many friends who cannot all be named here. But I especially want to thank Constance FitzGerald, O.C.D., Mary Milligan, R.S.H.M., and Kathleen O'Brien, I.H.M., for their participation in my life and work in ways they know and that I treasure.

Finally, my special thanks to my research assistant, Ms. Jan Richardson, whose electronic wizardry, copy-editing skills, and library sleuthing were crucial to the production of this volume; to James LeGrys, my editor at Crossroad, whose care and commitment to the project have been immensely helpful in bringing it to completion; and especially to Maurya Horgan, of The HK Scriptorium, Inc., whose intelligence, biblical scholarship, and editorial care in copy-editing and indexing the book will make it much more useful to readers than it would otherwise have been.

To all these people, living and dead, and others whom I carry in mind and heart, my deepest gratitude for all you have done to make this book better than it would otherwise have been even as I willingly assume responsibility for all that is still wanting in it.

Grateful acknowledgment is offered to the following publishers for permission to use portions or versions of previously published material:

In chapter 5: "Reflections on Commitment in the Gospel According to John," *Biblical Theology Bulletin* 8 (February 1978): 40–48.

In chapter 6: "Women in the Fourth Gospel and the Role of Women in the Contemporary Church," *Biblical Theology Bulletin* 12 (April 1982): 35–45.

In chapter 7: "Born Anew," *Theology Today* 44 (July 1987): 189–96.

In chapter 9: "To See or Not to See: John 9 as a Synthesis of the Theology and Spirituality of Discipleship." In *Word, Theology, and Community in John,* edited by John Painter, R. Alan Culpepper, and Fernando F. Segovia, 189–209. St. Louis: Chalice, 2002.

In chapter 10: "Death in the Community of Eternal Life," *Interpretation* 41 (January 1987): 44–56.

In chapter 11: "The Foot Washing (John 13:1–20): An Experiment in Hermeneutics," *Catholic Biblical Quarterly* 43 (January 1981): 76–92.

In chapter 12: "The Face Veil: A Johannine Sign (John 20:1–10)," *Biblical Theology Bulletin* 8 (July 1983): 94–97.

In chapter 13: "John 20:11–18: The Encounter of the Easter Jesus with Mary Magdalene—A Transformative Feminist Reading." In *What Is John? Readers and Readings of the Fourth Gospel,* edited by Fernando F. Segovia, 155–68. Atlanta: Scholars Press, 1996.

In chapter 14: "John 21:1–14," *Interpretation* 43 (January 1989): 70–75.

In chapter 15: "'Because of the Woman's Testimony . . .': Reexamining the Issue of Authorship in the Fourth Gospel," *New Testament Studies* 44 (1998): 513–35.

Abbreviations

RB	*Revue biblique*
RelS	*Religious Studies*
RevScRel	*Revue des sciences religieuses*
RSV	Revised Standard Version of the Bible
SE	*Studia Evangelica*
SJT	*Scottish Journal of Theology*
SNTS	Society for New Testament Studies
SNTSMS	Society for New Testament Studies Monograph Series
TS	*Theological Studies*
TU	*Texte und Untersuchungen*

Introduction

THE PROJECT

The interpretive chapters that form the main section of this book were all published in some form before they were revised and brought together in this project. However, what unites them is not simply that they are all concerned with symbolic narratives in the Fourth Gospel and were all written by the same author but that they represent a single, particular, and (in a way to be explored later) original approach to the Johannine material. I realized, in rereading the studies prior to revising them, that I have been developing this approach over more than two decades of work on this "spiritual gospel."[1] I actually began to explore its potential in my doctoral dissertation, an exegetically based interpretation of the Johannine resurrection narrative as a synthesis of Johannine spirituality,[2] and it has been operative in everything I have written on this Gospel since then.

Although I have never named this approach, it could be described as an attempt to engage the spirituality of the biblical text through rigorously critical study undertaken in the context of living faith.[3] This approach is not

[1] According to Eusebius (*Historia Ecclesiastica* 6.14.7), Clement of Alexandria in the second century referred to the Gospel of John as "the spiritual gospel." Although the use of this epithet in the history of Johannine commentary has not always been positive, intended at times to suggest that the Gospel was without historical substance, the real significance of the name has stuck for the very good reason that, of the four Gospels, the mystical or unitive character of Christian discipleship is most salient in this Gospel.

[2] Sandra M. Schneiders, *The Johannine Resurrection Narrative: An Exegetical and Theological Study of John 20 as a Synthesis of Johannine Spirituality* (Ann Arbor, Mich.: University Microfilms, 1982).

[3] Bruno Barnhart, in a commentary on John that uses an approach quite similar to mine (*The Good Wine: Reading John from the Center* [New York: Paulist, 1993]), refers to his

1

individualistic, homiletic, or devotional. Rather, it is an engagement of the text which is rooted *simultaneously* and *equally* in the faith of the Christian community, past and present, and in the best critical biblical scholarship of which I am capable or upon which I can draw. This engagement has as its objective to contribute both to the faith life of readers (myself included) and to the ongoing enterprise of biblical scholarship.

At the beginning I had few companions in this enterprise. This lack was the manifestation not simply of a lack of interest in this aspect of biblical work but of a historically understandable suspicion on the part of most serious biblical scholars that any effort to engage the biblical text as Sacred Scripture rather than as a purely historical artifact and record would lead to subjective and distorting "piety" or fantastic medieval allegorization. In some quarters there was also a fear that making manifest the implications of modern scholarship for faith or church life might reactivate official ecclesiastical strictures very recently abrogated.

However, the climate in the biblical academy is slowly shifting. For complex reasons that need not detain us here, both students and their teachers are realizing that studying this text as if it were devoid of contemporary religious significance and/or as if the challenge to the reader that such significance raises were not integral to the meaning of the text itself is to falsify rather than to interpret the text. Furthermore, the intense search for personal meaning and specifically for life-integrating spirituality that has been a marked characteristic of the second half of the twentieth century has led many Christians back to the Bible with an explicit hope for transforming engagement with this foundational text of their faith.

Although in their original form most of the studies that make up parts 2 and 3 of this book were written for biblical colleagues and published in academic journals, I have discovered, in using the material in teaching and in lectures to nonacademic audiences, that solid scholarship need not necessarily render material inaccessible (or uninteresting!) to nonspecialists. With adequate preparation, motivated literate adults, both students and lay readers, can understand and profit from the kind of work that appears in these studies. Consequently, although I hope the gathering of these studies into a single volume will make them accessible to colleagues, my primary intended readership is students and serious believing adults who are willing to take the time and make the effort to enter into the spirituality of the Fourth Gospel in a way that respects the integrity of the text. This involves entering a historical world, that is, the community of the Beloved Disciple, which is dis-

---

approach as "sapiential." The term stems from the monastic tradition of *lectio divina* and captures as well as any I have seen this type of reading.

tant in time and thought from our own; a literary world that is created by this masterpiece of religious writing but is fraught with linguistic challenge; and the spiritual world of mysterious mutual indwelling of Jesus and his disciples that shaped the spirituality of that early community, comes to expression in the text, and is intended to shape the spirituality of the reader.

THE PLAN OF THE BOOK
AND SUGGESTIONS FOR READING IT

In order to provide the necessary background for the nonspecialist reader, part 1 consists of six introductory chapters, which may or may not be of interest to scholars already familiar with the field of Johannine studies. In these chapters I attempt to condense, in relatively nontechnical language, the best current scholarship on the Fourth Gospel in relation to those questions which are pertinent to the themes and texts discussed in the interpretive chapters of parts 2 and 3. While occasionally indicating points of significant disagreement among scholars, these chapters do not intend to describe, much less engage, the endless array of scholarly positions on virtually every aspect of the Johannine text. Consequently, the positions presented necessarily represent my judgment about what is most reliable, credible, and helpful in current Johannine research. The reader is forewarned that there are other positions on almost every topic covered and is invited by means of selected references in the notes and the bibliography to explore further if she or he is intrigued by the questions.

The first three chapters, unlike a traditional introduction to the Gospel, do not constitute a systematic march through the background questions of author, date, place of composition, structure, themes, and so on. Rather, they offer three synthetic treatments of the Fourth Gospel as a whole from three different points of view with the intention of plunging readers into the Johannine world, immersing them in the powerful literary techniques, unique perspective on Jesus, community ethos, theological stance, and spiritual sensibility that pervade this Gospel so that they develop a "feel" for this very different Gospel.

Two suggestions flow from this approach. First, readers will be very well repaid if they take the time, before approaching the studies in parts 2 and 3 of this book, to do an attentive, unhurried reading of the whole of the Fourth Gospel from beginning to end in order to develop a feel for its language, rhythms, themes, characters, and issues, many of which are repeated again and again throughout the Gospel. Second, it would be well worth their while to choose a good commentary on John, to read the "Introduction" section, which will deal in some detail with such questions as date, place, authorship, history of interpretation, and other areas of dispute, and to keep the commentary handy for consultation when they are unsatisfied with the scope or content of my presentation or are curious about the current state of scholarship on an issue.[4]

In chapter 1 I deal, segment by segment, with the Fourth Evangelist's stated intent in writing the Gospel given in its conclusion, John 20:30–31, namely, that it function for the reader as *Sacred Scripture*. This provides the opportunity to present some of the central themes and concerns of the Gospel and to familiarize the reader with some of the vocabulary of Johannine scholarship that will be used in the rest of the book.

In chapter 2 I discuss three topics that help to situate this Gospel as *literature* within the New Testament as a whole, within its own historical setting, and theologically. In discussing the uniqueness of the Gospel of John in relation to the other three Gospels I take up first its particular content, structure, and language. Special attention is given to the last category, the very striking linguistic features of John which contribute both to the difficulty some people encounter in reading this Gospel and to its immense power to engage the deepest spiritual dynamics of the reader. Second, I take up the pervasive influence in the Fourth Gospel of the composition and historical setting of the community out of which this Gospel emerged. Third, I briefly indicate certain theological traits that characterize the Gospel, which are taken up in greater detail in the third chapter.

Chapter 3 is devoted to the *theology and spirituality* of the Fourth Gospel. It is organized around two central categories, revelation (the relationship between Jesus and his disciples) and the continuation of that relationship throughout history after the return of Jesus to God on the cross (resurrection, the Paraclete, and community).

After these introductory chapters, intended to situate the reader in the world of the Fourth Gospel, come three global chapters on general themes in

---

[4] A few commentaries that could be useful are the following: John Ashton, *Understanding the Fourth Gospel* (Oxford: Clarendon Press, 1991); C. K. Barrett, *The Gospel According to St. John*, 2nd ed. (London: SPCK, 1978); Raymond E. Brown, *The Gospel According to John*, 2 vols., Anchor Bible 29, 29A (Garden City, N.Y.: Doubleday, 1966, 1970); Robert Kysar, *John*, Augsburg Commentary on the New Testament (Minneapolis: Augsburg, 1986); Francis J. Moloney, *The Gospel of John*, Sacra Pagina Series (Collegeville, Minn.: Liturgical Press, 1998); Mark W. G. Stibbe, *John, Readings: A New Biblical Commentary* (Sheffield: JSOT Press, 1993); Pheme Perkins, *The Gospel According to St. John: A Theological Commentary* (Chicago: Franciscan Herald Press, 1978); Charles H. Talbert, *Reading John: A Literary and Theological Commentary on the Fourth Gospel and the Johannine Epistles* (London: SPCK, 1992).

John: symbolism and sacramentalism, the role of women, and commitment within Johannine spirituality.

Part 2, which is the heart of the book, is devoted to interpretive studies of seven symbolic narratives of encounter between Jesus and his actual or potential disciples, two from the public life of Jesus, one from the transition from the public life to the passion, one from the passion itself, and three from the period of the resurrection. All of these interpretations embody the interdisciplinary method I have proposed as most effective for transformative reading of the text, and in most of the chapters I make explicit the method I am using in hopes of helping readers not only understand and appropriate the interpretation in question but also learn how to approach biblical texts in general.

The interdisciplinary approach, which will be seen in each chapter, involves historical criticism, literary criticism, theological analysis, and ideology criticism from a feminist perspective. Historical-critical questions bear on such issues as the concerns of the Johannine community to which the pericope responds, the agenda of the evangelist insofar as this can be discerned, the tradition history of the pericope, and the relation of the pericope to historical facts. Literary criticism involves a very close reading of the text with attention to structure, vocabulary, form, and rhetoric as these function to engage the reader at the level of faith. Theological analysis is especially concerned with situating the pericope under discussion within the theological framework of the Gospel as a whole and in relation to the Old Testament, which is a kind of background music running through the whole Gospel. Finally, there is a continuous concern to detect and expose gender bias in the text and/or the history of interpretation and to highlight the liberating potential of the text, especially when it has been blunted or veiled by patriarchal interpretation.

In the last chapter, which constitutes part 3, I present a hypothesis about the authorship of the Fourth Gospel which synthesizes much of the foregoing material in relation to one of the knottiest problems in Johannine scholarship while attempting to open the imagination of readers to new dimensions of discipleship.

Anyone who reads the chapters in order will be aware of the repetition of themes and motifs. For example, I return in almost every chapter to the hermeneutical key to the Gospel, John 20:30–31, in which the evangelist states the purpose and intention of the Gospel; to the important difference between sign and symbol and the crucial revelatory function of Jesus' symbolic actions in the Gospel; to the notion of representative figures who occur in all of the pericopes studied. It is hoped that this continuous circling back over familiar material will gradually habituate the reader to look for and to recognize the techniques and concerns of the Gospel as she or he studies other sections of the Gospel not dealt with in this book.

SOME WRITING CONVENTIONS

In order to avoid an overload of scholarly apparatus that might discourage potential readers at the outset, I have deliberately kept notes in the first three chapters to a minimum and thereafter have relegated to the notes material that would be of interest more to scholars than to general readers. Where notes are used, they indicate direct dependence on a source that requires acknowledgment, supply the necessary data for a work mentioned in the text, or offer supplementary bibliography on a major topic for those with more scholarly interests. The bibliography and index of scriptural citations can assist such readers to pursue topics treated in the text.

Occasionally I supply the Greek for a particular translation or interpretation because it is the only or at least the best way to make the point at issue, but the Greek is either transliterated into English letters so the reader can pronounce the terms or/and translated so that the meaning will be clear even for those who do not have Greek at their command.

Throughout the text I use various accepted terms to speak about the agent(s) involved in the production of the Fourth Gospel, a topic with which we will deal in detail in the final chapter. However, for purposes of introduction, the Fourth Evangelist is considered to be the individual who actually composed the Gospel of John. This evangelist's identity has never been deciphered, but this person's name was, in all likelihood, not John. In particular, scholars are almost unanimous in holding that the Fourth Evangelist was not John the son of Zebedee, one of the twelve disciples whom the other evangelists call "apostles." The Fourth Evangelist, furthermore, is not identical with the Beloved Disciple, who was, in all probability, an eyewitness companion of the earthly Jesus but not one of the Twelve. It is the Jesus tradition (the gospel) as remembered, interpreted, and transmitted by the Beloved Disciple that was authoritative for the Johannine community and was the basis of the written Gospel. Consequently, the terms *John, Johannine, Gospel of John,* and so on should not be taken to mean that there was someone named John involved in the foundation or formation of the community or in the writing of the Fourth Gospel. It is simply convenient language for denoting this Gospel, which has traditionally been entitled the Gospel according to John.

With these few suggestions and signposts I invite you, the reader, to enter, with reverent anticipation and even excitement, into the richly mysterious world of the Fourth Gospel.

Part 1

Entering the World
of the Fourth Gospel

1

The Fourth Gospel as Sacred Scripture

The approach to Sacred Scripture briefly described in the Introduction is actually the very approach that the Fourth Evangelist explicitly encourages in the conclusion of the Gospel. The evangelist ends the Gospel[1] with these words:

> Now Jesus did many other signs in the presence of his disciples, which are not written in this book. But these are written that you may come [or may continue] to believe that Jesus is the Messiah [or Christ], the Son of God, and that through believing you may have life in his name. (John 20:30–31)[2]

Let us unpack this very important text by way of introducing the approach characteristic of the studies in this book.

The Gospel Is Selective and Unique

First, the evangelist acknowledges the existence of "many other signs" which Jesus did that are not included in the Fourth Gospel. John's Gospel, by its own admission, is one "take" on the much larger Jesus tradition, which

---

[1] The Gospel as we have it has twenty-one chapters, but chapter 21 has long been regarded by scholars as an "epilogue" added after the death of the Beloved Disciple either by the evangelist or a later redactor. Consequently, the conclusion in John 20:30–31 seems to have been the original conclusion of the Gospel before the addition of the final chapter, which ends with a very similar conclusion, probably written in imitation of 20:30–31.

[2] Unless otherwise noted, biblical texts are cited from the New Revised Standard Version (NRSV). The material in brackets indicates another reading of the text that is well supported by the Greek and/or adds some nuance that is helpful for understanding the fullness of its meaning.

included many miracles, especially exorcisms, that are not included in this Gospel. This suggests that the evangelist has both a project and a point of view, that is, an approach to the Jesus tradition that is unique. It leads the evangelist not only to include some things and forgo including others but also to arrange the selected material in a particular order and to emphasize certain aspects of the tradition, certain discourses and events from the life of Jesus, while minimizing or excluding others. It is therefore very important for a fruitful reading of this Gospel to get into its spirit and not to conflate it with the Synoptics, whose "take" on the Jesus tradition is very different. On the other hand, however, it is important to read John in relation to the Synoptics precisely because the Fourth Evangelist does not include everything, and slants what is included in a particular way.

The Text Is the Locus of Revelatory Encounter

The "other signs" (and we should take this term broadly to include all that Jesus said and did) not recorded were done "in the presence of his disciples." In other words, they were part of the earthly life of Jesus and helped form his first followers into disciples. But in the mind of the evangelist those not recorded are not crucial for later disciples, however much we might want to know everything about Jesus. Rather, *only* those things that "are written" in the Gospel, and *as* they are written in the Gospel, are necessary and sufficient for later disciples, who will come to believe through their reading (or hearing) of the text and thus become and remain disciples of Jesus just as truly as his first disciples. This is very important because it locates the revelatory encounter with God in Jesus, not in one's experience of the words and actions of the earthly Jesus (which was available only to a few followers in first-century Palestine) but in the engagement with the Gospel text (which is open to all people of all time). Revelation is *rooted* in the life of Jesus in Palestine in the first century. But it *occurs* in the faith life of believers in the community shaped by the text of scripture.

The Text Is Written for Its Contemporary Readers

The evangelist then goes on to say that "these [events and words of Jesus] are written" to bring "you," that is, the reader, to believe. In other words, the Gospel, which undoubtedly served a purpose in the Johannine community of the second century, has in view primarily those who would encounter it later, namely, readers who had not been part of the life of the earthly Jesus or of the Johannine community. We are not assigned to try to extract from recalcitrant ancient materials historical information that can then be remolded into religiously significant material for contemporary faith. We are not, in other words, eavesdropping on a past conversation or spying on an ancient community of which we are not a part. The Gospel was written *for us*. And it addresses itself to us, not primarily as scholars or historians but precisely as *readers*. While scholarly historical-critical work is crucial for the church's understanding of the background of the sacred text, it is primarily in the literary experience of reading (or hearing), of allowing ourselves to get caught up in the Jesus-story that is being told, that we are drawn into the salvific revelation dynamic.[3]

Beginning with the work of the "redaction critics" in the 1970s and 1980s, who focused on the theological content of the Gospels as it was differently manifested in both the content and style of each evangelist,[4] biblical scholars have paid increasing attention to the literary character of the Gospel text: its structure, rhetoric, narrative modes, literary features such as irony and symbolism, and the way in which the literature as literature mediates meaning. The Fourth Gospel fits well into this development because of its insistence on the interaction between written text and reader or hearer as the locus of revelatory encounter.

The Purpose of the Encounter:
That You May Believe

The purpose of the encounter between reader and text, according to John, is "that you may believe." In this Gospel, as we will see later in more detail, the noun "faith" never occurs. John always uses the verb "to believe," because the interaction between Jesus the teacher and his disciples is never something acquired, achieved, possessed. It is an ongoing relationship that either incessantly deepens or ceases. It is a friendship, a love relationship, which cannot

---

[3] This is the burden of an important book by Gail R. O'Day, *Revelation in the Fourth Gospel: Narrative Mode and Theological Claim* (Philadelphia: Fortress, 1986).

[4] For a good overview of the development in this century of literary approaches to the New Testament, see the preface by Amos Niven Wilder in his *Jesus' Parables and the War of Myths: Essays on Imagination in the Scriptures*, ed. James Breech (Philadelphia: Fortress, 1982), 15–38. See John R. Donahue, "Redaction Criticism: Has the *Hauptstrasse* Become a *Sackgasse?*" in *The New Literary Criticism and the New Testament*, ed. Edgar V. McKnight and Elizabeth Struthers Malbon (Valley Forge, Pa.: Trinity, 1994), 27–57, for a history of the development and present state of redaction criticism and a useful bibliography on the subject.

remain static without stagnating. This suggests that reading the Gospel, by which we engage in this relationship, is not a once-for-all action. The Gospel is meant to mediate, facilitate, nourish this relationship, and therefore reading it must be an ongoing activity. As friends or lovers do not cease to talk, even when they have communicated all the "news," so Jesus and his disciples are involved in an ongoing dialogue mediated by the Gospel text the way letters and phone calls mediate the conversation between physically separated friends. The evangelist presumes that we will read and reread the Gospel. And "reader response critics"[5] tell us that every time we reread a text we change our relationship with it, precisely because we have been formed by our previous reading.

The Object of Believing:
Jesus Who Is Messiah and Son of God

What the evangelist intends us to believe is not historical facts about the earthly Jesus but "that Jesus is the Messiah, the Son of God." This is supremely important. It is the succinct statement of the identity of Jesus according to the Fourth Gospel. Jesus is the Messiah, the expected savior of Israel, a radical position that not only caused a painful and bitter separation between the Johannine community of the late first century and the Jewish community from which many members of John's community came, but it also situates Jesus within the revelation tradition of ancient Israel as both a product of and the ultimate fulfillment of that tradition. The Johannine Jesus cannot be understood apart from the Hebrew Scriptures, which formed his religious imagination and schooled his faith and spirituality. But the Hebrew Scriptures, for John, have become the Old Testament, that is, the living background of a new revelation in Jesus, and can only be properly understood in terms of Jesus.

The Johannine Jesus is not only the Messiah or Christ but also the Son of God. By the time the Fourth Gospel was written, around 100 C.E., the Christian church had become a faith community distinct from Judaism and had

---

[5] A somewhat difficult treatment of reader-oriented biblical criticism that is, nonetheless, well worth the effort it requires is Edgar V. McKnight, *Post-Modern Use of the Bible: The Emergence of Reader-Oriented Criticism* (Nashville: Abingdon, 1988). It includes a selected but helpful bibliography. A much briefer treatment is McKnight's essay "Reader-Response Criticism," in *To Each Its Own Meaning: An Introduction to Biblical Criticisms and Their Application,* ed. Stephen R. Haynes and Steven L. McKenzie (Louisville, Ky.: Westminster/John Knox, 1993), 198–219.

come to believe that Jesus was truly and fully divine.[6] It would take another
two to three centuries for the church to elaborate, in the categories of Greek
philosophy, what came to be called the doctrine of the Trinity, that is, three
divine persons (Father, Son, and Holy Spirit) in one divine nature (God).[7]
But the seeds of that very important theological development are found, in
the most explicit form of any of the New Testament writings, in John's
Gospel.

For the Fourth Evangelist Jesus is the personal manifestation of God in this
world. In Jesus, according to this Gospel, the Word of God, holy Sophia or
Wisdom in the Old Testament, through whom and in whom God created all
things, became incarnate (John 1:14). The gospel is the story of Jesus' living
out of this divine-human identity. The invitation as well as the challenge to
discipleship is to believe that Jesus is who he says he is, the Son of the one
God who sent him, the one in whom that divine Sender is seen and known.
"Whoever has seen me has seen the Father" (John 14:9), Jesus claims, because
"the Father and I are one" (John 10:30).

The Gospel ends with Thomas proclaiming, in the name of all who will
read this Gospel and come to believe, "My Lord and my God" (John 20:28).
This confession of fully Christian faith is accepted by Jesus not only from
Thomas, one of the original eyewitnesses of the earthly Jesus, but from all disciples of all time: "Blessed are those who have not seen and yet have come to
believe" (John 20:29). Coming to know who Jesus is, accepting who he is in
himself and for us, is the very essence of discipleship according to the Fourth
Gospel. "Knowing" in John is not merely intellectual assent to some propo-
sitional truth. It is personal affective commitment and self-donation to the
Truth incarnate. It carries all the interpersonal resonance that it does in the
Old Testament, where it is used for sexually expressed union between lovers.
For this Gospel, which actually contains no explicit moral commandments
such as we find in Matthew's version of the Sermon on the Mount (see
Matthew 5–7), all salvation lies in the relationship of the disciple to Jesus, the
abiding in Jesus that expresses itself in love of all those whom Jesus loves.

---

[6] For a very nuanced discussion of how early Christian christological faith developed and
culminated in the incarnational theology of the Fourth Gospel, see James D. G. Dunn, *Christology in the Making: A New Testament Inquiry into the Origins of the Doctrine of the Incarnation* (Philadelphia: Westminster, 1980), esp. chapter 7, on "The Word of God," pp. 213–50,
and the summary and conclusion, pp. 251–68.

[7] The doctrinal formulation of the mystery of the Trinity emerged from the Council of
Nicaea (325 C.E.) in the Nicene Creed, whose primary purpose was to affirm the divinity of
the Son. It was further developed at the Council of Constantinople (381) with the addition of
explicit affirmation of the equality of the Holy Spirit with the Father and the Son. Finally, the
doctrine was fully formulated at the Council of Chalcedon (451).

The Fruit of Believing:
That You May Have Life in His Name

The fruit of believing in Jesus is "that you may have life" (John 20:31). In John's Gospel, life, usually qualified by the word "eternal," is a central category. Jesus, who lives by the divine life of God, was sent by God into this world to give eternal life to all who believe in him (see John 6:47; 17:2; and elsewhere). This divine life, already enjoyed by believers in this world, makes them children of God (see John 1:12–13),[8] brothers and sisters of Jesus (see John 20:17), who can call Jesus' God and Father their own God and Father. It makes the disciples living branches of Jesus, the true Vine (see John 15:1–11). It makes them participants, even now, in the life shared by Jesus and God in the Holy Spirit (see John 14:18–26). And this divine life is so real, so powerful, that it will triumph over the death of the disciple as it triumphed over the death of Jesus, who proclaims: "I am the resurrection and life. Those who believe in me, even though they die, will live, and everyone who lives and believes in me will never die" (John 11:25–26). The eternal life that those who believe in Jesus begin to live now will carry them beyond physical death because it is already a real participation in the infinite life of God.

The life of God that the believer enjoys is life "in his name," that is, in Jesus' name. This is a phrase that opens upon the deep mystery of the mutual indwelling of God, Jesus, and his disciples through the gift of the Holy Spirit. In the Old Testament the name of God was so sacred that it was never pronounced. To know someone's name was to have some kind of power, either dominative power such as a master might have over a slave or the power of intimacy as a friend or lover might have with the beloved, in relation to that person. When Moses asked God's name at the theophany of the burning bush, God replied only "I am who I am" or "I am who I shall be" (Exod. 3:14)—in other words, "None of your business." God alone knows the divine identity. Thus, the Jewish "name" for God, יהוה (*Yhwh*), is an unpronounceable symbol for the One who is completely beyond human knowing, naming, or control.

In John's Gospel Jesus not only knows God's name (see 17:12) but uses it as his own. Jesus' claim to have God as his Father (see John 5:18) and to be himself the great "I am" (e.g., John 4:26; 8:58) leads his enemies to seek to

---

[8] It is interesting, and important, that John does not use the Pauline notion of adoption to talk of the Christian's filiation. John says that, to all who believe in Jesus' name, Jesus gives the right or power to become τέκνα θεοῦ (*tekna theou*), literally, "children of God." They are "born of God" (John 1:12).

kill him because they recognize it as a claim to "equality with God" (see John 5:18; 8:59). Jesus not only knows God's name and uses it for himself but makes it known to his disciples (see John 17:6) precisely in order to assimilate them to himself in the Father's love: "I made your [God's] name known to them [the disciples], and I will make it known, so that the love with which you have loved me may be in them, and I in them" (John 17:26).

Once Jesus has completed the work that the Father has given him to do, he can claim that his disciples, who from the beginning belonged to God and whom he had kept in God's name while he was on earth, have now been given by God to him (see John 17:6–8, 12, 23) to receive life in his name.

Consequently, when the evangelist says that the whole point of the Gospel is that its readers may have life in Jesus' name, he is explicitly applying to future readers what Jesus asks of God in his final prayer before his glorification on the cross:

> I ask not only on behalf of these [the disciples present at the Last Supper], but also on behalf of those who will believe in me through their word [all future disciples who will read the gospel] that they may all be one. As you, Father, are in me and I in you, may they also be in us, so that the world may believe that you have sent me. The glory that you have given me I have given them, so that they may be one, as we are one, I in them and you in me, that they may become completely one, so that the world may know that you have sent me and have loved them even as you have loved me. Father, I desire that those also, whom you have given me, may be with me where I am, to see my glory, which you have given me because you loved me before the foundation of the world. (John 17:20–24)

In this passage is summed up the whole message of the Gospel. Its point is to bring those who contemplate the Gospel into a union with Jesus which will plunge them into the depths of God's very life, the life Jesus shares with his Father. There is no question that the purpose of the Gospel is the mystical union of the disciples with Jesus in God through the Spirit.

INTERPRETATION FOR TRANSFORMATION

If this is the purpose of the Gospel, then the appropriate approach to the text is one that seeks to achieve this purpose. I said in the Introduction that the approach I have taken to the Gospel is "in some sense" original. In fact, it is actually in substantial continuity with the approach to scripture that characterized the first fifteen centuries of Christian history. What makes it original is not its objective of allowing the biblical text to function as Sacred Scripture for the reader, that is, as a mediation of the encounter between God and the believer in the dynamic of revelation.[9] Nor is it original in its commitment to critical rigor, which characterized the work of all the great patristic and medieval commentators, who used all the scholarly methods available to them. It is original only in that this objective must now be pursued in the wake of the development of modern critical scholarship from which there can be no retreat even as we modify some of its most extreme developments.

The history of biblical interpretation is not the point of this volume, or even of this chapter. However, some awareness of how biblical interpretation, which began as an effort to hear and respond to the Word of God, became a strictly academic pursuit of historical knowledge that regards any personal involvement of the reader with the subject matter of the text as, at best, a distraction and, at worst, a failure in academic rigor will clarify both why, on the one hand, a reappropriation of the spirituality approach is necessary and why, on the other hand, it cannot consist in a simple return to pre-Enlightenment methods.

Premodern Biblical Interpretation: Reading for Transformation

The type of reading that has personal and communal transformation as its ultimate purpose, what I might call a biblical spirituality approach, was actually the type of reading that was characteristic of the patristic and medieval periods of church history.[10] The fathers of the church—that is, the first Christian theologians, notably Origen and Augustine—developed a theory of the biblical text modeled on the mystery of the incarnation and a theory of interpretation that corresponded to their theory of the text.[11] They believed

---

[9] A good, brief history of interpretation of the Bible is Robert Grant and David Tracy, *A Short History of the Interpretation of the Bible*, 2nd ed., revised and enlarged (Philadelphia: Fortress, 1984). A more detailed study of patristic and medieval approaches to the Bible is Beryl Smalley, *The Study of the Bible in the Middle Ages* (Notre Dame, Ind.: University of Notre Dame Press, 1964).

[10] For a brief overview of the development of biblical spirituality, see Sandra M. Schneiders, "Scripture and Spirituality," in *Christian Spirituality: Origins to the Twelfth Century*, ed. Bernard McGinn and John Meyendorff, World Spirituality: An Encyclopedic History of the Religious Quest (New York: Crossroad, 1985), 1–20. David C. Steinmetz, in an important article, "The Superiority of Pre-Critical Exegesis," *Theology Today* 37 (1980): 27–38, argues that the multiple-sense theory of scripture of the early and medieval scholars was actually more true to the nature of the text than the single-sense theory of historical criticism even if the actual practice of precritical scholars was not as sophisticated as modern scholarship.

[11] Origen's classic treatment of the interpretation of scripture is book 4 of his *De Principiis*,

that just as Jesus' divinity is mediated by his real bodily humanity so in the biblical text the Word of God is mediated by human language. Consequently, for them the text had at least two senses,[12] one historical or "literal" (what the text says about facts, events, persons, etc.) and the other spiritual or "allegorical" (what the text means morally, theologically, or eschatologically).[13]

Although these early interpreters in their search for the spiritual meaning sometimes departed so far from the historical sense that modern exegetes find their interpretations farfetched or fanciful, these ancient interpreters actually took the exegetical task very seriously and never believed that the reader could or should evade the arduous task of discerning the literal sense before moving on to the spiritual sense. But these early readers would have found a modern, purely exegetical approach that never got beyond the literal or historical sense truncated and pointless. It would amount to carefully preparing and combining the ingredients of a delicious meal and then failing to cook and eat it.

The approach to reading the Bible that corresponded to this theory of the text was a four-step process that proceeded from *lectio*, or careful, meditative reading of the text, to *meditatio,* which involved deep rumination on the meaning, to *oratio,* or personal response in prayer to what had been understood, to *contemplatio,* in which the reader surrendered to the action of the Spirit drawing her or him into the divine mystery through the meaning of the text.[14]

---

in which he insists on the use of all the scholarly techniques available in his day. It is available in critical English translation as "On First Principles," in *Origen,* trans. by Rowan A. Greer, with a preface by Hans Urs von Balthasar, Classics of Western Spirituality (New York: Paulist, 1979), 171–216.

Augustine's work on the same subject is his *De Doctrina Christiana,* which is available in English translation as *On Christian Doctrine,* trans. D. W. Robertson, Jr. (New York: Macmillan, 1958). In this work Augustine says that there are two things necessary to the treatment of the scriptures: "a way of discovering those things which are to be understood, and a way of teaching what we have learned" (p. 7). Discovering is the work of study, using all available resources.

[12] For a brief explanation of the theory of the multiple senses of scripture, see Sandra M. Schneiders, "Senses of Scripture," in *The HarperCollins Encyclopedia of Catholicism,* ed. Richard P. McBrien (New York: HarperCollins, 1995), 1175–76. A much more detailed treatment can be found in Grant and Tracy, *A Short History,* especially in chapters 5–7.

[13] The ancients used the term "allegory" to cover all more-than-literal senses of language, including symbol and metaphor. Consequently, much of what they called allegorical interpretation would be what we today would regard as appropriate attention to the actual meaning of the text as it is conveyed by symbolic and metaphorical use of language.

[14] The two locales in which biblical study was done in the Middle Ages were the monastery and the university. In the former *meditatio* often meant interior repetition, "rumination" over

The process involved, at least in the university setting, the kind of serious exegetical study with which moderns are familiar, even though the ancients and medievals lacked many of our more sophisticated critical tools. For the scholar the study of the text, then as now, demanded knowledge of the biblical languages, textual criticism, historical criticism, and literary and theological analysis of content. But these earlier interpreters also recognized that the biblical message was intended not only for the scholar but for all the people of God. It was, therefore, the task of educated preachers to make the exegetical results of scholarship available to the community. The volumes of homilies by many of the fathers and medieval theologians, which contain lengthy, continuous expositions of whole books of both testaments, witness to the seriousness with which they regarded that duty. All, whether specialist or lay, were expected to meditate on the text, either through their own scholarship or by using that of scholars and preachers. Biblical literacy was considered a *sine qua non* for the serious Christian of any walk of life.

Modern Biblical Interpretation: Exegesis for Information

This integrated approach to biblical reading began to disintegrate in the high Middle Ages as biblical scholarship moved from the monastery schools into the great universities. The unified synthesis of learning rooted in scripture study and crowned by theology began to be divided into distinct sciences, each with its own object and method. This laid the foundation for eventually regarding biblical study as a specialized discipline concerned primarily with the historical investigation of the reliability of the biblical text in relation to the events it purported to describe while assigning to theologians the task of determining the meaning of what was historically ascertained and to pastors the task of finding the relevance of that meaning to the life of believers. It also inaugurated the movement toward the proof-text use of scripture as theology was gradually uprooted from its biblical grounding and replanted in philosophical soil.

The Reformation in the sixteenth century, which fractured the western church, also challenged the authority of the church and its tradition in bibli-

---

the text being considered. In more academic environments study in the sense in which we understand the word was integral to the process. Study might consist primarily in listening to the exposition of the text by a learned teacher or preacher or the actual work of personal study for those equipped to do it. But the point is not which word, *lectio* or *meditatio*, covered which process but that intellectual engagement with the text by all available means was integral to but not the only component of the process of interpretation.

cal interpretation. The defensive reaction of the Catholic Church, which sought to preserve orthodox interpretation by reserving it to clerical specialists, alienated ordinary believers from direct contact with the scriptures. Thus, the living *context* of biblical interpretation was subverted from the Protestant side, while living *contact* with the biblical text was restricted from the Catholic side.

As a result of many factors in intellectual history, the Enlightenment, which began in the seventeenth century, signaled the definitive demise of the unified system of faith, thought, and social organization that had been at least the ideal and to some extent the reality in the western world from the triumph of Christianity in the fourth century until the Protestant Reformation. In the academic world, theology was dethroned from its controlling position as queen of the sciences and critical reason replaced faith as the norm of truth. The pursuit of critically established, mathematically certain, experimentally verifiable, true knowledge led, in virtually every sphere of investigation, to ever more refined specialization. The Renaissance ideal of education as a synthetic, universal grasp of all things in their principles gave way to the ideal of analytical knowledge of ever smaller units which could be exhaustively investigated. Scholars became specialists in restricted areas, which they controlled with an exactitude and rigor never before imagined but which they were increasingly unable to relate to other areas of knowledge, much less to the whole of knowledge.

In biblical studies this gave rise to what came to be called "the higher criticism," the philological, historical, anthropological, social, and literary analysis of texts in order to obtain the best possible answer to what was considered the prime question about the biblical text, namely, how exact was the correspondence between what the text said and what actually happened. The higher criticism became, in effect, historical criticism.

Although this development led to an astounding increase in our actual knowledge of the Bible, its origins, its content, and its meaning for the people to whom it was originally addressed, it also produced some less desirable effects with which we struggle today. As scholars specialized ever more rigorously, few were able to attend to the Bible as a whole (and often they were not interested in doing so), to its relevance for faith, or to the communication of the results of scholarship to ordinary believers. These tasks were assigned to religious professionals such as pastors or catechists who were generally not taken seriously as scholars. The gap between scholars and pastors and the estrangement of ordinary believers from both the text itself and the best biblical scholarship (which they were increasingly unequipped to follow), not only deprived the faithful of the fruits of academic work on the biblical text but led to increasing religious and theological sterility of academic work on the Bible.

In the wake of two World Wars, the Second Vatican Council, the social cataclysm of the 1960s, the electronic revolution, and other developments, major changes began to occur in society, church, and the academy that have, in many ways, begun to undermine certain features of the Enlightenment.[15] The overspecialization in rigorously defined areas of study is being balanced by an interdisciplinarity that is broadening the focus of scholars. Students are increasingly interested not just in facts, information, and marketable skills but in meaning, the significance of what they are studying for their lives and the world that is falling apart (or perhaps being reborn) all around them.

My attempt to use the best critical methods of biblical scholarship not simply to increase piecemeal information about the text and its historical referents but to allow the message and method of the biblical text to influence its readers in spiritually transformative ways flows from this development. The Enlightenment espousal of critical reason and its application to biblical studies cannot be simply repudiated, much less reversed. But it must be combined with, indeed integrated into and transformed by, an agenda of spiritual transformation that is both personal and communal, aimed at both the holiness of the reader and the fostering of the reign of God in this world. Meaning in and for the present must take precedence over, without undermining or ignoring, knowledge of the past. Historical questions and methods must be integrated with contemporary literary, sociological, and theological concerns and methods. And the critique of ideology that has developed in the wake of twentieth-century experiences of hegemonic domination, whether racial, ethnic, sexual, cultural, or economic, requires serious engagement of the liberationist agenda, particularly the feminist agenda, which is permeating postmodern consciousness.

THE APPROACH OPERATIVE IN THIS BOOK

The approach that is operative in the studies of John's Gospel presented in this volume is, therefore, a reappropriation of a more global project that has a long tradition but which virtually disappeared from the academic horizon during the past three centuries. However, it is a reappropriation that rejects none of the advances of modern critical biblical scholarship developed dur-

---

[15] This phenomenon is often referred to as "postmodernism," a complex cultural transition the discussion of which is beyond the scope of this chapter.

ing those centuries. On the contrary, it affirms the absolute necessity of solid, multidisciplinary, ideologically sophisticated exegesis as the basis for interpretation.

The approach I am using involves four operations whose importance in the interpretation of particular passages may vary but none of which may be ignored. First (not necessarily in importance or time), is *historical* interrogation of the text. The text must be correctly translated and its vocabulary and grammar properly assessed. It must be situated in the context of first-century Christianity and specifically in that of the Johannine community. If there are crucial questions about the historicity or factuality of what is recounted, they must be addressed. The sources and evidence of redaction need to be examined. It is not mandatory to deal with every historical question that can be raised about a text. Since the number of such questions is virtually infinite, the answer to one giving rise to a plethora of further questions whose importance is often minimal, the interpreter has to decide which historical questions must be answered and which can be left aside.

Second, and perhaps most important in the critical work of interpreting the passage, is *literary* criticism of the text. The term "literary" covers an enormous range of questions. The text must be situated in the literary context of the Fourth Gospel, the four Gospels, the New Testament as a whole, and the Bible. Its structure, special vocabulary, and narrative or rhetorical features must be examined. The operation in the text of such literary devices as symbolism, irony, double-meaning expressions, and repetition, as well as structural and stylistic features such as rhythm, inclusion, and parallelism must be studied. The genre of the passage, such as miracle or revelatory discourse, must be discerned, since the genre shapes the traditional or original material in particular ways. Author and reader work together in construing the meaning of the text, and the text in all its literary specificity is the script that governs that interaction. Consequently, the analysis of the text as text—that is, as a literary entity—is extremely important.

Third, the text must be analyzed for its *theological* content. The theological construction of the evangelist is our primary ingress into the transformative meaning of the text. What people (including Jesus' first disciples and the earliest Christian communities) experience with God comes to expression in many ways: personal prayer, liturgy, community interaction, and action in the world. But when it is explicitly thematized and taught, it is usually formulated and expressed theologically. Consequently, to discern the spirituality, that is, the religious experience, that gave rise to and comes to expression in a particular text usually involves going "through" its theological interpretation and formulation. The great contribution of redaction criticism to contemporary biblical interpretation is that it called attention to the theological agenda of each of the evangelists and thus sensitized us to the presence and overwhelming importance of theology in the creation of and in the understanding of the biblical texts.

Finally, the culmination and fruit of the interpretive project is the engagement of the transformative potential of the text, that is, the appropriation of its *spirituality.* What possibilities for an enriched faith life does this text open for the reader?

It will be clear from the foregoing that I am invoking the now-familiar categories of the world "behind," the world "of," and the world "in front of" the text.[16] Historical interrogation investigates the world behind the text, not in the sense of a historical reality chronologically or causally anterior to the text (which is actually a point of convergence of a variety of contemporaneous forces), but in the sense of conditions of possibility of a text emerging at this point in time and in this place. Literary and theological analyses investigate the text as it stands, both in terms of what it is saying (theologically) and how it is saying it (literarily). Finally, attention to the spirituality of the text attends to the life possibilities that the text opens out before the reader, the faith reality or world of commitment into which the reader is invited.

These operations are not necessarily successive, and they are not all equally important in every interpretive project. Historical interrogation, for example, may reveal that historical questions are of minor importance in a particular case. Also, literary and theological examinations may coincide. Finally, other types of interrogation may become particularly important in regard to given texts, for example, the history of its interpretation, ideological distortion or exploitation of certain texts, or the role some texts have played in the liturgical or mystical tradition. The important point is that, in an adequate and integral interpretation of the text, none of the four basic operations can be bypassed.

In the next chapter I will attempt to supply a minimum of background information about the Gospel's historical setting and to explain briefly how this Gospel functions as a literary text in order to equip the reader to deal with the first two operations. In chapter 3 I will lay out a synthesis of Johannine theology and spirituality in order to facilitate the third and fourth operations. The hope is that this material will enable the reader to understand and appreciate the interpretive chapters in part 2.

---

[16] I have delved into this schema at full length in my book *The Revelatory Text: Interpreting the New Testament as Sacred Scripture,* 2nd ed. (Collegeville, Minn.: Liturgical Press, 1999).

2

The Fourth Gospel as Text

The Gospel of John has always been distinguished from the other three (Matthew, Mark, and Luke) by the fact that, whereas they are "synoptic," that is, they strongly resemble each other in viewpoint, content, and order of their narratives, and often in the very language they use, John is strikingly different. Unlike the Synoptic authors, who tell the story of the earthly Jesus to lead readers to the realization that this man is more than a mere human being, the Fourth Evangelist writes from a heavenly or divine viewpoint, beginning with the preexistence of the Word of God, who becomes human in Jesus, and placing on the lips of Jesus a divine discourse, which he claims to have directly from God. This gives the Fourth Gospel not only a distinctive tone but a very different content, structure, and language.

In order to get a feel for this difference before considering it in enough detail to prepare for the chapters that follow, I suggest that the reader of this book stop at this point and take the time for an unhurried and meditative reading of the Fourth Gospel from beginning to end. This will recall, or introduce, some of the Johannine passages that do not occur in the Synoptics; get the typical Johannine vocabulary "into the ear" of the reader; introduce into the imagination the striking symbols and images that are crucial to understanding the Johannine approach to Jesus; and introduce the cast of characters which, in this Gospel, includes a number who do not appear in the Synoptics and gives a very different picture of some who do, while not mentioning some who play a role in the other Gospels.

The reader will notice that John's Gospel omits some very familiar episodes from the Synoptic Gospels such as the birth of Jesus, his baptism, his temptations in the desert, stories of Jesus expelling demons, parables, the "institution narrative" at the Last Supper, the agony in the garden, and some of the resurrection stories. On the other hand, it includes a number of passages that have no Synoptic parallels, such as several intense and prolonged encounters between Jesus and individual characters including Nicodemus,

the Samaritan woman, Martha and Mary at the grave of Lazarus, Mary Magdalene at the tomb, Thomas the Twin, and Simon Peter on the shore of the
Sea of Tiberias after the resurrection; a number of long, highly theological,
mystically oriented discourses of Jesus; a very limited number of miracles
most of which do not occur in the other Gospels, for example, the story of
the water made wine at Cana, the cure of the paralytic at the pool of Bethzatha, the story of the man born blind, the raising of Lazarus; as well as episodes
that are not recounted by the Synoptics, such as Jesus' conversations with his
first disciples, the foot washing, the scene between the dying Jesus and his
mother and the Beloved Disciple at the foot of the cross, and the story of
"doubting Thomas."

Reading the Gospel from beginning to end, rather than in the form of isolated texts as they are presented in the liturgy, will consolidate the sense of
John's uniqueness, which I want now to describe in some detail in order to
highlight important features of the text that will influence interpretation.

Content

As just mentioned, John recounts events (e.g., the story of the Samaritan
woman in chap. 4) that do not occur in the other Gospels, and he omits
many events (such as exorcisms) that play a major role in the Synoptics.
Although John and the Synoptics share some events (such as the feeding of
the multitude and the death of Jesus), John's account of these events is usually strikingly different. In John, for example, Jesus' crucifixion is not his ultimate humiliation or *kenōsis* but his ultimate "exaltation," which changes the
meaning of the resurrection in the Fourth Gospel from the triumphant vindication of the humiliated one to the intimate return of Jesus to his own.
Even the order of the life of Jesus is quite different. There is no birth narrative in John at all; Jesus' "agony" takes place not in the Garden of Olives
before his death but in public before the beginning of the passion (in John
12:27–34); Jesus cleanses the temple in Jerusalem at the beginning rather
than at the end of his life, thereby giving the episode a very different meaning and function in the narrative.

Structure

Although John, like the Synoptics, intends to tell the story of Jesus, the
Fourth Evangelist's version is less a quasi-biographical story[1] than a narrative

---

[1] For a succinct discussion of and bibliography on the literary form of the Gospels and their
reflection, to some extent, of the genre of Greco-Roman popular biography, see Larry W.

drama. Scholars continue to debate the structure of John, some suggesting that it is a forensic or trial drama, others that it is concentric or chiastic in structure, others that it is organized as symbolic "weeks" of symbolic "days," and some that it is a combination of such structures.

Virtually all scholars agree that it has a basic textual structure: a prologue (1:1–18), a body (1:19–20:31), and an epilogue (chap. 21). For many decades it has been customary to regard the body of the Gospel as divided into two parts, a "book of signs" (chaps. 1–12) and a "book of glory" (chaps. 13–20). This division reflects the clear literary break between the first twelve chapters, which recount Jesus' public life, including his miracles, which in John are called "signs," and the last eight (or nine) chapters, beginning with the Last Supper in chapter 13, which recount the passion and resurrection. In the first part Jesus refers repeatedly to his "hour" which is coming; beginning in chapter 13 he talks about his "hour" which has now come. Jesus' hour, which is the passion and resurrection, is called glorification in John. Hence, the naming of the first part the book of signs (or miracles) and the second part the book of glory (or the paschal mystery).

This division is convenient as a structural marker, but it is increasingly called into question theologically since, while all Jesus' miracles are signs, it is not at all clear that all his signs are miracles. In fact, Jesus' greatest sign would seem to be his glorification on the cross, which occurs not in the first part but in the second. The reason scholars struggle over the issue of structure is because the way a literary work is put together both determines to some extent what it means and communicates that meaning to the reader.

It is probably true, and more useful, to say that there are several structures, overlapping and interrelated, holding this Gospel together and moving it forward, depending on how one looks at it. Just as we might analyze a film in terms of the relationships among the characters, or the relation between the main character's flashbacks and present experience, or as a gay film or a woman's film or both simultaneously—and all of these structures and motifs might interact—so with John. Each structure, if indeed a valid case can be made for its presence and operation, allows the reader to see different aspects of the Gospel in a clearer light.

It is possible, for example, to read John as a trial narrative[2] in which the world puts Jesus on trial and Jesus puts the world on trial until, in the glorification of Jesus, the Paraclete or Advocate (a lawyer-like persona John gives

---

Hurtado, "Gospel (Genre)," in *Dictionary of Jesus and the Gospels*, ed. Joel B. Green and Scot McKnight (Downers Grove, Ill.: InterVarsity, 1992), 276–82.

[2] E.g., A. E. Harvey, *Jesus on Trial: A Study in the Fourth Gospel* (Atlanta: John Knox Press, 1976).

to the Spirit) eventually convicts the world of sin and exonerates Jesus as Son. It is also possible to see the Gospel as a sequence of dramatic personal encounters between Jesus and individuals who typify all who accept or refuse Jesus' offer of life.[3] From another point of view the Gospel appears as a "new creation" of six symbolic "days," after which Jesus rests in the tomb on the "seventh day" before inaugurating the transcendent "eighth day," which is simultaneously the resurrection of Jesus, the beginning of the new eschatological era, and the day of the church's eucharistic participation in Jesus' paschal mystery.[4] It is equally possible to see the Gospel as a concentric or "mandala"-type structure centered on a new exodus, which takes place when Jesus, the new Moses, walks on the water after the feeding of the multitude, thus giving the whole Gospel a certain meaning as the inauguration of a new Israel, which must make a definitive choice for Jesus just as the ancient Israelites had to choose life in the desert.[5] The Gospel also seems to be structured by the use of the bride-bridegroom symbolism of the Canticle of Canticles, which emphasizes the covenant character of the relationship between Jesus, the true bridegroom pointed out by John the baptizer and the community of believers who are "given" to Jesus by God as a bride to her husband. These are not the only possible structural motifs, but they suffice to show why attention to structure is important and how rich this Gospel is from a literary standpoint. To choose one against all the others is actually an unnecessary impoverishment of one's reading.

Language

The most striking characteristic of John's Gospel is perhaps the way the evangelist uses language. By language here I mean not just the words used (although, as we will see, John's characteristic vocabulary is a very significant

---

[3] Raymond E. Brown discusses some of the extraordinary "encounter stories" in John in *A Retreat with John the Evangelist: That You May Have Life* (Cincinnati: St. Anthony Messenger, 1998), 41–54.

[4] This theory that John is organized according to symbolic days was originally proposed by M.-E. Boismard in *Du baptême à Cana (Jean 1,19–2,11)*, Lectio Divina (Paris: Cerf, 1956) and was taken up and developed by P. Van Diemen in "La semaine inaugurale et la semaine terminale de l'évangile de Jean: Message et structures" (doctoral diss., Rome, 1972). A similar thesis has been integrated with changes into a basically chiastic/mandalic structure by Bruno Barnhart in *The Good Wine: Reading John from the Center* (New York: Paulist, 1993).

[5] The most thoroughgoing example of this approach is Peter F. Ellis, *The Genius of John: A Composition-Critical Commentary on the Fourth Gospel* (Collegeville, Minn.: Liturgical Press, 1984). Ellis's work has been taken up and modified in terms of the mandala by Barnhart, *Good Wine*.

feature) but all the linguistic features such as rhetoric (in both senses: stylistic and persuasive),[6] literary devices such as cyclical development and repetition, double meaning, literal misunderstandings, irony, parallelism, paradox
and dialectic, symbolism, and so on. John's superbly effective and highly
charged use of language makes the Gospel not only singularly rich but also
very dense. It seems deceptively easy to read (in Greek as well as in translation!) until one suddenly realizes that what is being proposed through the
"simple" language is earth-shaking in its implications. What does it mean to
say that one person "dwells in" another? For Jesus to claim to have existed in
God's glory "before the world was made"? That he gives "living water"? That
he is "bread of life" to be eaten? That he will raise his followers on the last day?
The power and density of the Fourth Gospel's language have driven some
people away from the text to the more manageable categories and story line
of the Synoptics. But for those willing to immerse themselves contemplatively in the Johannine text, the artistry of the Gospel will draw them into the
mystery of divine union. It is well to be prepared, however, for what one will
encounter.

Vocabulary. The Johannine vocabulary might be characterized as "concretely abstract." It is remarkably simple. Surprisingly, this is clearer in English
than in Greek because in English almost all the pivotal terms in the Fourth
Gospel are one-syllable, everyday words that no one needs to look up in a dictionary: life, death, love, hate, light, dark, see, hear, speak, know, seek, truth,
one, in, dwell, believe, sign, work, word, glory, kill, rise, son, father, born,
child, come, go, send, eat, drink, bread, water, world, where, name, joy, sin,
hour, I am, peace. All of these very simple words are quasi-technical terms in
the Fourth Gospel whose meaning is gradually built up over the course of the
narrative until, by the end, they are charged with an astounding depth of
meaning.

This vocabulary is concrete in that everyone knows what the words mean,
but abstract in that the words carry whole realms of significance that must be

---

[6] The term "rhetoric" or "rhetorical" can refer either to the art of composition or to the art
of persuasion, that is, the techniques by which a discourse seeks to achieve its end. Both understandings have their proponents in the biblical academy today. For an introduction to the sub-
field of rhetorical criticism, see Phyllis Trible, *Rhetorical Criticism: Context, Method, and the
Book of Jonah* (Minneapolis: Fortress, 1994), especially chapters 1 and 2, pp. 5–52; Yehoshua
Gitay, "Rhetorical Criticism," in *To Each Its Own Meaning: An Introduction to Biblical Criticisms and Their Application*, ed. Stephen R. Haynes and Steven L. McKenzie (Louisville, Ky.:
Westminster/John Knox, 1993), 135–49; C. Clifton Black, "Rhetorical Criticism," in *Hearing the New Testament: Strategies for Interpretation*, ed. Joel Green (Grand Rapids: Eerdmans,
1995), 256–77. All of these contain bibliographies for further study.

arrived at and deepened by life experience and thus are simultaneously universal and highly personal. Even a small child, for example, knows the difference between her doll and her dog, namely, that the dog is alive and the doll
is "make believe." But how much more does the word "life" mean to the adolescent who advises a fixated companion to "get a life," or to the parents who
watch helplessly as the bright future of their child ebbs away in deadly dis-
ease, or to the couple celebrating their golden wedding anniversary who can
say to each other, "You are my life." It is largely because of this powerful
vocabulary that it has been said that the Fourth Gospel is a body of water in
which a child can wade and an elephant can swim, that is, that even the sim-
plest reader can understand it at one level whereas its meaning continues to
deepen the longer one deals with it.

Cyclical repetition. A second linguistic feature of the Gospel that mediates
meaning to the reader is its cyclical repetitive quality, which some commentators have called its spiral quality. The attentive reader will quickly realize
that she or he is hearing the same ideas, even the same expressions, over and
over throughout the Gospel. Sometimes the repetition is within a single passage such as

> In the BEGINNING was the WORD
> And the WORD was with GOD
> And the WORD was GOD.
> He was in the BEGINNING with GOD. (1:2)

Sometimes it is in the form of an *inclusio*, in which the same words,
thoughts, or motifs occur at the beginning and at the end of a passage or section, thus both unifying the passage and calling the reader's attention to its
real meaning. For example, in the prologue we are told that Jesus came to give
the power to become children of God to those who believe in him (see 1:12)
and at the end of the Gospel, when Jesus appears to Mary Magdalene after
his glorification, he tells her: to "Go to my brothers and sisters," and tell them
that "my Father" is now "their Father" (see 20:17). The purpose of Jesus' life
and paschal mystery is succinctly indicated: to give divine life as children of
God to human beings. The entire Gospel is also enclosed in the great *inclusio* between "The Word was God . . . became flesh, and dwelt among us" (1:1,
14) and the final confession of Thomas, "My Lord and my God" (20:28),
which tell the reader unambiguously who Jesus is: God for and with us.

Sometimes the repetition occurs throughout the Gospel in various contexts. For example, the theme of seeking begins in 1:38, when Jesus asks the
two disciples of John the baptizer who followed him, "What do you seek?" It

continues throughout the Gospel as people seek Jesus for the right reasons (like the first disciples), for the wrong reasons (see 6:26, where Jesus accuses those who follow him after the multiplication of the loaves of seeking him in order to satisfy their physical hunger), even to kill him (see 5:18), until Mary Magdalene hears the initial question repeated differently in the garden of the resurrection, "Woman, why are you weeping? Whom do you seek?" (20:15). By this point the reader has been thoroughly steeped in the significance of the theme of seeking Jesus and notes that the opening question to the first disciples, "*What* do you seek?" has now become focused on the person of Jesus, "*Whom* do you seek?" The reader has gone through the transformation from simple religious seeker investigating Jesus among other possibilities to Christian disciple whose spiritual seeking has found its final home in Jesus.

The cyclical repetition in the Fourth Gospel is like a spiral staircase that takes the reader up higher, down deeper, passing again and again the same familiar points, giving an ever clearer and richer view of the One who stands in the center. But each time, because of previous encounters with the words, ideas, and themes, the reader is deeper into the mystery of Jesus and more able to appreciate the meaning. Above all, the reader is, as one commentator has said, always standing contemplatively before the figure of Jesus.[7] One moves, but does not really move, as one is repeatedly brought back to the place of encounter. This is a text that the writer intends the reader to read, reread, and read again. And each time the work will be new because the reader is being educated by the text, initiated into a mystery that deepens as one participates in it.

Destabilizing literary techniques. John's Gospel is rife with techniques designed to destabilize the reader's conventional religious knowledge and commitments: double meanings, literal misunderstandings, irony, paradox, and dialectical tensions.

Double-meaning expressions in John (such as *pneuma,* which can mean "spirit" or "wind"; *anōthen,* which can be "again," "anew," or "from above"; *nyx* and *skotia,* which can be "night" or spiritual darkness/sin; *hypsoō,* which can mean "exalted in glory" or "lifted up" as on the cross; *paradidomai,* which can mean "given" or "handed over" in the sense of betrayed) are sometimes explained by the evangelist. For example, in 2:19–22 where Jesus says to the Jewish authorities who protest his action in the temple, "Destroy this temple and in three days I will raise it up," the evangelist explains that the temple of

---

[7] Barnabas Lindars, "The Fourth Gospel an Act of Contemplation," in *Studies in the Fourth Gospel,* ed. F. L. Cross (London: Mowbray, 1957), 23–35.

which Jesus was speaking was "his body," which he would raise up in his resurrection. Jesus' use of a second meaning for temple occasioned a typical
Johannine *misunderstanding*. The Jewish authorities immediately take his
statement literally and declare incredulously that it took forty-six years to
build the temple Jesus promised to rebuild in three days. In this case, the misunderstanding is cleared up not for Jesus' immediate interlocutors but for his
disciples, who, after the resurrection, "remembered that he had said this" and
believed in Jesus and the scriptures. And the evangelist clarifies it for later disciples who read the account.

There is also a touch of *irony* in this episode, when the authorities, irate at
Jesus' expulsion of the money changers, demand that he show a "sign" that
would establish his authority. The sign, ironically, is the very prophetic action
Jesus is performing which they do not understand, but which the reader
understands through a kind of literary "wink" by the evangelist, who makes
the obtuseness of the authorities perfectly clear. Jesus compounds the irony,
seeming to accede to their demand, by offering another sign, the rebuilding
of the temple in three days, which they also misunderstand.

The purpose of irony is both to mock and discredit the victim and to create a community of understanding among those who are "in the know."[8] The
richest text for experiencing Johannine irony is chapter 9, the story of the
man born blind. The Pharisees, insisting arrogantly that "we know" who is
sent by God and who is a sinner, repeatedly say the "right thing for the wrong
reason," digging themselves deeper into stubborn, real ignorance as their
"ignorant" victim, the healed blind man, works his way into the light. They
challenge him to "give the glory to God" by denouncing Jesus while he is, in
fact, giving glory to God by confessing Jesus. When they contemptuously say
they "do not know where this man [Jesus] is from" (meaning he has no credentials) they ironically condemn themselves because salvation consists precisely in knowing Jesus' true origin, namely, God. The blind man, with
feigned ignorance that is deliciously ironic, marvels at their lack of knowledge
and, while professing to know nothing himself about complicated theological questions like sin, in which they are, of course, the experts, he draws
exactly the right conclusion from the sign, namely, that Jesus comes from
God. The whole ironic drama comes to a climax when Jesus says that he has
come so that the blind might see and the seeing become blind and the Phar-

---

[8] For a full-scale study of irony in the Fourth Gospel, see Paul D. Duke, *Irony in the Fourth
Gospel* (Atlanta: John Knox, 1985). A very good brief treatment can be found in Gail R.
O'Day, *Revelation in the Fourth Gospel: Narrative Mode and Theological Claim* (Philadelphia:
Fortress, 1986), especially chapter 1, "The Essence and Function of Irony."

isees, suspecting he is targeting them, protest, "Surely we are not blind, are we?" Jesus replies that if they were, that is, if they were simply ignorant, they would be capable of salvation but that because they insist that they know they are impervious to revelation. The reader, like the blind man, moves through the story catching on at each point that Jesus' enemies are saying what they do not understand and failing to understand what they are saying. The irony discredits the pseudo-wise, who think they know, while building a community of the truly wise, who know that they do not know and are thus open to Jesus' self-disclosure.

This story also provides examples of *paradox,* or seemingly contradictory indications, in which the truth lies hidden. The argument between the healed man and the Pharisees is over Jesus' identity. The Pharisees insist that one non-negotiable indication that a person is from God is fidelity to the law of Moses which forbids work (such as healing) on the sabbath. They conclude that since Jesus broke the sabbath and is therefore a sinner he cannot be "from God" without making God's law self-contradictory. Theologically this seems a perfectly valid argument. The healed man agrees in principle and resigns on the question of whether Jesus sinned (which gives the reader a clue to the flaw in the Pharisees' argument). But he then proceeds to draw the opposite conclusion about Jesus: Jesus comes from God, credentialed by the very Moses who gave the law and whose own credentials from God were not his sinlessness but the signs he did by God's power in Egypt. The reader is caught up in the paradox that the very requirement God has established, namely, obedience to the law, is leading its adherents into unbelief, while breaking the law seems to be a sign of doing God's will. This involves the reader in the thorny question of authority, which is central to the Fourth Gospel: Moses or Jesus? The law or the gospel? Human knowledge or divine revelation?

Dialectic is akin to paradox in that it presents the reader with apparently irreconcilable claims that challenge her or him to transcend the available options and embrace a new truth.[9] For example, when Jesus' disciples ask whether the man was born blind because of his own sin or that of his parents Jesus rejects the notion that physical handicaps are the result of sin: "Neither this man nor his parents sinned." But in 5:2–15, after Jesus cures the paralyzed man by the pool of Bethzatha, he warns him to sin no more "so that

---

[9] C. K. Barrett, in a seminal article, "The Dialectical Theology of St. John," in *New Testament Essays* (London: SPCK, 1972), 49–69, proposed the theory that John's theology was essentially dialectical. Most recently the thesis has been taken up and exploited by Paul Anderson in *The Christology of the Fourth Gospel: Its Unity and Disunity in the Light of John 6* (Valley Forge, Pa.: Trinity, 1996).

nothing worse happens to you," implying that the man's paralysis was due to his sin. What is the reader to make of the two stories? The first thing the dialectic does is destabilize our commonsense convictions. The relationship between disability and sin cannot be reduced to either "sin causes disability" or "there is no causal relationship between sin and disability." It calls for a much more nuanced theology.

Another example of dialectical theology is Johannine eschatology. Jesus declares that anyone who believes in him has eternal life in the present and will never die (see 11:25), but he also promises to raise up on the last day (implying that they have died and need to be raised) those who already have eternal life, symbolized in their eating and drinking his flesh and blood (see 6:54). One is forced to ask what relationship there is between the "realized eschatology" that seems to preclude death altogether and the "final eschatology" that seems to presume that the believers do indeed die.

Even more difficult to hold simultaneously are such statements as "the Father and I are one" (10:30) with "the Father is greater than I" (14:28), or "no one comes to the Father except through me" (14:6) with "no one can come to me unless drawn by the Father who sent me" (6:44; see also 6:65).

The purpose of these techniques is not to confuse the reader or to demonstrate the cleverness of the evangelist. It is strictly theological and spiritual. Salvation in John consists in coming to share in the divine life that Jesus has from God. The way in which we come to share in that life, that is, to become disciples of Jesus and children of God, is captured by the central theological category, revelation, which we will examine in chapter 3. Revelation, the encounter between the witnessing Jesus and the believing disciple, cannot take place unless the potential believer can be shaken loose from the convictions, the verities, the prejudices, the commonsense assumptions that constitute our everyday "knowledge." The purpose of the literary techniques discussed above (and others such as wordplays and rhetorical questions) is to destabilize, to subvert, to undermine that knowledge so that the reader becomes vulnerable to revelation, open to considering the "unheard of" that comes to us in Jesus. Consequently, learning how to recognize and respond to these techniques is crucial to learning how to read the Fourth Gospel for personal and communal transformation.

Representative Figures

One of the striking features of John's Gospel, in contrast to the Synoptics, is that the Johannine Jesus almost always deals not with crowds or groups but with individuals.[10] In this respect John uses the convention of Greek drama which requires that only two characters be "on stage" at a time. Even when Jesus' interlocutor is plural in John, the "group" is usually a single voice, more like the Greek chorus expressing a particular point of view or idea necessary for the audience's understanding. For example, the two angels at the tomb of Jesus speak as one, "Woman, why are you weeping?" (20:13).

The individuals with whom Jesus engages are strikingly well-drawn, rounded figures. We get to know them as people. Simon Peter, Nathanael, Nicodemus, the Samaritan woman, the paralytic at the pool, the man born blind, Martha, Mary of Bethany, Judas, Mary Magdalene, Thomas the doubter, and others are all characters so well developed that the reader identifies with them. This is the intention of the evangelist. The New Testament scholar Raymond Collins coined the phrase "representative figures" for these Johannine personalities,[11] and many scholars have accepted his theory. I would go a bit further and call them "symbolic figures."

The evangelist does not invent these characters out of whole cloth but develops them by both using and transcending their historical identity. Most of them are familiar to us from the Synoptic tradition, suggesting that they were real people who associated with Jesus during his earthly lifetime. But the evangelist focuses their identity and intensifies it, often by stressing one or a collection of traits to the exclusion of everything else, in order to turn the character into a symbolic carrier of a particular feature of relationship with Jesus. For example, Judas in John is the very incarnation of the ultimate evil of unbelief. Nathanael is the "true Israelite" without guile in contrast to "the Jews" who refuse the truth.[12] The Samaritan woman, the royal official, and the man born blind (all of whom, significantly, are "nameless" so that the reader will insert her or his own name) are symbolic presentations of the journey, by a "heretic," a Gentile, and a Jew respectively, to believing in Jesus. Thomas, who is a mere name in the Synoptic Gospels, appears in three scenes in John, symboling the eager and generous disciple of Jesus who must (and does) accept the new type of relationship with Jesus that must be that of the postglorification disciple, believing without seeing the historical signs of the

---

[10] The major exception to this rule is John 6, the Johannine version of the feeding of the multitude. It is interesting that this is one of the very few clear Johannine parallels to the Synoptics.

[11] Raymond F. Collins, "The Representative Figures in the Fourth Gospel," *DRev* 94 (1976): 26–46, 118–32.

[12] The problem with John's use of "the Jews" in this negative sense will be dealt with below.

earthly Jesus but relying on the ever-active testimony of the believing community, now incarnated in the text of the Gospel.

By identifying, positively or negatively, with these symbolic figures, the reader of John is educated in believing. She or he learns both what to do and what not to do in relation to Jesus. Essentially, the mother of Jesus gives the principle, "Do whatever he [Jesus] tells you" (2:5). But how that must work itself out in relation to Jesus' self-revelation, religious authority, community life, and so on we learn from these symbolic characters, who embody the dynamic.

Old Testament Allusions

An enlightening paradox of John's Gospel is that its bitter polemic against "the Jews" occurs in a text that is extremely rich in Old Testament references. This paradox is enlightening because it tells us that the object of the polemic was not Israel, which was God's chosen people; nor Judaism as a religious tradition, which was as dear to John's community as it was to Jesus himself; nor Jews, of whom Jesus was one, but all those who reject the light that Yahweh, the One God, had sent into the world in the person of Jesus.

At the time this Gospel was written, around 100 C.E., the definitive break between the synagogue and the originally Jewish sect whose followers came to be called "Christians" was occurring, and, like any intrafamilial conflict, the struggle was intense and the bitterness on both sides vitriolic at times. Consequently, the real, historical Jewish authorities who were persecuting the Johannine community as some of them had persecuted Jesus are turned by the evangelist into the symbolic carrier of the mystery of unbelief and violent rejection of Jesus. John refers to the religious authorities with which his community is in bitter conflict as "the Jews" the way Catholics often refer to Vatican officials, especially when the latter are acting violently toward members of Christ, as "the Church." In both cases it is not the people of God but certain hierarchs in the institution who are called by the name of the whole community.

Unfortunately, throughout succeeding centuries Christian readers of the Gospel who knew nothing of the historical situation of John's Gospel took the term "the Jews" literally as applying to all the Jews of Jesus' time (which is absurd, since Jesus, his mother, his immediate followers, and many in the Johannine community were Jews) and of later centuries and concluded that since Jesus was in conflict with these people so must Christians be. The horrendous result of this total misunderstanding, which has led to centuries of Christian persecution of Jews, reached its nadir in the Nazi Holocaust, and it is incumbent on all who read, pray, teach, or preach the Gospel of John to do their utmost to combat this misunderstanding and inculcate in themselves and others the love and respect for Judaism and its adherents that Jesus himself, a faithful Jew, always had.[13]

The evangelist's love for the Jewish Scriptures, as well as the principle that Jesus is the hermeneutical key to their meaning (see 5:39), is clear. But unlike the Synoptics, who frequently cite Old Testament passages verbatim (e.g., Matt. 2:6, 18; 3:3; 4:6, 15–16, etc.) John rarely cites but usually alludes to Old Testament themes, motifs, events, characters, or even collations of texts without citing exactly.[14] Only the reader who is as steeped in the Hebrew Scriptures as were the evangelist and the Johannine community will really pick up most of these allusions. But to miss them is to miss the real depth of the Gospel itself.

For example, the first four chapters of John contain numerous evocations of the nuptial theme of the covenant relationship between Yahweh and Israel that runs through the Old Testament, especially in the prophets Jeremiah, Ezekiel, and Hosea, and culminates in the Canticle of Canticles. The theme is now applied to Jesus, the divine spouse, and the new Israel, his beloved. John the baptizer points Jesus out as the "one who has the bride" (3:29); the chief steward at the wedding feast inadvertently identifies Jesus as the true bridegroom who sets forth the good wine in the end time (see 2:9–10); the whole of the story of the Samaritan woman in John 4 is laced with nuptial imagery. This theme will reach its climax in the resurrection narrative of Jesus' appearance to Mary Magdalene, in which the exchange of names, "Mary . . . Rabbouni (which means Teacher)" (20:16) expresses the new covenant union between Jesus and the symbolic representative of the Johannine community.

Scholars have pointed out the ubiquity in John of the themes of the new

---

[13] Some useful resources for understanding the problem of John's presentation of "the Jews" are the following: Urban C. von Wahlde, "The Johannine 'Jews': A Critical Survey," *NTS* 28 (1982): 33–60; Judith Plaskow, "Anti-Judaism in Feminist Christian Interpretation," in *Searching the Scriptures*, vol. 1, *A Feminist Introduction*, ed. Elisabeth Schüssler Fiorenza, with Shelly Matthews (New York: Crossroad, 1993), 117–29; Rosemary Radford Ruether, "Christology and Jewish-Christian Relations," in *To Change the World: Christology and Cultural Criticism* (New York: Crossroad, 1981), 31–43; James E. Leibig, "John and 'the Jews': Theological Antisemitism in the Fourth Gospel," *JES* 20 (1983): 209–34; George M. Smiga, *Pain and Polemic: Anti-Judaism in the Gospels* (New York: Paulist, 1992), chapter 4 on John; Norman A. Beck, *Mature Christianity in the 21st Century: The Recognition and Repudiation of the Anti-Jewish Polemic of the New Testament*, expanded and revised ed. (New York: Crossroad, 1994), chapter 9 on John.

[14] The classic study of this issue is Edwin D. Freed, *Old Testament Quotations in the Gospel of John*, NovTSup 11 (Leiden: E. J. Brill, 1965).

creation, new covenant, and new Israel. Jesus is presented in myriad ways as
the new Moses, who feeds the people in the wilderness, gives the new law of
love, and above all incarnates the presence of God among the people as light
of the world. A major motif of the Fourth Gospel is that Jesus replaces for
Christians the law, temple, sabbath, and feasts with himself.

Because, unfortunately, many contemporary readers of the Gospel are not
as steeped in the Old Testament as were our forebears in the faith, it is important to use commentaries in studying this Gospel so that one does not miss
this important "background music," which, like the soundtrack in a film,
often forms and guides the sensibility of the reader in ways that deepen and
clarify the explicit text. Gradually, as one immerses oneself in the text, these
themes and motifs become more familiar and the reader more sensitized to
their presence.

Symbolism

The most important literary-theological feature of John's Gospel is symbolism. Since chapter 4 will be devoted to this topic I will not discuss it here
except to say that this Gospel does not merely *contain* symbols; it *is* itself symbolic. In John the great symbol of God is the Word made flesh, that is, Jesus.
The Gospel is the literary symbol of Jesus, that is, the "place" of our
encounter with him and through him with God, just as his humanity and
earthly activity were the place of encounter with God for his first disciples.
Understanding what a symbol is and how symbols function is crucial to
understanding John's Gospel.

The most important misunderstanding to avoid is thinking of symbol as
a "stand-in" for an absent reality, like an exit arrow standing for a door that is
both something and somewhere else. The symbol does not stand for an
absent reality; it is a way of being present of something that cannot be otherwise expressed. The best example of symbol in the strong sense, as it functions
in John's Gospel, is our own bodies. The body and its self-symbolizations in
words and acts and other such extensions are the sensible dimension of the
present person, that which creates and offers a place of encounter between the
person and all other reality, both personal and nonpersonal. The body makes
the person present, active, intersubjectively available.

Symbols in John all originate with and derive from the great symbol of
God, Jesus. In Jesus, God becomes present, active, intersubjectively involved
with us. Jesus generates symbols of himself: his works and words, which he
calls not miracles but "signs" in the very sense in which I am here using the

term "symbol."[15] These "signs" (i.e., symbols), such as the feeding of the multitude, the enlightening of the blind man, and the raising of Lazarus, in turn reveal Jesus' identity in symbolic terms including bread of life, light of the world, resurrection and life. Finally, after the "departure" of Jesus, the evangelist created a text, the Gospel, which becomes, with such symbols as baptism and Eucharist, the symbolic medium of the encounter between later disciples and Jesus. As long as the Gospel is among us, the evangelist claims, Jesus himself is present, active, available to us. And furthermore, we are at no disadvantage in relation to Jesus' first disciples. Those who believed because they "saw" are equally blessed with those who do not see but "hear." In both cases revelation is mediated symbolically. What the flesh of the earthly Jesus was to his first disciples the text of the Gospel is to his later disciples. In this sense, all disciples are "first generation." All encounter Jesus directly in and through his symbolic self-offering. What differs is not what is mediated, namely, Jesus; nor how it is mediated, that is, symbolically. What differs is the symbolic "material," which, in one case, is the earthly life of Jesus and, in the other, the text which is written that we may believe.

THE JOHANNINE COMMUNITY
AND ITS SETTING

Background Data

Understanding the Fourth Gospel is greatly facilitated by some familiarity with its setting and with the original community out of which it arose. Today, because of the work of Johannine scholars from Rudolf Bultmann to Raymond Brown and others of this century, we know a great deal more about the provenance of this Gospel than did our ancestors.[16]

The Gospel of John was written, in all likelihood, sometime between 90 and 110 C.E. We derive the earlier date from the fact that there are references in the Gospel to Jews being persecuted and even excommunicated from the

---

[15] This is a bit confusing because modern language uses "sign" for that which is other than the signified, whereas symbol is a way of being present, not a stand-in for what is absent.

[16] Rudolf Bultmann's great commentary on John (1941), *The Gospel of John: A Commentary,* trans. George R. Beasley-Murray (Oxford: Blackwell, 1971) was the work that initiated modern critical study of the Fourth Gospel and remains a touchstone for all subsequent work.

Raymond E. Brown, *The Gospel According to John,* 2 vols., Anchor Bible 29, 29A (Garden City, N.Y.: Doubleday, 1966, 1970) is the "gold standard" of modern scholarship.

synagogue because of their belief in Jesus (see 9:34; 12:42; 16:2). This did not happen until sometime after the fall of Jerusalem in 70 C.E., the subsequent relocation of the authoritative Jewish sanhedrin to Jamnia, and the provision, around 90 C.E., for Jews who confessed Jesus as Messiah to be cut off from the Jewish community. The latter date derives from the fact that fragments of John's Gospel dating from about 135 C.E. were found in Egypt,[17] which means that the Gospel had to have been written before that date and some time allowed for it to be taken from its place of composition (probably Palestine or Asia Minor) to Egypt and copied there.

This dating makes John the last of the four Gospels to be written and raises the question of its relationship to the Synoptics.[18] Every possible hypothesis about this relationship has been proposed and explored in the course of Johannine scholarship: that the Fourth Evangelist knew and used the Synoptics; knew but did not use them; did not know or use them. It has even been suggested that John was written to correct what the Fourth Evangelist saw as inadequacies in the other Gospels.

No one has solved this riddle to the general satisfaction of scholars, but a reasonable hypothesis might be the following: that the Fourth Evangelist was familiar with a tradition like that from which the Synoptics worked. In other words, the Fourth Evangelist knew the basic tradition about Jesus as it eventually appeared in the other Gospels. But just as Matthew and Luke each had "special material," which they used in conjunction with the common tradition they knew from Mark and which was not known apparently to the other two, so the Fourth Evangelist had a unique source of the Jesus tradition, which is symbolized in the Gospel by the mysterious figure of the "disciple whom Jesus loved" or the Beloved Disciple. What is very different about John is that rather than supplementing or modifying a common tradition (as Matthew and Luke work with Mark) John's special material constitutes virtually the whole of the Gospel, governing its content and to a major degree even its structure, with occasional textual traces of contact with the Synoptic-like traditional material.

The Fourth Evangelist seems to assume that the readers of the Fourth

---

[17] The fragment, known as John Rylands Papyrus (P 52), contains part of John 18.

[18] The scholar who has done the most extensive and balanced work on the subject of the relationship of John to the Synoptics is D. Moody Smith, who has written a book and several articles on the subject. See, e.g., *John Among the Gospels: The Relationship in Twentieth-Century Research* (Minneapolis: Fortress, 1992) and "John and the Synoptics in Light of the Problem of Faith and History," in *Faith and History: Essays in Honor of Paul Meyer*, ed. John T. Carroll, Charles H. Cosgrove, and E. Elizabeth Johnson, Scholars Press Homage Series (Atlanta: Scholars Press, 1990), 74–89.

Gospel did know the Jesus-story, and there is some reason to believe that the evangelist does want to present an alternative to or a different reading of some of that material. For example, John's Gospel presents a much "higher" Christology than the Synoptics, insisting that Jesus is the preexistent Word of God, something that we do not find in the other three Gospels. And there is clearly a difference between John's theology of the relationship between seeing signs and believing in Jesus and the Synoptics' theology of the relationship between miracles and faith.

While John's Gospel, since it intends to tell the Jesus-story, follows the basic structure of Jesus' life from beginning to end, it differs from the other three not only in the arrangement of some of the events of the public life but especially by having Jesus' "life" commence in the bosom of the Father before all time and end not with his physical departure into heaven after the resurrection (cf. Mark 16:19; Luke 24:50–53) but with his return to the Father on the cross and his return to his own through the Spirit on Easter night. Within the Gospel itself a number of episodes are rearranged. For example, the cleansing of the temple in Jerusalem is the opening confrontation between Jesus and his adversaries rather than the final challenge that precipitates the passion as in the Synoptics. The final challenge in John is the raising of Lazarus, which the Synoptics do not relate at all. As already mentioned, Jesus' "agony" takes place not in the Garden of Olives on the night of his arrest but in John 12, before the beginning of the book of glory.

Finally, there is the question of the identity of the Fourth Evangelist. Ancient authorship was a very different phenomenon from modern authorship. The modern author is one person (or sometimes a group), who sets out to write a single piece of literature, revises it until she or he is satisfied with it, and then publishes it under the name of the author, who retains control of the material through copyright. The closest thing to this kind of authorship in the New Testament is probably the epistles of Paul. But even in Paul's case there is considerable debate over the authenticity of some of the letters that come to us under his name; he clearly seems to have dictated some of his letters; others wrote letters or, in the case of Hebrews, a theological treatise, and attributed them to Paul in order to invoke his authority for the contents. In the case of the Gospels there were at least two phases to the composition. First, a specific community with particular features, concerns, problems, and sensibilities lived the Christian life for some time in response to the preached gospel. This resulted in the choice of certain parts of the Jesus tradition as particularly apt for this community, the shaping of the stories by the homiletic, liturgical, and pastoral practice of the community, and the loss of some other material that was less adaptable to the community's agenda. After decades of such "shaping" by community use and practice, the gospel tradition of the community was committed to writing, probably first in fragments that were later put together into a sequential composition. This writing might have been done by an individual (like Luke) or by a small "school" (such as Matthew). The final version might have been the result of several "redactions" or revisions made necessary by any number of factors in community life.

In the case of John's Gospel it seems that something like the following took place. The Beloved Disciple, an eyewitness of the life of Jesus but not one of "the Twelve," was the source of the special tradition about Jesus that was lived in the Johannine community from sometime after the death of Jesus until the 90s, perhaps at first in Palestine but finally in Ephesus in Asia Minor.[19] The Beloved Disciple probably did not actually write the Gospel. This was done by the evangelist, who may well have been a member of a "Johannine school" or group of theologians in the community.[20] The evangelist was younger than the Beloved Disciple, it would seem, and probably was a second-generation Christian rather than a companion of the earthly Jesus. The evangelist, who was a highly gifted theologian and a very effective narrative and discursive writer, composed the text sometime shortly before the death of the Beloved Disciple. After the death of the Beloved Disciple the text seems to have undergone some "redaction" or revision, probably to smooth out some of the more glaring theological and pastoral discrepancies between the Fourth Gospel and the teaching and practice of the "Great Church," that is, the emerging and increasingly organized early Christian community, in which the primacy of the Twelve and especially Peter had begun to emerge. Many scholars see the evidence of this "ecclesiastical redaction" in John 21, which seems to be an addition or epilogue after the conclusion in 20:30–31. Chapter 21 tells of Simon Peter's rehabilitation by Jesus after his denials during the passion and Jesus' commissioning of Simon Peter to some kind of special pastoral ministry (see 21:15–19) and seems to refer not only to the physical death of the Beloved Disciple but also the ongoing relevance of the special tradition stemming from the Beloved Disciple's witness which is not subject to Simon Peter's control (see 21:20–23). In the Gospel proper there is an

[19] We do not know where the Johannine community was located. Tradition assigns it to Ephesus in Asia Minor, and no one has made a better case for anyplace else. However, the strong Samaritan influence on the theology of the Gospel, as well as the firsthand knowledge of Jerusalem and Palestine that the Gospel betrays, suggests that the Beloved Disciple at least lived in Judea before the writing of the Gospel and perhaps spent some time in Samaria.

[20] This theory is well treated in R. Alan Culpepper, *The Johannine School: An Evaluation of the Johannine-School Hypothesis Based on an Investigation of the Nature of the Ancient Schools*, Society of Biblical Literature Dissertation Series (Missoula, Mont.: Scholars Press, 1975).

ongoing, often competitive, juxtaposing of Simon Peter and the Beloved Disciple with the latter always coming out as the superior. The scene between Simon Peter and Jesus in chapter 21 seems to resolve this tension by admitting that Simon Peter received from Jesus a special pastoral ministry but that that ministry does not include control of the Beloved Disciple's tradition and community.

In summary, John's Gospel, written by an anonymous, second-generation member of the Johannine community, was the last of the four to be written and is so different in content, structure, and theological concerns that it has always been regarded as unique. However, it is still a Gospel, that is, a quasi-biographical witness to the good news of the salvific life, death, and resurrection of Jesus of Nazareth. It bears witness to substantially the same tradition that comes to expression in the other three Gospels. However, it draws primarily on a unique version of that tradition, namely, that of the Beloved Disciple, to which the other evangelists did not have access; its structure is theologically rather than chronologically determined; it contains events not recounted in the Synoptics, omits many that the latter do recount, and revises or relocates some of those they have in common. This means that the reader must avoid collating or harmonizing John with the Synoptics or reading John through Synoptic lenses.

The Johannine Community

Because the Fourth Gospel is so different from the other three, the techniques of redaction criticism, which consist mainly in comparing the three Synoptic Gospels among themselves in order to discover what is peculiar to each, cannot be easily applied to the Gospel of John. This lack of comparative material from outside the Gospel itself made it very difficult to discern much about the specific concerns, and therefore the character, of the community that produced the Fourth Gospel. In the late 1960s, however, a major breakthrough on this problem occurred when J. Louis Martyn published his theory that evidence internal to the Gospel itself, specifically the texts referring to the expulsion of Jewish Christians from the synagogue for confessing Christ, something that, as noted above, could not have happened in the lifetime of the earthly Jesus (John 9:22, 34; 12:42–43; 16:2),[21] located the Gospel his-

---

[21] The language in John 9:22 is technical. The cause for expulsion is ἐάν τις αὐτὸν ὁμολογήσῃ Χριστόν, "if anyone should profess or confess [in the sense of making a formal declaration] him [Jesus] to be the Christ [i.e., the Messiah]." And the penalty is ἀποσυνάγωγος γένηται, "he would be cut off from the synagogue [i.e., excommunicated]."

torically around the time of the consolidation of Jewish orthodoxy at Jamnia in the early 90s C.E., and suggested that a major theological concern of the community was its identity in relation to Judaism.[22] This opened up a period of intense scholarly investigation into the Gospel text itself as a source of knowledge about the Johannine community.

Raymond Brown, building on Martyn's work, collated all the traces within the text of the Gospel that seemed to offer some hints about the composition and historical development of the community and worked out an elaborate hypothetical reconstruction of the Johannine community, including the stages of its history, the types of people who made up the community at each stage, and the issues that exercised the community.[23] Although scholars dispute one or another feature of Brown's reconstruction, most agree that, in general, the picture he paints is probably fairly accurate in its major lines. I cannot describe in detail or even summarize Brown's hypothesis, but I will set forth those features of the community (both those he discerned and others drawn from other sources including my own work) that are important for understanding the theological and spiritual concerns of the Gospel. Readers will greatly enrich their understanding of the Gospel if they take the time to read Brown's relatively short but crucial book.

The Johannine community probably was originally made up of highly religiously motivated Jews, such as the eager followers of John the baptizer we meet in chapter 1. Most of these would have been Galileans, like Jesus, rather than Jerusalem types like the Pharisees.[24] At some point a fairly large and powerful contingent of Samaritans joined the community. Diaspora

---

[22] J. Louis Martyn, *History and Theology in the Fourth Gospel,* revised and enlarged, 2nd ed. (1968; reprint, Nashville: Abingdon, 1979).

[23] Raymond E. Brown, *The Community of the Beloved Disciple: The Life, Loves, and Hates of an Individual Church in New Testament Times* (New York: Paulist, 1979).

[24] In John's Gospel it is significant that Jesus is portrayed as born where he was raised, in Nazareth of Galilee, not in Bethlehem in Judea. This is significant because it makes Jesus a "northerner" rather than a Judean Jew. In John "Israel," which historically denoted the ten northern tribes, is the positive term for the chosen people, whereas "Jewish" or "Judean," which historically originated with the two southern tribes, is usually negative. Although Galileans were orthodox Jews (unlike the Samaritans, who considered themselves descendants of the northern tribes and "true Israelites"), they were more open to contacts with both Samaritans and diaspora Jews. There is a subtle use of "in-house" Jewish language and geography in John to associate the north with "good" Israelites and the south with "bad" Judeans. Jesus is a Galilean, and those, like Nicodemus in John 7:52 when he defends Jesus, are also "Galileans" at least symbolically. When Jesus is accused of having a demon and being a Samaritan (see John 8:48–49), he denies having a demon but does not deny being a Samaritan. An interesting study of this question is Robert T. Fortna's article "Theological Use of Locale in the Fourth Gospel," *ATR* Supplement Series 3 (1974): 58–95.

Jews (i.e., Greek-speaking Jews who lived outside Palestine and, therefore, seldom or never went up to Jerusalem for the feasts celebrated at the temple) and Gentiles also belonged to the community by the time the Gospel was written.

John's community was threatened by dissension from within and rivalry and persecution from without, which led to something of a siege mentality that one would associate today with a sect. In such communities there is a strong need for unity within the community, unqualified commitment to its faith and practice, and separation from threatening forces from without. The Johannine insistence on love of one another, total commitment to Jesus, fully developed Johannine faith, and separation from the "world" stem from this situation.

Brown discerns traces within the Gospel of a number of groups that played a role, from within or outside the community, at various stages of its development and with many of whom the evangelist has some quarrel. Within the community there were Christians who had originally been *followers of John the baptizer* and who struggled to decide whether John or Jesus was the "true light" they should follow. The evangelist has John the baptizer himself confess formally, "I am not the Messiah" (1:20). Jesus proclaims without equivocation that he alone is the "light of the world" (9:5), while John was a "lamp" pointing the way to Jesus (see 5:35).

The community also included *Jewish believers* in Jesus who wished to "sit on the fence," that is, to belong to Jesus in their hearts but to avoid the break with the synagogue involved in openly confessing Jesus as Messiah. These "closet Christians" (like the parents of the man born blind in John 9) the evangelist considered inadequate in their faith and cowardly.

Still other Jews who had come to believe in Jesus and who openly confessed him were, in the evangelist's view, too attached to their Jewish roots. Jesus challenges these "Jews who had believed in him" to continue in his word so that the truth [Jesus himself] would make them free, but they balked at the suggestion that Jesus, not their physical descent from Abraham, was the key to freedom (see 8:31–47). We probably see traces of this group also in John 6, where Jesus and those Jews who want to believe in him struggle over the question of who gives the true bread from heaven, Moses or Jesus' Father, and whether the bread that Jesus gives can be truly himself. At that point a division takes place between those Jews who "no longer go about with Jesus" because his teaching on the Eucharist is "difficult" and those who, like Simon Peter and the Twelve, say "Lord, to whom can we go? You have the words of eternal life" (6:68). In other words, the problems for Jewish converts were the high Christology, the eucharistic realism, the birth from above through believing in Jesus, and the supersession of Judaism. In the view of the Fourth Evangelist, these were also problems in some other Christian communities, specifically those founded by Simon Peter and others of the Twelve.

Within the community there were other groups whose positive influence on Johannine theology seems fairly clear. Interestingly enough, these are converts to Christianity who, for one reason or another, were marginal to Judaism. Some of these were *Jews from the diaspora* who had long resided, some from birth, in locations outside Palestine and who spoke Greek rather than Aramaic. These diaspora Jews resented the centralization of Judaism in Jerusalem and the insistence of the authorities on worship in the Jerusalem temple, which made these faraway Jews second-class citizens in relation to Palestinian Jews. The anti-temple attitude of these diaspora Jewish Christians increased the animosity of the community toward official Judaism after the community's break with the synagogue. Jesus' declaration that the temple was to be replaced by his own resurrection body (see 2:19–22) as well as his proclamation to the Samaritan woman that worship in Jerusalem as well as at Shechem had been superseded by worship in "spirit and in truth" (4:23) are probably textual traces of the concerns of this group.

Samaritans, some of whom became members of the Johannine community, were apostates and even heretics, according to official Judaism. But their unique understanding of Israel (the Samaritans considered themselves true Israelites, not Jews) and its tradition (which they traced to Moses, not to David) actually constituted an alternative "take" on identity within the chosen people that was very fruitful for Johannine theology as it tried to work out its relationship with the tradition from which it had been expelled. Although Jesus insisted to the Samaritan woman (who probably represents in the text this contingent) that "salvation is from the Jews," he nevertheless claimed that since God had relocated true worship in Jesus himself, the dispute between Samaritans and Jews over whether to worship at Shechem or in Jerusalem was transcended. As we will see in chapter 8, Samaritan theology powerfully influenced Johannine Christology, which remained deeply rooted in Jewish monotheism even as it developed its confession of Jesus' divinity.

Finally, *Gentile converts* to Johannine Christianity (perhaps represented by the Greeks who want to "see Jesus" in 12:20) seem to have brought a refreshingly universalist influence to a community that could have become very introverted. The Jesus of the Fourth Gospel, who came to "enlighten everyone" (1:9) was sent by God to save "the world" (3:17) and will, when he is lifted up in death, "draw all people" (12:32) to himself, "the Savior of the world" (4:42).

Outside the Johannine community were other groups with whom the community had to deal. First were the *other Christian communities,* founded by members of "the Twelve" and already beginning to recognize a certain primacy in Peter. The rivalry between Simon Peter and the Beloved Disciple in the Fourth Gospel probably reflects the reserve of the Johannine community toward these "other sheep" (see 10:16) of Jesus, whose Christology and eucharistic theology, in the Fourth Evangelist's view, are orthodox but inadequate. It also reflects the Beloved Disciple's claim to mediate a Jesus tradition that came directly from Jesus and had no need of Petrine validation. The virtual absence of "the Twelve" from the Fourth Gospel, their replacement in Jesus' inner circle by "the disciples," and the exalted position of many of these disciples (like Nathanael, the Samaritan woman, the man born blind, Martha and Mary of Bethany, Mary Magdalene) who are not among "the Twelve" probably reflects the sense of superiority of John's community in relation to the other churches.[25] There is no break with these communities but the distinction from them in theology and practice is clear.

The situation is quite otherwise with "*the Jews,*" who are the symbolic representatives during the lifetime of the earthly Jesus and the Johannine community of "*the world,*" which hates Jesus, seeks to kill him, and will die in its sins because of its refusal to believe in him (8:24). As already discussed, the Jews in question are not a historical ethnic, religious, or racial group and are certainly not the Jewish people as a whole. Rather, they are the Jewish authorities from Judea turned by the Fourth Evangelist into a symbolic representation of a particular attitude toward Jesus, namely, one of having been exposed to his testimony from God and refusing it out of malice. On the eve of his death the Johannine Jesus equates the Jewish authorities who will participate in his own condemnation, those who will expel his followers from the synagogue and even kill them (see 16:1–3), with "the world," which hates not only Jesus, who comes from above, but also his followers, who, like Jesus, are "not of this world" (see 8:23; 15:19; 17:14).

From this thumbnail sketch we can see how complex was the composition of this unusual community and how involved its theological and spiritual issues were with real people and positions. The animosity of the community toward "the Jews," the anti-Jerusalem/temple polemic contrasted with the positive attitude toward Galileans and Samaritans, the continual contrasting

---

[25] Raymond Brown coined the term "apostolic churches" for these non-Johannine communities. I consider this an unfortunate choice because it suggests either that "apostolic" refers uniquely to the Twelve, a mistaken equation that has caused all kinds of mischief in the church down to our own day, or that John's church was not apostolic, that is, founded on the faith of the first witnesses, and the very powerful claim of the Gospel is precisely that the tradition of the Beloved Disciple is every bit as apostolic as that of the Twelve.

of Jesus and his teaching with Moses and Judaism, the utter rejection of "the world," the careful positioning of Jesus in relation to John the baptizer, the Samaritan cast to the Gospel's theology, the rivalry between Simon Peter and "the Twelve," on the one hand, and the Beloved Disciple and "the disciples," on the other, and the universalist soteriology are all probably reflective of the actual life of the Johannine community prior to, during, and after the writing of the Gospel.

Because of the beleaguered state of the community it developed an intense, sect-like, life among its members. Characteristic of sects (Christianity itself was a Jewish sect prior to its split from the synagogue) are features easily recognized in the Fourth Gospel. Sectarians typically see themselves as a persecuted minority that must leave the world, which does not accept them, and create an alternative world for themselves. Sects are usually highly egalitarian because all those who commit themselves to the project have made major sacrifices to become members and are equal sharers in the life of the group which is bound together by their mutual love and their resistance to the pressures from without. The sect is a voluntary association into which members are not born but to which they freely choose to belong, always at great personal cost. Initiation is, therefore, very important, and nothing less than total commitment to the project, its beliefs and its practices, is acceptable. Sects have little tolerance for timidity in publicly declaring one's membership.

On the other hand, the Johannine community was not a true sect for two very important reasons. First, the community did not deny the orthodoxy of the other churches founded by the Twelve, Paul, and his associates. In other words, they broke from Judaism but did not break *koinōnia*, or communion, with the Great Church. Second, there is a distinct universalism in John's Gospel. God's salvation, in Johannine theology, is meant for the whole world, and it is Jesus, not the community, who is the "Savior of the World" (4:42). Although the community's focus was on its own life in Jesus, it was not a self-enclosed enclave.

SOME THEOLOGICAL TRAITS
OF THE FOURTH GOSPEL

As redaction criticism allowed Synoptic scholars not only to delineate rather clearly the features of the communities of Matthew, Mark, and Luke but also to discern the particular theological and pastoral concerns of these communities, the analogous internal analysis of John's Gospel allows us to glimpse not only something of the history, composition, and struggles of the Johannine community but also some of the particular theological, spiritual, and pastoral concerns of this unique early church.

As we will see in later chapters, John's community, bound together by their absolute commitment to Jesus as Son of God and their love for one another as Jesus' sisters and brothers, is highly egalitarian. The Spirit is given without measure (see 3:34) to all the members, male and female, Jewish, Samaritan, and Gentile. No one holds Jesus' place in relation to his members, who are equally branches of the one vine, sheep of the one shepherd. Even in John 21, where Simon Peter is commissioned to "feed" Jesus' lambs and sheep, he is not made the shepherd of the sheep. Discipleship, not office, is what is important. Their ecclesiology, therefore, is one of communion rather than of institution, and their sacraments are the action among them of the glorified Jesus, who has not left them orphans (see 14:18), not rituals instituted and left behind by a departed Jesus. Because Jesus, who is the resurrection and the life (11:25), dwells in them, his disciples possess eternal life even now and can never really die. In other words, the eschatology of the community is "realized," or present, rather than oriented toward a future "end of the world." And they see their mission not as a going forth to preach the gospel to the ends of the earth (in contrast to Matt. 28:19–20 or Mark 16:20) but as a vocation to be the kind of community that will attract others to the One whose life they share as Jesus attracted them. In short, the spirituality of John's Gospel is essentially mystical and contemplative, giving rise to a theology that is very little concerned with institution and very much concerned with union and life. For this reason it has always been the favorite Gospel of the church's mystics.[26]

---

[26] For a good treatment of the spirituality-based ecclesiology of John, see Raymond E. Brown, *The Churches the Apostles Left Behind* (New York: Paulist, 1984), especially chapter 6, "The Heritage of the Beloved Disciple in the Fourth Gospel: A Community of People Personally Attached to Jesus."

3

The Theology and Spirituality of the Fourth Gospel

At the end of the last chapter I gave a brief sketch of important theological traits of the Fourth Gospel that make it unique in relation to the Synoptics: its ecclesiology, pneumatology, sacramental theology, soteriology, Christology, and missiology. In this chapter I want to focus on a collection of closely intertwined theological themes and the spirituality they express, which create the context within which this very different Gospel can best be understood. It is crucial to recognize that the theology of the Gospel arises from, rather than generates, the spirituality of the Gospel. It is the theology, however, that gives us access to the spirituality. In other words, it was a particular *lived experience* of union with God in the risen Jesus through his gift of the Spirit/Paraclete within the believing community (spirituality) that gave rise gradually to a particular *articulated understanding* of Christian faith (theology). This theology was encoded in the Gospel text, and through it we gain access to the experience, the spirituality, that gives this Gospel its unique character. The particular approach to John's Gospel embodied in the interpretive essays that make up part 2 of this book is governed by a concern to explore this spirituality as a resource for the spirituality of the contemporary reader.

THE GOVERNING CATEGORY:
REVELATION

The central category that governs the theology and spirituality of John's Gospel is revelation, a term that has been undermined in the history of theology by its practical equation with divine "information" transmitted from God by ecclesiastical authority and binding Christians to an intellectual assent to certain dogmatically formulated propositions. This is not at all what revelation means in the Fourth Gospel, and it is crucial for understanding this Gospel to move beyond this narrow caricature.

In John, revelation connotes a relationship, not a one-way communication of otherwise unavailable information that the hearer, at risk of her or his salvation, must take or leave. In relation to this Gospel it is helpful to think always in terms of *self-revelation* rather than of the "unveiling" of information. Self-revelation is always an invitation to another to enter intimately into one's life, to participate in one's selfhood. Wise people do not engage in indiscriminate self-revelation. They gradually reveal themselves as the other is judged trustworthy, discreet, appreciative, and ready to reciprocate with a responding revelation of her- or himself. In other words, self-revelation is an invitation to a shared life. This shared life, when it reaches a critical depth, is what we call friendship which, as we will see, is another important Johannine category.

John's Gospel begins not with "In the beginning was *God*" but with "In the beginning was the *Word*." In other words, God is not a self-enclosed monad, knowing and loving "himself" from all eternity and only later deciding to let others in on the divine secret. Rather, in the Johannine view, God's very nature is self-communication, self-opening, self-gift, that is creative of the other. Divine Wisdom, which had poured herself out in creation, in the salvific history of the chosen people, in the testimony of the prophets and the teaching of the sages, and which had been at times received and at times rejected by humanity, goes to the very limit in entering human history in the person of Jesus. The Word, Holy Wisdom, God's self-revelation becomes human, incarnate, in order to speak to humanity in a language we could understand.

Revelation in John is the dialectic between Jesus' self-giving through his witness to himself and to God and the receptivity through believing and reciprocal self-giving of the disciples. It is never a one-way communication but always an interchange, a mutual self-giving, leading to an ever-deepening sharing of life and love.

Revelation is therefore never "complete." One does not collect the requisite information about God and then go on to live one's Christian life accordingly. Rather, Jesus' self-revelation is his ongoing and progressive opening to his disciples of his own inner life, the life of divine filiation, which is infinite in its depth and breadth and richness. Discipleship, or the life of believing, is correspondingly progressive. The Fourth Evangelist developed a quasi-technical theological vocabulary to talk about this ever-deepening relationship between Jesus and his disciples. It is captured in the terms *witness* (divine self-gift), *believing* (the human response), *life-light-love* (the dynamic of shared life), and *discipleship* (the living of the vocation to divine life).

Jesus' Self-Gift: Witness

Jesus' self-revelation in John is actually the whole of his "ministry." Everything he says and does is calculated to make known to potential disciples who he is, where he comes from, and who it is who sent him. Friendship is essentially mutual knowledge, which is why one way of saying we are close to someone is to say that we know each other very well. This knowledge is not primarily intellectual. It is a kind of union by sharing of selfhood. As Jesus shares in the very being of God and can therefore say that he knows the Father and the Father knows him (10:15), so Jesus wants his followers to know him as he knows them, to share in his very being and life. As Jesus knows God through God's self-revelation to him of the divine works, so Jesus' disciples will come to know Jesus through contemplation of what he does and says.

Evoking the Old Testament theology of God's great works or *magnalia Dei,* John calls Jesus' actions, collectively, his "*works.*" Some of these works are miraculous, such as the multiplication of the loaves or the healing of the man born blind. Others of Jesus' works such as the passion itself are not miraculous but are equally symbolic of where he comes from and who he is.

In John Jesus' miracles are called "signs" (i.e., symbolic actions). Because Jesus, in this Gospel, does only seven such miraculous signs and they are almost all different from the miracles recounted in the Synoptic Gospels, scholars have speculated that John had a special "signs source," that is, a document composed of accounts of miracles Jesus did. The evangelist selected from this source seven signs, which are redacted, that is, revised by the evangelist in function of the theology of the Gospel. This hypothesis, which has a certain plausibility, arose because the first two of Jesus' signs are numbered. The reader is told that the wine miracle at Cana was the "first of his signs" (2:11) and the raising of the royal official's son was "the second sign that Jesus did" (4:54). Possibly the "signs source" had a numbered list of Jesus' miracles. Another possibility is that the evangelist numbered the first two so that the reader would keep counting and realize that Jesus did exactly seven miraculous signs, just as he speaks seven great "I am" statements about himself. Seven, the symbolic number for divine plenitude, emphasizes that the works Jesus did and the sayings Jesus spoke constitute the fullness of divine witness to his identity.

Complementing the works are Jesus' *words.* In John, unlike in the Synoptics, Jesus gives a number of long, theological discourses. There is little doubt that the earthly Jesus did not talk in this exalted and mysterious theological language. These discourses are the evangelist's composition, meant to convey the meaning of Jesus' self-revelation as the community came to understand it from many years of meditating on Jesus' words and works. The discourses often occur in connection with an encounter between Jesus and potential disciples and especially in connection with signs. We find one, for example, after the encounter with Nicodemus in chapter 3, another during the encounter with the Samaritan woman in chapter 4, another after the sign of the multiplication of the loaves in chapter 6, and one that extends from chapter 13 to chapter 16 at the Last Supper. However, in John we find very few of the short, pithy sayings characteristic of the Synoptic Jesus.

The purpose of the works and words of Jesus is to manifest to his hearers who he is, namely, the Word of God, and where he comes from (which is essentially the same thing), namely, from the bosom (i.e., the interiority) of God. The sharing of life that is true friendship is always based on, indeed consists in, knowing the other intimately. Jesus initiates his disciples into that intimate knowledge of God by revealing who he, Jesus, is because anyone who has truly seen Jesus (i.e., come to know him) has seen the Father (see 14:9) for Jesus and the Father are one (10:30). Jesus maintains always that he does nothing except what he sees God doing and speaks nothing on his own authority but only what he hears from God (see 5:19 and many other texts). Ultimately, what Jesus knows and testifies to is that God so loved the world as to desire its salvation even unto the pouring forth of God's very self in the incarnation (3:16). Jesus' witness is an invitation to accept this unreserved divine love, to respond in love, and thus to create a shared life with God. God, says Jesus, desires intimate friendship with us. The "place" of that relationship is Jesus himself, in whom God is present and available. The disciple is invited to a mutual indwelling with Jesus as Jesus and the One who sent him indwell each other, as a branch inheres in a vine. And out of this mutual indwelling love will come the works of the disciple, the lasting fruit that the disciple in union with Jesus will bear to the glory of God (see 15:1–11).

The Disciple's Response: Believing

Scholars have long recognized that John developed a special vocabulary for exploring and explaining what it means to respond to Jesus' self-revelation. The human pole of the revelation dynamic is "believing." It is striking that John uses the verb "to believe" ninety-eight (or possibly ninety-nine) times in comparison with the Synoptics, who together use it only thirty-four times. Furthermore, John never uses the noun "faith" or "belief." For John faith is not a spiritual acquisition or a state of being but an activity, an ever-active relationship in the present.

John uses several different grammatical constructions of the verb "to believe," each with particular theological overtones. Thirty-six times the Fourth Evangelist uses a construction not found elsewhere in Greek literature, πιστεύειν εἰς (*pisteuein eis*) followed by a noun in the accusative case, meaning literally "to believe into." Although it is usually translated "believe in" (since English, like Greek, has no expression such as "believe into"), it is not equivalent to simply giving credence to someone. There is a perfectly normal construction in Greek for this banal meaning, *pisteuein,* followed by the dative, that is, "to believe something," and John uses it at times. But his special accusative construction is a dynamic expression in which the evangelist tries to capture the progressive entrance of the believer into the life of Jesus.

There are stages in this process illustrated by the call of the first disciples in John 1:35–51: coming to Jesus, being recognized (and sometimes named) by Jesus, remaining with or dwelling in Jesus over time, until one finally comes to "know" him in the deepest sense. Some who come to Jesus do not remain but walk away, as is illustrated by some of the crowd after the multiplication of the loaves in John 6. This is the mystery of unbelief in the Fourth Gospel, obviously a very troubling phenomenon for the Johannine community.

Another construction of the verb "to believe" is the absolute *pisteuein,* "to believe," with no object expressed, in order to capture the unqualified character of the act of believing. One way this absolute believing expresses itself is as an original, fundamental openness to the divine initiative even before one knows precisely who Jesus is or what he can do. The royal official in John 4, a Gentile who does not know who Jesus is but comes to him for help for his dying son, and the man born blind, who obeys Jesus' command to wash in the pool of Siloam even before he knows Jesus, are examples of such unqualified openness to divine intervention in one's life. Another way this unqualified faith appears is in the attitude of the person who has been with Jesus long enough to place no limits on what one can expect of him. The disciple is one who simply believes, much as we might talk of believing without reservation in a friend, regardless of what might seem to be problematic. We believe not this or that specific thing about the friend but in the person him- or herself because of the quality of our relationship.

Finally, there is the expression *pisteuein hoti,* "to believe that . . . ." The object of "that" is some proposition such as that God sent Jesus or that Jesus is from God. Although formulated differently in different texts the proposition always amounts to the same thing: to believe that Jesus is who he says he is, the One sent by God, the Son in whom one encounters God. This is the total and explicitly thematized faith of one who is "confirmed" in the relationship with Jesus. This believing is equivalent to "knowing" in John, truly knowing Jesus and being known by him as Jesus knows and is known by God (see 10:15). Jesus says, in his last prayer to God before his passion, that he has made known to his disciples everything that God has made known to him and thus that they have come to know God in truth. Jesus declares, "This is eternal life, that they may know you, the only true God, and Jesus Christ whom you have sent" (17:3). There is a great deal of irony in John around the word "know." Those who claim to know, for example, Nicodemus or the Pharisees in the encounter with the man born blind, are usually precisely those who do not know who Jesus is and are not really open to finding out even though they may seem to be inquiring. Those who know that they do not know, like the man born blind, are the ones whom Jesus can and does progressively enlighten (see the clear statement of this in 9:39–41).

The knowledge of Jesus that the disciple gradually achieves is not, therefore, primarily intellectual or informational. It is the kind of knowledge one has of a friend that makes one say, "We know each other intimately." It is, quite simply, a deep sharing of life with Jesus. And sharing in the life of Jesus is participation in the life of God. This is why in John salvation comes not by way of expiatory sacrifice or substitutionary suffering by Jesus for us but by way of revelation.[1] To be saved, in John, is not to be rescued from evil (although that is included) so much as to be born into eternal life. When Jesus dies, John says that he is glorified, that is, that his very being as God's love incarnate is fully manifested to those with eyes to see. Revelation achieves its consummate expression and full efficacy in Jesus' ultimate witness, through his laying down of his life for those he loves, to who he is and the active acceptance of and entrance into that life by the representative disciples at the foot of the cross, the mother of Jesus and the Beloved Disciple.

Living the Revelation Dynamic

Because salvation is revelation in the Fourth Gospel, the great trilogy of Johannine terms—life, light, and love—captures the entire dynamic. Jesus, as

---

[1] John does not deny the sacrificial theology that had become the "mainstream" theology of the paschal mystery by the time this Gospel was written. But it is clear that he prefers his revelational theology of salvation. A full-scale treatment of this subject is J. Terence Forestell, *The Word of the Cross: Salvation as Revelation in the Fourth Gospel,* Analecta Biblica 57 (Rome: Biblical Institute Press, 1974).

Son of God, has been given God's own *life* in all its fullness and has been authorized by God to give that life to whomever he wills (see 5:21, 26). In Jesus as Word incarnate that life of God blazes forth, becomes available, is manifested, as *light* shining in the darkness (1:4–5). And those who receive it, who are enlightened by this light, who come to Jesus and remain in him, participate in the *love-life* between Jesus and God. As Jesus says in his final prayer, such disciples know that God has "loved them even as you [God] have loved me" (17:23).

To participate in the love-life of Jesus and God through the Spirit whom Jesus gives to his disciples is what it means to be "born of God." In the Fourth Gospel, this birth from God is not metaphorical or fictive. Those who believe in Jesus are not adopted but are actually given power to "become children of God, who [are] born, not of blood or of the will of the flesh or of the will of a male [*andros,* i.e., male, not *anthrōpos,* i.e., person], but of God" (1:12–13). Like Jesus, his disciples are not of this world, even though, like him, they are in the world. Rather they are born from above, born of the Spirit (see 3:3).

The life of Jesus in which his disciples participate is the life of children of God, divine *filiation.* Since the disciples share Jesus' filiation, they not only can call God their Father (see 20:17) and Jesus' mother their own (see 19:25–27), as Jesus did, but they also become sisters and brothers of Jesus and of one another. The intense love-ethic of the Johannine community is rooted in this *fraternal/sororal relationship,* which is the fruit of Jesus' sharing of his life with them. The ultimate realization of this mystery of loving union is *friendship.* Jesus says that he no longer calls his disciples "servants" but he calls them "friends" because he has shared with them everything he has received from his Father (see 15:15). This extraordinary union in friendship between Jesus and his disciples, a friendship that calls for laying down one's life for the beloved, connotes an equality in the relationship, a mutual indwelling, a total sharing of being and life, which grounds the mystical spirituality into which this Gospel invites its readers.

Discipleship

In the Fourth Gospel, "the Twelve," whom the Synoptics call apostles (Matt. 10:2; Mark 3:14; Luke 6:13) and who play such an important role in these three Gospels, have virtually no role at all. Some of Jesus' disciples in John can be recognized as members of the Twelve, for example, Simon Peter, Judas, and Thomas. But they are not identified as members of the Twelve except when they are in trouble because of their doubt, betrayal, or denial of Jesus. The message seems to be that it is not important to hold a special position of leadership or authority in the community. All that is truly significant is being a disciple of Jesus. Thus, Jesus' question to the repentant Peter is simply, "Do you love me?" (21:15ff.), since office without love is meaningless whereas love without office lacks nothing. As disciples, all in the community are equal. In fact, the representative ideal figure of the Gospel is called only, "the disciple whom Jesus loved."[2]

This insistence on discipleship carries several messages besides the equality of all in the community in their relationship with Jesus. A disciple is a student, a learner, one who goes from not knowing to knowing under the guidance of a teacher or master. Jesus says, just after washing his disciples' feet at the Last Supper, "You call me Teacher and Lord [master]—and you are right, for that is what I am" (13:13). Jesus' revelatory witnessing, which draws his disciples into the life of God is, in fact, a teaching. It is not a purely intellectual activity but an initiation of the disciples into Jesus' own life by their prolonged association with him. It is an apprenticeship in divine filiation, a being "taught by God" (see 6:45–46). The "final examination" in this "course" on love is the willingness to lay down one's life for those one loves after the example of Jesus. When Mary Magdalene, who thinks that she has lost Jesus in death, recognizes her Beloved when he calls her by name, "Mary," her faith rebounds in a joyous exclamation, "Rabbouni," which the evangelist translates lest the reader miss its significance: "which means Teacher" (20:16). Because salvation in John is accomplished through revelation, the relationship between Jesus and those who believe in him is most appropriately one of discipleship, which fructifies in friendship.

THE MYSTERY CONTINUES
IN THE PRESENT

Because in John there is no "institution" to carry on the work of Jesus among later disciples, the Fourth Gospel is particularly concerned, especially after the death of the Beloved Disciple, with the question of how people who had never known the earthly Jesus could become and remain disciples. This question is raised in anguished tones in the Last Supper conversations between Jesus and his disciples as a concern of those who were soon to experience Jesus' "going away" in death. They want to know where he is going, how they

---

[2] On this point, see Raymond E. Brown, *The Churches the Apostles Left Behind* (New York: Paulist, 1984), especially pp. 90–95; idem, *A Retreat with John the Evangelist: That You May Have Life* (Cincinnati: St. Anthony Messenger, 1998), 55–68.

can follow him there, why they cannot go with him now. And Jesus tells them to calm their hearts because he goes to prepare a dwelling for them in his Father's house "so that where I am, there you may be also" (14:1–3). But the problem remains in regard to the "little while" between Jesus' going away and their joining him in the Father's house. Of course, since the Gospel was written "the little while" has stretched into twenty centuries, and disciples today have the same problem. How do we enter into Jesus' life, dwell in him and he in us, when we no longer see (or never have seen) him in the flesh, witnessed his works, and heard his words?

The response of Jesus in John is the most profound exploration of this aspect of Christian faith in the New Testament. It weaves together a theology of the resurrection, a theology of the Holy Spirit, and a theology of Christian community into a seamless whole that is essentially mystical and immediate rather than ritual or institutional. Failure to understand and appreciate this aspect of John's Gospel makes the Gospel as a whole unintelligible, as it is indeed to people who want to read it for information about divine realities but who do not open themselves in prayer to the necessary transformation.

The Resurrection in John: Jesus' Return to His Own

As is well known, the Jesus tradition was appropriated by each of the evangelists in function of the concerns of a particular community and in terms of a theology and spirituality that developed in that community. While most students of the New Testament easily accept this in relation to the birth of Jesus and his public life, it is less readily recognized in regard to the paschal mystery of Jesus, that is, his passion, death, and resurrection. It is particularly crucial, however, to read John's passion and resurrection account on its own terms and not through Synoptic lenses.

In the Synoptics Jesus' public life begins with his enthusiastic reception by the crowds, who are amazed at his miracles and energized by his words. As he continues to preach and teach, however, they become progressively more disillusioned and finally find him to be "too much for them" (see Mark 6:3), as one translation has it. Jesus is finally arrested, humiliated, tortured, condemned, and killed by the horrible and shameful Roman form of execution, crucifixion. Not only is crucifixion a human horror, but according to the scriptures it is a sign of divine rejection. Deuteronomy 21:23 says, "When someone is convicted of a crime punishable by death and is executed, and you hang him on a tree . . . you shall bury him that same day, for anyone hung on a tree is under God's curse." Critical to continued faith in Jesus is a divine vindication of him and his work. The resurrection, in the Synoptics, is Jesus' vindication by God, the divine reversal of the ultimate *kenōsis*, or abasement of Jesus in death by crucifixion.

In John, Jesus' death is never presented as *kenōsis*. Rather, Jesus is glorified in and by his death. His lifting up on the cross is his exaltation. It is the supreme manifestation, the final and definitive revelation of who he is and what God desires for humankind. Consequently, even though the Fourth Evangelist mentions the mockery of Jesus and tells of his crucifixion, the account of the passion is transformed into a victory march of Jesus to his enthronement on the cross. Jesus is calmly in charge of his trial, and it becomes clear that it is Pilate and the Jewish leaders who are actually on trial, while Jesus is clearly vindicated and his death patently unjust and seen as such by all the participants. Jesus' words from the cross in John are not cries of anguish but carefully scripted revelatory pronouncements that end with his self-possessed declaration: "It is consummated," that is, everything God had sent Jesus to do has been accomplished. With that proclamation Jesus imparts his final gift to his disciples as he bows his head and hands over his Spirit (19:30).

The transformation of the ignominious passion and death into a glorification of Jesus and God raises the question: What need is there in John for a resurrection? Some scholars have concluded that there is no need and that John appended a resurrection narrative because, given the development of the tradition by the time this Gospel was written, it would have been considered incomplete without such a narrative. This is a solution of despair, in my opinion. The Fourth Evangelist is a consummate theologian and writer and would hardly have allowed his great work to fizzle out in a pointless narrative command performance to keep the traditionalists happy. Furthermore, the Johannine resurrection narrative is one of the literary jewels of the New Testament and hardly an afterthought to a Gospel that ends theologically with Jesus' glorification on the cross.

John's transformation of the passion from *kenōsis* to glorification, however, did require a complete reinterpretation of the resurrection as something other than divine vindication. In effect, John reverses the resurrection–ascension schema of the Synoptics, in which God vindicates Jesus by resurrection and Jesus, after showing himself alive to his followers, ascends to "the right hand of God," that is, into the divine presence. In John, Jesus returns to the Father on the cross. His death, which is his passing over into divine glory, is his "ascension," or as John puts it, his exaltation. This is summarized in Jesus' prayer on the night before he died: "Father, the hour [of the passion] has come; glorify your Son so that the Son may glorify you. . . . So now, Father, glorify me in your own presence with the glory that I had in your presence before the world existed" (17:1, 5). Jesus is exalted, glorified, and ascends to God at the moment of his death, which is why he can, at that moment, hand over the Spirit, which the evangelist has told the reader earlier could not be given until Jesus was glorified (see 7:39).

It is his glorification that makes Jesus able to return to his own as he had promised at the Last Supper. He had told them, "I will not leave you orphaned; I am coming to you. In a little while the world will no longer see me, but you will see me; because I live, you also will live. In that day you will know [recall what "know" means in John] that I am in my Father, and you in me, and I in you" (14:19–20). Jesus goes on to explain that his return to them will be interior, through the gift of the Spirit/Paraclete.

The resurrection narrative in John, therefore, is not really about what happened to *Jesus* after his death. That has already been narrated in the account of his glorifying death, namely, that he has *returned to God*. The resurrection narrative is about what happened to *Jesus' disciples* after Jesus' glorification, namely, that the Jesus who had gone to God has also *returned to them*.

Through the four episodes of chapter 20 the mystery of Jesus' return to his own is unfolded. First, the Beloved Disciple at the tomb "sees and believes" (note the absolute use of "believe") even though they (Simon Peter and the Beloved Disciple) do not yet understand about the resurrection. What the Beloved Disciple believes is that Jesus has indeed been *glorified*. He is not dead, not defeated, but alive with God. What they do not yet understand is that this glorification will include a resurrection, a return of Jesus to his own.

Next, Mary Magdalene sees the glorified Lord and goes to announce to those who are now his "brothers and sisters" that Jesus is indeed alive, that she has seen him, and that he has commissioned her to announce to them that he is both with God and again with them. In other words, Mary, and through her the community, is enlightened about the *resurrection*.

Jesus then "stands into the midst" of his gathered disciples, grants them his paschal peace, and commissions them as a community to share what they have received from him, namely, the taking away of their sins and their unification into a community of disciples. In other words, the community, filled with the Holy Spirit, has become the *risen body of the glorified Jesus*, the temple in which God and humanity will meet.

Finally, Thomas, representing all later disciples, first refuses to believe unless the preglorification dispensation of physical presence is restored, and then accepts Jesus' challenge to cross over into the postglorification dispensation of "believing without seeing" or *believing through the testimony of the community*.

The evangelist concludes the Gospel by telling the readers that the testi-

mony of the community, written in the *Gospel,* is for them what the signs and
words of the earthly Jesus were for the first disciples. As the latter had "seen
and believed," so later disciples will "hear [read] and believe."

In summary, the progression is from Jesus' glorification/exaltation on the
cross (his return to the Father) to his resurrection (his return to his own) to
their receiving his Spirit and becoming his risen body in the world to the
incorporation of all who will believe through their testimony by means of the
Gospel.

The Holy Spirit/Paraclete

At the Last Supper, when Jesus' disciples are expressing their anguished concern that his "going away" will separate them from him and thus from eternal life, Jesus reassures them that his going away will be a new coming to
them (see 14:28: "I go away and I come to you"—both in the present tense
as simultaneous) and that he can only come to them in this new way if,
indeed, he goes away as the historical, physical presence they have so far experienced. Therefore, rather than being troubled and sad, they should rejoice
because he is going to the Father, for only from and with the Father can he
send them the Advocate (15:26) who will be his new presence within them.
Jesus says that "it is to your advantage that I go away, for if I do not go away,
the Advocate will not come to you; but if I go I will send him to you" (16:7).

There are five Spirit/Paraclete texts in the last discourses Jesus speaks at the
Last Supper.[3] This living Gift which Jesus promises to send is, in the felici-
tous expression of Raymond Brown, the real presence of the glorified Jesus
within them. This new presence of Jesus will be in no way inferior to his
earthly presence, something that first Mary Magdalene and then Thomas
have to accept in order to cross over from the preglorification to the postglorification dispensation. This presence is called by Jesus the Holy Spirit, the
Spirit of Truth, the Paraclete (or Advocate or Comforter).

The Spirit will first of all give the disciples an interior and abiding conviction of the reality of Jesus' presence within them: the Spirit of Truth "abides
with you, and . . . will be in you. . . . On that day you will know that I am in
my Father, and you in me, and I in you" (14:16–17). Second, this abiding
Holy Spirit/Paraclete will teach the disciples all they will need to know in the
future by reminding them of what the earthly Jesus taught them (14:26).
Third, the Paraclete/Spirit of Truth will testify on Jesus' behalf and will enable
the disciples to do so (15:26). Fourth, the Paraclete will vindicate Jesus and

---

[3] The texts are the following: John 14:16–17; 14:26; 15:26; 16:7–11; 16:13–15.

his disciples against the accusations and persecutions of the world (16:7–11). And finally, and as a kind of summary, Jesus says that the Spirit of Truth will have the same relationship to him as he, during his earthly life, had to the Father. Just as Jesus received everything from God and shared it with his disciples, so the Spirit receives everything from Jesus and shares it with Jesus' disciples (16:13–15). In other words, the Spirit will be the interior presence of Jesus within his disciples, maintaining their union with him, leading them moment by moment, as they are able to bear it, into all truth, and uniting them to the Father. Jesus will be more intimately and powerfully present to them in this new way than he was during his earthly life when he was limited, like all humans, by space, time, gender, race, age, ethnicity, and even death itself. What Jesus is saying to the disciples is that it is not the reality of his presence to them that is changed by his "going away," but only the mode. He had been present to them in the flesh only in order to prepare them for his presence in the Spirit.

The Community

The intensely personal character of Jesus' relation to his disciples in the Fourth Gospel has led some commentators to talk of this Gospel as "individualistic."[4] In fact, this Gospel has some of the strongest language in the New Testament about love of one another in the Christian community. Here we find Jesus' own sign of Christian identity: "By this everyone will know that you are my disciples, if you have love for one another" (13:35). The Johannine Jesus gives no revision of the Decalogue and no moral instruction. He gives only one commandment, a new commandment, which he calls his own commandment, that we love one another as he has loved us (see 13:34–35; 15:12–14), namely, unto the laying down of our lives for those we love.

The Fourth Gospel shows little interest in the institutional aspects of "Church," a word we do not find in this Gospel. As already mentioned, office and titles are not significant in this community. On the contrary, the only preferential status is closeness to Jesus, and that is equally open to men and women, Samaritans, Gentiles, and Jews. This seems to have been a thoroughly egalitarian community.

---

[4] Raymond Brown captures well the nuance of the position of the Fourth Gospel on "the relation of the individual Christian to Jesus Christ," not in the American sense of rugged individualism or fundamentalist "personal savior" piety but that, within a strong sense of community reflected in the vine and branches similitude, "there is an unparalleled concentration on the relation of the individual believer to Jesus" (*Churches*, 84–85). I would prefer to say the emphasis is on the "personal" rather than the individual.

There are references to what later came to be known as "sacraments" of baptism and Eucharist, but in the Fourth Gospel they are not presented as rituals presided over by officials and occurring punctually on certain days. Rather, being "born of water and the Spirit" is a way of talking about the filial identity of Christians by which they enjoy eternal life, ongoing union with Jesus, even now. Eating Jesus' flesh and drinking his blood connotes receiving him continuously into one's life through his Word and the community's sharing of the meal. If there was a particular eucharistic ritual in the Johannine community, it may well have been the one that Jesus told his disciples to do in imitation of him, "So if I, your Lord and Teacher, have washed your feet, you also ought to wash one another's feet. For I have set you an example, that you also should do as I have done to you" (13:13–15).

The love of the community members for one another, according to this Gospel, is the fruit and manifestation of the outpouring of the Spirit of Jesus upon them by the glorified Savior. In 20:19–23, Jesus "returns to his own" as he had promised. We are not told that he passed through closed doors (as the popular versions sometimes suggest) but that he "came" and "stood into the midst of them," despite their self-enclosure out of fear of the authorities who had put Jesus to death. This language is important because it is the fulfillment of Jesus' own promise that in his going away he would *come* to them. But it is also the fulfillment of Jesus' prediction at the commencement of his public ministry: "Destroy this *temple* [that is, his earthly body], and in three days I will raise it up" (2:19). These two features resonate against the Old Testament promise, made just after the vision of the dry bones, of the new covenant that God would make with the new Israel:

> I will make with them a covenant of peace; it shall be an everlasting covenant with them, and I will multiply them, and put my sanctuary among them forever. My dwelling shall be with them; I will be their God and they shall be my people. Thus the nations shall know that it is I, the Lord, who make Israel holy, when my sanctuary shall be set up among them forever. (Ezek. 37:26–28)

Jesus, rising up in the midst of his disciples, giving them his peace, pouring out his Spirit upon them, after having told them through Mary Magdalene that his God is now their God (note the covenant language) and that, therefore, they are the new Israel, is fulfilling the ancient promise in a most unexpected way.

The glorified Jesus, uniting his disciples to himself by his Spirit, is indeed setting up God's sanctuary in the world. The temple is the community, the risen body of Jesus, which has replaced his earthly body, the temple destroyed by his enemies. Out of that temple will flow, as it flowed from the side of Jesus on the cross (see 19:34), the living water of the Spirit. There is a remarkable, deliberate ambiguity in John 7:38–39, where Jesus cries out in the temple in Jerusalem, "let the one who believes in me drink. As the scripture has said, 'Out of *his* (emphasis added) heart shall flow rivers of living water.' Now he said this about the Spirit, which believers in him were to receive; for as yet there was no Spirit, because Jesus was not yet glorified."[5] The αὐτοῦ (*autou,* "his") can refer either to the "one who believes in me," that is, the disciples, or to Jesus himself. In fact, it is doubly fulfilled because the living water of the Spirit flowed from the heart of Jesus on the cross just after he was glorified in death, and it now flows from the heart of believers through whose word others will come to believe (see 17:20).

The community, then, is the key to Jesus' ongoing presence in the world. The task of the community is to *be,* through love, Jesus' bodily presence, and thus the giver of his Spirit, to all who will come to believe down through the ages. Jesus has gone to prepare a place for his disciples because, as he prays on the night before his death, "Father, I desire that those also, whom you have given me, may be with me where I am, to see my glory, which you have given me before the foundation of the world" (17:24). In the time between Jesus' going away and his coming again to take us to himself so that where he is we also may be (see 14:3), the community is the place of encounter between Jesus and his disciples. There we are born again of the Spirit, eat and drink the life of Jesus, and share that life with fellow believers and with all those to whom we testify about him. As Jesus promised, his disciples will do even greater works than he had done because they will not be limited as he was during his earthly life to a single place and time (see 14:12). During this "little while" the Gospel of the Beloved Disciple illuminates our path. Interpreting it is a never-ending enterprise because it deepens as our experience of union with Jesus deepens. And so, with this brief introduction to the Gospel I invite you to explore certain aspects and themes of the Gospel as well as some of its texts, in the light of your own lived experience.

---

[5] The NRSV translates this verse by coming down on the side of its application to the believer: "As the scripture has said, 'Out of the believer's heart shall flow rivers of living water.'" The Catholic Study Bible leaves the ambiguity intact: "Whoever believes in me, as scripture says: 'Rivers of living water will flow from within him.'" Leaving it ambiguous requires a gender exclusive use of "his" because it has to apply equally to Jesus and the believer. But in this case, the theological issue seems to demand the use of the generic masculine.

4

Symbolism in the
Fourth Gospel

THE ISSUE OF SYMBOLISM
IN THE FOURTH GOSPEL

Few issues in twentieth-century Johannine scholarship have been more vigorously disputed than that of the presence and function of symbolism in this Gospel. However, the state of the question has changed dramatically over the past three decades. Because symbolism is not only intrinsic to the Fourth Gospel but is *a* if not *the* primary hermeneutical key to its interpretation, it is important to address this issue at the outset of our study of this text and to establish some basic concepts and terminology.

From the end of the nineteenth through the first decades of the twentieth century scholars tended to regard the Fourth Gospel as a very late (end of the second century C.E.) composition in comparison with the Synoptics, which were written sometime between 60 and 90 C.E. They also tended to regard John as "inauthentic," meaning that it was historically unreliable,[1] supplying little if any factual data about the life of Jesus. For that very reason they tended to regard it as heavily "symbolic," by which they meant without factual content but primarily concerned with theological reflection by a writer who had had no direct contact with the earthly Jesus.

Toward the middle of the twentieth century this judgment underwent serious revision because of new evidence supplied by archaeology and manuscript discoveries. Internal and external evidence made it nearly certain that the Gospel was written not in the late second century (and therefore several generations after Jesus) but toward the end of the first century, while some of

---

[1] Raymond Brown, in a series of lectures given in 1998 and available on tape, explains very accessibly the meaning of "inauthenticity" as the term is used by historical critics and the history of the issue in relation to the Fourth Gospel ("The Paraclete: Spirit's Gift to the Church," The Audio File, P.O. Box 93, Glenview, IL 60025).

Jesus' first disciples and/or their immediate disciples were still alive.[2] Furthermore, the Fourth Evangelist's knowledge of Palestine in general and especially of Jerusalem at the time of Jesus, as well as of first-century Jewish tradition and customs, suggested that the Fourth Gospel might be even more historically reliable than the Synoptics.

The more historical the Gospel was judged to be, however, the more reserved scholars became about its symbolic character. There was (and in some quarters still is) a nearly visceral conviction that there is an inverse ratio between the historical and the symbolic, that is, the more historical the less symbolic and vice versa. This conviction arises from an erroneous tendency to equate historical with factual and factual with true. Because the symbolic is not concerned primarily with facts in the sense of "what actually occurred" but with truth in the sense of meaning, it is often assumed that the symbolic and the historical are contrary (if not contradictory) categories. If it is literally factual (i.e., true) then it is not symbolic, and if it is symbolic it is not factual (i.e., not true). We are increasingly aware today that fact and truth are not identical and that often enough the truth is best conveyed by the nonliteral, for example, by symbol, myth, or story.

Beginning in the late 1960s New Testament scholars under the influence of form and redaction criticism became increasingly aware of the literary character of the Gospels, and therefore that categories which are relevant to the analysis of literature in general are also relevant to Gospel study.[3] Literary

---

[2] See the discussion of the date of John in chapter 1.

[3] Among the most influential scholars in the emergence of literary approaches to the New Testament was Amos Wilder, whose *Early Christian Rhetoric: The Language of the Gospel* (Cambridge, Mass.: Harvard University Press, 1971) was first published in 1964. His *The Bible and the Literary Critic* (Minneapolis: Fortress, 1991) is both a summary and a criticism of the developments in the field since that beginning. A useful overview of the field and an extensive basic bibliography are provided by William A. Beardslee, "Recent Literary Criticism," in *The New Testament and Its Modern Interpreters,* ed. Eldon J. Epp and George W. MacRae, vol. 3 of *The Bible and Its Modern Interpreters,* ed. Douglas A. Knight, Society of Biblical Literature Centennial Publications (Philadelphia: Fortress, 1989), 175–98. A useful collection of essays on various kinds of literary criticism is *The New Literary Criticism and the New Testament,* ed. Edgar V. McKnight and Elizabeth Struthers Malbon (Valley Forge, Pa.: Trinity, 1994)

Major literary studies of John's Gospel include R. Alan Culpepper, *Anatomy of the Fourth Gospel: A Study in Literary Design* (Philadelphia: Fortress, 1983); Paul D. Duke, *Irony in the Fourth Gospel* (Atlanta: John Knox, 1985); Gail R. O'Day, *Revelation in the Fourth Gospel: Narrative Mode and Theological Claim* (Philadelphia: Fortress, 1986); Jeffrey Lloyd Staley, *The Print's First Kiss: A Rhetorical Investigation of the Implied Reader in the Fourth Gospel,* SBL Dissertation Series (Atlanta: Scholars Press, 1988); Mark W. G. Stibbe, *John as Storyteller: Narrative Criticism and the Fourth Gospel* (Cambridge: Cambridge University Press, 1992); *The Gospel of John as Literature: An Anthology of Twentieth-Century Perspectives,* selected and intro-

approaches to the Gospels such as structural, narrative, and rhetorical criticism necessarily brought into focus such literary techniques and devices as metaphor, irony, and symbolism. No matter how slippery such terrain originally appeared to be to scholars trained in a highly positivistic historical-critical type of exegesis, it became necessary to reengage the issue of symbolism in the Gospel of John. If a text is intrinsically symbolic, there is no such thing as a valid, purely "literal" interpretation of it. Nonsymbolic interpretation of a symbolic text is not literal; it is inadequate.

Taking symbolism seriously, however, raised questions about how to handle it. Unlike purely factual historical questions such as Did this really happen? questions about symbolism are much more difficult to formulate and to answer. First is the question of whether something in the text is symbolic or not. And does that depend on whether the author intended it to be symbolic or whether, in interacting with it, readers experience it as symbolic? And which readers are to be given credence, medieval (or contemporary) spiritual interpreters or modern literalists? And once it is determined that a text is intrinsically symbolic, how is it to be read? These questions have led some Johannine scholars to engage seriously the contemporary work on symbolism of philosophers and literary critics, and this has given rise to a number of serious studies of symbolism in John.[4]

THE MEANING OF SYMBOL

Before discussing the nature of symbol and symbolism in the Fourth Gospel it would be well to call attention to the semantic confusion sometimes occasioned by John's use of the term σημεῖον (*sēmeion*), which is usually translated "sign." John's choice of σημεῖον rather than σύμβολον (*symbolon*) perhaps reflects the Septuagint's use of σημεῖον to translate אוֹת (*'ōt*), "sign," the Old Testament designation of the great revelatory and salvific acts of God in the history of Israel (e.g., in Exod. 10:1–2; Num. 26:10; Deut. 34:11). But

---

duced by Mark W. G. Stibbe, New Testament Tools and Studies (Leiden: E. J. Brill, 1993); *The Fourth Gospel from a Literary Perspective,* ed. R. Alan Culpepper and Fernando F. Segovia, *Semeia* 53 (Atlanta: Scholars Press, 1991).

[4] Dorothy A. Lee, *The Symbolic Narratives of the Fourth Gospel,* SNTS Supplement Series 95 (Sheffield, England: JSOT Press, 1994); Craig R. Koester, *Symbolism in the Fourth Gospel: Meaning, Mystery, Community* (Minneapolis: Fortress, 1995); Larry Paul Jones, *The Symbol of Water in the Gospel of John,* JSNTSup 145 (Sheffield: Sheffield Academic Press, 1997), all of which contain extensive bibliographies on symbolism in general, in scripture, and especially in the Fourth Gospel.

whatever the reason for John's choice of *sēmeion*, there is growing consensus among scholars in the semantic disciplines that "sign" and "symbol" are very different realities[5] and that using the two terms interchangeably leads to substantial confusion. The Johannine *sēmeia* are, in contemporary terms, not signs but symbols.[6] Therefore, to avoid confusion I will call them *sēmeion/ sēmeia* (pl.), and reserve "sign" and "symbol" for that which they respectively denote in contemporary discourse.

Although there is much theoretical diversity among those working in the several disciplines concerned with symbolism, there is today broad consensus at least on the nature and function of the symbol, and the following definition would, I think, be generally acceptable.[7] Symbol can be defined as (1) a sensible reality (2) which renders present to and (3) involves a person subjectively in (4) a transforming experience (5) of transcendent mystery. Of the five elements of this definition only the first is common to both sign and symbol. A brief consideration of each of the five elements of the definition will clarify this point.

1. Both sign and symbol are *sensible realities*. Not only things (such as bread, wine, and water) but also words, gestures, and combinations of things, words, and gestures can constitute the sensible dimension of the symbol. The importance of the sensible element in the symbol is that it renders the transcendent, which is by nature purely spiritual, intersubjectively available. The human body, for example, is the symbol by which the personality can be experienced. In the Fourth Gospel Jesus of Nazareth is the great symbol of God. John's audacious and fundamental affirmation that the "Word became flesh" (1:14) is the basis for regarding the incarnation as genuinely symbolic. In it the Wisdom of God, invisible by nature, becomes that which "we have looked upon and touched with our hands, concerning the word of life . . .

---

[5] For a good discussion of the difference, see T. Fawcett, *The Symbolic Language of Religion: An Introductory Study* (London: SCM, 1970), especially p. 26.

[6] W. Nicol takes the opposite position on terminology but comes to the same conclusions on content, that is, on the significant difference between sign and symbol (*The Semeia in the Fourth Gospel: Tradition and Redaction*, NovTSup [Leiden: E. J. Brill, 1972], 123).

Because the terminology in respect to symbolism remains fluid and different authors use the two terms differently, the student must simply read each author on his or her own terms keeping in mind the distinction in concepts even if the terms are used differently.

[7] When I developed this definition of symbol I was making use of the monograph of G. Durand, *L'imagination symbolique*, Initiation philosophique 66 (Paris: Presses Universitaires de France, 1968), which unfortunately is not available in English. Although I have since refined my definition, my debt to this text remains.

that which we have seen and heard" (1 John 1:1–3) and in Jesus the God whom "no one has ever seen" (John 1:18) is revealed.

2. Unlike the sign, which merely points to or stands for an absent reality that is totally other than itself, the symbol *renders present* the transcendent because and insofar as it participates in what it re-presents. The symbol is an epiphany of present reality,[8] not an indication of an absent one. Nevertheless, although the symbol renders the transcendent really present, it renders it present in a limited and sensible mode, thus simultaneously revealing and concealing what it re-presents. This is the basis of the essential ambiguity of the Johannine *sēmeia,* in the face of which the blind see and those who see become blind (see John 9:39). The symbol, although sensibly perceptible, is by nature revelatory only to spiritual intuition. Everyone present could see Jesus, but not everyone could see in him the glory of the only Son.

3. The symbol, unlike the sign, is not an objective communication of information. Rather, it reveals by involving the person in a *subject-to-subject relationship* with the transcendent. This characteristic of the symbol has two implications. First, unlike the sign, which designates the known by means of an unambiguous one-to-one correspondence (the exit sign means only one thing), the symbol leads a person into the unknown by rendering present the mystery of the transcendent, which is essentially many-faceted. Because the symbol involves a one-to-many relationship, it resists translation or explana-tion.[9] The question What does this symbol stand for? shows that the ques-tioner takes the symbol for a sign. The symbol not only does not "stand for" anything; it cannot be reduced to signifying one thing only. Second, the sym-bol does not give objective information; it initiates one into an experience that is open-ended. The man born blind (John 9), in the *sēmeion* of his heal-ing, encountered the glory of the living God in Jesus and progressed in that experience even before he could name his healer (9:17, 30–31, 33, 36). The Pharisees wanted an explanation: "What did he do to you? How did he open your eyes?" (9:26). The healed blind man realized that it was useless to repeat what he had said (see 9:27). A symbol cannot be explained because it is not

---

[8] This is the point made by Paul Ricoeur when he distinguishes between metaphor, which is a purely linguistic reality, and symbol, which stands on the threshold between reality and language participating in the former and giving rise to the latter (*Interpretation Theory: Discourse and the Surplus of Meaning* [Fort Worth: Texas Christian University Press, 1976], 45–69).

[9] See Paul Ricoeur, *The Symbolism of Evil,* trans. Emerson Buchanan (Boston: Beacon, 1967), 347–57.

simply an appeal to the intellect but a locus of experience. His interlocutors were resistant to the experience and therefore impervious to the revelation.

4. The involvement of a person with the transcendent rendered present in the symbol is necessarily a *transforming experience*. By nature, the symbol demands involvement[10] as a condition for entering into the revelation of which it is the locus. The healed blind man knew that only those who also wished to become Jesus' disciples could understand the *sēmeion* of his healing (see 9:27). However, the initial commitment that enables one to encounter the transcendent in the symbolic is only the beginning of the relationship that must develop in a continuously deepening commitment or die. It is this relationship of ever deepening commitment that gradually transforms the person. All of the encounter narratives in the Fourth Gospel illustrate this characteristic of the symbol as dynamically involving. The contrast between Nicodemus in John 3 and the Samaritan woman in John 4 is especially illuminating.[11] Nicodemus, by his insistence on objectifying, indeed literalizing, the symbolic, was in fact refusing the involvement demanded by the symbolic discourse. The Samaritan woman, by her request for the living water, which as yet she did not understand (see 4:15), entered into the symbolic dynamic. She signified her initial commitment and was drawn into the fullness of revelation. The difference between Nicodemus and the Samaritan woman was not in their capacity for knowledge (Nicodemus being presented as clearly superior in this area) but in their capacity for involvement and commitment.

5. Finally, the symbol mediates the *transcendent* or some aspect of the transcendent, that is, the spiritual or mystery. From all that has been said, it is clear that only the personal can be symbolized, either a person him- or herself, or some aspect of personal existence such as thought, life, truth, or love. Therefore, all symbolism is potentially religious in that the symbolic opens out on personhood and therefore ultimately on the divine. However, only in the incarnation, according to the Fourth Gospel, did God adequately self-symbolize in the human sphere. It was the Word of God, Holy Wisdom, that became flesh. And that symbol, Jesus of Nazareth, constituted the sensible locus of relationship with God.

It is only in terms of symbol, correctly understood, that we can grasp John's presentation of the incarnation as salvation. According to John, the

---

[10] Fawcett, *Symbolic Language of Religion*, 42–46.

[11] Koester, *Symbolism*, 45–51; Mary Margaret Pazdan, "Nicodemus and the Samaritan Woman: Contrasting Models of Discipleship," *BTB* 17 (October 1987): 145–48.

incarnation was the inauguration of a symbolic or sacramental economy of salvific revelation in which the history of Jesus, and eventually the history of his disciples, constitutes the symbolic material. Jesus himself, and by extension his works (including both his *sēmeia* and his words), was the symbolic locus of the transforming relationship between God and the human person.

The transformation wrought in the person by his or her symbolic involvement with God in Jesus is the communication of the Spirit by which the person becomes in reality a child of God (see 1:12–13) born from above (see 3:3) into the eternal life (see 6:40) of the only Son. Participating in that life empowers the disciples to do Jesus' works and even greater works than the earthly Jesus had done (see 14:12). In other words, the disciple individually and the community of believers as a body become the real symbolic presence of the glorified Jesus in the world. The community is not a stand-in for the absent Jesus but Jesus' way of being present in every time and place. Through the actions and words of the disciples, as once through the works of Jesus, later generations will be brought to the encounter with God in Christ (see 17:20). The church is a realization of the same relationship between history and symbol as was the earthly Jesus. This amounts to saying that the church as community is sacramental in a much more fundamental sense than simply being the agent of certain sacramental rituals.

HISTORY AND SYMBOLISM
IN THE FOURTH GOSPEL

The Gospel of John, which mediates the encounter between Jesus and the contemporary believer, is not simply a historical work that includes an occasional, or even many, freestanding "symbols," but it is an essentially symbolic text in which the historical material itself functions symbolically. The Gospel mediates the encounter between God and Jesus' disciples of all time by being for readers the symbolic locus of that encounter.[12] As the earthly humanity of Jesus was the symbolic locus of the encounter between Jesus' first disciples and God, so his textual presence in the Gospel is a locus of that encounter for

---

[12] I develop this thesis fully in *The Revelatory Text: Interpreting the New Testament as Sacred Scripture,* 2nd ed. (Collegeville, Minn.: Liturgical Press, 1999). See the similar presentation by Marcus Borg in *The God We Never Knew: Beyond Dogmatic Religion to a More Authentic Contemporary Faith* (New York: HarperCollins, 1997), 117.

later disciples. This places the Gospel text in the category of "sacrament," or symbolic mediation of divine reality.[13]

As just explained, the crucial difference between sign and symbol is that whereas a sign stands for, or *stands in for,* something other than itself, a symbol is the *way of being present* of something in whose reality it participates. An "exit" sign stands for a door but attempting to leave through the exit sign would result in frustration if not injury. A kiss, by contrast, is a symbol. The very unitive character of the action itself mediates the love of which it is the expression. The task of the symbol is to make that which, by nature, is spiritual or transcendent, and therefore sensibly unavailable in itself, intersubjectively available by giving it a "body," a sensible form. The human body, in which the person becomes available, is perhaps our best example of symbol in the strong sense. Speech is a symbolization of inner experience. Art symbolizes the beautiful. The church is the symbolic presence of Christ in the world. Most importantly for our purposes, Jesus is the symbol of God, and the Gospel itself the symbol of Jesus. In short, a symbol does not stand for something. It *is* the "something," available in sensible expression. Therefore, it is the locus, the place, of revelation and encounter, whether human or divine.

The most characteristic feature of the Judeo-Christian tradition is its conviction that God's self-revelation to humanity took place in history. History itself, for Christianity, is the symbolic locus of encounter with the divine. This realization of the symbolic dimension of history was implicit and operative among the Old Testament writers. For them their history was salvation history. We see this clearly, for example, in Wisdom 10–19, where the whole of Israel's history is presented as the action of Holy Wisdom, that is, of God, in its midst.

In the Fourth Gospel, however, the notion of symbolic revelation becomes even more focused and explicit. The Fourth Evangelist concentrates the mystery of divine revelation in the person of Jesus of Nazareth, whom the evangelist designates as the Word (the Wisdom of God) *become* flesh. Revelation is the dynamic of manifestation and response, or, as John says, divine witness and human believing, both of which are constitutive of the reality. Both dimensions are emphasized in John's characteristic treatment of Jesus.

First, Jesus is the manifestation of the one who sent him, God, whom he calls his Father. Jesus is the sensible expression of the glory of God (see 1:14).

---

[13] I am talking here not about particular rituals that different Christian denominations have designated as "sacraments," for example, baptism or Eucharist, but about the revelatory and salvific character of symbolic reality participated in through faith.

His words and works reveal that glory (2:11). The Father dwells in him doing God's works (see 5:36; 14:10). In short, to see Jesus is to see the Father (14:9) for Jesus and the Father are one (10:30). Second, Jesus is the locus of the disciples' response, which initiates them into participation in the glory of God. Jesus is the temple where the people meet God (2:19–21) and where true worship will be offered (4:21–24). He is the way to the Father (14:6). To be in the hand of Jesus is to be in the Father's hand (10:28–29). To be possessed by Jesus is to belong to the Father (17:10). To receive Jesus is to become a child of the Father (1:12).

Although in the Synoptic Gospels Jesus is the center and high point of a history of salvation that is implicitly recognized as symbolic, it is only in the Fourth Gospel that Jesus himself is presented as the unique and totally adequate symbol of God. The exclusive centrality of the person of Jesus in the Fourth Gospel, which virtually all Johannine scholars recognize,[14] is due precisely to John's reflectively explicit consciousness of Jesus as the symbol of God, totally relativizing all other revelation, even that of the Old Testament which, according to this Gospel, can only be truly revelatory to one who has come to Jesus (see 5:39–40).

According to the conclusion of the Fourth Gospel (see 20:30–31) John intended what he *wrote* to have the same revelatory function for his readers that the symbolic activity of the earthly Jesus had for the first disciples. In other words, the Fourth Gospel is not simply a record of symbolic revelation but *is* itself symbolic revelation. "These things are written that you may believe." This is the key to the relation between history and symbol in the written Gospel. The Gospel is a literary symbol of Jesus in which history itself supplies the symbolic material.

The essence of the artistic or literary symbol is not that it copies or reproduces the natural symbol. John's Gospel does not copy the historical Jesus. The essence of the artistic symbol is to be *another* symbol of that which the natural symbol revealed. The Gospel is *another* symbol of the Word of God. This new symbol has been called the "Johannine Jesus,"[15] that is, the textual version of Jesus as John presents him. The question is, What is the relation between the earthly Jesus (i.e., the natural symbol) and the Johannine Jesus (i.e., the textual or literary symbol)? The relation is that both are true sym-

[14] See, e.g., Barnabas Lindars, "The Fourth Gospel an Act of Contemplation," in *Studies in the Fourth Gospel,* ed. F. L. Cross (London: Mowbray, 1957), 23.

[15] The expression is frequently encountered. An excellent treatment of the meaning of the term is Franz Mussner, *The Historical Jesus in the Gospel of St. John,* trans. W. J. O'Hara (1965; reprint, London: Burns & Oates, 1967).

bolic expressions of the same person, the Word of the Father. They are two symbols of one reality.

The artistic symbol of something in nature or history is always, in some way, influenced by the material of the natural symbol. The physical features of the face of the person influence the portrait artist's choice of color, use of line, and so on. The physical features of the countryside influence the landscape artist's painting. But the artist liberates the symbolized transcendent (the person or the beauty of nature) from its overparticularization in the natural symbol. The artist releases the transcendent by selecting only certain elements of the material of the natural symbol, and modifying even those, so that the glory of the symbolized reality subsumes the material of the artistic symbol making it exist with such fullness of being that it is literally transfigured.[16] The artistic symbol has a universality that the natural symbol cannot have. A person's face is his or hers alone; a countryside is singular and particular. But the portrait or the landscape painting universalizes the particularity without erasing it.

The Fourth Evangelist tells the readers of the Gospel that only some of Jesus' symbolic activity has been included (see 20:30) in the Gospel. And it is obvious, from the few parallels that we have between John and the Synoptics, that the Fourth Evangelist has substantially transformed even these few.[17] More exactly, John has used them in such a way that the glory which the historical events originally mediated in muted tones has now totally transfigured the historical material. To ask how the Johannine account corresponds to what "actually happened" is like asking how van Gogh's self-portrait corresponds to his historical face. The question is misplaced. The significant question is how the self-portrait of van Gogh corresponds to the person of van Gogh. Any amateur artist on Montmartre could have copied van Gogh's face. Only the artist could create a new symbolic expression of his person.

However, if we were to meet van Gogh today, and if we were sufficiently perceptive to read his soul in his face, we would recognize him from the self-portrait, not because the portrait exactly reproduces the physical face but because that face is the natural symbol of the same person we know from the artistic symbol. The marvel is that the artistic symbol is, in fact, more immediately and totally revelatory than the physical face itself because of art's peculiar power to release the transcendent and universal. This is exactly what is

[16] A good treatment of this subject is J. M. Tézé, "La gloire du sensible," *Christus* 17 (1970): 380–91.

[17] For example, the cure of the official's son in John 4:46–54 seems to be a genuine parallel of Matt. 8:5–13 and Luke 7:1–10, but the introduction of the seeing-believing problematic in John 4:48 and the *sēmeion* theme in 4:54 substantially modifies the Johannine account.

meant by the beauty of the work of art and why it has the peculiar universality of the beautiful.

By the same token, if we were to find ourselves suddenly transplanted to first-century Palestine, and if we were sufficiently spiritually perceptive, we would recognize the historical Jesus from our contemplation of the Johannine Jesus, not because the Gospel has reproduced the history with literal facticity but because both history and Gospel are symbolic expressions of the same person, the Word of God made flesh and text.

In summary, the history of the earthly Jesus, in John, has become artistic √ material. That is why, on the one hand, there are such surprisingly accurate historical details in the Fourth Gospel and, on the other hand, why it is so difficult to use this Gospel in the quest of the historical (meaning the earthly) Jesus. Into the spare outline of the Johannine Jesus, the Fourth Evangelist has poured the entire revelation of the Word of God experienced in the words and deeds of the earthly Jesus. Exactly how this textual figure corresponds to the earthly Jesus we will never know. Nor is this a loss. On the contrary, John has performed the service of the artist. In the intensity of artistic liberation the evangelist has given us the transcendent beauty of the Word of God as it transfigured the face of the earthly Jesus and now transfigures the language of the text.

Several consequences flow from the realization that the Gospel text as a whole is thoroughly symbolic. First, there is not an inverse proportion between the historical and the symbolic in the Fourth Gospel. On the contrary, the proportion is direct. Because history itself is John's symbolic material, the more historical something is, the more symbolic potential it possesses.

Second, symbolism in John is not an element in the Gospel but a dimension of the Gospel as a whole, namely, its characteristic revelatory mode.

Third, and following directly from the foregoing, because the Fourth Gospel is thoroughly symbolic, the individual parts have to be understood in function of the whole rather than the whole in function of the parts.

Fourth, Johannine symbolism is not extrinsicist allegorism.[18] Fifth, symbolism is not a slippery terrain where all interpretation is equally arbitrary and equally undemonstrable. The symbolic character of the Fourth Gospel

---

[18] Actually, the term "allegory" as it was used by the patristic writers included all figurative or more-than-literal uses of language and not merely the kind of one-to-one correspondence of the *roman à clé* that the term suggests today. For a fuller treatment of the ancient theory of "senses of scripture," see my article "Scripture and Spirituality," in *Christian Spirituality: Origins to the Twelfth Century,* ed. Bernard McGinn and John Meyendorff, World Spirituality: An Encyclopedic History of the Religious Quest (New York: Crossroad, 1985), 1–20.

does mean that it is literature, and one of the marks of true literature is its potentiality to enrich itself endlessly by the interpretations of successive generations. The genuine symbol is polyvalent by nature and therefore the source of a surplus of meaning that grounds multiple valid interpretations. But this does not mean that all interpretations are valid or even equally insightful. There are no rules for the "decoding" of symbols, because symbols, which are not signs, cannot be decoded. They do not stand for something that, once grasped, makes the symbol unnecessary. Rather, only through and in the symbol is the reality encountered. But there are criteria for the valid interpretation of symbolic works.[19] In this domain the Johannine exegete has much to learn from artistic criticism in general and especially from literary criticism, from philosophy, from comparative religion's study of symbolic expression, and from the sciences of language in general and of religious language in particular.

All of these consequences merely explicitate the basic hypothesis, namely, that the Fourth Gospel is essentially symbolic and that taking this fact into account in its interpretation is not an optional exercise but a condition of validity.

SYMBOLIC CHARACTERS
IN THE FOURTH GOSPEL

So far we have seen that Jesus himself is the foundational symbol, the very revelation of God, and that his works, including both the *sēmeia* he performs and the words he speaks, are his own self-symbolization. The Gospel text is the literary resymbolization of Jesus for successive generations.

Another feature of Johannine symbolism that has long been recognized but that has caused considerable debate among scholars concerns the characters in the Gospel. John's characters, a number of whom are specific to this Gospel, are remarkably well drawn and engaging. They do not appear as semi-anonymous members of a crowd, like the woman lifting her voice in praise of Jesus' mother in Luke (see Luke 11:27), but in intense, usually individual, interaction with Jesus. A number of these characters, for example, John the baptizer, Judas, Simon Peter, the Samaritan woman, Mary Magdalene, the man born blind, the paralytic, the mother of Jesus, Thomas,

---

[19] An excellent start in developing criteria for the handling of Johannine symbolism was made by J. Leal, "El simbolismo histórico del IV evangelio," *EstBib* 19 (1960): 329–48. See also Ricoeur, *Interpretation Theory*, 78–79, on validation.

Martha, Mary of Bethany, the royal official, Nicodemus, Nathanael, and the Beloved Disciple are good examples of the relationship between history and symbolism in John.

Virtually all of these characters (except Nathanael, the Samaritan woman, and the Beloved Disciple) are known from extra-Johannine sources and in all likelihood are real figures from the lifetime of the earthly Jesus. Furthermore, we recognize in them character traits, such as the impetuosity of Peter, the perfidy of Judas, and the devotion of Mary of Bethany, that link them to their personae in the other Gospels giving further evidence that they were real people in the lifetime of Jesus and/or the early Christian community. However, in John they are transformed into what Raymond Collins called "representative figures"[20] or, more exactly, symbolic characters. The evangelist concentrates the character of these figures into a single or a couple of traits that are highlighted and intensified. The character becomes a kind of incarnation of the feature or trait. Thus, the Beloved Disciple is the personification of loving insight into the mystery of Jesus; Judas, of refusal of the light that has come into the world; the man born blind, of the dynamic of coming to believe in Jesus, and so on. The trait that is highlighted and personified is something historically associated with the real person. The evangelist is using history symbolically, not inventing "symbols" out of whole cloth.

This literary technique is highly effective. The reader identifies with the character, positively or negatively, and thus enters into the dynamic of the narrative in a deeply personal way. We do not simply read about Thomas refusing to believe without seeing; we discover our own unbelief and thus hear Jesus' words, "Be not unbelieving but believing" (John 20:27), addressed to ourselves. We live through the process of coming to believe as our own infidelities and religious rigidities are revealed in the Samaritan woman (see 4:1–42). Our own love and longing for an absent Jesus are felt as we identify with Mary Magdalene searching in the darkened garden for the one she loves (see 20:1–18).

This character symbolism, however, has an unintended negative effect in the case of the collective symbolic personality of "the Jews." The Jews were, of course, a real historical factor both in the life of the earthly Jesus and in the life of the Johannine community. Jesus and his disciples were Jews, and certainly a large proportion of John's community were Jews. But it was also the Jewish authorities in Jerusalem who collaborated with the Roman authorities in condemning Jesus to death. And the Jewish authorities at Jamnia after the fall of the temple in 70 C.E. were the ones who finally excommunicated the

[20] Raymond F. Collins, "The Representative Figures in the Fourth Gospel," *DRev* 94 (1976): 26–46, 118–32.

Johannine Christians from the synagogue. It was these historical Jewish authorities in the life of Jesus and of the community who were personified by the evangelist in the collective person of "the Jews" in the Gospel.

This transformation of the historical Jewish authorities into a symbolic agent of evil, combined with two other features of the Gospel, has fed the destructive anti-Judaism of Christians down through the centuries. The first feature is the high Christology of John's Gospel, in which Jesus is the Son of God, God incarnate. Consequently, anyone who participates in the persecution and execution of the historical Jesus is a deicide. Whatever the historical Jewish authorities thought about Jesus and however unjust their persecution or threatening of that human being might have been, they certainly did not know that he was divine and did not intend to kill God. But the combination of the high Christology in John and the symbolic concentration of malice in the Jewish authorities is deadly because it makes them appear as deliberately intending to kill the one who was clearly God's Son.

The second feature of the Gospel that promotes anti-Judaism is the use of the unspecified term "the Jews" for a small group of authorities who certainly did not include or even represent the whole people at the time of Jesus, much less Jews of subsequent generations. But the symbolic technique actually concentrates in "the Jews" the whole of Judaism and then reduces the latter to a single highlighted trait, namely, rejection of the light who has come unto his own.

Undoubtedly, the evangelist would today repudiate absolutely this generalized anti-Judaism and its horrendous anti-Semitic progeny.[21] But they arise from the internal literary dynamics of the symbolic text and thus are extremely powerful. Therefore, a heavy obligation is incumbent on anyone who teaches or preaches this Gospel to deal explicitly with this issue and to counter the natural tendency of readers to take "the Jews" in John as a literal designation of all Jews, either of the time of Jesus and the Johannine community or of later times.[22]

CONCLUSION

Symbolism is the primary hermeneutical key to understanding the Fourth Gospel. Its theology is based on the incarnation itself, the self-symbolization

[21] Raymond E. Brown, *A Retreat with John the Evangelist: That You May Have Life* (Cincinnati: St. Anthony Messenger, 1998).

[22] See Francis J. Moloney, *The Gospel of John*, Sacra Pagina Series (Collegeville, Minn.: Liturgical Press, 1998), 9–11, on the subject of "the Jews" in John.

of God in the Word become flesh. The incarnation is the sacramental principle of all that follows from it: the sharing in divine life of Jesus' disciples through the gift of the Spirit; the church community as the symbolic presence of the glorified Jesus in subsequent history; the effectiveness of the words and deeds of that community in manifesting and communicating divine life to believers down through the ages. The symbolic character of the Gospel text itself is rooted in the incarnation of the Word of God.

Because the symbol is never a stand-in, never something "left behind" by one who has departed, but the mode of presence of one who is here and now, Christians of subsequent ages are not, in the Johannine perspective, heirs of a revelation they receive secondhand. There are, in John's theology, no "second-generation" Christians. All are, as were the original disciples, in direct relationship with Jesus, who is present and active in the community. They are branches in the vine (see 15:1–11), sheep of Jesus' flock (see 10:11–15), whom Jesus himself feeds with his own flesh and blood.

No one takes Jesus' place in the community or mediates between Jesus and his own. He knows his own and they know him, and he calls them each by name (see 10:1–5). Thus, mediation in the Christian community takes on a meaning very different from that of a hierarchical transmission. Jesus does not entrust the riches of salvation to some members of the church who represent him and pass on his message and grace to those they deem worthy. All receive the Spirit directly from Christ and thus mediate the riches of divine life to one another. And anyone who presumes to ask, "And what about that one?" (whoever "that one" following Jesus might be) is told by Jesus, "What is that to you? You, follow me!" (see 21:22).

The symbolic principle in the Fourth Gospel is, in other words, the basis of the extraordinary realism of its theology and spirituality rather than, as some positivist exegetes have feared, the source of confusion and obscurity. What it precludes is not clarity but detachment. This Gospel cannot be understood by simply reading it as a detached observer. The only path to understanding is participation and such participation is supremely dangerous. One who sees the light of the world in Jesus is caught up in the existential crisis of choosing or refusing to believe. And this is a choice for or against eternal life.

Commitment
in the Fourth Gospel

Fidelity in commitment is a perennial human and religious concern, both because the quality of life of an individual person is largely determined by the type of relationships he or she establishes and because the quality of any society, secular or ecclesial, is partly a function of the quality of the relationships that constitute it. Nevertheless, it must be recognized that this perennial concern has taken on an unprecedented importance in our own times, especially within communities of faith. Vocational instability, both in marriage and in religious life and ordained ministry, has reached epidemic proportions.[1] Although it is not altogether certain that this instability reflects a substantial loss of conviction about the value of fidelity in interpersonal commitments, it is clear that many people assign little importance to maintaining commitments beyond the point at which they seem to "be working for me." However, many people struggle valiantly, against very heavy odds, to preserve their marriages, honor the religious vows they have made, and maintain their ministerial commitments. And it cannot be denied that many persons who have, with serious deliberation, responsibly decided to terminate an interpersonal and/or institutional commitment go on to make new commitments which endure, the quality of which belies any simplistic judgments about the validity of their decisions.

Both Old and New Testaments reveal that loving fidelity (*ḥesed* and *'emet*) is a defining characteristic of the God of the Judeo-Christian tradition. For

---

[1] Almost half of marriages in the United States end in divorce, and many divorced persons have been divorced more than once. The number of religious women, which was roughly 190,000 in the preconciliar period, is now down to fewer than 80,000, a major proportion of the decline due to women requesting dispensation from their vows; and there has been a similar decline in brothers. The decline in Catholic ordained ministers due to resignations from the clergy is similarly steep. Margaret Miles referred to American society as one in which "people are disastrously inept at maintaining committed love relationships" (*Seeing and Believing: Religion and Values in the Movies* [Boston: Beacon, 1996], 191).

the Christian, then, fidelity is the ideal in all interpersonal relationships and especially in those that are specifically undertaken as lifetime commitments. But the complexity of contemporary experience precludes any simplistic assumptions about the meaning and implications of this ideal. The anonymity of modern Western society, the multiplication of options through education and media exposure, the loss of familial and community support and social control, the liberation of women and other minorities, and many other factors are unique to the late twentieth century.

The situation invites us to scrutinize the Word of God as it is mediated to us in the biblical text and to bring to bear on our questions the light of divine revelation. In doing so, we cannot naïvely address these peculiarly contemporary questions to the scriptures in hopes of straightforward answers. Our biblical forebears did not live in our circumstances nor face the questions these circumstances raise, and consequently they did not write answers to our questions into these ancient documents. The theological and pastoral impasses to which a noncritical proof-text approach to the questions of vocation and commitment has led in the past should warn us against biblical fundamentalism, anachronism, and accommodation in this matter. However, although the Bible is not an answer book for contemporary questions, it is a source of light for all of the perennial religious concerns of humankind. The contemporary question of commitment has a particular form that the Bible does not address, but the concern itself is as ancient as the relationship between God and the human race.

In what follows I will focus on what the Gospel of John might contribute to contemporary Christian reflection on the subject of commitment. Because the historical situation of the community for which this Gospel was written raised the question of Christian commitment in a particularly acute way, the Fourth Gospel's reflection on the subject might throw some light on our contemporary questions. At the very least it might help us more accurately formulate our own questions and therefore stand a better chance of more adequately addressing them.

HISTORICAL SITUATION OF THE FOURTH GOSPEL: A CONFLICT OF COMMITMENT

The Gospel of John probably received its final form somewhere in Asia Minor at the turn of the first century and was addressed to a community composed primarily, though not exclusively, of Jews. It was written during the time when Jewish authorities were attempting to consolidate Judaism in terms of belief and practice following the destruction of the Jerusalem temple in 70 C.E. Christianity, which had developed up to this time as an accepted Jewish sect among many such sects, increasingly came to be regarded as heretical because of its belief that in Jesus the awaited Messiah had come and also because Christianity, as it began to attribute divinity to Jesus, seemed a threat to the monotheism that is the heart of Jewish faith. The conflict between an increasingly normative Judaism and a Christianity that was becoming increasingly aware of its own distinctive beliefs reached a bitter climax in the excommunication of Jewish Christians from the synagogue during the period when the sanhedrin of Jamnia, which had replaced the sanhedrin of Jerusalem, was under the leadership of Gamaliel II (ca. 90–110 C.E.).

The importance of this historical situation for the Johannine community, and thus for the theology and spirituality of the Fourth Gospel, can hardly be exaggerated.[2] These Christians, living at the end of the first century, faced an agonizing choice between surrendering their membership in Judaism, the religious community of the chosen people, and abandoning their new faith in Jesus of Nazareth as the Christ and the Son of God (see 20:31). They faced the conflict of religious commitments in its starkest form.

It is difficult for a Christian who has never been a Jew to realize the magnitude of this choice. The Jew who became a Christian belonged to Israel, the chosen people whom God rescued from slavery in Egypt and led through the desert, to whom God gave the Torah on Sinai, and who entered the promised land under God's own leadership. Israel's kings had ruled in God's name and her prophets had spoken in God's name. God had recalled this people from exile and had promised them a savior. God dwelt in their midst, heard their cries, and was close to them, they believed, as to no other people on earth. To voluntarily cut oneself off from the community of Israel, from synagogue worship and observance of the law, from rabbinic leadership and table fellowship with God's people was a radical severance from one's past, one's corporate identity, one's whole historical understanding of the truth of revelation and its divine institution in Israel. Many passages in the Gospel of John are concerned with this agonizing experience and are calculated to strengthen the Christians in their choice of Christ by assuring them that the true Israelite was not necessarily a Jew nor the Jew necessarily a true Israelite (e.g., John 8:33–40). Being a true Israelite was not a matter of biology but of faith as,

---

[2] See J. Louis Martyn, *History and Theology in the Fourth Gospel,* revised and enlarged, 2nd ed. (1968; reprint, Nashville: Abingdon, 1979), 147–56, for a fuller explanation of this experience.

indeed, it had been for Abraham (cf. Gen. 15:6, to which Jesus refers in John 8:39–40).

Because the problem of Christian commitment was so urgent for the Johannine community, the Gospel's reflections on the question are explicit and radical. They are especially pertinent to the contemporary situation because the conversion with which the Fourth Gospel is concerned is not a conversion from evil to good or from idolatry to belief, but a conversion from a legitimate but no longer viable religious commitment within Judaism to a total and exclusive commitment to Jesus as Messiah and Son of God, which was now seen to be both the will of God and, for historical reasons beyond their control, incompatible with their prior commitment in Judaism. The members of the Johannine community were called to transcend the very commitment to which they had once been called by God. The conflict involved in this new call was not unlike the conflicts experienced by many sincere Christians in our own times who acknowledge the authenticity of the commitments they have made and yet feel called, by circumstances beyond their control, to leave those commitments behind. If anything, the Johannine conflict was more radical because it involved not merely an interpersonal relationship but their fundamental religious identity within the believing community of Israel.

There is no evidence in the Gospels that the historical Jesus intended to abolish Judaism, much less to found a new religion.[3] On the contrary, Jesus came to call to salvation the lost sheep of the house of Israel (see Matt. 15:24). The conflict between Jesus and his adversaries (the chief priests, scribes, and Pharisees in the Synoptics, usually simply "the Jews"—meaning the Jerusalem authorities—in the Fourth Gospel) arises not because Jesus' message was discontinuous with the revelation of the Old Testament but because the hierarchy, the official authorities of Judaism, were impeding the relationship between God and the people that their offices existed to foster. As Jesus says, "If you were Abraham's children [that is, faithful Jews], you would do what Abraham did" (John 8:39). Or even more explicitly, "Do not think that I shall accuse you to the Father; it is Moses who accuses you [of infidelity to the law], on whom you set your hope" (5:45). In other words, Jesus was not attempting to destroy Judaism but, like the prophets of the Old Testament, to recall her leaders to fidelity to the covenant. And while condemning the

---

[3] This point was made forcefully many years ago by Hans Küng, *On Being A Christian* (New York: Doubleday, 1976), 295–300. Today it is the solid consensus of scholars of Christian origins. See, e.g., Marcus J. Borg, *The God We Never Knew: Beyond Dogmatic Religion to a More Authentic Contemporary Faith* (New York: HarperCollins, 1997), especially 88–91.

abuses of the authorities he appealed to the ordinary people who were being oppressed by them to reclaim their identity, freedom, and power as children of God.

In the Fourth Gospel "the Jews" and "the world," when the terms are used pejoratively, are nearly synonymous.[4] They designate those who refused to receive the Word when he came into the(ir) world (see 1:10–11). John begins by analyzing the refusal of the truth among "the Jews," who, in the experience of the historical Johannine community, were the collective embodiment of this refusal. Nevertheless, although the evangelist's particular interest in the Jewish authorities is a function of the historical situation of the Johannine community, the reflection remains relevant because the phenomenon of refusal of the light one is offered is not limited to any time, place, or people. It is through the meditation on the refusal to believe of "the Jews" that the evangelist comes to understand the real nature of believing and, therefore, of commitment, whether of Jew or Gentile.

"The Jews" in the Fourth Gospel, who become the enemies of Jesus, are the Jerusalem officials. And those who later persecute the Johannine community are the successors of those officials. It should be noted that all those who accept Jesus in the Fourth Gospel, with the possible exception of the royal official in 4:46–54, are also Jews or, in the case of the Samaritans, originally Israelites. And a large segment of the Johannine community were also Jews by birth. Consequently, it is not Jewishness, in either its ethnic or its religious sense, that is the source of conflict.

The conflict, according to the Gospel, is between an idolatrous attachment to the Jewish religious institution and the inbreaking of divine revelation in Jesus. Attachment to their own interpretation of the law rendered the officials of Judaism incapable of responding to divine revelation, impervious to the truth to which the Law and the Prophets witnessed. The Jewish authorities had become committed to their commitment rather than to God. Jesus came as the one sent by God, the one "of whom Moses in the law and also the prophets wrote" (see 1:45), and they would not accept him. What is most striking about Jesus' conflict with the Jewish authorities is that at no point does Jesus call them to anything other than fidelity to the covenant relationship with God which was at the heart of Israel's faith, but the authorities pre-

---

[4] Both terms are open to misinterpretation. "Jews" can be taken to mean all Jews of the time of Jesus, the Johannine community, and later history when, in fact, it refers to specific Jewish authorities. "World" can be taken to mean all people of all time who are not Christian when, in fact, it refers to those, Jews, Christians, or Gentiles, who have come to know who Jesus really is and have chosen freely to reject him.

fer to cling to the institutional letter rather than to embrace the truth. What engages the evangelist's reflection is why the authorities resisted the truth.

Conflicts over Jewish Institutions

In John 2 Jesus drives the merchants and money changers out of the temple,[5] not because he condemns the temple cult but because he truly understands and loves it, because "zeal for [God's] house" consumes him (see 2:17). He recalls the Jewish leaders to the real meaning of the temple: it is the Father's house (see 2:16), the meeting place of God and the people, not a place for institutional religious business. The authorities refuse this simple and straight-forward statement of the truth and focus instead on the right of Jesus to question the current institutional practice: "What sign have you to show us for doing this?" (2:18). This is a typical ploy of threatened institutional authority, the deflection of the challenge to deal with the issue by appeal to correct procedure. Jesus' right is simply the right of truth to name flagrant infidelity and to demand righteousness. But because the temple authorities refuse to confront the mystery of the temple in all its gracious exigency they are incapable of understanding either the cleansing of the historical temple or the abundant accomplishment of the mystery of the temple in the body of the glorified Jesus (2:19–22).

The conflict over the sabbath, recounted in John 5:2–18, reveals the same pattern. Jesus cured a paralyzed man on the official Jewish day of rest, even though he could easily have done so on another day, for the man had been at the pool of Bethzatha for thirty-eight years (see 5:5). Unlike the Synoptic Jesus, who cures on the sabbath to show that religious observances were instituted for human beings and not vice versa (e.g., Mark 2:27), the Johannine Jesus cures on the sabbath in order to reveal the essential continuity between God's creative activity at the beginning of the world and his ongoing salvific activity in Jesus. When the Jewish officials object to the cure on the sabbath Jesus replies, "My Father is working still, and I am working" (5:17). Like God, who never ceases to give life, Jesus gives life whenever he chooses. That the Jewish authorities understood the revelational claim is clear from the fact

---

[5] Many scholars believe that Jesus' cleansing of the temple was really the act that precipitated the decision of the authorities to kill him. In the Synoptic Gospels it is the last public act of Jesus, apparently the "last straw." In John, however, it is Jesus' first public act, which, in effect, puts his whole public ministry under the sign of conflict with the authorities over the meaning of God's presence in Israel. The final act that precipitates Jesus' arrest, in John, is the raising of Lazarus in which Jesus acts as God to give life. Thus the whole Gospel is about who really speaks and acts for God.

that they immediately tried to kill Jesus because he was "making himself equal with God" (5:18).

The real reason for the Jewish sabbath observance was the imitation of God who, according to Torah, rested on the seventh day from the divine work of creation (see Gen. 2:2–3) and who fulfilled that work by making Israel God's covenant people. By entering into the divine rhythm, so to speak, the Jews were to become and to remain sensitive to the revealing action of God, which presided not only at the origin of the universe and at the creation of the covenant people but continuously in the life of Israel. But the religious officials, by their idolatrous attachment to the letter of sabbath observance, had become blind to the meaning of the sabbath and were therefore unable to receive the truth offered to them in the saving work of Jesus in their midst.

Conflicts over Jesus' Identity and Works

The Jewish officials are shown repeatedly attempting to cast suspicion on Jesus, undermining the openness to him of those who could not deny what they had seen and heard in his signs and words. The officers sent by the chief priests and Pharisees to arrest Jesus return saying, "No man ever spoke like this man!" They are rebuked for credulity, for lack of religious sophistication (7:45–49). If they knew the law they would not so easily accept Jesus' credentials, namely, that he does the will of God and seeks only God's glory (7:16–19); they would not be so easily convicted by his challenge to honor the Mosaic law by judging righteously (7:19–24); they would not be led astray into believing his promise of living water to those who believe (7:37–39). To Nicodemus, who pleads with the authorities to apply the law justly by at least giving Jesus the benefit of a hearing, they declare that Jesus is already discredited by the law, for it gives no indication that a prophet will arise in Galilee (see 7:50–52). The authorities have decided which indications in the scriptures are to be heeded and which ignored. Geographical provenance and acceptance by the institutional authorities take precedence over justice.

On another occasion, after trying repeatedly to intimidate the man born blind, whom Jesus had healed, into denying the plain fact that Jesus had cured him, they finally expel the man from the synagogue because he, an unlettered and sinful man, had dared to teach them, the official interpreters of the law (see 9:34). The healed man had simply exclaimed in surprise at their refusal to see the work of God in the action of someone who opened the eyes of a man born blind (see 9:30). Again, the appeal is not to the content of the law but to the institutional credentials of those who interpret it.

When many of the Jews are drawn to believe in Jesus because of his raising of Lazarus from the dead, the chief priests and the Pharisees decide to kill not only Jesus (see 11:45–53) but also Lazarus (see 12:10), who was living evidence that Jesus did indeed do the works of his Father as he had claimed. Once more, rather than engage the challenge, the authorities decide to eliminate the evidence.

In the bitter confrontation with the Jewish authorities recounted in John 8:39ff., a part of the lengthy controversy that extends from chapter 5 through chapter 10 and is a kind of synthesis of the whole struggle, Jesus challenges their claim to salvation on the basis of their biological descent from Abraham. Jesus accuses them of replacing the interior reality of descent from Abraham, namely, being a believer and doing the works of faith, with the external reality of physical birth from Jewish parents. Earlier, in 5:39–40, Jesus convicts "the Jews" of preferring the letter of the scripture to the Word of God that it mediates. If they had allowed the scriptural Word to enter their hearts, they could not have failed to recognize the Word speaking to them in person.

THE IMPEDIMENT TO BELIEVING:
SEEKING ONE'S OWN GLORY

What each of these episodes makes clear is the Fourth Evangelist's understanding of unbelief[6] as the great impediment to salvation. Unbelief, in John, is a deep perversion of the spirit that makes a person incapable of accepting the truth because of an idolatrous commitment to something other than God. Its predecessor in the Old Testament is the idolatrous attachment to the temple and sacrifices, the sabbaths, feasts, and new moons, which the prophets say that God abhors because they are being substituted for the justice that God truly demands (see Isa. 8:4–17; Jer. 7:1–16, and elsewhere). In the Fourth Gospel this idolatrous commitment is called "seeking one's own glory," as opposed to seeking the glory of God. Jesus demands of the Jews, "How can you believe, who receive glory from one another and do not seek the glory that comes from the only God?" (5:44). In contrast, Jesus can say of himself, "I do not seek my own glory" (7:50). Rather, he seeks the glory of the one who sent him (7:18).

---

[6] It is difficult to render in English John's vocabulary of believing. The evangelist never uses the nouns "belief" or "faith" but only verbal forms of "to believe." This is theologically very important because, in this Gospel, faith is not a condition or state of being or possession but an active engagement with God.

In the Fourth Gospel ζητέω (*zēteō*), "to seek," is a theologically freighted term. It is typical of John to denote fundamental attitudes and dispositions by verbs rather than by nouns. The verb "to seek" denotes the goal-determined dynamism of a person's life. What one seeks reveals one's deepest concerns. The first disciples who, at John the baptizer's indication, follow Jesus are asked what they *seek* (1:38); Jesus' disciples wonder what Jesus *seeks* with the woman of Samaria (4:27); Jesus is the one who *seeks* the glory of the one who sent him (7:18); "the Jews" are accused of *seeking* to kill Jesus (7:19) even before they had become conscious of their own desire; in the garden on the night of his arrest Jesus demands of those sent to seize him, "Whom do you seek?" (18:4); and in the garden of the resurrection Jesus asks the distraught Mary Magdalene, "Why are you weeping? Whom do you seek?" (20:15).

That which one seeks in this profound sense is the motive force of one's actions, and this explains the radical incompatibility between seeking one's own glory and being open to God's revelation. Only the person who truly seeks the glory of God can be open to the totally unexpected, even to that which calls into question one's understanding of sacred traditions and institutions and relativizes the laws and practices that have seemed absolute. Only a total and single-minded determination to seek God above all things, regardless of where the divine invitation leads, can enable a person to move beyond absolute reliance on the secure structures of religious institution and allow God to be God in one's life.

The perennial threat to genuine religion is the "Grand Inquisitor syndrome," the conviction of authorities that they must protect people from direct contact with God, which presumably they are unequipped to handle, by institutional "hedges." Despite the claim that these hedges are erected for the protection of the religiously and spiritually weak, their real purpose is to maintain the power of the religious elite.[7] Because the Jewish officials were fundamentally motivated by the desire to preserve their own power and position (see 11:48) they had a non-negotiable stake in the religious *status quo* which made them incapable of seeing the truth in the signs and words of

---

[7] Borg says that Jesus "rejected the notion of a brokered kingdom of God and enacted the immediacy of access to God apart from institutional mediation" (*God We Never Knew,* 142). There is a very important distinction between a haughty contempt for the human mediation that can facilitate our openness to God and a subservient conviction that access to God is absolutely controlled by an institutional elite. The abiding temptation of institutional authority is to foster, even to impose, the latter. Hannah Arendt in her important treatise *The Human Condition* (Garden City, N.Y.: Doubleday, 1959), 236–43, says that those in any society who control forgiveness control the capacity of people to act. Control of forgiveness is the ultimate form of control of access to God.

Jesus when these spoke of something new. They were "blind" in the deepest spiritual sense of that word (see 9:39–40).

THE MEANING OF COMMITMENT: UNRESERVED OPENNESS TO GOD

The unbelief of the Jewish authorities is the foil against which the Fourth Evangelist elaborates the true meaning of Christian commitment, namely, to believe unreservedly in Jesus. John never uses the noun "faith" but characteristically speaks in dynamic, verbal fashion. The verb "to believe" occurs ninety-eight times in the Fourth Gospel in contrast to thirty-four times in the three Synoptics combined. The subtle uses of the various constructions in which the verb occurs constitute an original and radical theology of believing as the essence of Christian commitment.[8]

John uses the verb "to believe" in the absolute, that is, without an object, twenty-five times. "To believe," in these texts, denotes a fundamental disposition of openness to the truth, which makes the person capable of seeing the glory of God whenever and wherever it is revealed. The man born blind, for example, did not know who Jesus was, but he staunchly maintained that only perversity could refuse to acknowledge that God was at work in one who healed blindness (see 9:16–17, 30–33). He was still ignorant of the identity of Jesus when the latter found him after he had been excommunicated from the synagogue and asked him, "Do you believe in the Son of Man?" The cured man could only ask, "Who is he, sir, that I may believe in him?" This readiness of spirit is identical with his willingness to accept the cure in the first place and to attribute it to the action of God.[9] Such a disposition makes possible the full self-revelation of Jesus, "You have seen him, and it is he who speaks to you." The man replied unhesitatingly, "Lord, I believe," and he worshiped him (9:35–38).

It is this unreserved readiness to accept the truth, this unqualified loyalty to reality as one experiences it, that Jesus tells Martha, prior to the raising of Lazarus, is the condition of receiving divine revelation: "Did I not tell you

---

[8] See Robert Kysar, *The Fourth Evangelist and His Gospel: An Examination of Contemporary Scholarship* (Minneapolis: Augsburg, 1975), 227–33.

[9] It is interesting to compare the immediate obedience of the blind man to Jesus' command to "go and wash in the pool of Siloam" (9:7) with the demurring of the paralytic at the pool of Bethzatha who never actually agrees to his own healing (see 5:6–8). Not surprisingly, the healed blind man defends Jesus and comes to believe in him while the healed paralytic turns Jesus in to the authorities.

that if you would believe you would see the glory of God?" (11:40). It is the disposition of the woman of Samaria, who was not deterred even by Jesus' exposure of her immorality from acknowledging him as a prophet (4:19) and seeking loyally to know what the true worship of God required of her and her people. In response to her genuine desire for the Messiah, regardless of the changes his coming might entail for her and her people, Jesus answers with the first great revelatory ἐγώ εἰμι (*ego eimi*) ὁ λαλῶν σοι of the Fourth Gospel, literally, "I am, the one speaking to you" (4:26).

The examples could be multiplied, but the meaning of "to believe" is clear from these few. It is the fundamental openness of heart, the basic readiness to see and hear what is really there, the fidelity to one's experience no matter how frightening or costly it appears to be, the devotion to being that refuses to tamper with reality in order to preserve the situation with which one is familiar. This basic disposition to accept the truth is what enables the person, regardless of moral weakness and lapse, regardless of ethnic or religious background, regardless of orthodoxy, regardless of religious education or lack thereof, to be interiorly "taught of God" (6:44–45). Such a person, no matter how far astray he or she might have wandered, remains tractable and can be drawn by the Father to Jesus (see 6:44).[10]

Only the person who has been taught of God is able to see in the words and works of Jesus the glory of the Word. It is this seeing which leads the person to believe in Jesus. "To believe in" is a Johannine construction, foreign to classical Greek, which appears thirty-six times in the Fourth Gospel. John seems to have coined the expression to denote the dynamic interpersonal relationship set up between Jesus and the person to whom he reveals himself. To believe in Jesus is to accept him, to identify with him, to follow him, to grow in discipleship. It is, in brief, to commit oneself to Jesus with that totality of self-giving that is suitable only in relationship to God and the one whom God has sent. By the fact and the quality of one's adherence to this human being one is proclaiming that Jesus is indeed the Son of God. This is not a theological proposition, an assent of the mind. It is a life stance which could only be legitimate if Jesus is indeed who he claims to be, the one sent by the Father.

It is this personal and total commitment to Jesus as the unique and absolute revelation of God in this world[11] that enables the believer to formu-

---

[10] See the rich explanation of this theme by Albert Vanhoye, "Notre foi, oeuvre divine d'après le quatrième évangile," *NRT* 86 (1964): 337–54.

[11] Increasingly Christians are coming to realize that their faith in Jesus as "unique," "definitive," "absolute" revelation of God need not mean "only" and must allow for the possibility and indeed the actuality of other saving manifestations of God in other religious traditions. This is the central challenge of an adequate theology of religions, which most theologians agree is still

late faith propositions about him. Eleven times in the Fourth Gospel the construction "to believe that" appears, followed by a theological proposition about Jesus. The disciples are the ones who believe that Jesus is the "Holy One of God" (6:69); "I am" (8:24; 13:19); "Christ, the son of God" (11:27; 20:31); the one sent by the Father (see 11:42; 17:8; 17:21); the one who is in the Father and in whom the Father dwells (see 14:10); the one who came forth from God (see 16:27; 16:30). All of these propositions are, from the standpoint of the believer, substantively identical. Although there are various aspects under which it can be considered, the mystery that is central to and all-inclusive of Christian faith is that Jesus and the Father are one. It is this that justifies an unqualified commitment to him, a commitment that cannot validly be made to law, temple, scripture, sabbath, hierarchy, tradition, or even to the covenant community itself.

The nuanced Johannine exploration of believing as the essence of religious commitment is meant for a Christian community, but it is radical enough to be universally enlightening. What God asks of every human being, regardless of time, place, or circumstances, is a loyal openness to reality that is incompatible with "seeking one's own glory." To seek one's own glory is to assign to oneself an absolute value in the order of being and action, to make oneself the center of the universe, which is fundamentally false. To do this is to close oneself to the truth. The only way a person can maintain such an existentially false stance is to invest with absoluteness those factors which support and sustain the illusion. One makes a total commitment to oneself, a commitment that cannot fail eventually to conflict with God's claim on one's life. When God's claim is made, it is seen as blasphemy because it is, in fact, a challenge to what the person has erected as absolute. God's revelation is experienced as darkness and sin. This is the blasphemy against the Holy Spirit in Markan terms (see Mark 3:29). In the Fourth Gospel it appears as the total blindness of the one who claims to see (see John 9:39–41) but who has made his or her own vision the measure of the visible.

In contrast, the person who refuses the diabolic temptation to absolutize the self remains inwardly open to reality. God educates the spirit of this person who does the truth and comes into the light (see 3:21). Such a person knows that he or she is not the measure of possibility, and it is this attitude that makes divine revelation possible. If and when Jesus stands before this person, doing the works of God, she or he, like the first disciples at Cana, will

---

in the future. No matter how it is eventually formulated, it must take account of two seemingly incompatible but necessary facts: on the one hand, one cannot really believe in a "relative" God; on the other hand, one cannot believe in a God who is not available to all people.

see his glory and believe in him (see 2:11). John, of course, is dealing only with people who have seen Jesus, whether in his earthly career or in the ecclesial community. Consequently, the evangelist regards each person as involved in the crisis situation that dominates the perspective of the Fourth Gospel, namely, the choice to accept or reject Jesus. To those who accept him, he gives the power to become children of God (see 1:12), while those who refuse him are condemned by that very refusal (see 3:18).

Although John does not explicitly take into account those who may never have been exposed to the revelation that is Jesus, the Gospel's treatment of the subject of commitment includes, in principle, all human beings.[12] What differentiates those who come to the light from those who remain in darkness is not their actual explicit exposure to and/or thematic faith in Jesus but their deeds, manifesting their basic disposition of heart. Those who do the truth will respond to the light, whenever and however it shines in their lives. Those who do evil will flee from the light (see 3:20–21). In other words, it is one's fundamental commitment to the truth, expressing itself in deeds, which opens a person to God's revelation, however that revelation enters the individual's life.

IMPLICATIONS FOR CONTEMPORARY
REFLECTION ON COMMITMENT

Although it is true that the author of the Fourth Gospel did not have our contemporary questions about permanent commitment, the evangelist was writing for a community facing a crisis of commitment: whether to abandon their hereditary religious commitment to institutional Judaism or to abandon their commitment to Jesus as Messiah and Son of God. John tries to help them deal with this dilemma by examining, in a very profound way, the meaning of religious commitment. Although we do not face precisely the same dilemma, the Fourth Gospel's elucidation of the meaning of commitment has important implications for twentieth-century Christians, who also face the challenge of conflicting commitments.

First, *religious commitments are partially conditioned by historical circumstances.* It was God who had originally called the Jewish Christians of the

---

[12] As Raymond Brown in his final book has the evangelist say, "Quite frankly I never gave thought to Jews (or others) who had never heard of Jesus or Jews of future generations, and I sincerely regret that my words were applied to them" (*A Retreat with John the Evangelist: That You May Have Life* [Cincinnati: St. Anthony Messenger, 1998], 71).

Johannine community to membership in the chosen people, including commitment within institutional Judaism. But the leaders of Judaism at the time of Jesus had progressively transformed the religion of Yahweh into a commitment to the institution, which guaranteed their own status and power, rather than to God. Continued commitment within institutional Judaism became impossible for the Johannine Christians. Paradoxically, fidelity to the meaning of the original commitment entailed abandoning it because of the changed historical situation over which the Jewish Christians had no control. John depicts the historical Jesus accusing his contemporaries of an idolatrous commitment to their commitments rather than to God in order to clarify the community's understanding of their own action as not infidelity but deep fidelity to the covenant. To be an Israelite was to believe that "the Lord is God; there is no other besides him" (Deut. 4:35). Consequently, it was precisely in order to remain a true Israelite that the first-century Christian had to abandon institutional Judaism.

Second, and very closely related to the first, *the only absolute commitment is the commitment to God,* which for the Christian means commitment *in Jesus.* All other commitments, however sacred, remain relative to this absolute commitment. Relative commitments can certainly be permanent. It is not only legitimate but necessary to shape one's life by permanent interpersonal commitments to which one remains faithful over a lifetime. But if any commitment takes on such absoluteness that we become incapable of moving beyond it if it should become a real hindrance to our love of God and our growth in Christ, then it has become idolatry. This is easy to understand in theory, but when the conflict is between a sacred and a permanent commitment, like that of John's community to Judaism, and fidelity to God in Jesus, the theory can be heartbreaking in application. And the application must frequently be made, as it was by the man born blind, at the price of religious rejection.

Third, *every commitment, insofar as it is authentic, is a relative expression of our absolute commitment to God.* This is the source of the sacredness of our commitments and the justification of their permanence. But it is also consolation in the situation in which a permanent but relative commitment must be relinquished. In such a case the deepest reality of the relinquished commitment is not lost, however psychologically agonizing the experience might be. The Christians of the Johannine community had to relinquish their institutional affiliation with Judaism, but the essence of what it meant to be an Israelite remained at the heart of their new commitment to Jesus.

Fourth, *the inner disposition of openness to the truth is ultimately our only protection against self-deception and the tyranny of others.* For the mature person, there is only one real guarantee that one's attitudes toward commitments are valid. A calm and trusting openness to the truth, a loyalty to life and to being wherever they lead, is the disposition of one who can and will be "taught of God." No outside agency, however sacred, can be substituted for conscience trained to the truth. Nor can we ever substitute someone else's vision or interpretation of the truth for our own, even though the prudent and humble person will take careful account of the input from religious authority as well as from other sources. The man born blind, the woman of Samaria, and the officers sent to arrest Jesus are all examples of people who resisted the pressure of "authority" in order to respond to the truth as they saw it.

Against the man born blind the Jewish officials invoked the law of Moses given by God, their own hierarchical authority sanctioned by tradition, and even the man's own ignorance and sinfulness to induce him to betray his experience and its revelatory implications. Both the consciousness of his own limitations and the weight of a lifelong commitment to Judaism favored a surrender to the authority of law, hierarchy, learning, and tradition. The healed paralytic in chapter 5 capitulated to these very pressures. But the man born blind chose to follow the truth that he saw, and Jesus' finding of and self-revelation to the excommunicated man is our assurance of the rightness of his choice. In contemporary terms, conscience remains the sole final arbiter in the case of conflict of commitments. Our fundamental challenge is not fidelity to our commitments, but fidelity to the truth. It is this fidelity that discerns and actualizes our commitment to God in the heart of our finite choices and which, finally, justifies our relative commitments and strengthens us to live them in hope.

6

Women in the Fourth Gospel

In recent years, beginning with a very provocative article on the subject by Raymond Brown in 1975, there has been increasing interest in the women characters in the Fourth Gospel.[1] Earlier scholarship had tended to see Luke, which mentions women more often than the other Gospels, as "the Gospel of women," but feminist analysis has progressively unmasked the pervasive subordinationism of Luke's presentation of women.[2] John, on the other hand, does not present women in tandem with men and subordinate in comparison with them but in stark contrast to men, with the women appearing in the more positive light. The Samaritan woman contrasts favorably with Nicodemus; Martha with the Jewish leaders; Mary of Bethany with Judas; Mary Magdalene with Simon Peter.

Two recent monographs have attempted to temper the enthusiasm of feminists for John's presentation of women by pointing out that the Fourth Gospel shares the patriarchal and androcentric bias of the culture in which it was produced.[3] While it is obviously true that the Fourth Evangelist was not,

---

[1] Raymond E. Brown, "Roles of Women in the Fourth Gospel," App. II in *The Community of the Beloved Disciple: The Life, Loves, and Hates of an Individual Church in New Testament Times* (New York: Paulist, 1979), 183–98; originally published in *TS* 36 (1975): 688–99. A recent, very helpful article that carries forward some of Brown's insights and supplies recent bibliography is Turid Karlsen Seim, "Roles of Women in the Gospel of John," in *Aspects on the Johannine Literature: Papers Presented at a Conference of Scandinavian New Testament Exegetes at Uppsala, June 16-19, 1986,* ed. Lars Hartman and Birger Olsson, Coniectanea Biblica: New Testament Series 18 (Uppsala: Uppsala Universitet, 1987), 56–73.

[2] Elisabeth Schüssler Fiorenza challenged the interpretation of women in Luke in "A Feminist Critical Interpretation for Liberation: Martha and Mary: Lk. 10:38–42," *Religion and the Intellectual Life* 3 (1986): 21–36; she has been followed by a number of other authors, most recently by Barbara Reid, *Choosing the Better Part? Women in the Gospel of Luke* (Collegeville, Minn.: Liturgical Press, 1996).

[3] Adeline Fehribach, *The Women in the Life of the Bridegroom: A Feminist Historical-Literary*

and could not have been, free of cultural assumptions and patterns of thought to which there was no alternative, much less critique, in the first century, denying the originality and power of John's contribution to Christian reflection on women in church and society on these grounds seems to me somewhat anachronistic and overly historicist.[4] The primary questions of the reader of the New Testament, as I have been trying to suggest, are not What actually happened in the first century? or What was the intention of the author? but What does the text actually say about Jesus? How does it present him and his work? and What light does this throw on contemporary Christian faith and life?

In regard to women in the New Testament this issue of how and for what purpose we read scripture is particularly acute. The primary motivation for the intense study of women in the New Testament in recent years has been the very contemporary struggle over the role of women in society and church. Because the equality of women with men, rather than their previously assumed "natural" subordination to men, has become a basic premise of the liberation struggle in society, it is hardly surprising that women and men in the church who are committed to justice want to promote such equality in the ecclesial community. But obviously the church is not simply a voluntary society. It is a faith community grounded in the life and teaching of Jesus. Consequently, those interested in the liberation and equality of women in the church as well as those in power who wish to perpetuate women's subordination to men and especially sexual apartheid in relation to the sacrament of Orders have turned to the New Testament for resources in defending their positions.

It seems especially important, therefore, to clarify how the New Testament in general, and the Fourth Gospel in particular, can and cannot contribute to this struggle. The Gospel is normative of Christian life. But this does not mean that whatever was done in the first-century Christian communities must be done by all subsequent communities nor that anything that was not done in the first century can never be done. If the contrary were true we would have to maintain the legitimacy of slavery today since Paul obviously and quite explicitly (however reluctantly) accepted it, and we would have to dismantle the Vatican since there is certainly no trace in the New Testament of Jesus founding a divine-right monarchy. Consequently, searching the New

---

Analysis of the Female Characters in the Fourth Gospel (Collegeville, Minn.: Liturgical Press, 1998); Martin Scott, *Sophia and the Johannine Jesus* (Sheffield: JSOT Press, 1992).

[4] In the chapter in this book on the Samaritan woman I try to bring out how, in this very liberating presentation of a woman in the life of Jesus, patriarchal assumptions are nevertheless present and sound a warning for the contemporary reader that the eternal life Jesus announced is both already present and not yet fully realized.

Testament for concrete prescriptions applicable to the present is not only futile but wrongheaded. In fact, the most responsible position on this subject was probably articulated by the Pontifical Biblical Commission in its 1976 report on the question of women's ordination[5] when they found, after exhaustive study of the relevant New Testament data, that the New Testament simply does not provide the answer to this question. The attempt to prove that the New Testament data demand either the admission of women to or the exclusion of women from Orders (or any other form of participation in the life of the church that is rooted in baptismal identification with Christ) should be abandoned.

But this being said, if the New Testament throws no light on the most excruciating questions and issues of our time, then it can hardly be considered the foundational document of our faith. This raises the question of how the New Testament can function as revelatory text in a community living in circumstances and with a historical experience vastly different from those of the communities which produced this text. This is the issue of biblical hermeneutics, of how an ancient document can be brought into fruitful dialogue with believers of subsequent ages without distorting the text or imprisoning it in the first century.[6] It cannot be discussed at length here, but the basic principle is that the New Testament is not a catechism or an answer book supplying prescriptions for the solution of problems not even envisioned by its authors. Rather, our engagement with the biblical text is meant to form in us the mind of Christ, so that we can confront the issues of our own time in the spirit of Jesus, who is for all Christians throughout the ages the way, the truth, and the life.

The purpose of the exegetically based reflection on the women in John's Gospel that follows is to provide resources for the imagination of contemporary Christians as they deal with the issue of women in the church today. In one early Christian community, that of the Fourth Evangelist, we find women presented in an extraordinarily positive light in relation to Jesus and in relation to male members of the community. The patriarchal culture in which these stories arose makes them even more remarkable not only because of the way in which they transcend and call into question the androcentric

---

[5] Pontifical Biblical Commission, "Can Women Be Priests?" *Origins* 6 (1976): 92–96.

[6] I have dealt with this question at length in *The Revelatory Text: Interpreting the New Testament as Sacred Scripture*, 2nd ed. (Collegeville, Minn.: Liturgical Press, 1999). See the shorter presentation in "Living Word or Dead(ly) Letter: The Encounter Between the New Testament and Contemporary Experience," in *The Catholic Theological Society of America: Proceedings of the Forty-Seventh Annual Convention Held in Pittsburgh 11–14 June 1992, Volume 47,* ed. Paul Crowley (Santa Clara, Calif.: Santa Clara University, 1992), 45–60.

bias but also because of the fruitful use they make of patriarchal assumptions to subvert those very assumptions. In my opinion, the Fourth Gospel is a rich resource for those who are convinced that the restriction and subordination of women within the church is not a matter of divine revelation but a distortion of the gospel by the culturally based sexism of men who have monopolized power in the ecclesiastical institution from the earliest days of the church's history and have attempted to sacralize that monopoly by appeal to scripture.

THE MATERIAL ABOUT
THE MOTHER OF JESUS

The material in the Fourth Gospel involving women consists of the following passages:

1. The first sign at Cana	2:1–12	Mother of Jesus
2. Dialogue at Jacob's well	4:4–42	Samaritan woman
3. Raising of Lazarus	11:1–44	Martha and Mary
4. Anointing at Bethany	12:1–8	Martha and Mary
5. Word from the cross	19:25–27	Mother of Jesus, Mary of Clopas, Mary Magdalene
6. Discovery of the open tomb	20:1–2	Mary Magdalene
7. First Easter Christophany	20:11–18	Mary Magdalene

Obviously, there are a number of possible ways of dividing and organizing this material. One could divide it chronologically: women in the public ministry (nos. 1–4) and women during the Hour of Jesus (nos. 5–7); by character: the mother of Jesus (nos. 1, 5), the sisters of Bethany (nos. 3, 4), the Samaritan woman (no. 2), and Mary Magdalene (nos. 5–7). I propose a theological division between the material about the mother of Jesus and the other material. I am going to exclude the former from detailed consideration for both practical and theological reasons.

The practical reason is that the sheer quantity of scholarly work on the mother of Jesus in the Fourth Gospel precludes any exhaustive original treatment of it in an essay of this length, and I do not think such a treatment necessary at this point in the history of Johannine research. The studies made in the decade 1960–1970, which take account of those that preceded them, have been competently surveyed in a lengthy article by Raymond Collins.[7]

[7] Raymond F. Collins, "Mary in the Fourth Gospel: A Decade of Johannine Studies," *LS* 3 (1970): 99–142.

Subsequently, the subject of Mary in the Fourth Gospel has been thoroughly reexamined and judiciously presented (although almost exclusively from a historical-critical perspective and with a tendency to minimalism that is quite legitimate in view of its purposes) in the ecumenical study published at the end of the 1970s, *Mary in the New Testament.*[8] Most recently, an intriguing article by Judith Lieu reviews the entire question and supplies most of the pertinent bibliography from the 1980s and 1990s.[9]

The theological reason for excluding the material about the mother of Jesus from this study is that the femaleness of Mary as she is presented in the Fourth Gospel, although historically factual and symbolically important, is irrelevant for the issue under discussion here, namely, the Gospel's contribution to our imaging of women believers as women. First, it is obvious that the mother of Jesus, unlike his interlocutors in Samaria, at Bethany, or in the garden of the tomb, could not have been other than female. Second, whatever role Mary is assigned in the Fourth Gospel, it is either unique to her or universal, in neither of which cases is it more significant for women than for men.

John does seem to imply that the mother of Jesus had some special role in relation to the salvific work of Jesus. If she is understood as the new Eve in relation to the new Adam, or as Sion giving birth to the Messiah, her role is unique and is not shared by other Christians, women or men. Just as men do not participate any more than women in Jesus' unique role as Savior of the World, new Adam, or Messiah, so women do not participate any more than do men in Mary's unique role as new Eve or Lady Sion. If Mary is seen as a symbol of the church, as mother of the church, or as mother of all believers, these roles also are unique to her and not shared by other Christians of either sex. Finally, if Mary is seen as model of disciples she is equally so for men and women. As a representative figure in the Fourth Gospel,[10] Mary must be assigned the same universality as the figures of the Beloved Disciple and Judas. The historical Judas was a male, but this does not imply that men are more typically the locus of the mystery of unbelief and betrayal than women. The same must be said of Mary as model of conversion and discipleship.[11] In

---

[8] Raymond E. Brown, Karl P. Donfried, Joseph A. Fitzmyer, and John Reumann, eds., *Mary in the New Testament: A Collaborative Assessment by Protestant and Roman Catholic Scholars* (Philadelphia: Fortress, 1978).

[9] Judith M. Lieu, "The Mother of the Son in the Fourth Gospel," *JBL* 117 (1998): 61–77.

[10] Raymond F. Collins, "The Representative Figures in the Fourth Gospel," *DRev* 94 (1976): 26–46, 118–32.

[11] James M. Reese, "The Historical Image of Mary in the New Testament," *Marian Studies* 28 (1977): 41.

summary, the femaleness of the mother of Jesus is both a historical fact and an integral part of the symbolism attached to her in the Fourth Gospel, but it is theologically irrelevant for the contemporary question of the role of women in the church because Mary's role is either unique to her or universally significant for all Christians.

The only observation about the mother of Jesus in the Fourth Gospel that is truly significant for our study is the one on which the ecumenical task force was unanimous: John is in substantial agreement, theologically, with the Synoptics in presenting Jesus as relativizing the significance of physical relationship with himself (whether of motherhood, fraternity, or distant kinship) and recognizing discipleship, expressed in hearing the word of God in Jesus and keeping it, as the truly meaningful relationship with him.[12] If physically based human relationship with Jesus is regarded as salvifically irrelevant, it should be obvious to all that biological similarity to Jesus is even less relevant in the order of faith.[13]

GENERAL REFLECTIONS ON THE MATERIAL
ABOUT WOMEN IN JOHN

Let me begin with some general observations, which might be significant for discussion of women in the church, about the way women actually appear in the text of the Fourth Gospel. No claims are being made that the evangelist explicitly intended to present women in this way, or in any particular way, for that matter. Rather, just as art critics have observed that Michelangelo, whether or not he intended to do so, frequently presented women as amazons, so it is possible for scholars to discern some overall characteristics of the Johannine women as they appear in the text, regardless of the possibilities of demonstrating the evangelist's intentions in this respect.

First, all the women in the Fourth Gospel are presented positively and in intimate relation to Jesus. No woman is shown as resisting Jesus' initiatives, failing to believe, deserting him, or betraying him. This is in sharp contrast to John's presentation of men, who are frequently presented as vain (13:37), hypocritical (12:4–6), fickle (13:38; 16:31–32), obtuse (3:10; 16:18), deliberately unbelieving (9:24–41; 20:24–25), or thoroughly evil (13:2, 27–30).

However—and this is the second characteristic—John's positive presenta-

---

[12] Brown et al., *Mary in the New Testament,* 283–94.

[13] The significance of Jesus' birth from a human mother lies in what it says about the reality of his humanity, not in what it says about Mary's discipleship.

tion of women is neither one-dimensional nor stereotypical. Women do not appear in the Fourth Gospel as bloodless representatives of the "eternal feminine." On the contrary, John's women appear as strikingly individual and original characters, especially in contrast to the shadowy male figures who frequently appear in close proximity to them. Compare, for example, the stereotypical scribe Nicodemus (3:1–12) with the Samaritan woman (4:7–41), who realistically negotiates an incredible range of emotions from suspicion, to almost brassy defiance, to a complex mix of intelligent curiosity and blank misunderstanding, to halfhearted deviousness, to total and selfless enthusiasm and commitment. Or again, compare the shadowy Lazarus with his sisters, the warm and dominant Martha and the strong, contemplative Mary (11:1–12:8). The male disciples in the Easter narratives, with the exception of Thomas (20:2–8, 19–29), are not nearly so realistically drawn as is Mary Magdalene (20:1–2, 11–18), who displays the blind folly, tough-minded devotion, desperate despair, and rapturous joy of the ardent lover.

Whoever the author of the Fourth Gospel was, it was someone who had a remarkably rich and nuanced understanding of feminine religious experience. Historically, this knowledge could have been the product of an active literary imagination, but it seems much more likely that it was the result of actual experience of Christian women who played prominent roles in the community of the Fourth Evangelist.[14] If women Christians in John's community had been restricted to the domestic and religious roles of women in the Jewish world of that period, it is very difficult to imagine where the evangelist got such extraordinarily rich insights into the relationships of women with Jesus.[15]

The third characteristic of women in the Johannine text is the unconventionality of the roles they play. The Samaritan woman with her checkered past (about which she is not unduly embarrassed!),[16] her uncommon theological knowledge and interests, and her spontaneous assumption of the role of public witness to Jesus; Martha running the public aspects of funeral and mourning; Mary of Bethany extravagantly anointing the feet of Jesus over the protests of the devious Judas; Mary Magdalene roaming alone in a darkened

[14] This is the suggestion of Brown, "Roles of Women," 198.

[15] I cannot enter into debate in this essay with Fehribach, who contends that, in fact, John's women characters are presented in stereotypical roles of subordinate and supportive relationship with the hero-bridegroom. I would maintain, however, that even if such is the case (and I am not at all sure it is), the vivacity of their exercise of these roles and the originality of their presentation in the text is not simply homage to androcentric idolatry.

[16] In chapter 8 on the Samaritan woman I will argue that her "checkered past" is not one of personal sexual immorality but the history of idolatry in the Samaritan community.

cemetery, questioning a strange man, and responsibly bearing apostolic witness to the assembled disciples cannot help but suggest that the Christian women of the Fourth Evangelist's experience were not uneducated domestic recluses. Surprisingly, none of John's women figures except the mother of Jesus and Mary of Clopas is presented as mother or wife or in any way essentially defined in relationship to men.[17] On the contrary, Lazarus is identified through his relationship to Mary and Martha and is named after them in relation to Jesus in 11:5. Again, John's presentation leads to speculation about the roles of women in the community of the Fourth Gospel. It seems more than likely that real women, actually engaged in theological discussion, competently proclaiming the gospel, publicly confessing their faith, and serving at the table of the Lord, stand behind these Johannine characters.

These three general observations—that women in the Fourth Gospel are all presented positively and in particularly intimate relationship to Jesus, that they have richly complicated and various religious personalities and experiences, and that they play quite unconventional roles—suffice to suggest that the women Christians in at least one of the earliest communities, that of the Fourth Gospel, were fully participating and highly valuable community members.[18] It also suggests that the evangelist considered such feminine behavior to be fully in accord with the mind of Jesus, who is never presented as disapproving of the women and in two scenes, as we shall see, defends the women against explicit or implicit male objections. But quite apart from the evidence that the material concerning women in John's Gospel seems to supply about the historical community of the Beloved Disciple, the text as it stands is significant for what it suggests about the discipleship of Christian women regardless of time or place.

First, women, according to the Fourth Gospel, relate to Jesus directly and never through the mediation and/or by the permission of men.

Second, according to John's Gospel, there is no such thing as "women" whose "place" and "role" in the community or in relation to Jesus are to be decided and assigned once and for all by some third (male) party. There are only highly individual and original women whose place is wherever Jesus calls them and whose role is whatever their love for him suggests or his desires for them indicate, however unconventional. Their ministry to Jesus and to others in his name requires no approval or authorization of anyone.

Third, unlike most of the male disciples in the Fourth Gospel, the women

---

[17] I think Fehribach has contributed an important insight on this point: that the primary relationship of all of these characters is to Jesus, who, in John's Gospel, is the bridegroom. Consequently, they do not appear as spouses of other men.

[18] Brown, "Roles of Women," 198.

are remarkable for their initiative and decisive action. The Samaritan woman assumes on her own (and with Jesus' evident approval) her mission of bearing witness to the people of her town; Martha and Mary immediately send for Jesus when Lazarus is ill; they prepare and host the supper on the eve of the passion, and Mary performs the unusual anointing on her own initiative; Mary Magdalene is first at the tomb on Easter morning, determined to find and remove the body of her Lord; she alerts the male disciples to Jesus' disappearance, and she alone remains to continue the search while they hide for fear of the Jewish authorities. If leadership is a function of creative initiative and decisive action, the Johannine women qualify well for the role.

SPECIFIC REFLECTIONS
ON THE PERICOPES ABOUT WOMEN

It is beyond the scope of this chapter to undertake a detailed exegesis of the four pericopes in the Fourth Gospel involving these women. Excellent historical-critical and theological analyses of these texts are available in the standard commentaries.[19] What I will try to do here is highlight aspects of these passages that have been overlooked or underestimated but are potentially useful for the contemporary discussion of the role of women in the church.

The Samaritan Woman (4:4–42)[20]

Three aspects of this long and theologically rich pericope deserve special attention: the self-revelation of Jesus to the woman; the woman's role as witness; and the discomfort of Jesus' male disciples. Commentators generally agree that it is very difficult to place this scene within the public ministry of the historical Jesus, and especially within the Johannine account of that ministry.[21] We have no evidence from the Synoptic Gospels that Jesus carried on a ministry in Samaria. However, Samaria was one of the first missions under-

---

[19] E.g., Raymond E. Brown, *The Gospel According to John*, 2 vols., Anchor Bible 29, 29A (Garden City, N.Y.: Doubleday, 1966, 1970); Charles H. Talbert, *Reading John: A Literary and Theological Commentary on the Fourth Gospel and the Johannine Epistles* (London: SPCK, 1992); Stanley B. Marrow, *The Gospel of John: A Reading* (New York: Paulist, 1995); Francis J. Moloney, *The Gospel of John*, Sacra Pagina Series (Collegeville, Minn.: Liturgical Press, 1998).

[20] I treat this pericope at full length in chapter 8 so the treatment here is schematic in accord with the specific purpose of this chapter.

[21] Brown, *Gospel According to John*, 1:175–76.

taken after Pentecost (Acts 8:1–8), and John was involved in that mission. This John, of course, was the son of Zebedee, not the evangelist, but there was a conflation of the two in the early Christian imagination reflected in the naming of the Fourth Gospel after John. It is fairly certain that the Johannine community had a significant Samaritan component,[22] and, in all probability, the scene recounted in John 4 has its real context not in the ministry of the earthly Jesus but in the early history of the Johannine community. The conversion of Samaria is projected back into the ministry of Jesus to establish that this important element of the community was called directly by Jesus as were the Jews and, in the mind of the Fourth Evangelist, every disciple of all time.

The central concern of the Fourth Gospel is the saving revelation that takes place in Jesus. This revelation, however, must be understood as a dialogical process of Jesus' self-manifestation as the one being continuously sent by the Father (see 7:16–18), who is thereby encountered in Jesus (see 10:30; 14:9–11), and the response of belief on the part of the disciples (see 17:8). After the glorification of Jesus on the cross, through the gift of the Spirit this belief bears fruit in the disciples' bearing revelatory witness to Jesus and thereby bringing others to him (see 16:26). This process is anticipated three times in the account of the public ministry: in the witness of John the baptizer (see 1:29–36); in the calling of the first disciples (see 1:35–51); and in the conversion of the people of Sychar (see 4:39–42).

The story of the Samaritan woman is remarkable for the clarity and completeness of its presentation of this revelation process in the Fourth Gospel. Jesus' self-revelation to the woman as the Messiah whom the Samaritans expect (4:25) is given in the "I am" formula that has such christological importance in the Fourth Gospel. It is the first use of this absolute formula in the Gospel, and its impact on the woman is that she immediately leaves her water jar where it is and hastens into the town to bear witness to Jesus as the expected Messiah, that is, the one who would tell them all things (see 4:25 and 29). We should not fail to note the feminine version of the standard Gospel formula for responding to the call to apostleship, namely, to "leave all things," especially one's present occupation, whether symbolized by boats and nets (e.g., Matt. 4:19–22), or tax stall (cf. Matt. 9:9), or water pot.

---

[22] For the influence of Samaritan theology on the Johannine community, see Wayne A. Meeks, *The Prophet-King: Moses Traditions and the Johannine Christology*, NovTSup (Leiden: E. J. Brill, 1967); Oscar Cullmann, *The Johannine Circle*, trans. John Bowden (Philadelphia: Westminster, 1976); Brown, *Community of the Beloved Disciple*, 34–54. For a more detailed treatment of Samaritan history and theology, see the studies in *The Samaritans*, ed. Alan D. Crown (Tübingen: J. C. B. Mohr, 1989).

The witness that the woman bears is quite clearly apostolic in the Johannine perspective.[23] First, its effect is that those who hear her "come to him" (4:30), which is the Johannine expression for the first movement of saving faith in Jesus (see 6:37). In 4:39 we are told explicitly that many Samaritans "believed in him because of the word [διὰ τὸν λόγον, *dia ton logon*] of the woman witnessing." The force of this expression as apostolic identification of the woman appears when we compare it with Jesus' prayer in 17:20, describing, in essence, the apostolic mission: "I do not pray for these only [i.e., those present at the supper] but also for those believing in me through their word" (διὰ τοῦ λόγου, *dia tou logou*). John ascribes the conversion of at least one Samaritan town (probably symbolizing the whole Samaritan mission) to this woman apostle, who acts out of her belief in Jesus' self-revelatory word and whose own witnessing word brings others to believe in him.

That her apostleship is fully effective is indicated by 4:41–42, according to which the Samaritans come to full faith in Jesus as Savior of the World (a title indicating that this is a postglorification account retrojected into the historical ministry). They claim that their faith is no longer dependent on the words of the witness but is now based on Jesus' own word. In John's perspective the witness of a believing disciple brings a person to Jesus, but then the disciple fades away as the prospective believer encounters Jesus himself (see 1:35–41). Anyone who believes is personally called by name by the Good Shepherd (see 10:3) and becomes a branch directly enlivened by the True Vine (see 15:4–5). Essentially, no one mediates between Jesus and his own (see 10:3–5) in this Gospel's perspective, for the immediacy of their relationship is patterned on that of the Father and the Son (see 10:14–15).

The third item of note in this account is the reaction of Jesus' disciples (presumably male) who return from their errand in town and discover Jesus conversing with the woman (see 4:27). We are told that they "marveled" or "wondered." Raymond Brown is undoubtedly correct to translate it "they were shocked."[24] They are not shocked, as we might expect, because Jesus was violating the religious prohibition against a Jew conversing with a Samaritan. By the time this Gospel was written converted Samaritans were an integral part of the Johannine community. But if the members of the community were well beyond anti-Samaritan prejudice, some were evidently not beyond the cultural patterns, characteristic of Semitic societies in general, of excluding women from public affairs. It seems more than a little likely that this detail about the disciples being shocked at Jesus' dealing with a woman, since

---

[23] Brown, "Roles of Women," 188–89.

[24] Brown, *Gospel According to John,* 1:167.

it is in no way necessary to the story itself, is aimed at those traditionalist male Christians in the Johannine community who found the independence and apostolic initiative of Christian women shocking. The point is quite clearly made, however, that they knew better than to question the profound purposes (indicated by the verb "to seek")[25] of Jesus for his women disciples. Jesus alone decides to whom he will reveal himself and whom he will call to apostleship. Jesus is evidently filled with joy at the woman's work (see 4:35), which he recognizes as a realization of his own mission to do the will of the one who sent him (see 4:34), and as an anticipation of the later work of the other disciples (see 4:38).

In summary, the episode about the Samaritan woman shows us a woman apostle, presented as such within the lifetime of the historical Jesus but surely reflecting also the life of the Johannine community, in whom is fully realized the typically Johannine revelation process: Jesus' self-revelation to her as Messiah (or Christ) and "I am" (God), which is the content of Christian faith according to the Fourth Gospel (see 20:31); her believing in him and leaving all things to bear effective apostolic witness to him among the Samaritans; and the acceptance of her work by Jesus, who claims as his own those who come to believe in him though her word. The detail about the silent shock of the male disciples vindicates her discipleship, apostleship, and ministry in the face of the cultural patterns that might have challenged its appropriateness or even legitimacy.

In the history of exegesis and preaching a great deal has been made of this woman's irregular marital situation,[26] very little of the clear indications of her apostleship, and virtually nothing of the vindication of her role against the implicit disapproval of the male members of the community. The importance of this scene for the contemporary discussion about the role of women is obvious enough, but we can see that it is only when we put a new question to the Gospel text that certain heretofore unseen aspects of the New Testament message come to light.

Martha and Mary (11:1–53; 12:1–8)[27]

The Johannine material on Martha and Mary of Bethany, who are sisters of Lazarus according to John, probably stems from a cycle of traditional

---

[25] Rudolf Schnackenburg, *The Gospel According to John,* vol. 1, trans. K. Smith (New York: Herder & Herder, 1968), 444.

[26] See n. 16 above.

[27] I deal with this pericope in detail in chapter 10.

women-disciple material that was common to all of the evangelists.[28] The Fourth Evangelist, however, has made very original use of this traditional material. In John 11, the account of the raising of Lazarus, I will focus on Martha, who plays the leading role in relation to Jesus. Mary's part in this scene (see 11:28–32) serves merely to introduce her in preparation for her leading role in the anointing scene in 12:1–8, and to introduce the Jews, who witness the sign that will divide them into those who believe in Jesus (see 11:45) and those who report him to the authorities (see 11:46). Mary herself, in the Lazarus episode, simply repeats what Martha has already said.

Within the Gospel narrative the raising of Lazarus functions as the crisis that determines the Jewish authorities to kill Jesus (see 11:47–53). Within the Johannine community it probably functioned in the context of the death of believers, which constituted the ultimate crisis of faith for those left behind.[29] If to believe in Jesus is to possess eternal life in him (see 6:40), what is to be made of the fact that faithful disciples die? And what answer is to be given to outsiders, especially Jews, who challenge the Christian faith in the presence and power of the glorified Jesus by asking why, if the Jesus of their faith is really the same Jesus who worked the signs of the public ministry, he cannot save his disciples (symbolized by the representative figure of Lazarus) from death (see 11:37). Indeed, the "Jews" raise the question in a very "Christian" way by asking why the One who opened the eyes of the man born blind (a baptismal account) could not save Lazarus (one of the "brothers," that is, the baptized) from death. Lazarus, whom Jesus loved (see 11:5, 36), is the faithful disciple who has died. Martha is the representative of the community left behind, which must face the challenge to its faith in Jesus as the Life. This is the point at issue in the dialogue between Jesus and Martha in 11:17–27.

Martha expresses (see 11:21–24) the real but inadequately enlightened faith of the community, which must be purified by a new and deeper encounter with Jesus in the crisis event of physical death: if Jesus had been there, that is, with the community as he had been during his public life, the brother (Johannine terminology for a member of the community) would not have died. However, whatever Jesus asks from God will be granted, and here the implication is that Jesus should do something to remove the scandal of death, which, even given the promise of resurrection on the last day, cannot be integrated into the faith experience of the community of eternal life.

---

[28] My hypothesis about such cycles of "disciple material" and their use in the early Christian communities was developed on the basis of a significant article by Martin Hengel, "Maria Magdalena und die Frauen als Zeugen," in *Abraham Unser Vater: Juden und Christen im Gespräch über die Bibel,* ed. O. Betz et al. (Leiden: E. J. Brill, 1963), 243–56.

[29] I will treat this episode at full length in chapter 10, on John 11.

Jesus challenges Martha with the revelatory word that must finally be accepted by anyone who wishes to belong to Jesus (see 11:25–26): that he is the resurrection and the life and that the eternal life he gives to his disciples transcends physical death without abolishing it. This must be believed in and through the crisis experience of death, that of others and finally one's own. Jesus asks Martha for a total acceptance of his self-revelation and its implications for her: "Do you believe this?"

Martha rises to the challenge, giving the response that, according to the conclusion of John's Gospel (see 20:31), is the saving confession of faith, that is, that Jesus is the Christ, the Son of God, the one coming into the world. (In contrast, Simon Peter's confession in John's Gospel [6:68–69] of Jesus as "the holy one of God" lacks the fullness of Johannine faith).

Several points are to be noted here. First, Martha in this scene represents the Johannine community making the full Christian confession of faith in Jesus, as Simon Peter represented the community of the disciples in an analogous scene in Matt. 16:15–19. In the Matthean scene Jesus also posed the ultimate faith question about himself: "Who do you say that I am?" and Simon Peter answered, "You are the Christ, the Son of the living God." In the Matthean pericope this confession is the foundation of the primacy conferred on Peter in the following verses (Matt. 16:17–19). In John, the primacy seems to be a shared charism. The Beloved Disciple has primacy as the authoritative witness to revelation (see John 19:35); a certain pastoral primacy is recognized in Peter (see 21:15–17); and apostolic primacy as witness to the paschal mystery belongs to Mary Magdalene (see 20:17–18). In this scene Martha seems to be the locus of the primacy of faith as confession in response to the revelatory word of Jesus. She speaks the faith of the community as it overcomes the ultimate scandal of death by belief in the one who is Life itself. Faith in the glorification of Jesus is not mature until it enables one to face physical death with full confidence that one's possession of eternal life is not simply a guarantee of resurrection on the last day but is a present and ongoing participation in the life of the ever-living Jesus. Those who believe in him never die, despite appearances to the contrary.

Second, it is important to realize that Martha's confession of faith is in no way a response to the sign of the raising of Lazarus. It is a response to the word of Jesus revealing himself as the resurrection and the life. The sign comes after Martha's confession and does not function as a guarantee of her faith but as a crisis for the Jews who have gathered. Martha does not expect the sign (cf. 11:38–39) any more than the disciples of any time or place can expect physical death to be overcome by miracle. Her faith, like ours, responds not to the signs of the public ministry but to the revealing word of the present Jesus. It is those who believe who will see the glory of God (see 11:40), not vice versa. After the glorification it is not the seeing of signs that leads to faith (cf. the Thomas incident in 20:24–29) but faith that enables one to see the glory of Jesus in signs.

In summary, Martha appears in this scene as the representative of the believing community responding to the word of Jesus with a full confession of Christian faith. It is a role analogous to Peter's as representative of apostolic faith in Matthew's Gospel. This representative role of Martha is difficult to understand unless women in John's community actually did function as community leaders. But whatever role women held in the Johannine community, the Gospel text as it stands presents Jesus as addressing the foundational question to a woman and the woman as responding, on her own responsibility, with the Christian confession of faith. If this confession, given during the public life of Jesus, grounds the promise of the primacy to Peter, it is no less significant as foundation of community leadership when given by a woman.

Let us turn now to the scene in which Mary plays the major role, the anointing at Bethany (12:1-8). The scene has certain eucharistic overtones, which ought not to be overlooked. It is situated six days before the Passover, which according to John's chronology of the passion, falls on the following Saturday (see 19:31). The meal at Bethany, therefore, took place on Sunday evening, the customary time of the Eucharist in the early church. Those whom Jesus loved (see 11:3, 5) gave a supper for him, and we are told that Martha "served." The Greek verb for "serve" is διακονεῖν (*diakonein*). By the time John's Gospel was written at the end of the first century the term διάκονος (*diakonos*), "servant," had become the title of a recognized ministerial office in some Christian communities (see Phil. 1:1; 1 Tim. 3:8, 12–13; Rom. 16:1), and waiting on table a function conferred by the laying on of hands (Acts 6:1–6). Alf Corell has made the interesting suggestion that if any established ministry existed in the Johannine community it was probably that of deacon.[30] And it is certainly not unlikely that, if any Christian community had some form of foot washing in its eucharistic liturgy, it would have been the Johannine community. I do not wish to defend the hypothesis that the supper at Bethany is presented explicitly as a "sacrament" in the strict sense of the term.[31] But it does seem to be evocative of Eucharist, and within that

---

[30] Alf Corell, *Consummatum Est: Eschatology and Church in the Gospel of St. John* (London: SPCK, 1958), 40–42.

[31] For a good recent summary of Johannine scholarship on sacramentalism in the Fourth Gospel and the current state of the question, see Paul Anderson, *The Christology of the Fourth Gospel: Its Unity and Disunity in the Light of John 6* (Valley Forge, Pa.: Trinity, 1996), especially chapter 6 and his extensive bibliography.

perspective it is worth noting that Jesus is the guest of honor and Martha and Mary are the ministers, a presentation of Eucharist that would fit well in the setting of the Johannine community. A loved male disciple, Lazarus, was present, but simply as one of those at table with Jesus.[32]

A second characteristic of the scene's setting is that it evokes the entirety of the paschal mystery. It is a supper, Jesus' last with these disciples whom he loves. A beloved disciple is reclining with Jesus and Judas is also present, as he will be at the Last Supper. Mary performs an act that recalls Jesus' washing of his disciples' feet signifying his death for them, and for this act of lavish, even extravagant, love she incurs the money-motivated enmity of Judas, who will betray Jesus himself for money. Her act is connected by Jesus to his burial. The scene ends with Jesus' prediction of his imminent departure.

Within this scene we are particularly concerned with Mary's action of anointing the feet of Jesus with costly perfumed ointment and then wiping his feet with her hair. The act, a combination of the Mark-Matthew account of the anonymous woman's (messianic?) anointing of Jesus' head (Mark 14:3–9; Matt. 26:6–13) and Luke's account of the sinful woman washing Jesus' feet with her tears and drying them with her hair (Luke 7:36–50), is so strange if taken literally that we are virtually forced to attach primary importance to its symbolism.

Perhaps the reference to Mary's wiping Jesus' feet with her hair is an effort to attach her act not to that of the sinful woman in Luke but to that of Jesus, who, at the Last Supper, performs an act that normally would have been performed by a devoted disciple for his teacher by washing his disciples' feet and

---

[32] This feature presents an interesting example of how differently the same text can be read. Fehribach sees Martha's role at the supper as being a diminished one: "Martha is portrayed as a server of the meal (Jn. 12:2), not as an equal participant in that meal" (*Women,* 110). Seim agrees that Martha's serving role is a subordinate one, "a task for those at the bottom," and that the emphasis is on her humility as it is in Mary's anointing of Jesus' feet, but recognizes that in this humility they are assimilated to Jesus ("Roles of Women," 72–73). If, however, there are eucharistic overtones in the pericope, the role of service of Martha and Mary would reflect that conflation of characteristics that Jesus claims for himself: "You call me master and lord . . . and if I, being your lord and master have washed your feet . . ." (13:13–15). Unfortunately, in the history of eucharistic practice, the role of presider has become exclusively that of "lord" and the foot-washing aspect has been relegated to a brief ritual on Holy Thursday that usually does little to counteract the hierarchical practice. The three readings obviously are governed by three different hermeneutical starting points: that women in John are purely textual victims of androcentric and patriarchal cultural patterns; that women in John should be seen solely as textual figures; and that women in John should be read as textual figures within the context of Christian tradition.

wiping them with the towel he was wearing. The anointing with precious ointment, on the other hand, is a proleptic anointing of Jesus for burial (see 12:7), which occasions Judas's objection.

Three points are particularly worth noting. First, if Mary's wiping of Jesus' feet with her hair is meant to evoke the foot washing, then we have a presentation of Mary as a disciple of Jesus in the strict sense of the word. To wash the feet of one's master was an act of veneration by a disciple.[33] It is also the act that Jesus commanded his disciples to perform in imitation of himself (see 13:14–15). This presentation of Mary as a disciple would accord well with the picture of this same Mary that we get from Luke 10:39, where she sits at the feet of Jesus listening to his teaching in the attitude of a Torah scholar with a rabbi. John has separated the two aspects of discipleship, that of listening to the master's teaching and that of actively expressing devotion to the person of the teacher. In John 11, after her confession of faith, Martha runs to Mary and says, "The Teacher is here and is calling for you" (11:28) and Mary goes quickly to him and falls at his feet (see 11:32). In John 12, Mary anoints her teacher's feet in an act that resembles (because of her wiping them with her hair) a foot washing. In other words, it seems likely enough that John is deliberately presenting this woman as a disciple of Jesus the Teacher, a role generally forbidden to Jewish women of Jesus' time.[34] When we remember that discipleship is the primary relationship with Jesus according to the Fourth Gospel and that, as R. Alan Culpepper has shown, the community of the Beloved Disciple had the characteristics of an ancient "school" in which the members devoted themselves to the study of the scriptures and the teaching of Jesus,[35] it becomes especially significant that John presents a woman in this role. It seems unlikely that the evangelist would have done so unless women in that community were active members of the school who devoted themselves to sacred study and discussion.

Second, we have in this scene another example of a male objection to a woman's unusual expression of her relationship with Jesus. Judas objects to Mary's extravagant act of devotion and suggests a more conventional form of piety for her, almsgiving (see 12:4–5). The evangelist tells us that Judas's real motive was theft (see 12:6), but Jesus replies not to his hidden motive but to

---

[33] Brown, *Gospel According to John,* 2:564.

[34] Evelyn Stagg and Frank Stagg, *Women in the World of Jesus* (Philadelphia: Westminster, 1978), 53.

[35] R. Alan Culpepper, *The Johannine School: An Evaluation of the Johannine-School Hypothesis Based on an Investigation of the Nature of the Ancient Schools,* Society of Biblical Literature Dissertation Series (Missoula, Mont.: Scholars Press, 1975), 270–71.

his expressed objection. His defense of Mary's ministry to him is blunt and harsh, "Let her alone" (12:7).

What is important for our purposes here is the fact that Jesus approves of this woman's original religious initiative. Mary does not express her relationship to Jesus in a conventional way, nor does she ask the permission of anyone, either of Jesus' male disciples (represented by Judas), or even of Lazarus, who was presumably head of the house, to act as she does. She assumes the right, as a disciple, to decide what form her ministry to Jesus should take, and when another disciple objects, he is silenced by Jesus himself. It is to be noted that each of the Synoptics has a version of this element of the episode, each with a different male or group of males objecting (see Matt. 26:8–10; Mark 14:4–6; Luke 7:39), which makes one aware of how early the attempt of men to control the discipleship and ministry of women began in the Christian community. Jesus' opinion of male attempts to control the relationship between his women disciples and himself is so clear in the New Testament that one can only wonder at the institutional church's failure to comprehend it.

Our third point concerns the Martha and Mary material as a whole. Chapters 11 and 12 of John constitute a proleptic presentation of the "hour" of Jesus. The raising of Lazarus both foreshadows Jesus' resurrection and finalizes the intention of the authorities to kill him. The anointing at Bethany foreshadows Jesus' burial and exposes Judas as the one who will precipitate the hour by his betrayal. Throughout this anticipation of the paschal mystery women disciples play the leading positive roles not only as witnesses but as faithful participants. In the persons of Mary Magdalene and the mother of Jesus, women will participate in the reality of the hour in a similarly intimate and public way.

Mary Magdalene (19:25; 20:1–2, 11–18)[36]

Like the Beloved Disciple, Mary Magdalene does not appear in the Fourth Gospel until the hour of Jesus' glorification has come. Her role is that of witness to the paschal events. She is at the foot of the cross at Jesus' death (19:25), discovers the empty tomb on Easter morning (20:1-2), and receives the first Easter Christophany including the apostolic commission to announce the exaltation of Jesus and its salvific effects to the disciples (20:11–18). Mary Magdalene is, without any doubt, the disciple whose place in the paschal mystery is most certainly attested by all four Gospels. She holds a place in the tradition about Jesus' women disciples analogous to that of

[36] I deal with John 20:11–18 in detail in chapter 13.

Peter among the male disciples, and for the same reason, namely, the tradition that she received the first appearance of the glorified Jesus and the foundational apostolic commission.[37] Consequently, we will concentrate on these two aspects of the Mary Magdalene material.[38]

The question of who first saw the risen Jesus is theologically significant because the early church regarded the protophany as the manifestation of the primacy of apostolic witness which is the foundation of the church's faith.[39] According to Paul (1 Cor. 15:3–8) and Luke (24:34), Jesus appeared first to Simon Peter. According to John (20:14–17), Matthew (28:1, 9–10), and the Markan appendix (16:9–11), he appeared first to Mary Magdalene, who, in Matthew, is accompanied by another woman. There are no scholarly grounds for questioning the authenticity of the tradition that the first Christophany was to Mary Magdalene. In fact, since this tradition clearly challenged the Petrine tradition, there would have been strong motivation for suppressing it if the evidence for it were at all weak. The fact that it has survived in two independent witnesses, John and Matthew (the Markan appendage is a collage that cannot be considered independent) is excellent evidence that it was a primitive and authentic tradition, different from the Petrine tradition, carefully preserved by some churches.

In the history of exegesis (in contrast to the liturgy, which celebrates Mary Magdalene as "apostle to the apostles"),[40] the Christophany to Mary Magdalene has been consistently trivialized as a "private," that is, unofficial event without ecclesial significance. The only grounds for such a position, which is clearly contrary to the evidence of the text, is the longstanding and unjustified assumption that all of the early Christian communities shared the Jewish proscription of testimony given by women.[41] As we saw in regard to the Samaritan woman passage, John regarded the apostolic testimony of women as valid, effective, and approved by Jesus.

The only conclusion that an unbiased interpretation of the Mary Magdalene episode in John 20 can yield is that, according to the Fourth Gospel,

[37] Hengel, "Maria Magdalena," 256.

[38] Other features of this important pericope will be taken up in the chapter devoted to Mary Magdalene.

[39] Félix Gils, "Pierre et la foi au Christ ressuscité," *Ephemerides Theologicae Lovanienses* 38 (1962): 5–43. For a summary of the tradition of interpretation and an excellent marshaling of the data for reinterpretation, see Gerald O'Collins and Daniel Kendall, "Mary Magdalene as Major Witness to Jesus' Resurrection," *TS* 48 (1987): 631–46.

[40] See Brown, "Roles of Women," 190 n. 336.

[41] Robert G. Maccini, *Her Testimony Is True: Women as Witnesses According to John,* JSNTSup 125 (Sheffield: Sheffield Academic Press, 1996), on the validity of female testimony in Judaism and particularly in John's Gospel.

Jesus did appear to Mary Magdalene on Easter morning, and that appearance was the first Christophany. He assigns no individual Christophany at all to Peter. That the theological significance of this protophany to Mary Magdalene is the same as that intended by Paul and Luke in assigning the protophany to Peter, namely, that it identifies the "apostle to the apostles" in the respective traditions, will be clearer once we have examined Jesus' commission to Mary.

The commission that Jesus gives to Mary is "Go to my brothers and sisters and say to them: I ascend to my Father and [who is now] your Father, to my God and [who is now] your God" (20:17).[42] It is not necessary to enter into all the detail that a complete exegesis of this text would require in order to make the point that this message is the Johannine version of the Easter kerygma.

First, it is addressed to Jesus' "brothers and sisters," whom Mary understands to mean the "disciples" (20:18). This is the first time in the Fourth Gospel that Jesus refers to his disciples as sisters and brothers, because it is only by his exaltation that he accomplishes the purpose of the incarnation, namely, to give the power to become children of God to those who believe in his name (see 1:12). The message entrusted to Mary is precisely that Jesus' Father is now truly Father of the disciples and thus that they are now truly the sisters and brothers of Jesus.

The second part of the message is equally vital: that Jesus' God is now the God of the disciples. This is an expression of the new covenant mediated by Jesus, the new Moses, through whom comes the grace and truth (*ḥesed* and *ʾemet*) foreshadowed by the Sinai covenant (see 1:17).[43] Until his glorification Jesus alone possessed the Spirit of the new covenant (see 7:37–39), but the

[42] I am translating this text differently from the way it appears in the New Revised Standard version. *Adelphoi,* the plural of *adelphos* (brother) is, in Greek, an inclusive collective noun including siblings of both genders if applied to a group including both. Obviously, the community to which Mary Magdalene is sent includes both women and men, since Mary herself is clearly a part of it, and one would certainly assume that it included the mother of Jesus as well. Hence, my translation of *adelphous mou* as "to my brothers and sisters" (which was the sense of the older English translation, "brethren," a once inclusive English term). The word usually translated "I am ascending" in a future sense, *anabainō,* is present tense, "I ascend." I believe it would be clearer in English to translate it paraphrastically as "my ascension is to my Father who is now your Father, my God who is now your God." The ascension in John takes place on the cross (thus it is accomplished by the time Jesus encounters Mary Magdalene in the garden), and the emphasis is not on the ascension but on the disciples' sharing in Jesus' relation to God, which is effected by this ascending.

[43] Cf. John 1:16–18; see Xavier Léon-Dufour, *Resurrection and the Message of Easter,* trans. R. N. Wilson (New York: Holt, Rinehart & Winston, 1975), 180–81.

very meaning of his return to the Father is that the Spirit is now handed over
to his disciples (cf. 16:7; 19:30). In short, the message Jesus entrusts to Mary
Magdalene is that all is indeed accomplished and that by his exaltation Jesus
has become the source of the Spirit of filiation and of the new covenant for
those who are doubly his brothers and sisters, children of the same Father and
members of the same covenant. There can be no question of regarding this
message as anything but the good news of salvation in its characteristically
Johannine formulation.

Mary Magdalene, unlike the women in Mark (16:8), hastens to fulfill the
commission by announcing the gospel to her co-disciples. The formula with
which she opens her proclamation is the Fourth Gospel's technical credential
statement of revelation as the basis of one's witness: "I have seen the Lord"
(cf. 20:18 with 20:25, in which the disciples announce the Easter message to
Thomas; also 3:11; 19:35). The disciples in John, unlike those in Matthew
(28:17), the Markan appendix (16:11), and Luke (24:10–11), give no indication of not accepting Mary's testimony. Indeed, when Jesus appears to them
later that day, they are not astonished or unbelieving but rather filled with joy
(see 20:20).

The Mary Magdalene material in the Fourth Gospel is perhaps the most
important indication we have of the Gospel perspective on the role of women
in the Christian community. It shows us quite clearly that, in at least one of
the first Christian communities, a woman was regarded as the primary witness to the paschal mystery, the guarantee of the apostolic tradition. Her
claim to apostleship is equal in every respect to both Peter's and Paul's, and
we know more about her exercise of her vocation than we do about most of
the members of the Twelve. Unlike Peter, she was not unfaithful to Jesus during the passion, and, unlike Paul, she never persecuted Christ in his members.
But, like both, she saw the risen Lord, received directly from him the commission to preach the Gospel, and carried out that commission faithfully and
effectively.

SUMMARY AND CONCLUSIONS

Let us now briefly summarize our findings about the potential contribution
of the Fourth Gospel to our reflection on the role of women in the Christian
community. We have seen that both general impressions and analyses of
particular passages about women suggest to us a picture of a first-century
community in which original and loving women played a variety of unconventional roles that the Fourth Evangelist presents as approved by Jesus and

the community despite the grumblings of some men. These women do not appear dependent on husbands or other male legitimators, nor as seeking permission for their activities from male officials. They evince remarkable originality in their relationships with Jesus and extraordinary initiative in their activities within the community. They are the privileged recipients of three of Jesus' most important self-revelations: his identity as the great "I am" and his messiahship (Samaritan woman), that he is the resurrection and the life (Martha), and that his glorification is complete and its salvific effects now given to his disciples (Mary Magdalene).

Women are the two most important witnesses to him both during his public life and during his "hour." We have seen that women officially represent the community in the expression of its faith (Martha), its acceptance of salvation (Mary Magdalene), and its role as witness to the gospel (Samaritan woman, Mary Magdalene). Two women in John hold the place occupied by Peter in the Synoptics: Martha as confessor of faith and Mary Magdalene as recipient of the Easter protophany and the apostolic commission to proclaim the Easter kerygma to the church.

Women were disciples in the strict sense of the word, as students of the word of Jesus, perhaps functioning in the Johannine school, and as performing the service of a student to the teacher (Mary of Bethany). We have also seen that women played the leading roles, along with the Beloved Disciple, in the paschal mystery, and that one (Mary Magdalene) was the primary witness to all three dimensions of that mystery: death, empty tomb, and Easter appearance.

Finally, we saw two examples of male objections to the activity of women (the disciples in Samaria and Judas at Bethany), both of which were effectively suppressed by Jesus, and two examples of the acceptance and effectiveness of the witness of women (the Samaritans and the disciples after the glorification).

If the material on women in the Fourth Gospel were released from the shackles of a male-dominated exegesis and placed at the service of the contemporary church, there is little doubt that it would help to liberate both men and women from any remaining doubts that women are called by Jesus to full discipleship and ministry in the Christian community. Hopefully, our investigation of this concrete question has also helped to demonstrate that the Word of God given to us in the New Testament is a word of liberation intended not only for first-century Christians but for each succeeding generation of believers who will faithfully and creatively address new questions to the text in the well-founded expectation that this Word is indeed living and active.

Part 2

Encountering Jesus through Symbolic Narrative in the Fourth Gospel

7

Born Anew (John 3:1-15)

Probably no passage in John's admittedly mysterious Gospel is more ambiguous than the dialogue between Jesus and Nicodemus in John 3:1–15. Frustrating as that may seem, however, the ambiguity is the clue to how the passage functions—for it is profoundly and pervasively ironical. In the irony lies the text's capacity to engage the reader to the point that she or he participates in building up the multilayered meaning and, at the same time, comes to the decisions that involve him or her in the community of believers that the evangelist is trying to create.[1] The irony centers first on the figure of Nicodemus, with whom readers spontaneously identify even while knowing that they shouldn't! Second, the irony pervades the entire dialogue. The dialogue makes perfectly good sense if read in terms of the Old Testament; however, the reader knows it is not to be read on that level. Salvation now lies not in the signs of the Old Testament (the brazen serpent raised up by Moses in the desert, for example [v. 14]) but in Jesus, the one who has descended from heaven and will be lifted up in crucifixion/glory to reveal God's love for the world and to give life to all who believe in him (vv. 13-14, 16). The essence of irony is that it says one thing while meaning another. But simple translation is not possible, because the literal meaning is the only access to the real meaning, just as the flesh of Jesus is the only access to the Word of God (see John 1:14–18).

NICODEMUS

Who, then, is Nicodemus? It is beside the point to inquire whether Nicodemus was a real person with whom the historical Jesus had a conversation. We

---

[1] See Gail R. O'Day's excellent treatment of irony as the mode of revelation in the Fourth Gospel, *Revelation in the Fourth Gospel: Narrative Mode and Theological Claim* (Philadelphia: Fortress, 1986).

will never know the answer to that question. Our concern is with the "textual Nicodemus," who, as most commentators recognize, is a "type" or representative figure in the Fourth Gospel.[2] Commentators who see the text primarily as a kind of window on the world of Jesus and/or the Johannine community tend to see Nicodemus as a representative of either those Jews who did not accept Jesus when he came (and were thus the enemies of the Johannine Christians), or of those whose faith was inadequate (based on and terminating in the signs), or of those who knew who Jesus was and believed in him but would not confess him openly through fear of persecution.

However, the unbiased reader has trouble feeling toward Nicodemus the animosity toward the unbelieving, the superiority toward those whose faith is inadequate, or the contempt for the "closet Christian" which the Gospel text seems to encourage. Nicodemus comes to Jesus with a generous openness, acknowledging that Jesus is credentialed by God. He seems to be guilty of nothing more than befuddlement before a confusing revelation, a befuddlement the reader can easily understand! At the end, Nicodemus does not argue with Jesus or depart in protest. He simply throws up his hands, asking helplessly, "How can this be?" (v. 9).

The spontaneous sympathy of the reader for Nicodemus is a clue that perhaps something has been overlooked. In fact, Nicodemus is "suspended" in the text between Nathanael in chapter 1, the true Israelite without guile who immediately abandoned his skepticism and confessed Jesus as "Rabbi (or teacher)," "Son of God," and "King of Israel" (1:49) and the Samaritan woman in chapter 4, the apostate Jew who comes to believe in Jesus as "the Christ" (4:29) and brings her fellow townspeople to him by her testimony (see 4:39). At the beginning of the pericope, Nicodemus is one of those Jews who believe in Jesus because of the signs he does, but whose faith Jesus finds inadequate (see 2:23–25). At the end of the dialogue Jesus ironically salutes him as a "teacher in Israel" who does not understand even the basics of Old Testament revelation, much less what Jesus has come to reveal (see 3:10, 12). But, if the reader perseveres through the text, it becomes clear that Jesus' irony is not so much a condemnation as a challenge. Jesus goes on speaking to Nicodemus, and through him to the reader, about his own identity and mission. And Nicodemus, who seems to vanish from the stage at this point, will reappear twice more in the course of the Gospel.

In 7:50–52 Nicodemus appeals to the law of Moses to defend Jesus to his fellow Pharisees in the sanhedrin who declare Jesus guilty and dangerous:

---

[2] See Raymond F. Collins, "The Representative Figures in the Fourth Gospel," *DRev* 94 (1976): 16–46 for a good explanation of the concept of representation as well as for a specific treatment of Nicodemus as a type.

"Does our law judge a person without giving him a hearing and learning what he does?" The Jewish leaders immediately assimilate Nicodemus to Jesus and his followers by asking, "Are you also a Galilean?"[3] In other words, Nicodemus in this scene, although still dependent on the Old Testament, "does the truth" according to the law (see 3:21). We are not told how Nicodemus responds to the taunt, but the evangelist, in 7:50, is at pains to remind the reader that this is the same Nicodemus who had come to Jesus before.

Finally, in 19:39–42, Nicodemus aligns himself publicly with Jesus in his "lifting up" by joining Joseph of Arimathea in removing Jesus' body from the cross and burying him with an enormous outlay of spices that reminds the reader of Mary of Bethany's action in 12:3. The evangelist reminds the reader that this now public disciple is the same Nicodemus who first came to Jesus "by night" (19:39). By doing the truth, Nicodemus has finally come to the Light, and it "is manifest that his works are done in God" (cf. 3:21).

The reader's original sympathy for Nicodemus is vindicated for the textual Nicodemus is actually a type of the true Israelite, who progresses in faith from seeing the signs, to doing the truth according to the scriptures, to finally confessing Jesus openly as the one in whom the Old Testament finds its fulfillment.[4]

No doubt Nicodemus functioned in *John's community* as a hero of its Jewish Christian members, but his primary function in the *Gospel* is to catch the conscience of the reader. Nicodemus is the very type of the truly religious person, who is, on the one hand, utterly sincere and, on the other, complacent about his or her knowledge of God and God's will. Such people are basically closed to divine revelation. Like Nicodemus, they "know" who Jesus is, what his message means (see 3:2). And like Nicodemus, it is only after they have been reduced to the futility of their own ignorance that they can begin the process of coming to the Light not by argument or reasoning but by doing the truth, a process that gradually opens them to the true meaning of the scriptures.

THE DIALOGUE

Let us return now to the dialogue between Jesus and Nicodemus (3:2–10). This conversation is supremely ironical. Jesus returns Nicodemus's respectful

[3] See Robert T. Fortna, "Theological Use of Locale in the Fourth Gospel," *ATR* Supplement Series 3 (1974): 58–95, on Galilee as a positive symbol vs. Judea as a negative symbol in relation to Jesus.

[4] See J. N. Suggit, "Nicodemus—the True Jew," in *The Relationship Between the Old and New Testament,* Neotestamentica 14 (Bloemfontein, South Africa: New Testament Society of South Africa, 1981), 100-101.

but self-confident "no one can do the signs you do unless God is with him" with "no one can see the reign of God unless he or she is born *anōthen* [which can mean again, anew, or from above]." In a particularly ludicrous example of typical Johannine misunderstanding, Nicodemus asks if one, being old, can *enter* a second time into the maternal womb *to be born,* and Jesus in a wonderful wordplay replies that one *must be born* of water and spirit in order to *enter* the reign of God. Nicodemus has understood *anōthen* as "again," that is, "a second time"; but Jesus clearly means "anew." At the level of the text, Jesus could not have said "unless one be born from above" because this could not have led Nicodemus to think he meant reentry into the maternal womb.[5] Johannine misunderstanding is based on misplaced literalness in interpreting what is said, not on a failure to understand the actual words.

Jesus immediately clarifies the meaning of "born anew." There are two births, one of water and another of spirit. The first is human birth of flesh from flesh; the second is spiritual birth of spirit from spirit. And this is something Nicodemus should have understood on two levels.

First, as a number of exegetes have recently pointed out, the use of "water" to refer to the processes of human reproduction and particularly to the actual coming forth from the womb after the breaking of the mother's water was common in both the Old Testament and other literature of the period.[6] Nicodemus's problem is precisely that he thinks being a member of the covenant, which according to Jewish law he was by birth from his mother, is sufficient to qualify him to judge religious reality, including Jesus' identity and teaching. But Jesus, especially in John's Gospel, insists that being born as a "child of Abraham" is totally inadequate for salvation (cf. 8:33–40), even though it is a preparation for hearing the Word of Jesus. Thus, at the most literal level, Nicodemus should have understood that it is necessary not only to be born into the Covenant of Israel but also to be born anew in the Spirit because what is born of flesh is fleshly while what is born of the spirit is spiritual.

---

[5] A surprising number of modern exegetes insist that *anōthen* should be translated as "born from above." They base their interpretation either on the sacramental practice of the early church or on the biblical theology of John regarding Jesus' origin. But as Linda Belleville clearly shows, this makes no sense at the textual level ("'Born of Water and Spirit': John 3:5," *Trinity Journal* 1 [1980]: 138 n. 75).

[6] Ben Witherington summarizes the arguments from Old Testament and comparative literature ("The Waters of Birth: John 3.5 and 1 John 5.6–8," *NTS* 35 [1989]: 155–60). See also Robert Fowler, "Born of Water and the Spirit (Jn 3:5)," *ExpTim* 82 (1971): 159; Margaret Pamment, "John 3:5: 'Unless One is Born of Water and the Spirit, He Cannot Enter the Kingdom of God,'" *NovT* 25 (1983): 190; D. Spriggs, "Meaning of 'Water' in John 3:5," *ExpTim* 85 (1974): 149–50.

But second, the juxtaposing of water and spirit should have alerted Nicodemus to the true meaning of spiritual birth. In the Old Testament, especially in the promise of the new covenant in Ezek. 36:25–27, it is the washing of the people in clean water and the outpouring of the Spirit that will usher in the new age. Jesus is announcing the fulfillment of that prophecy not only in regard to the people as a whole but in relation to the individual believer who Nicodemus is challenged to become. Jesus makes this point clear with the little parable about the wind which blows where it wills. One cannot doubt its reality and presence but its origin and destiny are obscure. The same is true of the inbreaking of the new covenant in those who are born anew. Their new life is manifest, but those who encounter them do not understand the source or destiny of that life.

What Jesus said should have been clear to Nicodemus against the background of the Old Testament. He is being challenged to recognize the arrival of the new covenant in the person of Jesus, whose signs are meant to draw him into relationship with this Teacher-Revealer who surpasses Moses. Instead, Nicodemus, who begins with a confident assumption of spiritual wisdom expressed in his "we *know* who you are and whence you come," regresses through literal misunderstanding into total confusion. His final words are a defeated, "How can these things be?" And Jesus, with supreme irony, then turns back on him his opening recognition. He who called Jesus "Teacher," an address that the reader recognizes as the perfect title on the lips of a disciple (because the Johannine Jesus is the ultimate Teacher-Revealer) but which Nicodemus did not really understand when he uttered it, is now gently mocked as a "teacher in Israel" who does not understand even "earthly things" such as the literal meaning of Jesus' discourse and thus is totally incapable of believing in the "heavenly things" Jesus is about to reveal.[7]

The reader goes on to understand Jesus' self-revelation as the one who comes from above to reveal, through his lifting up in death, what he has seen and heard with God, namely, that God so loved the world as to will its salvation and eternal life for those who believe in the only Son (see 3:13–18). Equipped with this revelation the reader can now reread the passage and hear what it really says in and through the ironically literal message.

The birth *anōthen* is indeed a birth "from above," like that of Jesus, who comes as Son from above. This is a birth through water and the Spirit (per-

---

[7] Wayne A. Meeks shows that in contemporary literature this was a common rebuke or warning to the disciple who has arrogantly presumed to question beyond his or her capacity to understand. Its function is to put the disciple in his or her place, which is exactly how it functions in this scene ("The Man from Heaven in Johannine Sectarianism," *JBL* 91 [1972]: 53–54).

haps by baptism, which was probably practiced in John's community).[8] It both results from and opens one to Jesus' revelation, which is, elsewhere in John's Gospel, referred to by the conjunction of water and Spirit (cf. 4:10; 7:37–39; 19:30, 34–35). Now the little parable gives up its true meaning. It is the Spirit, given to the one who believes, whose voice is heard in and through the believer, whose origin and destiny, like that of Jesus, are hidden in God. Like Jesus, the disciples are not of this world, for they are born not of the will of the flesh, nor of human concupiscence, but of God; not of "water" or flesh but of water and Spirit.

THE READER

There is a twist to this pericope, however, that contemporary Christian experience brings to light if the reader is attentive. We are meant to identify with Nicodemus, thus recognizing ourselves as believers and at the same time mistrusting ourselves as those who too readily presume that they understand the Christian mystery. We, like Nicodemus, are religious people who tend to be overly confident in our faith-based religious knowledge.[9] Like Nicodemus, we tend to be enslaved by the theological assumptions of the religious establishment so that we are not prepared to hear what is really new in the revelation of Jesus.

For example, Christians have, for centuries, read this passage without realizing that the Fourth Evangelist here supplies us, through the voice of Jesus, with one of the clearest New Testament images of the femininity of God. The Spirit is the one of whom we are *born* spiritually in the waters of baptism, just as we are born physically of our mothers in the waters of natural birth. Nicodemus's literalism about entering a second time into the maternal womb allows the evangelist to emphasize that Jesus had indeed used the metaphor of coming forth from the womb to describe our new birth in the Spirit. Jesus was not speaking here of being "engendered" by God, as of a male principle, but of being "born" of God, as from a female principle.[10] We are, in John's Gospel, *tekna theou,* "children of God," engendered by the God who is both

---

[8] Cf. Marc Michel, "Nicodème ou le non-lieu de la verité," *RevScRel* 55 (1981): 236.

[9] See the contemporary reading of Francis J. Moloney, "To Teach the Text: The New Testament in a New Age," *Pacifica* 11 (June 1998): 159–80.

[10] In Greek the verb γεννάω (*gennaō*) means both "to beget" and "to give birth to," the meaning being determined by the gender of the subject. But in this text the subject's gender has to be decided by other criteria since "water" and "spirit" are both sexually and grammatically neuter. Nicodemus's question shows that he understood it as feminine.

Jesus' Father and our Father (cf. 20:17), but also born of the Spirit, who is our Mother (cf. 1:13 in addition to the present passage).

This is not a case of some kind of divine biologism suggesting an intra-trinitarian marriage, but a way of introducing us into the deep mystery of our spiritual origin in God, a mystery too rich to be rendered by a single metaphor, however expressive. We have a similar juxtaposition of the male and female parental metaphors for God in the Old Testament. In Deut. 32:18 God rebukes Israel: "You were unmindful of the Rock that begot you, and you forgot the God who gave you birth."[11]

The biblical presentation of God as feminine has been virtually suppressed by the male religious establishment, which finds it as difficult to accept God in feminine imagery as the Jewish establishment found it to accept God in human form. And it may be that accepting this revelation will revolutionize our God-experience as radically as the acceptance of Jesus' divinity revolutionized the God-experience of the Jews in John's community. Nicodemus is not a figure of the past. He lives in the heart of every believer who is tempted to settle down in the secure religious "wisdom" of the establishment and thus resist the challenge of ongoing revelation.

HERMENEUTICAL AND THEOLOGICAL IMPLICATIONS OF THIS INTERPRETATION

Three theological presuppositions underlie the foregoing interpretation of the dialogue between Jesus and Nicodemus. First, I am assuming that the locus of *meaning* of the text is the *text as it stands* in interaction with the reader. Thus, the meaning is not to be sought primarily in the history behind the text, either in the life of the historical Jesus or in the experience of the Johannine community. Although the text does enable us to glean a certain amount of historical information, which is useful both in interpretation and for other purposes, the primary meaning of the text lies not behind it in history but in it as text.

Furthermore, the real meaning of the text is not in the dogma or doctrine that it teaches. Although this passage is replete with theological content, that content cannot be extracted from the text, which can then be discarded as a kind of semantic husk. The layers of interweaving meaning in which the reader becomes involved by participation in the ironical dialogue between

[11] See Phyllis Trible, "Feminist Hermeneutics and Biblical Studies," *Christian Century* 99 (1982): 117, on this verse and the masculinizing translations of it.

Jesus and Nicodemus can only be grasped in and through the text. This is why the reader returns again and again to the text, entering more deeply in successive encounters with it into the mystery of conversion, discipleship, and divine filiation, which can never be adequately grasped as doctrine.

By the same token, the meaning of the text cannot be reduced to its proclamation. Although each proclamation that is historically, theologically, and pastorally informed leads the reader into the meaning of the text, no proclamation captures it fully. Rather, the text remains a fountain of meaning whose waters can be endlessly gathered but never exhausted.

My second presupposition is that the locus of *revelation* is the text as it stands *in interaction with the reader*. The first conclusion of John's Gospel tells us that the historical Jesus did many other signs during his earthly life that are not recorded in the text, but the Gospel is written so that we may believe (see 20:30–31). In other words, revelation for us lies not in the deeds of the earthly Jesus in their historical facticity but in our encounter with him through the written account of those deeds.

The text is for us what the signs of Jesus were for his first disciples. Just as the signs were ambiguous, leading some to belief and others to incredulity, so the text is filled with the ambiguity of irony, double meanings, symbolism, metaphor, and all the other forms of tensive language that engage the reader in the quest for meaning. In the Nicodemus passage the reader experiences both identification with and distance from Nicodemus and comes to recognize in him- or herself the split disciple who comes to the Light only through an ongoing doing of the truth. We are caught up in the textual reversals: Nicodemus who claims to know is played off against Jesus who truly knows; the one whom Nicodemus blindly calls "teacher" reveals that the self-confident scribe is not truly a teacher; the "signs" that brought Nicodemus to Jesus are revelatory only in the light of the new birth that he cannot understand, and thus his physical "coming to the Light" is really a remaining in darkness, and so on.

As the ironical character of the passage becomes clear to the readers, they are enabled to reread the text with Christian eyes, not only understanding it in depth but allowing it to raise the question, Do *we* really understand? Or are we, perhaps, like Nicodemus, secure in our already acquired religious wisdom and thus blind to the newness of ongoing revelation?

The third presupposition operative in this interpretation is the feminist "suspicion" that alerts the interpreter to the ignoring, neutralizing, distorting, or suppressing of women's experience and all that relates to it. The masculinizing of the Christian tradition in the course of two thousand years of androcentric and patriarchal interpretation necessitates a watchfulness on the part of the exegete for that which has been distorted or lost.

Those who are privileged by any social system tend to see that system and its products as self-evidently total and adequate. But those who have been marginalized by the system can see its inadequacies precisely because it does not include them. This is what is meant by the "hermeneutical advantage" of the poor. Among the poor of Christianity are women who view the tradition, including its sacred literature, from the edges to which they have been confined. From this vantage point they can see "new" things that are invisible from the mainstream perspective. One wonders how the clear birth metaphor in the Nicodemus episode could have failed over the centuries to evoke the recognition of the femininity of God until one remembers that virtually all biblical interpretation and preaching have been in the hands of men whose control of the ecclesiastical system was legitimated by a patriarchal God and who therefore had a vested interest in maintaining God's exclusive masculinity.

Encounter with the Nicodemus text is a perennial challenge to be born again, to enter ever more fully into the mystery of divine revelation and thus to appropriate anew our identity as disciples. The path to this new birth for us, as for Nicodemus, is the doing of the truth insofar as we can grasp it. Perhaps in our day part of that which is demanded if we are to come to the Light is the integration of the feminine into our God-experience and the full inclusion of women in the church that this implies.

8

Inclusive Discipleship (John 4:1–42)

In this chapter I will attempt not only to illustrate, through an interpretation of John 4:1–42, the type of integral interpretation that I described in the introductory chapters but also to make the process of such interpretation explicit. The interpretation will be methodologically limited by the approach I have selected, namely, feminist criticism. This approach has been selected because of the question about the story of the Samaritan woman that interests me, namely, the identity and role of the woman in the passage.

The goal of the interpretive process is not merely exegetical-critical but properly hermeneutical. In other words, I do not propose simply to discover what the text says about the Samaritan woman in relation to Jesus in the context of the first century (either in the life of the earthly Jesus or in the Johannine community) in order to extrinsically "apply" the results to current feminist concerns. I am interested in the truth claims intrinsic to the text as they are addressed to contemporary believing readers, both women and men, in relation to their own discipleship. The aim is to allow the world of Christian discipleship as it is projected by this text to emerge and invite the transformative participation of the reader.

THE APPROACH: FEMINIST CRITICAL HERMENEUTICS

By way of preparation for the actual interpretation of the text, I will briefly explain the feminist critical hermeneutical approach that controls the methodology I am using.

Starting Point of Feminist Criticism

Feminist biblical criticism, which dates back to the nineteenth-century efforts of scholars such as Elizabeth Cady Stanton, was in abeyance for decades before its revival in the 1970s by the present generation of feminist biblical scholars.[1] Twentieth-century feminist scholars are motivated, as were Stanton and her colleagues, by the awareness that, in Western society at least, the Bible is a major source and legitimator of women's oppression in family, society, and church. One need not be a Christian to be affected by the Christian ethos, and that ethos is pervasively androcentric (i.e., male-centered), patriarchal (i.e., male-dominative),[2] and sexist (i.e., discriminatory toward and oppressive of women). Although Christianity did not invent patriarchy and a case can be made that in some ways it has defended women from the worst implications of misogyny, it is a fact that the Bible has been and is invoked as a religious legitimator of women's oppression, and the invocation is not groundless.

The first reaction of Christian women in general and biblical scholars in particular to the realization of the Bible's role in women's oppression was denial that the Bible itself was to blame. If the Bible is God's Word, it could not be damaging to any of God's creatures. The fault must lie in misinterpretation of the text. However, the deeper women probed into the problem passages of scripture, especially the New Testament, the clearer it became that, while some problems were indeed due to mistranslation and misinterpretation, many were integral to the text itself.

It is the realization that the biblical text itself is ideologically biased against women that has raised the question that underlies all feminist criticism: Can

---

[1] For a history and description of the current situation of feminist biblical studies, see Elisabeth Schüssler Fiorenza, *In Memory of Her: A Feminist Theological Reconstruction of Christian Origins* (New York: Crossroad, 1983), 3–40, including the notes. See also Deborah F. Middleton, "Feminist Interpretation," in *A Dictionary of Biblical Interpretation*, ed. R. J. Coggins and J. L. Houlden (London: SCM; Philadelphia: Trinity, 1990), 231–34; and Elaine Wainwright, "In Search of the Lost Coin: Toward a Feminist Biblical Hermeneutic," *Pacifica* 2 (June 1989): 135–50.

[2] Patriarchy is not merely a system of male domination of females but the institutionalization of an ideology of "otherness" that interlinks sexism, racism, classism, and other forms of oppression. On this point, see the excellent article of Elisabeth Schüssler Fiorenza, "The Politics of Otherness: Biblical Interpretation as a Critical Praxis for Liberation," in *The Future of Liberation Theology: Essays in Honor of Gustavo Gutiérrez* (Maryknoll, N.Y.: Orbis, 1989), 311–25. For my purposes in this chapter, however, I will restrict my considerations to the male-female structure of otherness.

the biblical text function as revelatory text, as locus of salvific encounter with God, for women once their feminist consciousness has been raised? The answer to this question, both theoretically (i.e., in terms of hermeneutics) and practically (i.e., in terms of actual interpretation) is far from evident. It will only come, if it does, from the efforts now being expended by feminist scholars.[3]

Feminist Criticism as Liberationist Criticism

Elisabeth Schüssler Fiorenza and other leading feminist scholars have placed feminist biblical interpretation in the category of liberationist hermeneutics.[4] But, as Fiorenza and others have pointed out, while feminist interpretation does share with other liberationist approaches its starting point in the experience of the oppressed and its objective of social transformation, in contradistinction to the claim of traditional academic exegesis to neutrality and objectivity in the search for pure knowledge, it differs from other forms of liberationist interpretation in one very important respect. Whereas the Bible permits a fairly straightforward connection between the oppression of the poor and the stranger in the biblical story and analogous oppression of the poor and racial-ethnic minorities in contemporary society, the biblical text is not only frequently blind to the oppression of women in the Israelite and early Christian communities, but the text itself is pervasively androcentric and patriarchal, frequently sexist, and even misogynist. In other words, not only does the text frequently fail to supply women with resources for liberation; it is often enough itself the problem, demonizing women, degrading female sexuality, erasing women from the history of salvation, legitimating their oppression, and trivializing their experience.[5]

Even the great stories of salvation from oppression, for example, the exo-

---

[3] For the reader new to feminist biblical scholarship three collections of essays can serve as an introduction to both the commonality of the perspective and the diversity within the field: Mary Ann Tolbert, ed., *The Bible and Feminist Hermeneutics, Semeia* 28 (Chico, Calif.: Scholars Press, 1983); Letty M. Russell, ed., *Feminist Interpretation of the Bible* (Philadelphia: Westminster, 1985); Adela Yarbro Collins, ed., *Feminist Perspectives on Biblical Scholarship* (Chico, Calif.: Scholars Press, 1985).

[4] Elisabeth Schüssler Fiorenza, "The Function of Scripture in the Liberation Struggle: A Critical Feminist Hermeneutics and Liberation Theology," in *Bread Not Stone: The Challenge of Feminist Biblical Interpretation* (Boston: Beacon, 1984), 43–63.

[5] See Schüssler Fiorenza, *In Memory of Her,* 14–21; she criticizes what she calls neo-orthodox models of feminist hermeneutics for not attending sufficiently to this point. For an example of the problem, see T. Drorah Setel, "Prophets and Pornography: Female Sexual Imagery in Hosea," in *Feminist Interpretation of the Bible,* ed. Letty M. Russell (Philadelphia: Westminster, 1985), 86–95.

dus and the paschal mystery of Jesus, cannot be appropriated directly by women as paradigms of liberation. When the Hebrews were rescued from oppression in Egypt, only male Hebrews were actually liberated. Women remained male property, subject now to Hebrew males rather than to Egyptians, but subjugated and oppressed nonetheless. And within a single generation the universal salvation won by Jesus was appropriated by male Christians, who began to establish and enforce restrictive conditions for women's participation in Christian discipleship.

Because the biblical text itself is not purely and simply a text of liberation for women but is itself part of the problem, the transformational hermeneutic of feminism aims not only at the liberation of the oppressed through the transformation of society (the aim of all liberationist theology and interpretation) but at the liberation of the biblical text from its own participation in the oppression of women and the transformation of the church that continues to model, underwrite, and legitimate the oppression of women in family and society.

Suspicion and Retrieval

Feminist biblical interpretation, as an approach, belongs in the category of ideology criticism, which starts with the assumption that the text is not "neutral" or the interpreter "objective."[6] In other words, it is rooted in suspicion as we have learned it from the great molders of the modern mind: Freud, Nietzsche, and Marx.

First, the text is not neutral. The biblical text, like other historical documents, was written by the "historical winners," who virtually never write *the* story but *their* story. Women are the quintessential "historical losers" in that they are the doubly oppressed of every oppressed group throughout history. The result is that women in the biblical text are often marginalized when they are not omitted entirely, pornographically reduced to their sexuality (because they are presented as they are seen by and function for men), demonized (by male projection), or trivialized (as nonparticipants in the spheres of male activity that alone are deemed significant). One cannot assume, in other words, in reading the biblical text that it gives us an accurate picture of women in the community of salvation. We get the picture of women that men created, which corresponds to the male understanding of women and

---

[6] In the language of Jürgen Habermas, ideology produces "systematically distorted communication." For a succinct presentation of Habermas's position, see Paul Ricoeur, "Hermeneutics and the Critique of Ideology," in *Hermeneutics and the Human Sciences,* ed. and trans. John B. Thompson (Cambridge: Cambridge University Press, 1981), 78–87.

their place in society at the time of the writing of these documents. The feminist critic must, therefore, presume that she or he is dealing with a distorted record from which much has been omitted and in which much that is included is unreliable.

Second, the interpreters of the biblical text never have been, and are not now, objective, if by objective one means ideologically unbiased. Until very recently all the biblical scholars (exegetes and teachers), pastors, and homilists have been men living in, trained for, and ruling over patriarchal churches and society. They shared the mind-set of those who produced the biblical text and so noticed nothing, or very little, amiss in its presentation of women and men.

It is characteristic of ideology that it is invisible to the one whose bias it underwrites. Usually, only those who do not participate in the power system whose agenda is propagated by the ideology are aware that what seems to be simply "the way things are" is actually an oppressive conceptual, cultural, and social system. The "hermeneutical advantage" of the oppressed is precisely this ability to see, from the margins of social reality, what is second nature to those who are beneficiaries of the social system.

Feminist critics must, therefore, suspect of antiwoman bias both the text itself and the history of interpretation. This is not academic paranoia but realism. At the same time, they must propose an alternative stance to the false objectivity whose existence (and even possibility) they deny. Feminists, with other ideologically aware scholars, know that not only is there no presuppositionless interpretation but that there are no ideologically neutral presuppositions. In other words, everyone interprets from a perspective that is controlled to some extent by her or his social location. The only access to a relatively unbiased and therefore nonoppressive approach is to become self-aware of and explicit about one's social location and the effective historical consciousness to which it has contributed and then to methodically criticize and thereby neutralize as much as possible the ideological effects.

If feminist consciousness terminates in suspicion, however, it must end by repudiating the biblical text as hopelessly antiwoman and therefore without salvific potential for women. Some feminists have indeed come to this conclusion.[7] Those who continue to hope that the biblical text is susceptible of a liberating hermeneutic must pass by way of suspicion to retrieval. This

---

[7] The most well known perhaps is theologian Mary Daly, who is a self-described post-Christian scholar, but an increasing number of feminist scholars in the area of religious studies have abandoned the Christian tradition for various forms of goddess-centered religion. For a more detailed treatment of this phenomenon and a phenomenology of goddess-centered religious involvement, see my *Beyond Patching: Faith and Feminism in the Catholic Church* (Mahwah, N.J.: Paulist, 1991), especially chapter 1.

chapter is an exercise in the hermeneutics of retrieval, the effort to face without flinching the real problems in both the text and the history of interpretation and to move through the confrontation to the liberating potential of the text.

Feminist Critical Strategy

Numerous exegetical and critical strategies are employed by feminist biblical scholars in the effort to liberate the text from its own and its interpreters' ideological bias and women from the oppressive effects of that bias.[8] I will mention here five of the most common, but this list is illustrative rather than exhaustive, and different methods are appropriate to different texts.

1. Translation. Feminist interpretation often begins by challenging translations that privilege the male/masculine at the expense of the female/feminine.[9] For example, when the masculine plural in the Greek is plainly inclusive in meaning, many modern translations (although, happily, fewer) fail to use inclusive modern language, thereby perpetuating the fixation of the imagination on males as the normative and/or only important participants in the drama of salvation. A case in point is the NRSV translation of John 4:12–14, in which *hoi huioi* is translated Jacob's "sons" even though, if his daughters had not also drunk of the well, there would have been very few sons! The masculine plural is used in Greek, as it often is in English, as the inclusive term for a group including both men and women, that is, descendants, both sons and daughters in this case (cf. English "brethren"). To translate it as "sons" is, therefore, actually inaccurate, at least in modern English.

Likewise, in the RSV (happily corrected in the NRSV) in the same passage Jesus is presented as saying "whoever drinks of the water that I shall give *him* will never thirst; the water that I shall give *him* will become in *him* a spring of water welling up to eternal life" (emphasis mine). The translation of *autō* as masculine, given that Jesus is talking to a woman and plainly intends his

[8] Most typologies of feminist interpretation divide current scholarship into three hermeneutical types: revisionist, liberationist, and reconstructionist. As feminist scholars continue to interact, these classifications are breaking down. Whatever hermeneutical position a scholar embraces, however, certain strategies are shared. On this point, see Katherine D. Sakenfeld, "Feminist Uses of Biblical Materials," in *Feminist Interpretation of the Bible,* ed. Letty M. Russell (Philadelphia: Westminster, 1985), 55–64. I am concerned here with strategies.

[9] On the problem of translation, see Katherine D. Sakenfeld, "Feminist Perspectives on Bible and Theology: An Introduction to Selected Issues and Literature," *Int* 42 (1988): 5–18, especially 16–18.

message to have universal application, is literalistic and false to the meaning of the passage. Feminist consciousness recognizes and challenges the ideological agenda of rendering women textually invisible, which is an important factor in keeping them socially and ecclesially invisible.

2. Focusing on texts with liberating potential. One of the earliest types of feminist interpretation, which still has value provided that it is not used in isolation, consists in focusing on what has been called "woman material" in the New Testament. In other words, feminist scholars located and exploited texts in which women figure prominently, are presented positively, or overcome actual historical or textual attempts to suppress them. The story of the Samaritan woman has been used this way, and John 4:27, the episode of the disciples' return from the town and their confusion at Jesus' conversation with a woman, has often focused the attention of feminist interpreters. In my interpretation I will exploit this episode but within the context of a feminist interpretation of the passage as a whole.

The danger of this strategy is that it can unconsciously support the underlying ideological presupposition that women appear in history, as in life, by way of exception. In other words, it is falsely assumed that the biblical story, like all of human history, is basically about men. If women, by way of exception, are significant at some point, they must be singled out and raised to visibility. Thus, the question becomes, What does the Bible say about *women?* because the story as a whole is presumed to be *not about women* but about men. Nevertheless, there is value in focusing on material about women in the New Testament text because in these texts one can see clearly what is often completely hidden in the major portion of the text, namely, that women existed, participated actively, and were highly significant in Christian history from its first moments.

3. Raising women to visibility. A third strategy of feminist interpretation consists in raising to visibility the hidden feminine element in biblical texts. In other words, attention is called to the application to women specifically of texts that are obviously liberating but whose beneficiaries seem not to include women. For example, the proclamation by the townspeople of Sychar that Jesus is the "Savior of the World" (John 4:42) was not merely a vindication of the claim of Samaritans to equal participation with Jews in the salvation offered by Jesus but also of the equal participation of women in that salvation. "World" is a universalist term, and the invisible subgroup of every excluded group is women.

4. Revealing the text's "secrets." Feminist interpretation also attempts to reveal in the biblical text the "secrets" about women that are buried beneath its androcentric surface, especially the hidden history of women, which has been largely obscured and distorted, if not erased altogether, by male control of the tradition. Sometimes the feminist task involves pointing to that which is plainly in the text but has remained "unnoticed" or even been denied by exegetes. For example, there are enough ambiguities in the Fourth Gospel's few clues to the identity of the evangelist and/or the Beloved Disciple to at least raise a serious question about whether one or both might have been female.[10] The Gospel probably does not supply enough data to settle the question either way, but that in itself should suffice to undermine the nearly universal assumption that the Gospel is (of course) a male creation or that such is to be held until there is convincing evidence to the contrary.[11]

Rhetorical criticism is also used by feminist interpreters to "make the text reveal its context."[12] For example, the feminist rhetorical critic might well raise the following questions. What experience within the Johannine community would have suggested to the evangelist to make a woman the central character in two major missionary texts, that is, the story of the evangelization of Samaria in 4:1–42 and the commission to announce the resurrection in 20:11–18? Would such stories have been acceptable in a community that restricted apostolic identity and missionary activity to males? Who might have had a stake in preserving the little episode in 4:27 (the return of the disciples), since it plays no essential role in the story being told but clearly calls into question male hesitations about women's relationship to Jesus and to the apostolate? Would a male writer have done so or been allowed by other males to do so?

5. Rescuing the text from misinterpretation. A very important strategy of feminist interpretation consists in discerning and challenging the androcentric, patriarchal, sexist, and misogynist misinterpretations that pervade the history of New Testament scholarship and that have deeply affected the

[10] See chapter 15, where I explore this topic in greater detail.

[11] See Schüssler Fiorenza, *In Memory of Her,* 60–61. "The suggestion of female authorship . . . has great imaginative-theological value because it opens up the possibility of attributing the authority of apostolic writings to women and of claiming theological authority for women" (p. 61).

[12] I take this expression from Wilhelm Wuellner, "Where is Rhetorical Criticism Taking Us?" *CBQ* 29 (1987): 450. Elisabeth Schüssler Fiorenza elaborated the same point in her presidential address to the Society of Biblical Literature in 1987, "The Ethics of Biblical Interpretation: Decentering Biblical Scholarship," *JBL* 107 (1988): 3–17.

Christian imagination through the scholarly and homiletic tradition. For example, as I will attempt to show, the consistent identification of the Samaritan woman in John 4 as a duplicitous whore whom Jesus tricks into self-exposure and then, presumably, converts both violates the text and allows the woman's role in the evangelization of Samaria to be minimized while the (presumably male) townspeople emerge as virtual self-evangelizers who perspicaciously recognize Jesus while dismissing the woman's testimony.

HISTORICAL AND LITERARY PRESUPPOSITIONS

Although the approach I am taking to the story of the Samaritan woman is that of feminist ideological criticism, valid integral interpretation demands the explicitation of the basic historical- and literary-critical presuppositions that are operative throughout the interpretive process.

Historical Presuppositions

In what follows I will focus on the apostolic identity and missionary role of the Samaritan woman, but I start with certain historical-critical presuppositions about the pericope as a whole. First, the episode in Samaria is, in all likelihood, not a historical event in the life of the earthly Jesus. Although the Lukan Jesus makes a Samaritan the hero of one of his parables (Luke 10:29–37) and praises the Samaritan whom he had cured who was the only one of the ten healed lepers to return and give thanks (Luke 17:11–19), there is nothing in the Synoptic tradition to suggest that the earthly Jesus exercised any ministry among the Samaritans. In fact, in Luke 9:52–53 we are told explicitly that the Samaritans refused to receive Jesus, and in Matt. 10:5 that Jesus commanded the Twelve whom he sent on mission not to enter any town of the Samaritans. Furthermore, Acts 8 recounts what seems to be the first Christian mission to Samaria, and it was initiated after the death of Stephen.

The story in John 4, then, probably represents a reading back into the public ministry of Jesus the Johannine community's postresurrection experience of the Samaritan mission and the influence of the Samaritan converts within the community of the Fourth Gospel.[13] The basic purpose of the story of the

---

[13] See Raymond E. Brown, *The Community of the Beloved Disciple: The Life, Loves, and Hates of an Individual Church in New Testament Times* (New York: Paulist, 1979), 36–40, for a discussion of the entrance of the Samaritans into the Johannine community and their effect on Johannine theology as well as on the relations of Johannine Christians with the Jewish community.

Samaritan Woman in the Gospel itself is to legitimate the Samaritan mission and to establish the full equality in the community between Samaritan Christians and Jewish Christians. The story presents this equality as resting on the fact that both groups were evangelized by Jesus himself, who, in the theology of the Fourth Gospel, is no less immediately present to those who "have not seen and yet have come to believe" than to those who associated with him in his pre-Easter life (see 20:29). In the story the theological issues dividing Samaritans and Jews are faced and resolved with a reaffirmation of Jewish legitimacy as bearer of the covenant faith and a surprising recognition of the essential validity of the Samaritan faith tradition despite the very real failures in fidelity of these historical successors of ancient Israel.

Literary Presuppositions

Two literary characteristics of the story of the Samaritan woman are important for our purposes. First, in form the story is what has been called a "type story," that is, a narrative that follows a recognized biblical pattern.[14] In this case the pattern or paradigm is the story recounting the meeting at a well of future spouses who then play a central role in salvation history. We find the pattern in the story of Abraham's servant finding Rebekah, the future wife of Isaac, at the well of Nahor (Gen. 24:10–61); Jacob meeting Rachel at the well in Haran (Gen. 29:1–20); and Moses receiving Zipporah as wife after his rescue of the seven daughters of Reuel at the well in Midian (Exod. 2:16–22).

In the Johannine story, Jesus meets the woman at the most famous well of all, Jacob's well in Samaria, that is, ancient Israel. Jesus has already been identified at Cana as the true Bridegroom, who supplied the good wine for the wedding feast (see 2:9–10) and by John the baptizer as the true Bridegroom to whom God has given the new Israel as bride (see 3:27–30). Now, the new Bridegroom, who assumes the role of Yahweh, bridegroom of ancient Israel, comes to claim Samaria as an integral part of the new Israel, namely, the

---

Literature on the Samaritans, their history, theology, and influence on and in scripture is vast. Of particular importance is the seminal study of Wayne A. Meeks, *The Prophet-King: Moses Traditions and the Johannine Christology,* NovTSup (Leiden: E. J. Brill, 1967). See also Charles H. H. Scobie, "The Origin and Development of Samaritan Christianity," *NTS* 19 (1972–73): 390–414; John Macdonald, *The Theology of the Samaritans* (Philadelphia: Westminster, 1964). Samaritan studies are brought up to date and the most important bibliography given by James D. Purvis, "The Samaritans and Judaism," in *Early Judaism and Its Modern Interpreters,* ed. Robert Kraft and George W. E. Nickelsburg (Atlanta: Scholars Press, 1986). Specialists will want to consult *The Samaritans,* ed. Alan D. Crown (Tübingen: J. C. B. Mohr, 1989).

[14] See P. Joseph Cahill, "Narrative Art in John IV," *RelS Bulletin* 2 (April 1982): 44–47.

Christian community and specifically the Johannine community. The marital theme is underscored by the male–female dynamic of the scene, the conversation between the woman and Jesus about marriage, the abundant symbolism of fertility and fecundity of the episode (well, water, vessel, fruitful fields, sowing and reaping, etc.).[15]

Second, the Samaritan woman episode must be seen within the "Cana to Cana" literary development in John 2–4. This section of the Gospel, pervaded by the nuptial motif, begins with the wedding at Cana in chapter 2, where Jesus' *Jewish* disciples (presumably including his mother) come to believe in him through his *signs* (2:1–11), and ends with the healing of the royal official's son in Cana in chapter 4, in which a *non-Jew* and his whole household come to believe because of the *word* of Jesus (4:46–54). Within this literary unit the Samaritan woman is clearly contrasted with Nicodemus (3:1–15).[16] Whereas Nicodemus comes to Jesus at night and disappears into the shadows, confused by Jesus' self-revelation, the Samaritan woman encounters Jesus at high noon, accepts his self-revelation, and brings others to him by her testimony.

THE THEOLOGICAL FOCUS
OF THE STORY: MISSION

Although the story of the Samaritan woman is part of the presentation of Jesus as the Bridegroom of the new Israel, which pervades the first section of the Fourth Gospel, it is also clearly a missionary story. This is evident from Jesus' discourse to his disciples in 4:31–38 as well as from the denouement of the scene, the conversion to Jesus of the Samaritan townspeople in 4:39–42.

In the discourse that intervenes between the woman's departure to evangelize the town by recounting her encounter with Jesus and the coming of the townspeople to him, Jesus speaks to his disciples who have returned from their errand in the town. He attaches what is occurring before their eyes to his own mission from God by declaring that his deepest hunger, namely, to do God's will, has been satisfied (see v. 34) by his conversation with the woman and its consequences. He has no need of the earthly food they have

---

[15] See Calum M. Carmichael, "Marriage and the Samaritan Woman," *NTS* 26 (1980): 331–46, for detailed treatment of the Old Testament Yahweh–Israel marriage theme in John 4.

[16] Mary Margaret Pazdan, "Nicodemus and the Samaritan Woman: Contrasting Models of Discipleship," *BTB* 17 (1987): 145–48.

brought him. Furthermore, he calls the attention of the disciples to Samaria, "white for the harvest," and indicates that its conversion is part of the great missionary venture of the church, in which they participate but which they did not originate and do not control (see vv. 35–38).

When the townspeople come to Jesus, they do so, the reader is explicitly told, because of "the woman's testimony" (v. 39), and they finally confess him to be "the Savior of the World" (v. 42), which is clearly a postglorification Johannine formulation of Christian faith in Jesus. My question, then, is, What is the identity and role of the Samaritan woman in this missionary story?

THE IDENTITY AND THE ROLE OF THE
SAMARITAN WOMAN: CHRISTIAN DISCIPLE-APOSTLE

As anyone familiar with the major commentaries on the Fourth Gospel knows, the treatment of the Samaritan woman in the history of interpretation is a textbook case of the trivialization, marginalization, and even sexual demonization of biblical women, which reflects and promotes the parallel treatment of real women in the church. Rather than cite the commentators and argue with them, however, I will interpret the passage as a feminist who does not assume that most women (insofar as they are interesting at all) are whores and that Jesus' paradigmatic relationship with women is centered on saving them from sexual sins, and who does not accept the assumption that Jesus called only males to apostleship or that all missionary activity in the early church was done by men. The interpretation should serve to call into question the standard approaches to this text.

The first clue to the woman's identity is her placement between Nicodemus, the Jewish authority who fails to recognize Jesus as Messiah or to accept his self-revelation, and the royal official, the pagan authority who recognizes Jesus' life-giving power and comes to faith through and in his saving word. In other words, the woman, like Nicodemus and the royal official, is what Raymond Collins has called a "representative figure," that is, a symbolic character.[17] Very often the symbolic characters in John (e.g., the mother of Jesus, the Beloved Disciple, the royal official, the paralytic at the pool, the man born blind) are nameless, which enhances their power to represent collectivities without losing their particularity. This is the case with the Samaritan

[17] Raymond F. Collins, "The Representative Figures in the Fourth Gospel," *DRev* 94 (1976): 26–46, 118–32.

woman, one of the most sharply drawn characters in the Gospel. This woman is symbolic not only of the Samaritans who come to Jesus through the witness of the Johannine community but, as we have already seen, of the new Israel, who is given to Jesus the Bridegroom "from above." This symbolic identity should warn the reader against the sexual literalism to which so many commentators immediately leap, whether in regard to the woman's supposedly shady past or in regard to what one recent commentator described as the woman's attempt to seduce Jesus.[18]

The second clue to the woman's identity and role is her conversation with Jesus. It is important to note that the discussion, from the very first moment, is religious and even theological. The woman does not, as is often suggested, introduce extraneous theological issues as a smokescreen to distract Jesus from probing into her shameful sex life. She begins by questioning Jesus' breaking with Jewish tradition, first by speaking in public to a woman and asking to share utensils with a Samaritan, and second by his implication, in the offer of living water, that he is on a par with the patriarch Jacob, who gave the well to Israel. Characteristic of Samaritan theology was its Mosaic-patriarchal tradition as opposed to the Davidic-monarchical tradition of the Jews. Thus, for the woman, Jesus' implicit claim to be on a par with the patriarch Jacob has enormous theological implications.

Immediately after the exchange on the five husbands (to which we will return shortly), the woman recognizes Jesus, whom she had at first identified as merely a man and a Jew, as a prophet (v. 19), and she asks him where true worship is to take place, on Mt. Gerizim as the Samaritans held or in Jerusalem as the Jews believed. According to Samaritan theology the Messiah would be not a descendant of David but a prophet like Moses (as promised in Deut. 18:18–19) who, upon his return, would reveal all things and restore true worship, not in the temple of Jerusalem but in Israel, that is, in the northern kingdom. In other words, the woman is pursuing a careful investigation of the identity of Jesus, who has already indicated his affinity with the patriarchs and his prophetic capacity to "tell her all things." She wants to know where he stands on the issue of true worship, which, in Samaritan theology, is not only a prophetic concern but specifically a messianic one.

When Jesus, after vindicating the claim of the Jews to be the legitimate bearers of the covenant tradition, goes on to invalidate by transcendence both the Jewish claim for Jerusalem and the Samaritan claim for Mt. Gerizim in favor of worship in spirit and in truth, the woman suspects his messianic

---

[18] Lyle Eslinger, "The Wooing of the Woman at the Well: Jesus, the Reader and Reader-Response Criticism," *JLitTheo* 1 (1987): 167–83.

identity, that he is indeed the one who comes to restore true worship in Israel. Jesus confirms her intuition and reveals himself to her as not only the prophetic Messiah of Samaritan expectation but as *egō eimi,* that is, by the very designation that the Samaritans preferred for God, the "I am" of the Mosaic revelation (see Exod. 3:14). This is the first use of the "I am" revelation formula in the Fourth Gospel.

Within this context of careful theological scrutiny of Jesus by the woman, culminating in Jesus' self-identification as descendant of the patriarchs, prophetic Messiah, and Mosaic "I am"—that is, as the superabundant fulfillment of Samaritan expectation—the discussion about the five husbands takes on a completely different cast from the mildly salacious one usually evoked by commentators. Either it is totally out of place, a trivial bit of moralism, a display of preternatural knowledge on the part of Jesus, or it is an integral part of this highly theological exchange.

The woman has questioned Jesus on virtually every significant tenet of Samaritan theology. Through this process she has come to suspect that he is the Messiah in and through his own self-revelation as the new prophet like Moses (significantly, not a new David), thus vindicating the Samaritan claim to be spiritually a legitimate part of the chosen people and thus of the new Israel. Jesus has pointed the way beyond the controversy between Jews and Jerusalem, on the one hand, and Samaritans and Mt. Gerizim, on the other. Both are called to transcend their particularistic traditions and to find their common spiritual identity in Jesus, who is the Truth. If this story, as I have suggested, is meant to legitimate the presence of Samaritan Christians in the Johannine community and to affirm their equality with Jewish Christians, it could not have been more artistically constructed. I would suggest, then, that the dialogue on the five husbands is integral to the discussion of Samaritan faith and theology, and the "husbands" are therefore symbolic rather than literal.[19]

First, the exchange about the husbands occurs, as I have already pointed out, not as prelude to the theological discussion but in the midst of it, that is, after the woman has perceived Jesus' implicit claim to equality with the patriarchs and before she acknowledges him to be a prophet.

Second, if the scene itself is symbolically the incorporation of Samaria into the Johannine community, the new Israel, the bride of the new Bridegroom, which is suggested by the type scene itself, then the adultery/idolatry sym-

[19] This thesis was proposed decades ago by John Bligh in "Jesus in Samaria," *HeyJ* 3 (1962): 336. It has been regularly disputed by commentators who prefer the literal interpretation despite the context of the story and the high improbability that any Jew or Samaritan man would marry a woman who had been divorced several times.

bolism so prevalent in the prophetic literature for speaking of Israel's infidelity to Yahweh the Bridegroom would be a most apt vehicle for discussion of the anomalous religious situation of Samaria. Samaria's infidelity to the Mosaic covenant was symbolized by its acceptance, after the return of the remnants of the northern tribes from Assyrian captivity, of the worship of the false gods of five foreign tribes (see 2 Kgs. 17:13–34). Samaria's Yahwism was tainted by false worship and therefore even the "husband" she now has (a reference to her relationship with the God of the covenant) was not really her husband (see v. 18) in the full integrity of the covenantal relationship. Salvation, Jesus therefore insists, is "from the Jews" (v. 22), who worship what they know, that is, whose Yahwist faith is integral and orthodox, while the Samaritans worship what they "do not know." Thus, in claiming that Samaria, in reality, has no husband, the woman is correctly (even if unwittingly) using the prophetic metaphor to describe the religious situation of her people. Jesus confirms her answer: "What you have said is true!" (v. 18).

This brings us to the third point. Jesus' revelation to the woman, who symbolizes Samaria, of her infidelity is not a display of preternatural knowledge that convinces the woman of Jesus' power (and thus her helplessness before him), embarrassing her into a diversionary tactic in an effort to escape moral exposure. Rather, it is exactly what she acknowledges it to be when she says in response to his revelation, "I perceive that you are a prophet" (v. 19). Jesus' declaration that Samaria "has no husband" is a classic prophetic denunciation of false worship, like Hosea's oracle in which the prophet, expressing God's sentiments toward unfaithful Israel, says, "Plead with your mother, plead— for she is not my wife and I am not her husband—that she put away her harlotry from her face and her adultery from between her breasts" (Hos. 2:2).

The woman challenges Jesus' prophetic judgment by insisting that "Our fathers [i.e., the patriarchs] worshiped on this mountain" (i.e., the Samaritan tradition rests on the authority of the patriarchs), but Jesus vindicates his position, insisting that his prophetic judgment on Samaria is just but also that the question of where to worship has become irrelevant, because, just as Samaritan theology taught, the messianic era that has arrived in Jesus will be characterized by true worship of God in spirit because God is spirit (see vv. 20–24). The woman is overcome by this interpretation of Samaritan faith and recognizes that Jesus may be the very Messiah who, according to Samaritan eschatological hope, would "proclaim all things to us," which is what Jesus has just done (v. 25) and what the woman will eventually offer as evidence to her fellow townspeople: "Come and see a man who told me [i.e., us] all I [i.e., we] have ever done!" (v. 29). Jesus confirms her conclusion with his lapidary and unambiguous self-identification as Messiah and as the God of Mosaic revelation, "I am" (v. 26).

In summary, the entire dialogue between Jesus and the woman is the "wooing" of Samaria to full covenant fidelity in the new Israel by Jesus, the new Bridegroom. It has nothing to do with the woman's private moral life but with the covenant life of the community. Nowhere else in the Fourth Gospel is there a dialogue of such theological depth and intensity. Jesus' conversation with Nicodemus in chapter 3 ends in a long theological monologue by Jesus in which Nicodemus has ceased to participate. In chapter 6 Jesus, in response to occasional "foil lines" from his completely confused and/or resistant interlocutors, gives a lengthy theological monologue on faith. And at the Last Supper Jesus gives several lengthy theological discourses. But in this extraordinary scene the woman is not simply a "foil" feeding Jesus cue lines. She is a genuine theological dialogue partner gradually experiencing Jesus' self-revelation even as she reveals herself to him.

At the precise moment of Jesus' culminating self-revelation, the disciples, who had gone into the town to buy food, arrive. They are shocked to find Jesus talking to a *woman*. Interestingly enough, it is not his talking to a Samaritan that upsets them. This may indicate that in the Johannine community, by the time the Gospel was written, the issue of Samaritan integration was long settled, while the issue of women's role in the community was still a subject of lively debate. In any case, the disciples realize uneasily that Jesus "seeks" something in or of this woman, and they dare not question his intention.[20] The evangelist confirms the reader's intuition that what shocks the disciples is the woman's role by inserting a narratively unnecessary detail over which considerable exegetical ink has been spilled: "then the woman left her water jar and went back to the city." Like the apostle-disciples in the Synoptic Gospels, whose leaving of nets, boats, parents, or tax stall symbolized their abandonment of ordinary life to follow Jesus and become apostles, this woman abandons her daily concerns and goes off to evangelize the town.

In the Fourth Gospel *zēteō* ("to seek")[21] is often used as a quasi-technical theological term for the deep desire that finalizes religiously significant attitudes and actions. Jesus' first words in the Gospel, to his first disciples, are *ti zēteite*, "What do you seek?" (1:38). His question to Mary Magdalene on the morning of the resurrection, is *tina zēteis*, "Whom do you seek?" (20:15). Throughout the Gospel such themes as "seeking glory," "seeking to kill,"

---

[20] See Raymond E. Brown, "Roles of Women in the Fourth Gospel," in *Community of the Beloved Disciple*, 198.

[21] In this section I am translating *zēteō* as "seek" rather than using the NRSV translation.

"seeking the will of the one who sent me," and "seeking the truth" emphasize the theological import of the term by marking the ultimate motivations of various characters. In this case the disciples are made very uneasy by what Jesus seems to "seek" from this woman.

This little interlude of the return of the disciples undoubtedly tells us more about the Johannine community than about the earthly Jesus. The theological and missionary role of the woman is profoundly unsettling to the male disciples, who see themselves as the privileged associates of Jesus, who, nevertheless, seems to have gotten along quite well without them. He does not need the food they have brought him (see vv. 31–34) because his dialogue with the woman has satisfied both his hunger to do the will of the one who sent him and the thirst that symbolically mediated their encounter. And the Samaritan mission, plainly in the hands of the woman, is one in which Jesus says they (the male disciples) will participate as "reapers." But they do not initiate it, and it is not under their control (see vv. 35–38). It seems not unlikely that whoever wrote the Fourth Gospel had some experience of women Christians as theologians and as apostles, was aware of the tension this aroused in the community, and wanted to present Jesus as legitimating female participation in male-appropriated roles. Again, one cannot help wondering about the identity of the evangelist.

As the disciples lapse into silence, we are told that "many of the Samaritans . . . believed in him because of the woman's testimony" (v. 39). Literally the text says *dia ton logon tēs gynaikos martyrousēs,* that is, "through the word of the woman bearing witness." Remember, this scene is probably a description of the conversion of the Samaritans after the departure of Jesus. In John 17:20, at the Last Supper, Jesus on the eve of his going away prays for his disciples. The evangelist tells us that he prayed not just for those present with him at the supper, "but also for those who will believe in me through their word" (*alla kai peri tōn pisteuontōn dia tou logou autōn eis eme*). This woman is the first and only person (presented) in the public life of Jesus through whose word of witness a group of people is brought to "come and see" and "to believe in Jesus."[22]

The effectiveness of her ministry is underlined by the fact that the townspeople not only "come to Jesus," which is a Johannine expression for beginning to believe, but they entreat Jesus to "remain with them," and he "remained there two days" (v. 40). In the Fourth Gospel, *menō*, "to remain"

---

[22] In chapter 1, prior to Jesus' emergence into public life at the wedding feast in Cana, John the baptizer points Jesus out to two of his followers and they bring personal acquaintances and relatives to Jesus. But it is striking that in the Fourth Gospel Jesus does not call any "apostles" nor does he send his disciples out on missionary journeys.

or "to dwell," is a quasi-technical term for union with Jesus. These new believers are presented as coming to full Johannine faith in Jesus as the Christ (as the woman has suggested in v. 29), proclaiming him as "the Savior of the World" (v. 42). This clearly postresurrection confession of faith is another indication that this episode is a reading back into the life of the earthly Jesus of a post-Easter event. The evangelist has "narratized" as a single event the mission to the Samaritans so that it can be inserted into the Gospel itself, thus attributing the presence of the Samaritans in the Johannine community to Jesus' own initiative even while assigning the work of evangelization to a disciple.

Some commentators hasten to undermine this evident identification of the woman with Jesus' postresurrection disciple-apostles[23] by pointing out that the townspeople, once they encounter Jesus, proclaim that their faith is now based no longer on the word of the woman but on that of Jesus. "We have heard for ourselves, and we know that this is truly the Savior of the World" (v. 42). This position betrays an ignorance, if not suppression, of the characteristically Johannine pattern of faith development.

In the Fourth Gospel we see repeatedly people brought to Jesus by a disciple and coming to full faith in him on the basis of Jesus' own word to them. John the baptizer (see 1:35–39) testified to Jesus; two of his disciples followed Jesus and remained with him that day; and they came to believe in him on the basis of that interchange. One of them, Andrew (see 1:41–42), brought his brother Simon to Jesus. When Jesus recognized Simon and renamed him, Simon (now Peter) became a disciple. Philip (see 1:44–51) brought a reluctant Nathanael to Jesus, and again Jesus' word converted his hearer into a follower. Even after the resurrection it was the testimony of Mary Magdalene that prepared the disciples to recognize Jesus when he appeared in their midst on Easter night (see 20:18–20) and Thomas was reprimanded for his refusal to accept the word of witness of the other disciples, who claimed, "We have seen the Lord" (20:25).

In each case the pattern is the same: someone is brought to Jesus through the word of another but comes to believe in him definitively because of Jesus' own word. In a sense, there are no "second generation disciples" in John, because all are bound to Jesus by his own word. Thus, the role of the Samaritan woman in the coming to faith of the townspeople is precisely that

---

[23] As already pointed out, in the Fourth Gospel no one is called an "apostle." "Disciple" is the term that indicates one's relation to Jesus, who alone is the Sent One. But this woman plainly exercises the apostolic role which Jesus' followers assume only after his departure. Again, this is a clue that this scene does not recount an event of Jesus' earthly life but a post-resurrection experience read back into the public life.

assigned to his disciples by Jesus himself on the night before he died. She bore witness to Jesus as the Messiah of Samaritan expectation, the "one who told me everything" as the prophet-like-Moses was to do, and through her word the hearers came to believe in him.

RESULTS OF FEMINIST INTERPRETATION

We are now in a position to summarize the results of this basically feminist exegetical-critical analysis of John 4:1–42, which included historical, literary, theological, and ideological methods of investigation. My inquiry began with the question about the identity and role of the Samaritan woman in this episode. I began with a strong suspicion about the basic cast of much tradi-tional exegesis of this passage, which presents the woman as a disreputable (if interesting) miscreant who, failing in her attempt to distract Jesus from her sexually disgraceful past, surrenders to his overpowering preternatural knowl-edge of her, alerts her fellow townspeople to his presence, and then fades from the scene as they discover him for themselves and come to believe in him. Despite this critical picture of the woman, generations of believers have been deeply religiously moved by this story and drawn to this woman, a fact that testifies to its literary power and spiritual density and justifies our taking a second look at the data.

Given the male tendency, pervasive in the Bible as elsewhere, to reduce women to their sexuality and their sexuality to immorality, I entertained an alternate possibility about the woman, namely, that she was not a whore whom Jesus converted but a potential spouse whom he invited to intimacy. This hypothesis was suggested by two literary clues: the place of the episode in the Cana to Cana section of the Gospel and the meeting-at-the-well type story on which it is patterned.

The analysis of the episode from this alternative perspective revealed the woman as a symbolic figure representing the Samaritan element in the Johan-nine community, which understood itself as the new Israel, bride of the true Bridegroom, Jesus. In this role she engages with Jesus in a highly theological dialogue that mediates the significant religious differences between Jews and Samaritans, which undoubtedly had to be and were resolved in the Johannine community. She intuits Jesus' identity as the fulfillment of Samaritan (as well as Jewish) messianic expectations, and he confirms her intuition with the first "I am" self-revelation of the Fourth Gospel. The woman evangelizes her fel-low Samaritans, who, in the classic faith pattern of the Fourth Gospel, come to Jesus, accept his word, and acknowledge him implicitly as Christ and explicitly as universal Savior. He abides with them as they come to abide in his word and thus in the Johannine community, whose theology, especially in its high Christology and universalism, reflects the Samaritan influence on its origins.

In this context the dialogue about the five husbands, which hardly makes sense as a historical event since five successive marriages (as opposed to mere concubinage with several men) by a woman of that religious culture is totally implausible, assumes its theological character as symbolic discourse about the covenant. Jesus the prophet uses the familiar adultery/idolatry metaphor of the prophetic tradition to call Samaria to renounce its historical infidelity and to embrace the worship of the one God in spirit and in truth. The path to Christian identity for the Samaritans does not necessarily pass by way of Jerusalem.

While this interpretation, which seems to make better sense of the pericope than the hypothesis of a long digression on the woman's morals for the sole purpose of displaying Jesus' preternatural knowledge, allows the woman to function symbolically and theologically rather than merely sexually in the episode, it also raises a problem. Feminist biblical scholars have called attention to the underlying sexism of the prophetic tradition's marital metaphor for the covenant relationship.[24] Not only is it based on the model of patriarchal marriage, to which male domination and female subordination are intrinsic, but it always casts God as the faithful and forgiving husband and Israel as the faithless and adulterous wife, thus consolidating the entrenched tendency to divinize men and demonize women. Jesus, in this episode, does not exploit the pornographic potential of the prophetic tradition in that he neither accuses nor condemns the woman but merely confirms her self-identification. However, the fact that the evangelist uses the metaphor continues its legitimation in the Christian community.

The brief episode of the return of the disciples, viewed from a feminist perspective, reveals the all-too-familiar uneasiness of men when one of their number takes a woman too seriously, especially in the area of the men's primary concern. Jesus' discourse about his mission and its extension into Samaria only serves to confirm their worst fears, that they are neither the originators nor the controllers of the church's mission. The effectiveness of the woman's evangelization of her town caps this scene, in which any male claim to a privileged or exclusive role in the work of Jesus is definitively undermined by Jesus' own words and deeds.

[24] See Setel, "Prophets and Pornography."

HERMENEUTICAL APPROPRIATION

In this final section I will make explicit the culminating moment of integral interpretation, its termination in hermeneutical appropriation. Often this moment, which might emerge from a powerful, criticially based homily or a period of deep, critically informed meditation, as well as from critically responsible scholarly study of a passage such as John 4, is not and need not be made explicit. However, just as people who have shared the experience of a moving play might discuss it and its transformative effect on them without dissipating that effect, it is perfectly legitimate and often even necessary for the biblical interpreter not only to pursue the interpretive project to its transformative conclusions but to render them explicit.

In the foregoing interpretation I have assumed a number of things. The interpreter of John 4 (in this case, myself and my readers) that I have posited is a believer, that is, a participant in the Christian tradition that produced and claims as its own this book that it regards as scripture, that is, as the Word of God that is inspired, revelatory, authoritative, and normative for the church. On the basis of these operative theological convictions about the nature of the biblical text and its implications for interpretation, the interpreter, by means of historical and literary methods and ideological analysis, has achieved an interpretation of the text, which is summarized in the preceding section.

The questions now to be explicitly raised concern the "world in front of the text." What kind of world does the text project and invite the reader to inhabit? What are the coordinates and the dynamics of the faith world of Christian discipleship that has opened before the reader as this interpretation has unfolded? And, from the standpoint of the feminist approach adopted here, is this a life-giving world for women as well as men believers?

It is important to note here that the questions being raised are not about extrinsic "application" in the ordinary sense of the term. We are not asking what conclusions for contemporary Christian life one might draw from the foregoing interpretive work. Nor are we asking what might be the implications of this interpretation for modern male–female relationships or church order. We are asking about the transforming effect on the reader of the interpretation process itself. This effect is not some willed change in attitude or behavior brought about by an extrinsic process that follows from exegesis and criticism but rather the effect of interpreting itself on the interpreter. It is analogous to the effect on the audience of participation in the play. Watching the play participatively is an act of interpretation that terminates in the transformation of the viewer through the aesthetic experience itself. This transformation can be made explicit afterward (analogously to what I am doing here) and can even result in some decisions or actions to be carried out later, but it is itself not something added on to the interpretation but the terminating moment of the interpretation itself.

The interpretation of the John 4 passage initiates the reader into a world essentially characterized by an astonishing, even shocking, inclusiveness. Jesus goes to Samaria, the land of the hated "other," to confront and to heal the ancient divisions and to integrate into the new covenant not those who were merely ignorant of, but those who had been unfaithful to, the old covenant. No one is excluded, no one may be excluded, from the universalist reign of the Savior of the World.

The reader cannot fail to be affected by the fact that the recipient of Jesus' universal invitation to inclusion is a woman, universal representative of the despised and excluded "other" not only in ancient Israel but throughout history and all over the world. Not only is she included, but she is engaged with respect, even asked for a gift (water) that she might receive a greater gift (living water). Her legitimate inquiries, even her objections, are met and responded to with integrity. And even more strikingly, she is made an active participant in the establishment of the universalist reign of the Savior of the World.

The initiation of the reader into the inclusive world of discipleship is further developed by participation in a kind of reverse psychology of exclusion. The scene with the disciples, including both their shock at Jesus' inclusiveness and Jesus' discourse on the harvest that exceeds their control, delegitimates any ecclesiastical "buts" that might be raised in defense of exclusion based on ethnicity, morality, or gender.

But the reader, especially the feminist reader, will also experience the "not yet" quality of this new world. There is an intrinsic tension between the total inclusivity of this world as ideal and the lingering sexism in the idolatry/adultery prophetic metaphor, which carries a God/male/faithful versus human/female/faithless domination and subordination dynamic, at least potentially. Thus, the reader experiences the interpenetration of the world of discipleship that Jesus reveals and "the world" (in the Johannine sense) that is not yet fully transformed. They are not two worlds set side by side. And the disciple-reader cannot exit from one to enter the other. We inhabit a complex situation that is "already" and "not yet." In Johannine terms, we are in the world and not of it, because we were born from above, but this has not resulted in our being taken out of this world. Instead, it results in the necessity that we be preserved, by Jesus' prayer for us and by our own choices, from the evil one (see John 17:14–16).

By participation through interpretation in the world this passage projects, the reader knows both what inclusion means and how to recognize the evil that undermines the reign of God to which those born of the Spirit are called. We can recognize it in the exclusiveness of those who claim superiority in their relation to Jesus, or who arrogate to themselves control of the church and its mission. But we can also see that it is not always so blatant. Exclusiveness, domination, oppression, and discrimination are embedded in the language and metaphors of our most sacred traditions. Ideology is pervasive and will not be exposed, recognized, and repudiated except by incessant vigilance and courageous action. The feminist reader is not called to overlook the "flaw" in this passage, much less to appropriate it into her or his self-image as a Christian or to legitimate its effects in family, society, or church. She or he is called to struggle for the transformation of this world into the world of discipleship that the text, imperfectly but nevertheless really, projects.

The integral interpretation of any biblical text is the process of engaging it in such a way that it can function as locus and mediator of transformative encounter with the living God. In this process of interpreting the New Testament as Sacred Scripture we experience and claim it as the Christian classic par excellence: the revelatory text.

9

Choosing to See or Not to See (John 5:1-18 and 9:1-41)

INTRODUCTION

Since early in Christian history the ninth chapter of John's Gospel, the story of the man born blind, has been linked with chapters 4 and 11 (the Samaritan woman and the raising of Lazarus) in the church's initiation praxis.[1] In today's lectionary these narratives—unlike most New Testament passages which are read every third year—are read on the third, fourth, and fifth Sundays of Lent every year (not just in Cycle A where they occur in the normal rotation) in connection with the scrutinies of the catechumens preparing for baptism.[2] The reason is obvious. These are the archetypal New

---

[1] G. M. Lukken, *Original Sin in the Roman Liturgy: Research into the Theology of Original Sin in the Roman Sacramentaria and the Early Baptismal Liturgy* (Leiden: E. J. Brill, 1973), 328–37, discusses the role of these passages in the early church's baptismal liturgy: "In the Ambrosian rite this pericope is read on the fourth Sunday of Lent: it has also given its name to this Sunday 'De Caeco'. In the early liturgy of Rome the story of the healing of the man born blind is also read on a Sunday in Lent. For in Rome, certainly from the end of the fourth century this pericope—like that of the Samaritan woman (Jn. 4, 6–42) and the raising of Lazarus form [*sic*] the dead (Jn. 11, 1–45)—was linked with the Sunday Mass of the baptismal scrutinia" (p. 328). Lukken acknowledges the contemporary exegetical disputes over sacraments in John's Gospel but points out that for the early church the healing of the man born blind was clearly a type of baptism.

On the development of the lectionary in the early church, see *The Study of Liturgy*, revised edition, edited by Cheslyn Jones, et. al. (New York: Oxford University Press, 1995), 225–27.

[2] See Raymond E. Brown, *Reading the Gospels with the Church: From Christmas Through Easter* (Cincinnati, Oh.: St. Anthony Messenger Press, 1996), 33–43, for a treatment of the relation of the three narratives to each other and their place in the Lenten liturgy.

For an explanation of the rite of the scrutiny in the early church, see E. C. Whitaker, *The Baptismal Liturgy: An Introduction to Baptism in the Western Church*, Studies in Christian Worship 5 (London: Faith Press, 1965), 41–44.

Testament treatments of water, light, and life, the central motifs of Christian initiation which is understood as washing, illumination, and incorporation into the paschal mystery of Jesus' dying and rising.

The baptismal motifs of congenital blindness yielding to enlightenment through washing in the water symbolically named by the evangelist "the Sent [One]" (9:7), and launching the newly illuminated one on the challenging path to full Christian discipleship (see 9:38), suggest that the original *Sitz-im-Leben* of this story might well have been the sacramental initiation of believers in the Johannine community.[3] This hypothesis is supported by the fact that chapter 9 is the primary basis for the thesis of J. Louis Martyn that the historical setting of John's Gospel is the struggle which resulted in the final separation of emerging Christianity from the post-70 C.E. synagogue.[4] The critical indication of this historical setting is John 9:22 in conjunction with 9:34, that is, the expulsion of the man born blind from the synagogue because of his confession of Jesus as one who comes "from God," that is, as the Messiah. This narrative is recognized by virtually all commentators as not only an important clue to the historical setting of the Gospel but also as a literary masterpiece and highpoint of Johannine theology. Furthermore, it is also a primary locus for studying the distinctive spirituality of discipleship of the Fourth Gospel, which is the primary focus of this essay. The "baptismal" lens provides a hermeneutical entrance into this sphere of Johannine spirituality.[5]

THE HISTORICAL CONTEXT OF THE NARRATIVE

The question about the historicity of the event narrated in John 9 is raised by the fact that this is one of comparatively few episodes in John outside of the

---

[3] The issue of sacraments in John, or more broadly John's attitude toward sacramentalism, continues to be disputed. For a fine recent bibliography on the subject of the sacraments in John, see Paul N. Anderson, *The Christology of the Fourth Gospel: Its Unity and Disunity in the Light of John 6* (Valley Forge, Pa.: Trinity Press International, 1996), 291–93, as well as his brief summary of the current state of the question, 115–19.

[4] J. Louis Martyn, *History and Theology in the Fourth Gospel*, revised and enlarged (Nashville, Tenn.: Abingdon, 1979), 24–62. Contemporary Johannine scholarship is tending to relativize Martyn's thesis at least to the extent of questioning whether there was a particular, historically specifiable event or provision (such as the "Blessing" against the heretics) which sealed the separation of the two communities. But the increasing tension between them and the crisis this precipitated for some members of the Johannine community seems fairly clear.

[5] I am not proposing here to defend the thesis that the Johannine community practiced baptism by water as a specific rite but that the substance of the (perhaps later developed) rite, namely, initiation into the believing community implying identification with Jesus and entailing, at this point, separation from or perhaps shunning by the synagogue, was part of the community's practice.

passion (chaps. 18–19) which have synoptic parallels.[6] However, the differences between the Johannine and the Synoptic accounts are more significant
than the similarities. First, in John alone is the man "blind from birth." In
other words, this is not functional blindness or the possibly reversible result
of accident, injury, or age. The man's own statement that no one has ever
cured congenital blindness (see 9:32) testifies to the importance of this detail.
This blindness is symbolic of the universal congenital incapacity for divine
life that must be overcome through birth anew/from above/by water and the
Spirit (see 3:3, 5). It is not due to sin but provides the arena for God's salvific
work (see 9:3).

Second, the method of healing, that is, sending the man to a distant location to wash in the pool of Siloam, "translated" by the evangelist as *apestal-
menos* [Sent] which is virtually a proper name for Jesus in John, focuses
attention not on Jesus' healing action of putting mud on the man's eyes but
on the man's being "plunged into" Jesus, the Sent One. And as we will see, he
is narratively transformed into an *alter Christus*.

Third, the healing is clearly not a Synoptic-style miracle, a response of
compassion by Jesus to a request by the blind person(s), but an initiative on
Jesus' part so that the works of God might be revealed (9:3). It does not result
in astonishment by the bystanders and publication of Jesus' power. Rather, it
is a Johannine "sign" revealing God's works in Jesus who is the Light of the
World (9:3–5), and it immediately provokes a series of typical Johannine
"crises" or "divisions" in which people of various conditions and status are
confronted by the challenge of believing in the Sent One.

Fourth, the miracle itself is recounted extremely briefly (two verses!) but
the consequences of the healing, which take up the next 33 verses, concern
events that are scarcely plausible within the lifetime of the pre-Easter Jesus,
especially the interrogation/trial of the man's parents and the man himself for
something which is hardly a crime, being healed of blindness. The issue at
stake in the "trials" is not healing, or even healing on the Sabbath for which
the man is not responsible since he did not ask to healed, but profession of
faith in Jesus as the Christ and embarking on the path of discipleship.

In short, although it is highly probable that the evangelist knew of Jesus'
healing ministry and used it[7] as a basis for this narrative, the story of the man

---

[6] There are two independent healing of the blind episodes in the Synoptics: the healing of
Bartimaeus in Mark 10:46–52 with parallels in Matt. 9:27–31, Matt. 20:29–34, and Luke
18:35–43 and one healing involving Jesus' use of saliva: Mark 8:22–26.

[7] A variety of theses about the sources of John's Gospel continue to contend for acceptance
today. But whether or not John had a Synoptic-like source or a "signs source" (a compendium
of miracles) or some actual knowledge of the Synoptic Gospels themselves the evangelist

born blind is an original Johannine literary construction, a theological presentation of a "sign" or symbolic revelation of Jesus which probably does not correspond to any actual identifiable episode in the lifetime of the pre-Easter Jesus.

THE NARRATIVE AS LITERATURE

A. Global Considerations

1. Relation to John 5 and John 11: John 9 is related by the evangelist backward to the story of the healed paralyzed man at the pool of Bethzatha in 5:1–18 and forward to the story of the raising of Lazarus in 11:1–57.[8] Although the contacts and connections are far too numerous to discuss in a brief chapter, certain features provide important hermeneutical material for our purposes.

John 5:1–18, the story of the paralyzed man, is remarkably similar in structure, but strikingly dissimilar in outcome, to the narrative of the man born blind. This is a characteristic Johannine technique in which the contrast between two stories (or characters) presents, in negative and positive light, the point being made.[9] In this case the primary contrast concerns the relationship between election or divine initiative in salvation and freedom or human cooperation which is a theme that is central to my concern with this passage. We will return to this issue in the final section of the chapter. Here I am concerned with the literary technique of contrast itself and how it is used.

Both the blind man and the paralyzed man are "nameless," suggesting that

---

would surely have been aware of Jesus' healing ministry. For a brief summary of the current state of the question see R. Alan Culpepper, *The Gospel and Letters of John,* Interpreting Biblical Texts (Nashville, Tenn.: Abingdon, 1998), 37–41.

[8] I am not disputing the position expounded by Philip L. Tite, "A Community in Conflict: A Literary and Historical Reading of John 9," *Religious Studies and Theology* 15 (2–3, 1996): 77–100, esp. pp. 79–80, that John 9 is tightly connected to chapter 10, which functions as a discursive commentary on the healing and its aftermath for the community. My concern here is with the theological/spiritual rather than ecclesial connections. Both the historical/ecclesial connection of chapter 9 to chapter 10 and the theological/spiritual connection of chapter 9 to chapters 5 and 11 are features of the literary construction of the Gospel.

[9] The technique can be observed, for example, in the contrast between Nicodemus in chapter 3 and the Samaritan woman in chapter 4, between Nathaniel in chapter 1 and Thomas in chapter 20. It is interesting to note that in the early church chapter 5 was often linked to chapter 9 as another type-story of baptism. This reading is suggested by the fact that the man expresses a desire to be plunged into the healing waters of the pool. But, as we will see, the post-healing careers of the two characters present more contrast than similarity.

they are Johannine representative figures.[10] Both characters are *anthrōpos*, theologically "everyperson."[11] (Throughout the story in John 9 Jesus is referred to by his opponents as "this man" suggesting the identity between the man and Jesus.) In both cases Jesus takes the initiative in the healing. But unlike the blind man who cooperates with alacrity in his enlightenment the paralyzed man shows little real desire to be healed, does not trouble to ascertain even the name of his benefactor, and, when challenged by the authorities about carrying his mat on the Sabbath, he not only does not defend Jesus but blames him for the infraction of the Law and eventually turns him in to "the Jews."[12] In both cases the healing is clearly a *sēmeion*, a Johannine "sign" or symbolic action revealing Jesus' identity. Both stories engage the important question of the relation between sin and physical handicap, but offer very different conclusions (to be taken up later), and both highlight the animosity of the Jewish authorities aroused by Jesus' works (although in chap. 5 the animosity is toward Jesus himself, that is, within the historical framework of Jesus' earthly career, and in John 9 toward his followers, suggesting that the hostility is toward the Johannine community).

John 11, the raising of Lazarus, begins like John 9 (and like the ending of the story of the paralyzed man) with a theological reflection on the relation of sin to suffering and death, this time neither affirming a connection (as in the case of the paralysis in chap. 5) nor denying the connection (as in the case of the congenital blindness in chap. 9) but nuancing it by distinguishing between physical and spiritual death. In John 11 Jesus raises Lazarus to life revealing himself as the Resurrection and the Life as he reveals himself in John 5 as Creator (working until now, like the Father [5:17]) and in John 9 as the Light of the World. In both 9 and 11 a whole range of characters is challenged by the sign to believe in Jesus, with some choosing to believe and others deciding to persecute his followers (see 9:22) or even to kill Jesus himself (see 11:53). But the most important contact between the two narratives is supplied by "the Jews" who see Jesus weeping at Lazarus' tomb and ask, "Could not he [Jesus] who opened the eyes of the blind man have kept this man [Lazarus] from dying?" (11:37). In other words, how is it possible that one who has washed in the Sent One, who has been baptized into eternal life, be

[10] This category was suggested by Raymond F. Collins in "The Representative Figures in the Fourth Gospel," *Downside Review* 94 (1976): 26–46, 118–32, and has become a standard feature of Johannine scholarship.

[11] Although the character in this story is clearly male and from both a literary and an historical standpoint could not be otherwise, the generic term "human being" makes the story as applicable for women as for men.

[12] The reference to "the Jews" here is clearly to the Jerusalem authorities, not to the people in general or to Jews as a religious or ethnic group.

subject to death? Light and life are correlative and mutually implicating. The raising of Lazarus completes the theological treatment of Christian initiation begun in chapter 9 by showing that the inevitable implication of baptismal illumination (light) is resurrection (life).

2. *The fusion of horizons:* John 9, more clearly perhaps than any other narrative in the Gospel, fuses the horizons of the pre-Easter Jesus, the post-Easter Johannine community, and the readers of the Gospel. This is especially clear in the conclusion (9:35–41) in which Jesus brings the man to full Johannine faith in himself as Son of Man (horizon of the Johannine community), condemns the "Pharisees" for claiming to see even though they refused to believe (horizon of the earthly Jesus), and identifies himself as the point of decision for all who will come to believe or refuse to believe down through the ages (horizon of the readers). But the fusion is also clear in the successive inquisitions in chapter 9. The man and his questioning neighbors are presented as figures in the purported historical situation. The inquisition of the parents, whom Raymond Brown identifies as "crypto-Christians,"[13] reflects the life of the Johannine community threatened with expulsion from the synagogue for confessing Jesus as one who comes "from God." Interestingly, the "Pharisees," (i.e., the historical opponents of the pre-Easter Jesus) in the first interrogation of the man become, in the interrogation of the parents and the second trial of the man, "the Jews," (i.e., the representative figures in John's Gospel of culpable refusal to believe and violent hostility toward Jesus who are the opponents of the post-Easter Johannine community).[14]

B. Particular Literary Features

A number of well-known Johannine rhetorical and stylistic features calculated to involve the reader in the story are prominent in this narrative. As

---

[13] Raymond E. Brown, *The Community of the Beloved Disciple* (New York: Paulist, 1979), 71–73, discusses this hypothesized group within the Johannine community who seem to appear here in chapter 9 and in 12:42–43. Brown proposes that these characters in the Gospel who know who Jesus is and what he does, or who even actually believe in Jesus, but are afraid to confess him because of fear of the Jewish authorities, are "closet Christians" whom the evangelist is challenging to courageous self-identification.

[14] Tite, in "A Community in Conflict," 83–85, draws a horizontal distinction between "the Pharisees" who represent lay Jews who may not have accepted Jesus but were not necessarily or uniformly hostile to him and "the Jews" who were officials of the synagogue and aggressively hostile to Jesus. I consider this a plausible interpretation not in contradiction to the distinction I am drawing between the opponents of the pre-Easter Jesus and the religious officials who are the persecutors of the Johannine community (and who tend to be called "the Jews" in John). I find the latter distinction more relevant in relation to the subsequent interrogations of the man in chapter 9. See Robert Kysar, *John: The Maverick Gospel* (Atlanta: John Knox, 1976), 67–70, for a brief synthesis on this question.

already mentioned, the *anonymity* of the man born blind, like that of the Samaritan woman (4:1–42), the royal official (4:46–54), the paralyzed man (5:1–18), the Beloved Disciple (e.g., 13:23), and the "other disciple" (e.g., 18:15), is a Johannine literary technique for drawing the reader into the story as a participant in, rather than as an observer of, the action of the text. The nameless characters become "empty sets" into whom the readers insert themselves. In John 9 readers recognize themselves as those "born blind," that is, naturally and inculpably, but also really, incapable of "seeing the reign of God" unless they are born anew, born from above, born of water and the spirit (see 3:3, 5).[15] Like the man, we must be washed in the Sent One to experience the illumination, the opening of our eyes, that enables us to see who Jesus is, know him as the Son of Man who reveals and mediates God to us, and confess and worship him.

Few episodes in John's Gospel are as heavily *ironic* as this one.[16] The two most striking examples of this literary device by which the author "winks" at the readers over the head of the characters, drawing the readers into a community of collusion with the man (and the narrator/implied author) and against the authorities, are 9:24–25 and 27. When the man is called before the authorities the second time he is told to "give glory to God," by denouncing Jesus whom they "know" is a sinner because he does not fit the criteria established by their interpretation of the Law. The man replies by indeed giving glory to God, testifying that he "does not know" whether Jesus is a sinner or not (something only God can finally know about anyone) but that he "does know" that Jesus opened his eyes (something he experienced and will not be intimidated into denying). In John's Gospel it is spiritually dangerous to claim to know, especially things reserved to God (cf. Nicodemus in 3:2); but to testify loyally to what one has seen and heard, that is, to what is within the purview of one's own experience, is both a first step toward salvation and an expression of one's actual experience of revelation. The first is arrogance which estranges one from God by setting oneself up as judge of God's revela-

---

[15] The expression in John 3:3, "No one can *see* the Reign of God without being born *gennēthē*" is strange at first sight. One expects what, in fact, is said in vs. 5, "no one can *enter* the Reign." But if the reference in John 3 is to enlightenment or illumination, that is, if there are baptismal allusions, it makes better sense and throws some light on John 9.

[16] The basic modern study of irony in John is Paul D. Duke, *Irony in the Fourth Gospel* (Atlanta: John Knox, 1985). For a further development see Gail R. O'Day, *Revelation in the Fourth Gospel: Narrative Mode and Theological Claim* (Philadelphia: Fortress, 1986), esp. pp. 11–32 on "The Essence and Function of Irony." For a discussion of contemporary theories on Johannine irony, see R. Alan Culpepper, "Reading Johannine Irony," *Exploring the Gospel of John: In Honor of D. Moody Smith*, edited by R. Alan Culpepper and C. Clifton Black (Louisville, Ky.: Westminster John Knox, 1996), 193–207.

tion; the second is authenticity, fidelity to experience, which opens one to God's action in one's life.

The second piece of delicious irony is the man's reply to the question about his healing, which the authorities have already had adequately answered but which they now repeat with the implied threat that the man had better reconsider his first account and bring it into accord with their judgment. When they again ask, "What did he do to you? How did he open your eyes?" the man replies, "I have told you already. . . . Why do you want to hear it again? Do you also want to become his disciples?" As they have offered the man a temptation to lie, he now, seemingly innocently, offers them an invitation to the truth, posing the question that is central to the entire narrative, namely, of whom are you a disciple? It drives them into a fury in which they blurt out their real motive in trying to intimidate the man, namely, to discredit Jesus because he seems to pose a challenge to Moses and therefore to the religious status quo. Again, they insist "we know" that God spoke to Moses (and thus we have this under control), but we do "not know where this man [Jesus] comes from" (and thus have no control over him). The prospect of self-surrender to the action of God unscripted by their laws and customs is too much for them. And the man, with feigned simplicity dripping with irony, exposes the very essence of their rejection of revelation, namely, that they "do not know" what is plainly revealed in the fact of the healing, that they reject what God is offering them in and through an experience that challenges their construction of reality and especially their own place in that construction.

Paradox is another Johannine literary device directed toward the engagement of the reader in the story. In John 9 sight and blindness, physical and spiritual, are subtly and complexly played off against each other in an overarching paradox. The scene opens with the disciples' question about the nature of the man's blindness: is it divine punishment, and if so, for what? Jesus reduces the blindness to a morally neutral fact of birth that God will use for revelatory purposes. Our being "born blind," that is, having only the life "from below," is indeed a grievous situation, but God intends that the Light coming into the world will enlighten every human being (see 1:9) making us children of God (John 1:12–13) born not of human initiative but of God. Very quickly the reader begins to see that there is blindness and blindness. The blind man inchoately "sees" who Jesus is even before his physical sight is restored or he even knows Jesus' name; the people who witness the healing struggle "to believe their eyes" when the man returns seeing; the Pharisees refuse to see both what is clearly before their physical eyes, that is, that the man has been healed, and what demands spiritual sight to be accepted, that is, that the healing has implications for who Jesus is. To refuse the latter they have to deny the former, thus paradoxically implicating the body in soul-business as the man's soul-business implicates his body.

At the end, Jesus intensifies the paradox in terms of the Johannine "crisis and judgment" theme. He claims that he has come that the blind might see (not just, or even primarily, that the physically blind might be cured as has indeed happened in this case, but that the congenitally spiritually blind might have their eyes opened to divine revelation) and the seeing might become blind (i.e., that those walking in their self-assured knowledge might be progressively engulfed in the darkness of unbelief). When the authorities are caught in the paradox, sensing that they who are so confident in their knowledge of God's will and ways might be the blind Jesus is talking about, Jesus confirms their suspicion: "If you were blind [as are all coming into the world], you would not have sin. But now that you say, 'We see,' your sin remains" (9:41).

The whole Fourth Gospel has been seen as a forensic drama or collection of dramas,[17] and this chapter is a particularly clear example of this *dramatic and forensic* character which engages the reader by drawing her or him into the world of the text.[18] Throughout the narrative the classical dramatic convention of having only two characters on stage at one time prevails: Jesus and his disciples; Jesus and the blind man; the healed man and his neighbors (who function as a single character like a Greek chorus); the man and the Pharisees (again a collective character); "the Jews" and the parents (who speak with one voice); "the Jews" and the man; Jesus and the expelled man; Jesus and the Pharisees.

The cast of characters represents the Johannine community and its religious interlocutors in the period around 90 C.E. but embraces also the readers. The disciples are Christians of any time who agonize over the meaning of life's mysteries, e.g., innocent suffering, and turn to Jesus for enlightenment. The man born blind is "everychristian" in John's community who came into the world incapable of seeing the reign of God but who, by being plunged into the life-giving waters of the Sent One, is enlightened and enlivened by divine Light and Life and is able to respond to questions by friends or challenges by enemies as Jesus, that is, as an *alter Christus, egō eimi* (I am). The Christian, a child of God, is identified with the Son of God, the Sent One. The neighbors are inquirers who, in the face of what seems to speak of God, address their questions to believers. The Pharisees who, later in the text,

---

[17] See Neal Flanagan, "Gospel of John as Drama," *Bible Today* 19 (July 1981): 264–70.

[18] J. Louis Martyn, *History and Theology in the Fourth Gospel*, revised and enlarged (Nashville, Tenn.: Abingdon, 1979), 24–33, explains the narrative as a drama in seven scenes.

become "the Jews" are a group which initially included some who are impressed with the sign and some who do not accept it.[19] Thus, the work of Jesus creates a "division" among the observers. Those who are later characterized as "the Jews" are the community's persecutors who think that by persecuting Jesus' disciples they are giving worship (or glory) to God (cf. 16:2 in relation to 9:24). The parents are the crypto-Christians in the Johannine community who know who Jesus is but are afraid to confess him. And Jesus, of course, is the ever-present, unseen, mysterious figure who mediates the experience of the pre-Easter disciples, the Johannine community, and the readers for he is both Light of the World and source of eternal life for all who believe in him both during and after his earthly career.

The entire scene is a long trial in which different witnesses are called and interrogated. The man is the defendant, but the judgment falls strangely, leaving the reader caught in the toils of personal decision, that is, of spiritual crisis. The man is first questioned by seemingly well-disposed but confused neighbors who, unable to render a judgment, take the man to the religious elite, the Pharisees, who should be able to adjudicate such a situation. The Pharisees interrogate the man but come to no firm judgment about his witness. The man's testimony is a quintessentially Johannine witness to the truth. The first time he recounts the healing (which is narrated in two brief verses) to the neighbors the account takes one verse (9:11). The second time, to the Pharisees, it takes only half a verse (9:15b). And the third time (in a later scene), to "the Jews," he refuses to recount it at all (9:27) because it is clear that his questioners are not interested in the truth.

The man, in his first interrogation by the Pharisees, does not elaborate, exaggerate, or make himself the center of attention. He makes no claim to have had anything to do with his healing. It was a pure, unsolicited gift of God. It is revelation in Johannine terms, the manifestation of Jesus' identity in his works as invitation to salvation. The man's task is simply to bear witness to the truth, regardless of the consequences. The man is already conducting himself as Jesus will later at his own trial when he claims to have come into the world to bear witness to the truth (cf. John 18:37) but even-

---

[19] Recent scholarship on the Pharisees of Jesus' time and during the period in which the church developed has modified the virtually totally negative evaluation of the Pharisees that has characterized New Testament scholarship for generations. It is difficult, given the fragmentary and often polemical nature of the evidence, to arrive at an accurate picture of this group. However, in the Gospel of John the Pharisees are usually, though not always, portrayed as suspicious of or hostile to Jesus. For a good treatment of current research on the subject including a select bibliography, see Anthony J. Saldarini, "Pharisees," *The Anchor Bible Dictionary*, 5:289–303.

tually falls silent before Pilate whose concern for his own political position makes him impervious to the claims of the truth (cf. 19:9). The first interrogation sets the stage by supplying all the facts of the case and making clear what is in contention: the official authority of those whose allegiance is to the Law vs. the revelation of Jesus struggling for the allegiance of the man. No judgment is yet rendered.

The interrogation of the parents has no parallel in the other Gospels. This is the kind of story we might expect to read in the Acts of the Apostles, and it clues the readers in to the real setting of the story which is less that of the lifetime of the historical Jesus than that of the post-Easter Johannine community.[20] The central position of the episode in the concentric or chiastic structure of the seven scenes further emphasizes the significance of the scene for the Johannine community.[21] The crisis is set forth in bold colors: to identify with Jesus is to be rejected by the Jewish authorities; to reject Jesus is to be approved of and accepted by the authorities.[22]

The parents are ostensibly being asked to verify the facts of the case. The first question is straightforward: "Is this your son?" Then comes the veiled accusation: was he, "as you say" really born blind? The implication is that they are colluding in a hoax which the man is perpetrating. But the nefarious intent of the questioners becomes crystal clear in the third question—about which the parents could hardly have had first-hand knowledge—which is not at all in the same category as the first two questions: "How then does he now see?" The parents are really not being examined as innocent material witnesses. They are being trapped and surreptitiously put on trial themselves, not for having a son born blind, but for sharing in his confession that Jesus healed him with its implications for Jesus' messianic identity. They do not take the bait but execute a pre-emptive strike. Before they can be asked about

---

[20] This is substantially the position taken by Martyn in *History and Theology*, 27–30. Martyn says that the transposition of an account of a healing into a theological drama is the vehicle for fusing the horizons of the post-resurrection Johannine community experience with the *einmalig* healing episode in the life of the pre-Easter Jesus..

[21] Most commentators, for example, Martyn, *History and Theology*, 30–36, divide the drama into seven scenes, with the interrogation of the parents in the center. Recently, Gilberto Marconi, "La vista del cieco: Struttura di Gv 9,1–41," *Gregoriana* 79 (1998): 625–43, proposes that there are eight scenes. Although I tend to agree with the concentric structuration which places the interrogation of the parents at the center of the narrative I also see the plausibility of Marconi's segmentation and the logic of his structuration to make the point, with which I also agree, that the narrative presents a dialectic between knowledge based on religious conviction (the religious authorities) and that based on experience (the man born blind). The two analyses, in my view, are more complementary than contradictory.

[22] See Tite, "A Community in Conflict," 78–79.

Jesus they assert that they do not know either *how* the healing took place or *who* brought it about, thus saving themselves from the threatened excommunication. But the evangelist implies that the price they paid is much too high. Their fear makes them untrue to Jesus whom they know is the source of their son's (and as members of the Johannine community their own) enlightenment. The judgment has fallen not on the judges (the Pharisees) or the defendant (the man) but on the witnesses (the parents).

The second interrogation of the man is openly hostile. "The Jews" covertly threaten him, try to intimidate him by a sinister repetition and reformulation of their questions implying that his previous testimony was defective. They are trying to bring him to choose Moses over Jesus, the security of the Law over the freedom conferred by the Truth, their authority over his revelatory experience. But the form of the intimidation is the pressure on the man to deny his own experience. The man, like Jesus throughout the Gospel, refuses to testify to anything except what he has seen and heard (e.g., 1:18; 3:32; 8:26–28). He will not change his testimony. And he will not interpret it perversely. The man is being tempted to commit what Mark calls "the sin against the Holy Spirit" (Mark 3:29), the unforgivable sin of spiritual perversity, calling good evil and evil good. He resists the seduction. Instead, he calls his judges on their plot, declaring in mock amazement, "Here is an astonishing thing! You do not know where he comes from, and yet he opened my eyes. We know that God does not listen to sinners, but he does listen to one who worships him and obeys his will" (9:30–31).

The man is no longer on the defensive; he has become the judge and the authorities are condemned out of their own mouths and according to their own Law in a way parallel to the reversal of roles between Pilate and Jesus in the passion. "The Jews" respond violently by an attack *ad hominem*, "You were born entirely in sins." They abandon all pretense of exercising legitimate authority or dispassionate judgment and revert to raw power: "they cast him out." The evangelist makes sure the reader knows what is really at issue. Their final furious charge against the man is that of any corrupt authority defeated by the truth coming from an inferior, the withering demand, "Are *you* trying to teach *us*?" (emphasis added) [NRSV] or as another translation puts it, "How dare you lecture us!" [NIV] Truth is irrelevant; position and power is all.

Finally, the innocent man is condemned and punished, as Jesus will be. And the untruthful judges have been judged by the Truth as Pilate will be. It remains only for Jesus to bring the trial to its final conclusion. He finds the man and invites him to the fullness of Christian faith, to believe in the Son of Man. And the man replies in perfect continuity with his already demonstrated integrity, "Who is he, Sir, . . . that I may believe?" Jesus offers an equivalent of the great "I am," and the man responds, "Lord, I believe" and worships him.

The Pharisees, standing nearby, are still proclaiming their innocence and by implication invoking their authority. But Jesus unmasks their self-serving delusions, declaring that if they were really blind they would have nothing to worry about. As the prologue proclaimed, God has sent Jesus into the world to enlighten everyone and has given Jesus the authority to make children of God of all who believe in him. But since they claim to see, "your sin remains."

The shift from the pre-Easter story to the Johannine community's life to the situation of the reader is so subtle and pervasive, and the drama so powerful, that the reader is virtually forced to take a position. The reader is, of course, supposed to identify with the man born blind. But do we, perhaps, recognize something of ourselves in the parents who confess Jesus in private but become sophisticated evaders when that confession has consequences for our reputation or job or safety? Even worse, are we religious authority figures whose first allegiance is to the institution and who are willing to suppress the prophets among us when their testimony to their experience calls that institution or our position within it into question?[23]

THEOLOGY AND SPIRITUALITY OF DISCIPLESHIP

A. Original Sin

The question of "location" and "origins" pervades John's Gospel. The word "where" is a *leitmotif*. The first question addressed to Jesus in the Gospel is that of his first two disciples, "Where do you dwell?" (John 1:38) and the final question is that of Mary Magdalene to the risen Lord whom she does not recognize, "Where have you laid him [Jesus' body]" (John 20:15). Throughout the Gospel people are distinguished by whether they know where Jesus comes from, where he is, and where he is going, namely, from, in, and to God, or whether they do not know either his origin or their own. Jesus is the one who knows his origin and his disciples are those who come to

---

[23] Anne Thurston, "In a New Age, Whose Story Can We Trust?" *Doctrine and Life* 48 (10, 1998): 603, warns against too quickly identifying ourselves with the man born blind. The problem for the authorities is that the man's experience does not fit within their institutional system and so, to be read by them, "calls for self-questioning, calls for conversion." We also can be locked in an "old story," an institutional construction of reality which discounts experience that does not fit, no matter how obvious its truth or relevance.

this knowledge (see John 8:14). To know where Jesus comes from is to know *who* he is. To know where he dwells is to be *with* him. To know where he is going is to *follow* him.

The most important collection of "where" texts concerns origins. The difference between Jesus and everyone else is that he is by nature "from above," from God. The difference between Jesus' disciples and his opponents is that the former are, like Jesus, "from above," not by nature but by the new birth of water and Spirit which makes them children of God, and the latter are "from below" [i.e., of this world, unenlightened by the Sent One] or even more ominously "from your father, the devil" (John 8:44) [a text which must be handled very carefully because of its anti-Jewish potential].[24]

This issue of origins is focused sharply at the beginning of John 9 when the disciples ask Jesus if the man's blindness is due to his own or his parents' sin. This is a very interesting question in view of later developments in the church's theology around the question of "original sin" and its connection with baptism. The notion that all are implicated in the sin of the first parents and that baptism is a remedy for this congenital condition is, of course, Pauline in origin. Paul, in order to establish the universal need of salvation, posits that all are sinners, not necessarily through personal sin but as inheritors of the original sin which came into the world by "one man," Adam (see Rom 5:12–21). John's position seems to be quite different. We are not congenitally sinful but rather congenitally blind, unable to "see the reign of God," incapable of believing, that is, of sharing in the Light which is Life. Furthermore, this blindness is not due to sin, our own or that of our ancestors. Rather, our helpless situation is the "place" where God can reach us, the occasion for God's saving action in our lives: "Neither this man nor his parents sinned: he was born blind so that God's works might be revealed in him" (9:3). As the early church held, baptism is "illumination" and "rebirth." Our eyes are opened to the realities of faith, the reign of God; we become children of God, born from above.[25] In the Johannine perspective we are washing "in the Sent One" rather than being washed clean of sin. It is the Jewish author-

---

[24] This text, because in it Jesus is presented as speaking to "the Jews," has dangerous anti-Semitic potential. It is crucial to note and to teach that Jesus' opponents are not from the devil because they are Jews but because they are not open to the truth. In the same passage (8:39–47) Jesus contrasts Jews who are true children of Abraham with those who do not do what Abraham did, namely, believe. Hence the contrast is not between Jews (ethnic or religious) and non-Jews but between those (of whatever ethnic or religious background) who are open to the truth and those who are not.

[25] Early Christian baptismal catechesis and ritual texts conflate notions of baptism as washing from sin and as illumination in faith. However, this does not seem to be how John 9 presents the situation. Sin and blindness are explicitly disjoined.

ities who charge the man with "original" sin: "You were born entirely in sins" (9:34).

By contrast with the man born blind, the paralyzed man in chapter 5 is not congenitally paralyzed. He has been ill for thirty-eight years, a "long time" (5:5) but apparently not from birth. And Jesus warns him at the end to "not sin any more, so that nothing worse happens to you" (John 5:14), seeming to imply that his own sin was the cause of his paralysis. Just as the post-healing integrity and loyalty of the blind man in chapter 9 makes evident his openness to Jesus' revelation and his courageous assumption of responsibility for the gift he has been given, the post-healing vacillation and disloyalty of the paralyzed man makes the reader aware of his moral and spiritual paralysis, which seems to be reflected in his physical condition. When Jesus asks if he wants to be healed he demurs, making a feeble excuse about not being able to get into the pool (which is irrelevant since Jesus is offering help), and the reader gets the distinct impression that he does not really desire freedom. Had he wanted to be healed, surely in thirty-eight years he could have figured out how to get into the pool! But his lack of interest in who healed him (he does not even ascertain Jesus' name), his unprotesting taking up of his mat when ordered to do so by Jesus (even though he surely knew it was the Sabbath), which is swiftly followed by his disowning responsibility for the act as soon as it is questioned by the religious authorities, and his final act of turning Jesus in to the authorities give us the picture of a man morally and spiritually paralyzed. He is unable to take responsibility for himself, his actions, or his relationships. He apparently prefers to sit and beg, to feel sorry for himself, and imply that no one takes pity on him or helps him. But he does not readily accept help when it is offered.

Our own sins (not those of our parents) can indeed bind us, and even Jesus cannot really liberate the person who does not want to be healed. The difference between the blindness of the man in chapter 9 and the paralysis of the man in chapter 5 is striking. In one case the blindness is congenital and not due to or reflective of sin; in the other the paralysis is of long standing and apparently the result of personal sin. In the former case, Jesus heals and the man responds freely and responsibly, integrating his new-found vision into his spiritual identity. In the latter case, Jesus virtually imposes healing, which the man receives without enthusiasm and fails to integrate into his identity and actions. It seems that in John there is no such thing as original sin, only personal sin. Congenital incapacity for divine life is remedied by immersion in Christ and consequent believing, but moral and spiritual paralysis can only be finally healed by conversion.

It is interesting that when the man born blind returned seeing from the pool of Siloam and his neighbors disputed over his identity he "kept saying, 'I am'" (9:9). At the narrative level, of course, the expression means simply, "I am the one," that is, the same man who was blind. But in the context of John's Gospel, where "I am" is used by Jesus as a self-identification with God, it has overtones of divinization. The man, washed in the Sent One, is (as all Christians are) the presence of Jesus in the world. And throughout the rest of the story Jesus is invisible; the man plays the role of Jesus on trial, Jesus bearing witness, Jesus condemned and rejected. Coming to believe is not so much purification from sin as identification with the Lord.

B. The Identity of Jesus

Like the Samaritan woman in chapter 4 and unlike the paralyzed man in chapter 5, the man born blind makes steady progress in his knowledge of the identity of Jesus even as his persecutors entrench themselves progressively in their blindness. The man, in response to his neighbors, identifies the one who healed him as "the *man* called Jesus" (9:11). When he is first brought before the Pharisees, some of whom claim that Jesus is "not from God" because he does not keep the Sabbath, the man counters with "He is a *prophet*" (9:17). In the second interrogation "the Jews" claim outright that "this man [Jesus] is a sinner," and the man replies, "If this man were not *from God*, he could do nothing" (9:33). Finally, when Jesus finds him after his expulsion, he asks the man if he believes in the *Son of Man*, the one speaking to him, and the man replies, "*Lord*, I believe" (9:38).[26] The Pharisees lurking nearby protest that they, surely, are not blind, and Jesus assures them that they are indeed blind and will remain so. In contrast to the man's deepening faith, his progressive spiritual insight into the identity of his healer (from Jesus, to prophet, to One from God, to Son of Man, to Lord) the paralyzed man first does not know who cured him and gets no further than learning Jesus' name. He is as spiritually paralyzed at the end as he was physically in the beginning.

C. Crisis and Judgment

In John's Gospel Jesus' coming into the world instigates a great trial (*krima*), which is verified in the life of individuals as "crisis" or "judgment" (*krisis*). People faced with the revelation of God in Jesus must choose, like the Hebrews in the desert, between life and death. The poles of the crisis are var-

---

[26] In John being "from God" and being "Son of Man" are functionally equivalent, designating Jesus as the revealer sent by God. But narratively the man's final confession thematizes his faith at a higher level than his claim that Jesus is from God on the basis of the evident fact that God, who does not listen to sinners, "listens" to Jesus.

iously named: life vs. death, doing/abiding in the truth vs. remaining in sin, truth vs. lie, light vs.darkness, freedom vs. slavery, being from above vs. being from below, spirit vs. flesh, being children of God/Abraham vs. being children of the devil. In this episode the crisis is faced by each of the characters: the man who chooses light with unwavering integrity and courage; the neighbors who vacillate; the parents who try to have it both ways; "the Jews" who choose blindness and are lost in sin and darkness. The trial which Jesus underwent in his historical life is now being lived by the Johannine community in the person of the healed man and, Jesus promises, will be undergone by all his disciples throughout history (see 16:1–4). It is a trial in which the innocent are inevitably condemned but are finally victorious and in which the judges become the judged and are finally vanquished. It is a trial in which some will always try to slip out unnoticed, to equivocate enough to save their skin without becoming terminally guilty. But in the end, like Pilate, those who attempt to avoid the crisis will be consumed by it.[27]

ELECTION AND FREEDOM
IN A JOHANNINE PERSPECTIVE

A final dimension of the theology and spirituality of John which emerges from this pericope is a unique and enlightening position on one of the conundrums of the early church, and surely of John's community as signaled in the prologue itself (see 1:10, 17), namely, the nonacceptance of Jesus by some of "his own," people who had a long and intimate experience of God's saving work in their own history and who had been instructed by the Law and the Prophets. How, given this centuries-long preparation, could they have failed to recognize the one sent by God who now stands in their midst as one they do not know (see John 1:26)? This historical quandary has continued in the history of theology and spirituality as the issue of grace and free will or of election/predestination and freedom.

The traditional answer in the early Christian communities, as suggested by the formulaic use of the Isaian passage, is the one repeated by John at the end of the book of signs:

---

[27] See Raymond Brown's powerful reflection on Pilate's attempt to avoid making a decision. "Pilate is typical . . . of the many honest, well-disposed men [sic] who would try to adopt a middle position in a struggle that is total. . . . [i]t illustrates how a person who refuses decisions is led to tragedy." *The Gospel According to John (xiii–xxi)*, Anchor Bible 29a (Garden City, N.Y.: Doubleday, 1970), 864.

> Although he [Jesus] had performed so many signs in their presence, they did
> not believe in him. This was to fulfill the word spoken by the Prophet Isaiah:
> "Lord, who has believed our message, and to whom has the arm of the Lord
> been revealed?" And so they could not believe, because Isaiah also said, "He has
> blinded their eyes and hardened their heart, so that they might not look with
> their eyes, and understand with their heart and turn—and I would heal them."
> (12:36b–40)

In other words, the unbelief of some of Jesus' own people is a mystery of
divine election. For some reason God made some of the chosen people incapable of responding to the revelation present in Jesus. In the terminology of
some later theologies, they simply did not receive the gift of faith; they were
not predestined for salvation.

But, like many people down through the ages and perhaps especially
today, the Fourth Evangelist, who places such emphasis on the freedom of
people to respond to the light and their personal responsibility for the
response they make, seems to have been unsatisfied with this Job-like con-
signment of the problem to the depths of divine inscrutability. Several times
John returns to the question of why some people come to believe and others
do not. One answer is proposed in the context of the "hard saying" about the
bread of life in chapter 6. Jesus says to those who murmur at his claim to be
the bread come down from heaven,

> No one can come to me unless drawn by the Father who sent me. . . . It is writ-
> ten in the prophets, "And they shall all be taught by God." Everyone who has
> heard and learned from the Father comes to me. (6:44–45)

But, in a sense, this only pushes the conundrum back a pace. Why are some
taught by God and thus enabled to come to Jesus and others not?

John's original contribution to Christian reflection on this problem is dis-
persed throughout the Gospel but concentrated in the controversy chapters
5 to 8, and it comes to a head in chapter 9. Jesus repeatedly accuses his opponents—those who cannot accept his word (see 5:47; 8:43), those who do not
respond to the truth (see 14:24), those who seek to kill him (see 7:19; 8:37),
those who do not judge justly but according to appearances (see 7:24;
8:15)—of "seeking their own glory" (see 5:44; 12:43) in contrast to himself,
who "seeks only the glory of the one who sent him" (see 7:18; 8:50, 54) and
those who are of the truth who "seek the glory of God." Seeking one's own
glory seems to be the root of the incapacity of some people to believe. It bears
examination, especially because it is the turning point in the trial of the man
in chapter 9. The authorities command him to "give glory to God" by
denouncing Jesus as a sinner. The man gives glory to God precisely by con-

fessing that Jesus is "from God." There could hardly be a clearer Johannine formulation of the problematic.

Glory (*doxa*) is not merely a matter of splendor or dignity nor the honor accorded such dignity. Glory is God's very selfhood visibly manifest to humans (see Num 16:19, 42; Ps 102:16; Ezek 10:14).[28] The glory of God covered Sinai at the giving of the Law, hovered over the tabernacle, filled the Temple, and was revealed to the prophets. The response of humans to God's manifestation is to "ascribe glory and honor" to God (e.g., Pss 22:23; 29:2; 86:9; Isa 66:5), that is, to recognize God's presence, power, and works and correspondingly to acknowledge with praise that God alone is the source and the norm of all reality.

Conversely, to "seek one's own glory" is to ascribe to oneself what belongs to God, to make oneself the center of one's religious universe, the measure of what God can do in the world and in one's own life. It is to presume to set standards for God's work, criteria of approval for divine action. It is, by definition, to be impervious to revelation, which is precisely the inbreaking of what is truly new, beyond human power or even imagination. God doing a genuinely "new thing," something that has "never since the world began" been heard of such as opening the eyes of the congenitally blind, is what revelation means (see 9:32). The Hebrews' building a golden calf, something they could control, rather than surrendering themselves to the mystery being revealed on Mt. Sinai in the cloud and beyond their ken (Exod 32:1–6), the scribes in the Synoptic Gospels making void the law of God for the sake of their traditions (see Mark 7:8; Matt 15:3), the Pharisee in the temple telling God why God should be pleased with him, why—despite his smooth words of praise—God should glorify him rather than he glorifying God (Luke 18:11–12), and the crowd in John 6 murmuring that someone whose apparently ordinary father and mother they knew could not be the bread from heaven or give his flesh for the life of the world (see 6:42) are all seeking their own glory rather than the glory of God.

In John 9 Jesus manifests the glory of God in healing the man born blind. And the man responds appropriately, truly gives glory to God in Jesus, by testifying truthfully to what he has experienced, acknowledging that Jesus and not he is the source of the healing, and refusing to falsify his testimony under

---

[28] See the excellent article by Carey C. Newman, "Resurrection as Glory: Divine Presence and Christian Origins," in *The Resurrection: An Interdisciplinary Symposium on the Resurrection of Jesus,"* edited by Stephen T. Davis, Daniel Kendall, Gerald O'Collins (Oxford: Oxford University Press, 1997), 59–89, in which he argues that the real source of the eventual separation of the Jewish and Christian communities was the Christians' recognition of the glory of Jesus which was equivalent to recognizing his divinity.

threat. He "glorifies God" revealed in Jesus even as he refuses to seek his own glory, that is, to save himself at the expense of the truth. Thus, he is "taught by God" and grows ever more lucid in his knowledge of Jesus' identity and God's ways. He discovers that he knows not only much more than he thought he did but, indeed, more than his learned judges. When the man expresses frank amazement at their religious ignorance and spiritual hardness of heart they become blindly furious at his clarity.

What, we are led to ask, in the man's comportment supplies a clue to his capacity to be taught by God and thus drawn by God to Jesus? The answer is so obvious we can easily miss it. The man is not a religious professional. In fact, when Jesus approaches him to anoint his eyes with mud he does not even know who Jesus is. Prior to the healing he certainly does not have any kind of thematized or even inchoate faith in Jesus or his power to heal since he does not ask to be healed. The man's capacity for salvation seems to lie in his openness and utter fidelity to reality and to his own experience of it, a fidelity that perhaps reflects a lifelong practice of Torah, which forbids the bearing of false witness.[29] He does without hesitation what Jesus commands, and he recounts exactly what Jesus did to him and what resulted. He refuses to change, embellish, profit from, or deny that experience. He recognizes that God is at work in his life, however unaccountable and overwhelming that might be, and, come what may, responds to it with integrity. This is precisely what John seems to mean by "giving glory to God," making God rather than ourselves the center of our religious universe, God rather than our own or other peoples' expectations the measure of possibility and the norm of reality.

Throughout the Gospel Jesus commends those who, like Nathanael and the Samaritan woman, respond to him without guile even though they are resisting and questioning him. But he challenges those, like Nicodemus and the crowd seeking him after the sign of the bread, who, even though they are saying the right things, deviously seek their own advantage. Nicodemus is trying to make Jesus fit into the Mosaic scheme of things. The crowd is trying to gain some control over Jesus and some access to his power by making him fit into the religious categories with which they are familiar.

Coming to knowledge of God and the ability to recognize God at work in Jesus is not something of which human beings, prior to the new birth from above, are capable. Illumination in faith and the resulting knowledge of God

---

[29] My thanks to my colleagues at the Jesuit School, and visiting scholar Thomas Hughson, who discussed this paper with me at a faculty colloquium, for pointing out that the man was the product of a Jewish home and thus, most probably, schooled in the practice of the Law even if he was not what we would call "theologically educated" as were his accusers.

is a free gift of God. But it is not something God arbitrarily withholds from some people. God's intention, says John, is "to enlighten every human being" (1:9). "God so loved the world that he gave his only Son. . . . Indeed, God did not send the Son into the world to condemn the world, but in order that the world might be saved through him" (3:16–17). As Jesus tells the crowd in chapter 6: "This is indeed the will of my Father, that all who see the Son and believe in him may have eternal life" (6:39). In other words, divine election is synonymous with the universal salvific will of God. The impediment to salvation lies in the human heart, not in an inscrutable divine discrimination. It is not God who predestines some for faith and eternal life and others for hardness of heart and remaining in sin.

The Fourth Gospel seems to say that the impediment of the heart which renders some people incapable of entering into the relationship with God which is divine revelation is something for which humans are finally responsible. And it is something that has nothing to do with theologically thematized faith, professional religious knowledge, or institutional approbation. It is, in Synoptic language, the sin against the Holy Spirit, which is expressed in the perverse refusal to acknowledge the good, in the attempt to call good evil and evil good for one's own advantage. In Johannine language, it is seeking one's own glory rather than the glory of God, which manifests itself in willful infidelity to one's own experience, in bearing false witness in the face of the truth. It is the refusal to see what is life-giving as true and good because it threatens the religious or political status quo or calls into question the reality construction with which we are familiar or comfortable.

CONCLUSION

This chapter has been an attempt to apply to John 9 a hermeneutics of discipleship, beginning with baptism and culminating in full Christian confession of Jesus as Son of Man, that is, as the one sent by God for the salvation of the world. I have hypothesized that the *Sitz-im-Leben* of the story, although narratively the lifetime of the pre-Easter Jesus, is really the post-resurrection Johannine community struggling with the synagogue over the messianic identity of Jesus. But that socio-religious (and covertly political) struggle is the external manifestation of the underlying spiritual/theological struggle over the meaning of discipleship: what disposes one to be taught of God and come to Jesus, the identification with Jesus that baptism effects, the crisis evoked by the costly invitation to participation in the paschal mystery that such identification implies, the various responses people give to that invitation, and the decisive result of those choices in the opening of the eyes of the blind and the blinding of those who claim to see. The story of the man born blind is, in short, a synopsis of the theology and spirituality of the Fourth Gospel addressed to all, down through the centuries, who will be invited by this text to believe that Jesus is the Christ, the Son of God, so that by believing they might have life in his name (see John 20:31).

The Community of Eternal
Life (John 11:1-53)

INTRODUCTION
AND BACKGROUND ASSUMPTIONS

The narrative of the raising of Lazarus (John 11:1–54) has been recognized by commentators as the compositional zenith of the Fourth Gospel. In chapter 11 narrative and discourse are so intricately interwoven that they cannot be separated.[1] Although levels of composition can be detected,[2] and there is rough consensus among scholars in identifying a basic traditional oral or written narrative source underlying the evangelist's composition,[3] virtually every verse of the Lazarus story is so marked by Johannine style characteristics and theological concerns that, as Brian Henneberry con-

---

[1] R. Alan Culpepper, *Anatomy of the Fourth Gospel: A Study in Literary Design* (Philadelphia: Fortress, 1983), 73.

[2] Gérard Rochais, *Les récits de résurrection des morts dans le Nouveau Testament*, SNTSMS (Cambridge: Cambridge University Press, 1981), 133. Rochais, who has done the most painstaking recent historical-critical analysis of the narrative, concludes that there are three levels of composition: a simple catechetical resuscitation story much like that of 1 Kings 17 and 2 Kings 4, the point of which was Jesus' messianic identity and the general resurrection; the signs source redaction, which, by adding the delay of two days and the dialogue with the disciples, carried forward the Christian teaching on the fate of the deceased before the parousia; the evangelist's redaction, which introduced Martha and the Jews as carriers of the evangelist's own theology and tied the narrative into the chapters that precede and follow. E. D. Stockton isolates two strands, a "Martha Strand" and a "Mary Strand," originally separate stories that were conflated by the evangelist. The Mary story was originally in the Gospel, and the evangelist added the Martha story. See Stockton, "The Fourth Gospel and the Woman," *Essays in Faith and Culture* 3 (1979): 137–40.

[3] Brian H. Henneberry gives a consensus reconstruction of the source (*The Raising of Lazarus [John 11:1–44]: An Evaluation of the Hypothesis That a Written Tradition Lies Behind the Narrative* [Ann Arbor: University Microfilms, 1984], 64). Rochais proposes a reconstruction of the evangelist's redaction (*Les récits*, 137).

cludes in his 1983 Louvain dissertation, "The story can be seen as johannine throughout. Any attempts to separate a written tradition that was redacted by the Evangelist seems doomed to end in failure."[4]

The Lazarus narrative, remarkably unified within itself, is integrated into the Gospel in an intricate fashion. The raising of Lazarus, which is the culmination of the book of signs, is identified by the evangelist as the proximate cause of Jesus' arrest (see 11:47–50), the turning point that precipitates the Hour of Glory, whose arrival structures the Gospel as a whole.[5] The evangelist has introduced into the Lazarus narrative "the Jews," who play no essential role in the raising story itself but serve to lace the story tightly into its Gospel context. It is the Jews who relate the death of Lazarus to the healing of the man born blind in chapter 9 (11:37) and thus, by implication, to the dispute with the Jerusalem Jews in chapter 10. Likewise, some of the Jewish witnesses to the raising of Lazarus report Jesus to the authorities (11:46), who then not only plot to kill Jesus (11:50) but also to put Lazarus to death (12:10–11).[6] The strange proleptic "recall" in 11:2 that Mary was the same person who (in a story in chap. 12 that has not yet been recounted) anointed the Lord with ointment alerts the reader to the prolepsis of the paschal mystery constituted by chapters 11 and 12. In these two hinge chapters Jesus is symbolically executed by the decision of the authorities (11:47–53), symbolically buried in the anointing scene (12:1–8), and symbolically glorified by the triumphal entry into Jerusalem, which is explicitly attributed to his victory over death in the raising of Lazarus (12:17–18).[7]

My thesis in what follows is that John 11 is the high point of integration not only of style, composition, and narrative in the Fourth Gospel but also of history, theology, and spirituality. Spirituality is the ultimate concern into which history and theology are subsumed. I am using the term "history" to refer to the recounted events of the life of Jesus as well as those of the Johannine community, upon both of which the Gospel is a kind of textual window. By the term "theology" is meant the reciprocal reflection on Christian faith in the light of experience and on experience in the light of Christian faith. By "spirituality" is meant the personal appropriation of faith as the horizon for

---

[4] Henneberry, *Raising of Lazarus,* 203.

[5] John R. Jones, *Narrative Structures and Meaning in John 11:1–54* (Ann Arbor: University Microfilms, 1982), 11.

[6] See Rochais, *Les récits,* 115–17.

[7] C. H. Dodd, "The Prophecy of Caiaphas: John XI 47–53," in *Neotestamentica et Patristica: Eine Freundesgabe, Herrn Professor Dr. Oscar Cullmann zu Seinem 60. Geburtstag,* NovT-Sup (Leiden: E. J. Brill, 1962), 134. See also Herold Weiss, "Foot Washing in the Johannine Community," *NovT* 21 (1979): 298–325.

self-transcending Christian integration. Spirituality is lived participation in the paschal mystery of Christ. While history lies *behind* the text and theology is expressed *in* the text, spirituality is *called forth by* the text as it engages the reader.

In chapter 11 the story of Jesus and that of the Johannine community are completely fused in a touchingly human narrative that opens onto the experience of any believing Christian who has ever lived through the death of a loved one. The experience of the characters in the narrative is a vehicle for the exposition of the Fourth Gospel's sublime theology of eternal life. But the narrative so maintains the tension between the clarity of theology and the ambiguity of the human experience of death that it creates a horizon within which the reader of any time or place can integrate the human experience of death into his or her faith in Jesus as resurrection and life.

HISTORY

The first historical question is whether Jesus actually raised Lazarus from the dead. It is perhaps instructive that the endless efforts of exegetes have been unable to achieve consensus even on the historicity of Lazarus, much less of his resuscitation. Henneberry summarizes scholarly opinion under three headings:[8] (1) that the raising of Lazarus was a historical event; (2) that the story is a conflation of the Lazarus story in Luke 16:19–31 with the Martha and Mary material in Luke 10:38–42, the Synoptic story of the raising of the daughter of Jairus (Mark 5:21–43; Luke 8:40–56; par. Matt. 9:18–25), and the Lukan story of the raising of the son of the widow of Nain (7:11–17);[9] (3) that there is a common story behind the Lazarus narrative and the other New Testament stories of raisings from the dead.[10] Rochais, after investigating in minute detail all of the raising-of-the-dead stories in the New Testament against the background of the Old Testament stories in 1 and 2 Kings (1 Kgs. 17:17–24 and 2 Kgs. 4:18–37; 13:21), concludes that the historical Jesus probably did not raise anyone from the dead during his lifetime. The

---

[8] R. Dunkerley, "Lazarus," *NTS* 5 (1958–59): 321–27.

[9] Both the influence of Luke on John and the reverse have been proposed. Dunkerley maintains that the stunning miracle recounted in John gave rise to the Lukan parable about refusal to believe one who has returned from the dead ("Lazarus," 323). J. N. Sanders takes essentially the same position ("Lazarus of Bethany," *IDB*, 3:103). Most commentators who pursue this argument see the influence going the other way, that is, the parable about Lazarus in Luke having supplied the character for the Johannine account.

[10] Henneberry, *Raising of Lazarus,* xi–xxiv.

stories arose in the early Christian communities as a way of teaching that Jesus not only preached the coming reign of God but in his own person, through his resurrection from the dead, inaugurated that reign.[11]

In my opinion, the argument over historicity is completely misconceived. Brian McNeil was quite correct in stating that the meaning of the story is "affected in no way by the question of whether the matters [and I would add, the persons] it relates are 'historical'" or not.[12] The story is the evangelist's way of dealing with the question confronting the Johannine community: How is the death of believers to be understood and faced? The answer to that question is derived from Jesus' own resurrection and its efficacy in the experience of believers. The story of the raising of Lazarus is a powerful vehicle for presenting this theology.[13] In other words, the fusion of the history of the earthly Jesus with the history of the Johannine community is so complete that it is virtually impossible to distinguish, much less separate, them.

THEOLOGY

It has been suggested that the problem faced by the Johannine community in the Lazarus narrative is the same as that in other New Testament writings, namely, the delay of the parousia and the fate of Christians who die before the second coming of Christ (e.g., 1 Thess. 4:13–17; Rev. 6:10; 14:13).[14] While Jesus' delay in coming to Lazarus might suggest this, and while it is therefore perhaps a subordinate theme, I would suggest that this is a misfocusing of the Johannine perspective. Jesus' delay in chapter 11 follows the pattern that can be observed in his response to his mother in chapter 2, to the royal official in chapter 4, and to his brothers in chapter 7. The purpose of these refusals and/or delays in Jesus' response is to emphasize the sovereign independence of Jesus' action in relation to human initiative.[15] This is especially important in the raising of Lazarus, which is to be understood primarily not as a private favor conferred on the distraught sisters but as Jesus' culminating self-revelation on the eve of the passion.

Furthermore, the theology of the Johannine community would also sug-

---

[11] Rochais, *Les récits,* especially 2, 10, 190–91.

[12] Brian McNeil, "The Raising of Lazarus," *DRev* 92 (1974): 274.

[13] J. P. Martin, "History and Eschatology in the Lazarus Narrative: John 11, 1–44," *SJT* 17 (1964): 332–43.

[14] See ibid., 334.

[15] Charles H. Giblin, "Suggestion, Negative Response, and Positive Action in St. John's Portrayal of Jesus (John 2.1–11; 4.46–54; 7.12–14; 11.1–44)," *NTS* 26 (1980): 197–211.

gest that the primary issue is not the delay of the parousia. The whole message of the Fourth Gospel is that Jesus came to give divine life in all its fullness to those who believe in him (cf. 1:12; 3:16; 5:24; 6:50, 51; 10:10, etc.). Future eschatology plays a very minor role in this Gospel. The problem is not that Christians die too soon (i.e., before the last day) but that they die at all. How is death compatible with eternal life possessed now in all its fullness by believers? The real question is that of the Jews, "Could not he who opened the eyes of the blind man have kept this man from dying?" (11:37). In other words, how can the believer whose eyes have been opened by the baptismal bath in the Sent One (see 9:7) die? If Jesus is truly present, as he promised in the last discourses, indwelling his disciples as the principle of eternal life, death is an anomaly. Death, it would seem, can only mean that Jesus is absent. This conviction is expressed by both Martha and Mary: "Lord, if you had been here my brother would not have died" (11:21, 32). The theological concern of the Lazarus story, therefore, is not the delay of the parousia but the real meaning of death and life, of the absence and presence of Jesus. It is the problem of death in the community of eternal life.

The theological issue is taken up in the opening scene (vv. 1–16), including both the introduction and Jesus' discussion with his disciples, and in the closing scene (vv. 45–53), in which the authorities plot the death of Jesus. These two scenes frame the central narrative in which Martha, Mary, and the Jews symbolically incarnate the existential situation in which the human experience of death must be drawn into the horizon of the paschal mystery as faith in Jesus illuminates and transforms, but does not negate, that experience.

The first question concerns the real meaning of death. In the opening and closing scenes death is examined in its origin or cause, its nature as human experience and spiritual reality, and its finality or purpose. The finesse of the treatment both clarifies the theological meaning of death and leaves its experiential ambiguity completely intact.

The most fundamental question is, Who or what causes death? The first suggestion is that illness leads to death. Yet Jesus categorically rejects this: "This illness is not unto death" (11:4). Jesus' statement, which is plainly contrary to the phenomenological facts, since Lazarus's illness *will* lead to his own death and eventually to Jesus' death, opens up an ambiguity in the word "death" by calling radically into question its presumed univocal reference to the end of physical life. In some cases, what Lazarus will undergo as a result of natural causes and what Jesus will undergo as a result of human malice is not death. This is reinforced in vv. 5–10, and a hint of the true answer is given. The disciples protest Jesus' going back into Judea, where the Jews had just tried to kill him, but Jesus assures them that he is in no danger at the moment because "the night" of the passion, his hour, is not yet come. The will of his Father, not human volition, controls life and death. Therefore, whatever death means, nature and human intention cannot be regarded as its ultimate causes because what they bring about, that is, physical death, is in some sense not death; and they cannot bring about death at all except according to God's will and design.

In the conversation with the disciples in vv. 5–16 the question that has been answered negatively (we know what death is not and what does not cause it) is raised positively. If human death is, in some sense, not death, then death is perhaps an illusion, a mere falling asleep. In the early church death was often referred to as "falling asleep" (see 1 Thess. 4:13–16; 1 Cor. 7:39; 11:30; 15:6, 18, 51; Acts 7:60; 13:36; 2 Pet. 3:4), and Jesus says of Jairus's daughter that "the child is not dead but sleeping" (Mark 5:39). Rochais, after examining the use of sleep as a metaphor for death in the Old Testament and Jewish apocalyptic,[16] concludes that there is a fundamental difference between the Old Testament and the New Testament uses of the term. In the former the just dead were understood to be resting peacefully in Sheol awaiting the general resurrection. In the New Testament, the metaphor of sleep is not an attempt to describe the state of the deceased in the afterlife but to affirm that death is temporary because, finally, it will be overcome by the resurrection of Jesus.

In John, however, there is a somewhat different emphasis. Jesus tells the disciples, "Lazarus has fallen asleep, but I go to awaken him" (11:11). The disciples reply with a typically Johannine irony based on double-meaning words: *ei kekoimētai sōthēsetai,* "If he has fallen asleep [or died] he will get well [or be saved]" (11:12). This is, of course, the Christian understanding of death as passage to life, but the disciples, like Caiaphas later in the chapter, are unaware of the true meaning of their statement. The evangelist immediately clarifies, "Now Jesus had spoken of [Lazarus's] death, but [the disciples] thought that he meant taking rest in sleep. Then Jesus told them plainly, 'Lazarus is dead'" (11:13–14). This almost brutal announcement serves to correct any tendency to see death as illusory or unreal. Human death is brutally real. Referring to it as sleep is not recourse to a euphemism to soften or disguise its reality. Even though it is true that death is not a univocal term and that there is a sense in which death is not due to natural causes or human volition, there is also a sense in which death does result from sickness and human malice; and this death, though not ultimate, is real.

It has often been noted that John's vocabulary makes a consistent distinc-

---

[16] Rochais, *Les récits,* 192–99.

tion between *zōē*, eternal life, and *psychē*, natural life. It is significant that there is no such distinction between natural death and spiritual death. *Thanatos*, death, is used for both. The word remains ambiguous because the experience is profoundly ambiguous. Death cannot be relieved of its experiential character as enemy of humanity even though, conquered by resurrection, it has been deprived of its ultimate power. This ambiguity is caught by the comment of Thomas that closes the theological introduction. In response to Jesus' decision, "Let us go to him [Lazarus]," Thomas answers, "Let us also go, that we may die with him" (11:6). The grammatical antecedent of "with him" is Lazarus, although the meaning is clearly "with Jesus," who will surely be arrested if he returns to Judea. In fact, of course, both meanings are intended. The disciples, like the raised Lazarus, will become targets of persecution unto death because of their relation with Jesus (see 12:9–11); but their resulting deaths will be death with Jesus, that is, death which glorifies them by glorifying God.

In the closing scene (11:45–53) the primary question concerns the finality of death in both senses of the term. The council of the Jews has decided to put a final end to Jesus' signs, but the finality of death lies not in what it terminates but in what it inaugurates.

In the opening scene Jesus had declared that Lazarus's illness was "for the glory of God, so that the Son of God may be glorified by means of it" (11:14). In proposing to go to Lazarus, Jesus had declared, "Lazarus is dead; and for your sake I am glad that I was not there, so that you may believe" (11:14–45). The death of Lazarus, therefore, is for the manifestation of Jesus' glory in order that the disciples may believe. In the closing scene Caiaphas unwittingly prophesies that Jesus' death will be for the salvation of the Jewish nation, and the evangelist universalizes the prophecy to include the eschatological ingathering of the people of God, which was both the Old Testament sign of the arrival of the eschaton (cf. Isa. 11:12; 43:5; Ezek. 28:25) and the peculiarly Johannine understanding of the significance of Jesus as Savior of the World (cf. John 4:42; also 10:15–16; 12:32).[17] What, then, is the connection between the glory of God, the glorification of Jesus, the faith of the disciples, and the salvation of the world? In the Lazarus narrative all of these Johannine themes are brought together and clarified in relation to the death of Jesus and his disciples.

The glory of Jesus revealed during his lifetime by means of his works is his communion of being, life, and action with his Father; but his glorification on the cross, the *doxa* that will be given him when he is raised up from earth, is

---

[17] Dodd, "Prophecy."

his union with believers. The glory that is given to God by Jesus' glorification is the communion of life between believers and God,[18] that is, the salvation of the world through their becoming one as children of God (11:52). The death and raising of Lazarus will set this entire divine plan into motion,[19] beginning with the faith of the disciples, whose spokesperson is Martha. The exploration of the meaning of death thus comes to its conclusion. Human death, though real, is not victorious because, though caused at one level by natural and human factors, it finally serves the purpose of God, which is to bring all believers into union with God in Jesus.[20]

The second theological issue in the narrative concerns the meaning of presence. When the sisters send word to Jesus, they say, "The one you love is ill" (11:3). The implication is that Jesus, because he loved Lazarus and the sisters, should come. But the evangelist says the opposite: "Now Jesus *loved* Martha, and her sister and Lazarus. When *therefore* [*hōs oun*] he heard that [Lazarus] was ill, he stayed two days longer in the place where he was" (11:5–6, emphasis mine). Not only is absence compatible with love; it can even be the expression of love.[21]

Yet Jesus' physical separation from those he loves is not to be understood as complete absence. Jesus, though physically at a distance, knows everything that concerns Lazarus: the true significance of his illness (11:4–5) and the fact of his death (11:14). When Jesus finally goes to Bethany, it is not to become present to those he loves, for he has never really been absent. It is to reveal his glory and bring them, with the other disciples, to belief.

Nevertheless, Jesus' delay, like his physical absence before the parousia, is real; and the suffering it causes is real. Jesus does not rebuke the sisters for their suffering, either at their brother's death or at Jesus' absence. What he demands is that they, and all the disciples, realize and believe in his intimate real presence in and through his physical absence. This presence can sustain believers through all the sufferings of this life, even death itself. The death of Lazarus and Jesus' physical absence, both of which are real and yet not defin-itive of Christian experience, are the symbolic catechesis of the mutual indwelling of Jesus and his disciples, which gives them, even now and within the experience of death and absence, eternal life. The raising of Lazarus is the

---

[18] W. H. Cadman, "The Raising of Lazarus (John 10:40–11:53)," *SE* I = *TU* 73 (Berlin: Akademie-Verlag, 1959), 423–34; see especially 425–26.

[19] See McNeil, "Raising of Lazarus," 270.

[20] See Jones, who arrives at the same conclusion through structural narrative analysis (*Narrative Structures*, 317).

[21] Ibid.

gospel in miniature, reason enough for those who resist Jesus' revelation to decide to kill him.

SPIRITUALITY

In the Martha and Mary episodes that stand in the center of the narrative, we participate in the symbolic appropriation of Johannine faith as the horizon of Christian existence. Martha, Mary, some of the Jews, and, by implication, Jesus' other disciples, come to believe and from within this new horizon to understand both life and death in a new way. Christian spirituality is neither escape from real life nor denial of its pain but a way of living that is transfigured, even now, by the resurrection and the life which is Jesus.

The central section of the chapter is a triptych. First, Martha demonstrates true and perfect Johannine belief in the word of Jesus; second, Mary and the Jews anchor that believing in the ambiguity of human experience; third, Martha, Mary, and the Jews represent the full range of possible responses to the sign by which Jesus reveals his glory, that is, his identity as the resurrection and the life.

As Rochais correctly points out, Martha has been inserted by the evangelist into this narrative as the carrier of the evangelist's distinctive theology.[22] Her opening words are analogous to those of the mother of Jesus at Cana (John 2:3, 5). She indicates the problem and her own open-ended faith in Jesus: "Even now I know that whatever you ask of God, God will give you" (11:21–22). Jesus answers, "Your brother will rise" (11:23), which Martha understands inadequately in terms of the future eschatology which the early church took over from the Old Testament and reinterpreted in the light of Jesus' resurrection. Jesus replies with a lapidary self-revelation, "I am the resurrection and the life" (11:25), which he unfolds in a double explanation: The believer who dies will live; the living believer will never die (see 11:25–26). In both cases the life in question is eternal life ($z\bar{o}\bar{e}$), which does not yield to either physical death, however real, or the "death forever," which cannot touch the believer.

Jesus has not abolished final eschatology (some believers will die and Lazarus must eventually die again) but has given it a new dimension of depth, the experience of union with the risen Christ in this life, which constitutes the possession, here and now, of eternal life.[23] The resurrection on the "last

---

[22] Rochais, Les récits, 118–19, 121.
[23] See Martin, "History and Eschatology," 337–40.

day" is not a future purely beyond time that would defer life until the eschatological future[24] but a future already filling the believer's present with eternal life. As George MacRae has suggested, the juxtaposition of future and
present eschatology in the Fourth Gospel (e.g., 5:25–29 and 5:21–24; 6:40c,
54b, and 6:40b, 54a; 6:44 and 6:51) is neither inconsistency on the part of
the evangelist nor heavy-handed editing by a later redactor but a way of
asserting that all the diversified eschatological hopes that had emerged in
early Christianity meet and find their fulfillment in Jesus.[25] Jesus' revelation
to Martha, however, is not a presentation of eschatological propositions but
a self-disclosure calling for personal response. Faith at this point is not theological assent but personal spiritual transformation. "Do *you* believe this?"
(11:26, emphasis mine).

Martha's response is the most fully developed confession of Johannine
faith in the Fourth Gospel.[26] She recognizes in Jesus the Christ (Messiah), the
Son of God (a title that, by the time this Gospel was written, was freighted
with divinity), and the one sent into the world by the Father (which is what
Jesus later prays that those who witness the raising of Lazarus will come to
believe [11:42]). This is the faith that, according to its conclusion, the Fourth
Gospel was written to evoke (see 20:31). Especially significant is the fact that,
like Thomas's confession after the resurrection of Jesus (see 20:28), Martha's
confession is addressed directly to Jesus in response to his direct self-revelation
(*egō eimi*) to her: "Do you believe this?"—"Yes, Lord" (11:26–27). The difference between theology and spirituality is the difference between reflection
on revelation and personal commitment to the one who reveals. Martha's
belief in Jesus' word is her entrance into eternal life. The scene ends abruptly,
not because there is something inadequate in Martha's response but because
that response has initiated in her a new life that is the horizon of all further
experience.

The following scene between Jesus and Mary appears, at first sight, to be

---

[24] Jones, *Narrative Structures,* 313.

[25] George W. MacRae, "The Fourth Gospel and Religionsgeschichte," *CBQ* 32 (1970):
13–24; see especially 18–19, 23.

[26] Cadman says, "A confession such as this—the whole of it—cannot be an uncompre-
hending or half-comprehending response" ("Raising of Lazarus," 432–33). Raymond F.
Collins ("The Representative Figures in the Fourth Gospel," *DRev* 94 [1976]: 46) and Rochais
(*Les récits,* 118–19) take the same position. T. Evan Pollard considers the confession of
Martha inadequate because her later reaction shows that she did not fully understand Jesus'
self-revelation ("The Raising of Lazarus [John XI]," ed. E. A. Livingston, *SE* 6 = *TU* 112
[Berlin: Akademie Verlag, 1973], 440). In my opinion, this misses the point entirely. Like
Peter, who did not fully understand the bread-of-life discourse, Martha believes not in *what*
she understands but in the *one* who has the words of eternal life (cf. 6:68).

a useless and even impoverished duplication of the Martha scene. Such is not the case. The literary function of the episode is to bring onto the stage, with some narrative plausibility, Mary's companions in mourning, the Jews, who will report Jesus to the authorities. Yet what immediately strikes the reader about the Mary scene is her tears. The Jews who are with Mary in the house think she is going to Lazarus's tomb to weep (see 11:31). She comes to Jesus and falls at his feet weeping, her companions joining in her tears (see 11:33). Jesus, seeing their tears, is deeply moved and inwardly troubled (*enebrimēsato tō pneumati kai etaraxen heauton*), just as he is in 12:27 when confronted with the reality of his own death (*hē psychē mou tetaraktai*). Then we are told quite simply, "Jesus wept" (11:35). Rochais remarks that one of the characteristics of the New Testament raising narratives, in contrast to all other miracles, is the mention of tears.[27] Mary's function in this narrative is to weep, and Jesus joins her in her sorrow.

Mary greets Jesus with the news of her brother's death couched in a reproach of his delay that is itself an implicit act of faith. Mary's statement is that of every believing Christian in history who is overcome with sorrow at the death of a loved one, who believes firmly that God could have prevented that death, and yet who clings in bewildered grief to the source of all consolation, who is, paradoxically, the one who permitted the death. It has been suggested that Jesus' weeping was an expression of anger at Mary's and the Jews' lack of faith,[28] but the reaction of the bystanders (who voice the evangelist's interpretation) assures us that such is not the case. At the sight of Jesus' tears they exclaim, "See how he loved him" (11:36). Jesus' tears are an honest sharing in Mary's grief and perhaps in her anger at death, the enemy of all life. Jesus, in his most fully human moment in the Fourth Gospel, legitimates human agony in the face of death,[29] an agony he will feel for himself as he shrinks from the passion in chapter 12. This episode roots the spirituality of the community in the realism of human experience. Christian faith is neither Gnosticism nor stoicism. Death is real and so is the suffering it causes. Faith is not compatible with despair, but it is no stranger to tears.

Jesus then comes to the tomb, where Martha, the carrier of the evangelist's theology and spirituality, reappears. Her shock at Jesus' order to remove the stone shows that she did not in any way anticipate a resuscitation of Lazarus. This is not, however, due to lack of faith. She who now knows that Lazarus, even though he has died, yet lives, has no reason to think the final resurrection will be anticipated in his case. In this scene the evangelist summarizes the

---

[27] Rochais, *Les récits*, 15.
[28] See Pollard, "Raising of Lazarus," 440–41.
[29] Rochais, *Les récits*, 142.

Fourth Gospel's teaching on the relationship between signs and faith, between seeing and believing. Martha, who without seeing has believed in the word of Jesus, is able to see the glory in the sign (see 11:40). Mary and the well-disposed Jews, whose faith, though real, is still immature, come to full faith through their seeing of the sign (see 11:45). And some, the ill-disposed Jews, are confirmed in their unbelief by their blindness to the sign (see 11:46).

Jesus prays in thanksgiving to God, who has already heard his prayer, in order to make it clear to the bystanders that he does nothing on his own authority, that his works are the works of the One who sent him, for the purpose of the sign is to bring those who see it to believe in his glory, that is, his union with the Father who sent him. Then, in a scene carefully constructed to recall not only the prophet's description of the Servant of Yahweh who says to those in bonds "Come out" (Isa. 49:8–9) but also Jesus' own words about himself, "I say to you, the hour is coming when the dead will hear the voice of the Son of God and those who hear will live . . . when all who are in the tombs will hear his voice and come forth" (John 5:25, 28–29), Jesus calls out: "Lazarus, come forth" (11:43).[30] He then commands the witnesses to unbind Lazarus and let him go.

What is the purpose of this sign? On the one hand, Lazarus is not finally rescued from death since he must die again; on the other hand, Jesus' revelation to Martha was precisely that eternal life conquers death without abolishing it.[31] The raising of Lazarus, as a Johannine sign, is a revelation of the identity and mission of Jesus in and through a "historical" event. Just as Jesus gave physical sight to reveal himself as Light of the World (John 9) and physical bread to reveal himself as bread from heaven (John 6), so he here raises Lazarus to physical life to reveal himself as resurrection and life.[32] Jesus in this scene gives eternal life to those who believe in him, whether in response to his word or in response to the sign, whether because they see or without seeing. He symbolizes this eternal gift by raising the dead, which, at the end of time, will bring eternal life to full manifestation.[33] Lazarus can be raised because he is one whom Jesus loves, that is, a believer.[34] His new life speaks both of his

---

[30] Ibid., 132.

[31] See C. F. D. Moule, "The Meaning of 'Life' in the Gospel and Epistles of St. John: A Study in the Story of Lazarus, John 11:1–44," *Theology* 78 (1975): 114–25.

[32] Ibid., 121–25. L. Paul Trudinger argues against Moule that physical life given to Lazarus is not a sign of eternal life but a contrast offered to true life ("The Meaning of 'Life' in St. John: Some Further Reflections," *BTB* 6 [1976]: 258–63). This seems incompatible with the Fourth Gospel's theology of symbolic revelation.

[33] See Rochais, *Les récits*, 142.

[34] Cadman, "Raising of Lazarus," 430.

present possession of eternal life and of the final resurrection of those who die believing. It symbolizes the coincidence of present and future eschatology: the believer who dies yet lives; the living who believe will not die the everlasting death.

The end of the narrative is the supreme irony of the Fourth Gospel. The religious authorities decide to kill Jesus because he gives life (cf. Acts 3:14–15).[35] Yet his execution will be his glorification, the final revelation of the resurrection and the life.[36]

CONCLUSION

In the narrative of the raising of Lazarus the Fourth Evangelist achieves the ultimate integration of history, theology, and spirituality. The story of a historical community's tragedy, framed by two theological dialogues that explore the meaning of death/life and absence/presence, draws the reader, who identifies in turn with Martha and with Mary, into a new horizon of existence within which the ultimate human tragedy, death, is transfigured without being denatured. Christian readers are invited and enabled to integrate the ever-ambiguous experience of death, that of loved ones and their own, into their faith vision. The death of the beloved and the absence of the Lord are real, but they are neither ultimate nor final. Eternal life is unquenched by death, and the absence felt is Jesus' way of being present during the time of waiting. We are not asked not to weep but only not to despair, for the one in whom we believe is our resurrection because he is our life.

[35] Pollard, "Raising of Lazarus," 436.
[36] Rochais, *Les récits,* 146.

11

A Community of Friends (John 13:1–20)

HERMENEUTICAL PRESUPPOSITIONS

In the interpretation of the foot washing in John 13:1-20 that follows, the text from John will be treated primarily as a *work* rather than as an *object*.[1] This implies that the text is viewed not primarily as something to be analyzed but as a human expression that functions as a mediation of meaning; that the purpose of studying the text is not to decompose it into its constituent elements in order to account for its genesis but to appropriate the meaning of the text in its integrity; that the objective of interpretation is not empirically verifiable propositions about the historical-cultural references of the text, but the dialectical illumination of the meaning of the text and the self-understanding of the reader. In other words, the first presupposition is that, as a work, the text mediates a meaning that is not behind it, hidden in the shroud of the past when the text was composed, but ahead of it in the possibilities of human and Christian existence that it projects for the reader.[2]

---

[1] This distinction between "object" and "work" is fundamental to contemporary hermeneutical discussion. An object is a part of the natural world, whereas a work is a human expression. Texts are, of course, both object and work from different points of view. However, it is primarily as works that texts are a subject of interpretation. For further discussion of this distinction and its implications for interpretation theory, see Richard E. Palmer, *Hermeneutics: Interpretation Theory in Schleiermacher, Dilthey, Heidegger, and Gadamer*, Northwestern University Studies in Phenomenology and Existential Philosophy (Evanston, Ill.: Northwestern University Press, 1969), 3–11.

[2] Paul Ricoeur, *Interpretation Theory: Discourse and the Surplus of Meaning* (Fort Worth: Texas Christian University Press, 1976), 87. See also the fascinating article by Wilfred Cantwell Smith, "The Study of Religion and the Study of the Bible," in *Religious Diversity* (New York: Harper & Row, 1976), 41–56, in which he contends that to treat the Bible as scripture entails dealing with it more in terms of its effects than of what effected it.

Second, it is presupposed that the text is semantically independent of its author.[3] The meaning of the text is not limited to what the author intended, even though it was produced in function of such an intention. The text, in being exteriorized and established in independent existence by writing, open to anyone who can read, means whatever it actually means when validly interpreted, whether or not the author intended such a meaning.

Third, because the text is a linguistic work rather than an object of nature, it is, by virtue of its linguisticality, polysemous.[4] The meaning of a work of language (as distinguished from scientific formulae) cannot be reduced to a single, univocal, empirically verifiable (i.e., literal) sense; rather, because of the polyvalence of words and the semantic richness of larger linguistic units, the work generates various valid interpretations in different readers.[5] Together, the second and third presuppositions imply that the original audience's understanding of the text is neither exhaustive of meaning nor absolutely normative for all further interpretation.

Fourth, it is presupposed that the historical distance between the present interpreter and the text is not primarily an obstacle to understanding to be overcome by a self-translation of the interpreter into the world of the author but an advantage for understanding in that the tradition which is operative in the interpreter helps him or her to draw from the text richer meaning than was available to the original audience.[6] In other words, the original audience interprets a text within essentially the same historical horizon as the author. Subsequent readers interpret the text within a much wider horizon, one that

---

[3] The concept of semantic independence of texts is often associated with structuralism, for which the text is a closed system of signs whose structure is its meaning. See Daniel Patte, *What is Structural Exegesis?* (Philadelphia: Fortress, 1976), especially 9–17. Structuralism, however, tends to regard the text as an absolute and thus to reduce it to an object. Ricoeur distinguishes what he calls the "fallacy of the absolute text" from the concept of semantic autonomy, which is the effect of inscription on discourse (*Interpretation Theory*, 25–44). Ricoeur makes it clear that semantic autonomy does not imply the "absolute text." Rather, it means that in written discourse the "author's intention and the meaning of the text cease to coincide" in the way that the speaker's intention and the meaning do in oral discourse. The result is that "what the text means now matters more than what the author meant when he [*sic*] wrote it" (pp. 29–30).

[4] Ricoeur, *Interpretation Theory*, 31–32.

[5] For an excellent expansion of this presupposition, see Paul Ricoeur, "Creativity in Language: Word, Polysemy, Metaphor," *Philosophy Today* 17 (1973): 97–111.

[6] Hans-Georg Gadamer explains fully this concept of "effective historical consciousness" (*wirkungsgeschichtliche Bewusstsein*) (*Truth and Method*, 2nd rev. ed., translation revised by Joel Weinsheimer and Donald G. Marshall [New York: Crossroad, 1989], 300–307). Paul Ricoeur deals with this same phenomenon as "productive distanciation" in "The Hermeneutical Function of Distanciation," *Philosophy Today* 17 (1973): 129–41, and *Interpretation Theory*, 43–44.

results from the fusion of the horizon of the text and that of the later interpreter.[7]

A fifth presupposition has to do with the triple dialectic that structures discourse. As Ricoeur explains, discourse is both *event* and *meaning* (the first
dialectic).[8] As language-event, as the saying of something, it passes away with
the cessation of the speaking. But as meaning, as something said, it perdures.
The meaning, in other words, has an ideal quality that transcends the event
in which it was articulated. Now, meaning itself is dialectically structured (the
second dialectic). The meaning of discourse is, from one point of view, the
speaker's meaning, what the speaker intended to say. But, from another point
of view, the meaning belongs to the *sentence itself.* It transcends the speaker;
it outlasts its relationship to the speaker; it is no longer under the control of
the speaker. What is said, is said. Finally, the meaning of the sentence (in its
relative independence of the speaker) is also dialectically structured (the third
dialectic) as a relationship between *sense* and *reference*.[9] The sense is internal
to the sentence and is constituted by the relation of predicate to subject. A
sentence such as "Bananas are blue" makes "sense." But the reference, that is,
the relation of the sense to reality in which is located "discourse's claim to be
true,"[10] is falsified in this case because bananas are not blue.

In biblical interpretation (or any interpretation of texts) we are concerned
primarily with the meaning of the text itself, not with the author's meaning.
And we are concerned with the sense of the text only because of our concern
with its reference. This is an important difference between hermeneutics or
interpretation and traditional historical criticism. The latter assigned itself
primarily (or even exclusively) the task of reconstructing the author's meaning precisely by deciphering the sense of the text within its own historical circumstances.[11] It left the question of reference, the religious truth claims of

---

[7] The concept of "fusion of horizons" was developed by Gadamer (*Truth and Method*,
269–74) as an alternative to the notion, characteristic of nineteenth-century historical theory,
that the interpreter can and must escape from his or her own historical horizon and enter that
of the author. Gadamer maintains that this is neither possible nor desirable.

[8] Ricoeur, *Interpretation Theory*, 8–23.

[9] This distinction was first explored by Gottlob Frege in a now famous article, "Über Sinn
und Bedeutung," which has been translated by Max Black as "On Sense and Reference," in
Translations from the Philosophical Writings of Gottlob Frege, ed. Peter Geach and Max Black
(Oxford: Blackwell, 1970), 56–78. Ricoeur develops this distinction in relation to literary texts
(*Interpretation Theory*, 19–22).

[10] Ricoeur, *Interpretation Theory*, 20.

[11] A very clear articulation of this understanding of the exegetical task can be found in the
special issue of *JBL* 77 (1958) that was devoted to this question. The consensus of the authors,
among whom were such notables as Krister Stendahl, John L. McKenzie, and William A.

the text about God and humanity, to the theologian or the preacher. Hermeneutics assigns to the interpreter, as primary task, the understanding of the text precisely in its truth claims. The interpreter must engage those claims by uncovering the question to which the text constitutes an answer, and "dialoguing," from his or her own stance in history, with the text about the subject matter of the text.[12] Consequently, the primary question posed to the interpreter by the episode of the foot washing in John is not, Did Jesus actually wash his disciples' feet or actually speak the discourse that follows in the text? but rather, What interpretation of life and relationships does the text present? Is that interpretation true? And if so, what are the implications for the interpreter's own self-understanding?[13]

Lastly, it is presupposed that all literary texts are symbolic; that is, they are linguistic entities that have both a primary, direct, and literal signification and a deeper, secondary signification that is attainable only in and through the primary signification. This means, in regard to the Gospel, that the text is the symbolic locus of the revelation of God in Jesus.[14] Interpretation of the symbolic always consists in bringing to explicit formulation some of the thought to which the symbol gives rise,[15] but no categorization can exhaust the semantic possibilities of the symbol.[16] While this is true of all literary texts and therefore of the New Testament texts, it is especially true of the Fourth Gospel, in which the evangelist explicitly states the purpose of bringing the readers to salvific faith in Jesus through the presentation of "signs" (cf. John 20:30–31), that is, perceptible works that symbolically reveal the glory of Jesus.

Although some Johannine scholars limit the term *sēmeion* to the specifically miraculous works of Jesus, and therefore regard chapters 13–20 as devoid of "signs,"[17] this limitation seems too mechanical. If the signs are what

---

Irwin, was that the task of the exegete was to reconstruct as accurately as possible the meaning the human author intended to convey to her or his original audience. This meaning was understood to be univocal and fixed for all time.

[12] See Gadamer, *Truth and Method,* 325–41.

[13] Ricoeur, *Interpretation Theory,* 92.

[14] Paul Ricoeur, "Existence and Hermeneutics," trans. Kathleen McLaughlin, in *The Conflict of Interpretations: Essays in Hermeneutics,* ed. Don Ihde (Evanston, Ill.: Northwestern University Press, 1974), 12–13.

[15] Ibid., 13.

[16] Ricoeur, *Interpretation Theory,* 47.

[17] For a summary, critical appraisal, and selected bibliography of scholarship concerning the signs in the Fourth Gospel, see Raymond E. Brown, "Appendix III: Signs and Works," in *The Gospel According to John,* 2 vols., Anchor Bible 29, 29A (Garden City, N.Y.: Doubleday, 1966, 1970), 1:524–32.

Jesus did to reveal his glory so that his disciples would believe in him (see 2:11), then surely his paschal mystery, in which he is fully glorified (see 17:1, 5) and his disciples come to believe and to know who he really is (see 17:7–8), must be included among the signs.[18] In what follows, the foot washing is regarded as a sign par excellence, that is, a symbolic work of Jesus that reveals the meaning of salvation as the Fourth Gospel understands and presents it. The symbolic revelation of the act of the foot washing is resymbolized in the text. In other words, the sign that was done for Jesus' first disciples is, by being written into the Gospel, made a sign for all who can read with understanding. This means that the foot washing is not an event that has a single, univocal meaning coterminous with the intention of the Fourth Evangelist and/or the understanding of the original audience, but that it is a symbol, endlessly giving rise to reflection, generating an ever deeper understanding of the salvation it symbolizes as the horizon of the text fuses with the various horizons of generations of readers.

INTERPRETATION OF JOHN 13:1–20

The particular focus of interest in this section is the meaning of the controversy between Jesus and Simon Peter about whether Jesus would wash Peter's feet (John 13:6–10). The context of the dialogue, which is essential for any adequate interpretation of it, is the entire scene of the foot washing, including the solemn introduction (13:1–3),[19] the account of the sign itself (13:4–11), and Jesus' discourse which follows (13:12–20).[20]

As is indicated by the solemn introduction in vv. 1–3, this scene opens the second part of the Fourth Gospel, which has been called the "book of glory" or the account of the "hour of Jesus." Jesus is presented as acting in full awareness of his origin and destiny, that is, of his identity and of his mission as

[18] Although John calls Jesus' revelatory works "signs," the appropriate contemporary term would be "symbol." See chapter 4 on symbolism in the Fourth Gospel for a fuller explanation of the difference between sign and symbol.

[19] The distinction, which I think is correct, between v. 1 as an introduction to the entire second part of the Gospel (chaps. 13–20) and vv. 2–3 as the introduction to the foot washing and the following discourse (13:4–20), is not important for our purposes at this point. However, the interested reader can consult Brown, *Gospel According to John,* 2:563–64.

[20] I am not treating the discourse as a second, and substantially different, interpretation of the foot washing, as do a number of commentators, e.g., Marie-Emile Boismard, "Le lavement des pieds (Jn, xiii, 1–17)," *RB* 71 (1964): 5–24. The reasons for treating the passage, at least vv. 1–17, as a unity will become clear as the interpretation proceeds. For a summary of scholarly opinion on the unity of the passage, see Brown, *Gospel According to John,* 2:559–62.

agent of God's salvific will and work in the world (see 13:1, 3). The introduction, therefore, makes it clear that what follows is not simply a good example in humility but a prophetic action[21] that will reveal the true meaning of Jesus' loving his own unto the end (13:1) in fulfillment of his mission to bring to completion the salvific intention of God's boundless love for the world.

The evangelist's contemplative description of Jesus' elaborate, almost liturgical, preparation for his action of washing the disciples' feet (see 13:4–5) focuses the reader's attention on the essential characteristic of the sign. That which Jesus is about to do is an act of *serving*, of literally waiting upon his disciples. Many commentators have suggested, correctly in my opinion, that the foot washing in John is the analogue of the eucharistic institution narratives in the Synoptic accounts of the supper;[22] that is, it functions as the symbol and catechesis of Jesus' approaching death, his handing over of himself for and to his disciples. To characterize the passion and death as service is not peculiar to John. In the early church one of the most significant interpretations of Jesus' persecution and death consisted in identifying him with the Isaian Suffering Servant of Yahweh (Isa. 42:1–4; 49:1–6; 50:4–11; 52:13–53:12).[23] In the foot washing Jesus is presented as servant and symbolically characterizes his impending suffering and death as a work of service.

It is perhaps well to insist again at this point that we are attempting to interpret the *text*, to understand the meaning of the account given. We are not dealing with the question of the historical facticity of the foot washing (although this would be a valid and interesting question in another context and for other purposes).[24] Consequently, when we speak of what Jesus does,

---

[21] By "prophetic action" I mean an action that is presented as divinely inspired, revelatory in content, proleptic in structure, symbolic in form, and pedagogical in intent. I am not intending by this characterization to assert the historical facticity of the act but to call attention to its revelatory character.

[22] See Brown, *Gospel According to John*, 2:558–59; and Craig R. Koester, *Symbolism in the Fourth Gospel: Meaning, Mystery, Community* (Minneapolis: Fortress, 1995), especially 115–18, on the issue of the possible sacramental significance of the foot washing. For the purposes of the present discussion, the more important issue is not whether the foot washing is *equivalent in content* to the institution narrative (i.e., whether it is eucharistic) but that it is *analogous in function* within the context of the narrative of the supper—that is, both the action over the bread and wine and the foot washing serve as prophetic gestures revealing the true significance of the death of Jesus within the theological perspectives of the respective evangelists.

[23] The relevant Synoptic material is summarized in David M. Stanley, "Titles of Christ," *JBC* art. 78:22–23. Acts 3:13; 4:27, 30 also testify to this early interpretation.

[24] For a discussion of the historical and critical questions raised by the narrative, and appropriate references for further research, see C. K. Barrett, *The Gospel According to St. John*, 2nd ed. (London: SPCK, 1978), 435–37. I agree with Barrett's characterization of the account as a "symbolic narrative," which is best regarded as "a Johannine construction" (p. 436).

what Peter says, and so on, we are using shorthand for "what the text presents the characters as saying and doing." Our interest is in the meaning of the text as a literary work, not in the factual accuracy of the text as a historical document.

The action that Jesus performs seems so simple, so inadequate as an expression of his salvific work, that it challenges the reader to search for its deeper significance.[25] That there is indeed more to this scene than is immediately evident is confirmed by Jesus' reply to Peter's scandalized query, "Lord, do you wash my feet?" Jesus replies, "What I am doing you do not know yet, but after these things [i.e., after the glorification] you will come to understand" (13:6–7).[26]

The indication of the true meaning of Jesus' action is Peter's instinctive and profound scandal.[27] The Greek text, by the emphatic placement of the pronouns in v. 6b and the doubling of the emphatic negatives in v. 8, gives two important clues. First, Peter was not merely objecting to having his feet washed by another but specifically to the reversal of service roles between himself and Jesus: "Lord, do *you* wash *my* feet?" Second, his protest was not simply an embarrassed objection to Jesus' action but a categorical refusal to accept what this reversal of roles implied: "*By no means* will you wash my feet

---

[25] It is particularly the American authors working in parable interpretation who have pointed out that the "presence of the extraordinary in the ordinary" is an important clue to the presence of the symbolic. See, e.g., Mary Ann Tolbert, *Perspectives on the Parables: An Approach to Multiple Interpretations* (Philadelphia: Fortress, 1979), 89–91; Dan Otto Via, Jr., *The Parables: Their Literary and Existential Dimension* (Philadelphia: Fortress, 1974), 105–6. Paul Ricoeur also discusses this point ("Biblical Hermeneutics: The Metaphorical Process," *Semeia* 4 [1975]: 99–100). Although these authors are speaking specifically of parables, I think that the extension of this insight to other symbolic narratives, such as the foot washing, is legitimate.

[26] Brown in his commentary (2:559–60) calls attention to what seems to be a conflict or contradiction between v. 7, in which Jesus says the foot washing will not be understood until after the glorification on Calvary, and vv. 12, 17, which seem to indicate that it can be understood at the supper. I am inclined to think that even on the level of the narrative (not to mention the level of symbolic polyvalence) the tension is more apparent than real. In v. 7 Jesus says that what *he is doing,* that is, the relation of his action at the supper to his death, cannot be understood until after the crucifixion. Nevertheless, the disciples can understand immediately what *Jesus explains to them* in vv. 13–15, viz., that his relation to them in the foot washing is the pattern of their relation to each other. Only after the glorification will they understand that the relationship between Jesus and themselves was literally service unto death.

[27] In discussing the interaction of Jesus and Simon Peter, we will be referring to the emotional quality of that interaction *as it is presented in the text.* This is not a matter of "psychologizing" in the sense of trying to divine the intrapersonal states of the historical characters. It is a matter of taking seriously the literary text, including the described and implied reactions of the characters in the narrative.

ever" (literally, "unto the age," meaning "unto eternity"). In some way, Peter grasped that complicity in this act involved acceptance of a radical reinterpretation of his own life-world, a genuine conversion of some kind, which he was not prepared to undergo. Jesus confirms this by replying, "Unless I wash you, you have no heritage [or inheritance] with me" (13:8). As Raymond Brown points out, the "inheritance" (*meros*) in question is eternal life.[28] Now Jesus, who would declare Peter "clean" (13:10) despite his foreknowledge of the latter's triple denial (see 13:38), would certainly not declare him cut off from eternal life because he was unreceptive to an example of humility. Clearly, something much more serious was at stake.

A further indication of the true nature of Peter's refusal is perhaps supplied by an analogous scene from the Synoptics (Mark 8:32–33 and its intensified parallel in Matt. 16:22–23). In the Synoptic passage, Jesus has predicted his imminent death, and Peter categorically rejects this interpretation of salvific messiahship, "God forbid, Lord! This shall never happen to you" (Matt. 16:22). Jesus does not treat this statement as we might expect, that is, as the understandable shocked protest of a loyal companion frightened for his master's safety. Jesus answers harshly, "Get behind me, Satan! You are a stumbling block to me; you judge not according to God but humanly" (Matt. 16:23). Something very similar is going on in John 13. What sounds like a perfectly understandable expression of embarrassment or even humility is understood by Jesus as a fundamental rejection of the divinely chosen expression of the meaning of salvation. In both scenes Peter is presented as having taken a stance diametrically opposed to Jesus' salvific mission. In the Synoptic scene, Peter has done this by explicitly rejecting the passion. In the Johannine passage, Peter has taken his reprobate position by symbolically rejecting Jesus' salvific self-understanding expressed in service of his disciples.

To understand this scene, therefore, we must come to grips with the enigma of *Jesus' service* in order to understand both why he presented his salvific work by means of this symbol and why Peter so vehemently rejected the reality thus symbolized. We will try to facilitate the process of understanding by examining reflectively the nature of service, not in terms of historical forms of service (such as foot washing) but in its inner structure and realization in human relationships.

Service is generally understood quite univocally as something that one person does for someone else, intending thereby the latter's good. In service the server lays aside, temporarily or even permanently, his or her own project, goal, good, or at least convenience for the sake of fostering the good of the

---

[28] Brown, *Gospel According to John,* 2:565–66.

other. The finality of the served is allowed, at least for the moment, to take priority over the finality of the server. In its most extreme form, therefore, it would consist in the server's laying down his or her life for the sake of the served. Now, in John's Gospel Jesus says that the new commandment, and the sign of authentic discipleship, that is, that we love one another as Jesus has loved us, has no more perfect form than the laying down of one's life for one's friends (see 13:34–35; 15:12–14). To lay down one's life is the ultimate preferring of another's good to one's own. Service, in other words, by its inmost structure, is capable of expressing ultimate love, and the love commanded by Jesus has the inner form of service. Every act of service, however ordinary, because it consists in preferring another to oneself, is essentially an act of self-gift and, therefore, an expression of love, which, in principle, tends toward the total self-gift.

However, when we attempt to verify this transcendental or ideal concept in our real experience of giving and receiving service, it becomes abundantly evident that service as pure gift of self for another's good rarely, if ever, is realized in fact. A phenomenology of service as it occurs in our everyday experience reveals at least three different models of serving. The analysis and comparison of these models can provide a key to an understanding of the meaning of Peter's refusal of Jesus' service that will, perhaps, be more adequate to the extraordinary elements in the narrative than traditional historical-critical exegesis provides.

In the first model service denotes what one person (the server) *must do* for another (the served) because of some right or power that the latter is understood to possess. The server may be bound for any number of reasons, such as being a child in relation to parents, a slave in relation to an owner, a woman in a patriarchal society in relation to men, a subject in relation to a ruler, a poor person in relation to the rich, and so on. But whatever the situational reason, service in every such case arises from a fundamental condition of inequality between the two persons, and the service rendered expresses and reinforces that condition of inequality. In other words, service in this model is a basic element in a structure of domination, however benevolently exercised. It expresses not the free preference of another's good to one's own but the subordination of one person to another. Such subordination can, without doubt, be incorporated into one's participation in the paschal mystery of Christ (cf. Eph. 5:21–6:9). But the fact is that the structure of domination tends of its own weight to become exploitative and oppressive because the service is demanded as the right of the superior and must be rendered as the unavoidable duty of the inferior. Only a supreme inner freedom, such as Jesus exhibited before Pilate (see John 19:10–11), can enable a person to surmount such domination and infuse into the structure of oppression the reality of genuine service, namely, freely chosen preference of the other's (the oppressor's) good.

In the second existential model service denotes what the server *does freely* for the served because of some need perceived in the latter that the former has the power to meet. This is the service that the mother renders to her child, the professional to the lay person or client, the rich to the poor, the strong to the weak. At first sight, such service seems to realize the ideal, that is, the unforced seeking of another's good. But a deep flaw resides in the heart of this situation. The basis of the service is still inequality. The server is perceived by him- or herself and by the served as acting, however generously, out of genuine superiority to the other and the service situation lasts only as long as the server remains superior. This is why such seemingly altruistic situations have such an inveterate tendency to corruption. The mother turns her child into the answer to her own need to be needed, or to own and dominate another, or even to recover an unlived aspect of her own life; the teacher makes his or her students into trophies, sycophants, or academic pawns; the doctor mystifies patients in order to feed his or her own self-importance; the priest turns "his people" into substitute children or needy "sheep" over whom to exercise parental or pastoral power.[29] The dynamism at work in this second model is more subtle than in cases of outright domination (and, needless to say, not all such cases of service yield to the flaw in the situation), but it is no less distant from the ideal of service. The server seeks his or her own good by "detouring" through the good of the other. One reason people so often reject or rebel against the insistent "service" of parents, teachers, clergy, and professionals (sometimes using payment to neutralize the dependence incurred) is because they instinctively recognize such service as a subtle but powerful form of domination. They see clearly enough, even if they cannot articulate it, that the server intends to maintain the situation of inequality, not to liberate the served. The service rendered is a statement to both parties of the superiority of the server and the dependence of the served.

The third model is operative in the only situation in which service, of necessity, escapes this fundamental perversion, namely, *friendship*. Friendship is the one human relationship based on equality. If it does not begin between equals it quickly abolishes whatever inequality it discovers or renders the

---

[29] An interesting, basically Jungian, interpretation of service as a subtle exercise of power with a profound tendency to become domination is A. Gugenbühl-Craig, *Power in the Helping Professions,* ed. J. Hillman (Dallas, Tex.: Spring, 1971).

inequality irrelevant within the structure of the relationship.[30] In perfect friendship, which is indeed rare, the good of each is truly the other's good and so, in seeking the good of the friend, one's own good is achieved. But this self-fulfillment involves no subversive seeking of self; it is simply the by-product of the friend's happiness. This is why service rendered between friends is never exacted and creates no debts, demands no return but evokes reciprocity, and never degenerates into covert exploitation. Domination is totally foreign to friendship because domination arises from, expresses, and reinforces inequality. Service between friends, in other words, realizes the pure ideal with which we began this reflection.

It is now easier to see why the Johannine Jesus commands not love of enemies but love unto death of one's friends (15:13). It may be heroic to die for another, but it is only genuine service if the other is truly another self, a friend, for in this case the gift of one's life is experienced as an enrichment rather than as an impoverishment of oneself. To die that a friend might live is to live in a transcendent way. Therefore, John describes God's salvific intention not in terms of sacrifice or retribution but in terms of self-gift: God so loved the world as to give God's only Son to save us (see 3:16). Jesus, acting out of that salvific mission, so loved his own in the world that he laid down his life for them (see 10:17–18; 13:1). Jesus' self-gift was not, in John's perspective, the master's redemption of unworthy slaves but an act of friendship: "No longer do I call you servants . . . you I have called friends" (15:15).

Let us return now to the scene of the foot washing. Jesus symbolizes his impending death, his love of his disciples unto the end, by an act of menial service. He did not choose an act of service proceeding from his real and acknowledged superiority to them as teacher and Lord. Such an act would have expressed the inequality between himself and his disciples, their inferi-

---

[30] The Christian ideal of perfect friendship, perhaps most beautifully expounded by the early medieval monk Aelred of Rievaulx (*Spiritual Friendship* [Washington, D.C.: Cistercian, 1974]) is succinctly summarized by Thomas Aquinas (*Summa Theologiae*, I–II, 26, 4), who says that perfect friendship is distinguished from imperfect by the disinterested desire for the good of the friend, which is the basis of the former. This ideal can be traced back through Augustine into classical antiquity (see the summary in M. A. McNamara, *Friends and Friendship for Saint Augustine* [Staten Island, N.Y.: Alba, 1964], 21–23), where its most famous expositor was Cicero in his *De Amicitia* following Theophrastus's *Periphilias*. The use of the theme of friendship in the Fourth Gospel is unique in the New Testament and merits further study. It seems to me at least possible that John has made theological use of the classical concept in developing his unique presentation of love as the heart of the Christian experience. Since the original appearance of this chapter in *CBQ*, Josephine Massyngberde Ford has written a book on the subject, *Redeemer—Friend and Mother: Salvation in Antiquity and in the Gospel of John* (Minneapolis: Fortress, 1997).

ority to him. Instead, Jesus acted to abolish the inequality between them, deliberately reversing their social positions and roles. To wash another's feet was something that even slaves could not be required to do, but which disciples might do out of reverence for their master.[31] But any act of service is permissible and freeing among friends. By washing his disciples' feet Jesus overcame by love the inequality that existed by nature between himself and those whom he had chosen as friends. He established an intimacy with them that superseded his superiority and signaled their access to everything that he had received from his Father (see 15:15), even to the glory that he had been given as Son (see 17:22).

Peter's adamant resistance to what Jesus was doing can be seen now in a very different light. As in the presentation of Peter's rejection of the passion in the Synoptics, so here, Peter understands more than he articulates. At some level, the narrative suggests, Peter realizes that Jesus, by transcending the inequality between himself and his disciples and inaugurating between them the relationship of friendship, is subverting in principle all structures of domination, and therefore the basis for Peter's own exercise of power and authority. The desire for first place has no function in friendship. The desire of the disciples (and others) to dominate one another and establish their superiority over others was frequently the object of Jesus' instruction and reproach in the Synoptic Gospels (Matt. 20:20–28 and par.; Matt. 23:1–12; Mark 9:38–41 and par.; Mark 10:33–37 and par.; Luke 18:14; 22:24–27). There can be little doubt that this subject was a recurrent theme in the teaching of the historical Jesus. The foot washing is the Fourth Evangelist's dramatic interpretation of this theme. In the Johannine perspective what definitively distinguishes the community that Jesus calls into existence from the power structures so universal in human society is the love of friendship expressing itself in joyful mutual service for which rank is irrelevant. By the foot washing Jesus has transcended and transformed the only ontologically based inequality among human beings, that between himself and us. Peter's refusal of Jesus' act of service was equivalent, then, to a rejection of the death of Jesus understood as the laying down of his life for those he loved and implying a radically new order of human relationships.

It is now possible to take a renewed look at the discourse of Jesus which follows the foot washing (13:12–20). It no longer appears as a simple "doublet" of the first scene, a moralizing interpretation presenting Jesus' prophetic action as an example of humility. Jesus indicates that his action is mysterious and requires reflection, "Do you understand what I have done to you?"

---

[31] Brown, *Gospel According to John*, 2:564.

(13:12).[32] In helping them to understand Jesus calls attention immediately to the very aspect of his act which had scandalized Peter, the transcending of the inequality between himself and them through loving service: "You call me teacher and Lord, and you are right. That is what I am" (13:13). The superiorities and inferiorities of nature and grace are neither denied nor cloaked. They are simply transcended by friendship, rendered irrelevant and inoperative as the basis of their relationship. The principle of relationship between Jesus and his disciples is the love of friendship which transforms what would have been a humiliating self-degradation if performed under the formality of superiority and inferiority into an act of service, a revelation of self-giving love. Jesus goes on to say not that the disciples should wash the feet of their inferiors as an act of self-humiliation (for that is not what Jesus had done for them) but rather that they should "wash one another's feet" (13:14). They should live out among themselves the love of friendship, with its delight in mutual service that knows no order of importance, which Jesus has inaugurated.

CONCLUSIONS ON
HERMENEUTICAL THEORY

We are now in a position to interrogate the process of interpretation just completed in order to draw some conclusions about the methodology used. Of primary interest is the question of how this type of interpretation differs from traditional historical-critical exegesis and what effects flow from this difference.

The crucial difference lies in the role assigned to what has been called "appropriation,"[33] "application,"[34] or simply the discerning of the meaning of the text for the contemporary reader. In traditional exegesis appropriation is usually regarded as a secondary, detachable, and optional procedure to be carried out after the scientific work of historical-critical exegesis has provided the objective content of the passage.[35] The appropriation or application need not be done by the exegete who analyzed the passage, because the objective results of the exegesis are considered to constitute a body of univocal infor-

---

[32] See n. 26 above.

[33] This is Ricoeur's term for the process of making the distance between the world of the text and that of the reader productive (*Interpretation Theory,* 89–95).

[34] This is Gadamer's term for what he considers to constitute, with understanding and explanation, the hermeneutical process (*Truth and Method,* 274–78).

[35] This position is expounded quite clearly by Krister Stendahl in his now famous article, "Contemporary Biblical Theology," *IDB,* 1:418–32.

mation that can be used in various circumstances to ground various applications for contemporary Christians.[36] In other words, appropriation or application is not integral to the interpretive process. The meaning of the text can be ascertained in isolation from the issue of the present reader's transformation.

In the hermeneutical process carried out above the discerning of the meaning of the text for the contemporary reader operated as an integral part of the exegesis itself.[37] It should be noted (because there can be a tendency among exegetes to overlook the fact) that *any* attempt at interpretation is a quest for meaning, and meaning is always meaning *for someone*. Meaning does not exist in the abstract, nor is it "in the text" as if the latter were some kind of semantic container.[38] It is just that, in traditional exegesis, the quest for meaning that is operative in the interpretive process is the search for what the text meant *for the original audience*. The assumption is that this is the primary, objective, and normative meaning since it is supposed to correspond to what the author intended the text to mean and this is considered to be the only "literal" meaning. Therefore, meaning for subsequent audiences, including the present one, is secondary, derived, and valid or well founded to the extent that it coincides with the "original" or "literal" meaning.

By contrast, in the interpretation of the foot washing offered above, the semantic independence of the text in respect to the author's intention was assumed. Therefore, the quest for meaning that was operative was the effort to discern the contemporary meaning of the text, that is, the meaning *for the interpreter*. This led to a different process of interpretation involving a different use of the traditional tools of exegesis in combination with some less traditional methods.

The Different Process

The starting point of the interpretation was a certain preunderstanding which led to an educated guess about the meaning of the text and a subse-

---

[36] This particular attitude implies in a striking way one of the main differences between an exegesis that treats the text as an object to be analyzed and a hermeneutics, which treats the text as a work to be understood. The former regards the results of exegesis as acquired, scientifically substantiated data and application as the use of such data. Both Ricoeur (*Interpretation Theory*, 94) and Gadamer (*Truth and Method*, 278) insist that hermeneutics is not a taking possession of the text by the reader but a mutual submission or interaction between the reader and the text. As is well known, this is also the position adopted by the New Hermeneutic.

[37] Gadamer, *Truth and Method*, 274.

[38] Cf. Ricoeur, *Interpretation Theory*, 1–23.

quent effort to validate the guess.[39] The preunderstanding involved the assumption that Jesus, in this passage, was performing a revelatory sign in the solemn setting of "the hour" and, therefore, that the meaning of the passage would be related to the central preoccupations of the Fourth Gospel. The guess, based on familiarity with the well-known technique of misunderstanding in the Fourth Gospel, was that Peter's reaction was the indicator of the revelatory content. Peter is presented as scandalized by what Jesus was doing; Jesus is intransigent in requiring Peter to overcome the scandal and accept Jesus' action. The guiding question then became: What was Jesus really doing that caused this acute confrontation? What is the meaning of Jesus' action that presents the disciple with an ultimate choice between Jesus' world and that of the sinner?

If one contents oneself with an impersonal and objective reading of the text in its historical context, the answer appears simple enough: Jesus did an act of humble service, a symbolic presentation of his coming humiliation on the cross. This first meaning, complete in itself, is then "doubled" by a second, moral meaning: since Jesus humbled himself, his disciples should willingly do the same.[40]

However, the preunderstanding raises several problems regarding this seemingly obvious interpretation. First, in John's Gospel Jesus' passion is never presented as a humiliation or *kenōsis*, but as his definitive personal glorification and the full revelation of this glory to his disciples. Why then would he choose, as the symbolization of his glorification, an act of self-humiliation? Second, why would the Johannine Jesus give a moral lesson on humility in this solemn context? Mutual love, not humility, is the new commandment according to the Fourth Gospel (13:34–35). Finally, would a gratuitous act of self-humiliation actually constitute a good example of the kind of humility Christians are called upon by Jesus to practice? These problems confirmed a suspicion born of the relative irrelevance of the traditional interpretation, namely, that whatever this passage might have to say about freely chosen self-humiliation, its real point lies elsewhere.

Attention was then concentrated on the precise nature of Peter's refusal as indicated by the structure of his sentences in the Greek text. Peter objected not because Jesus' act was self-humiliating but because the superior was serving the inferior, thereby creating a confusion in the accepted social order that

---

[39] Ricoeur describes the process of guessing and validation of the guess as integral to the dialectic of explanation and understanding (*Interpretation Theory,* 74–79).

[40] See n. 20 above.

Peter could not handle. This reversal was proposed as the locus of the meaning of the text.

What followed, therefore, was not an examination of menial service in the historical-cultural context of first-century Palestine but an existential reflection on the phenomenon of service as it functions in the structures of human relationships as such, regardless of time or place. Such reflection revealed that the contrast between Jesus' understanding of his action and Peter's was really a contrast between service in its ideal form as an expression of love, and service in its corrupted form as an expression of domination. Jesus, as is clear from the teaching in the last discourse(s) on love of friends unto death, was proposing his action as an example of the former; Peter's refusal suggests that he understood it in terms of the latter. In the context of service as domination, Jesus' action was scandalously inappropriate. In the context of friendship it was an act of love. Because of the human situation in which we find ourselves, Jesus' action was subversive of the sinful structures in which not only Peter, but all of us, have a vested interest. This deep contrast in understanding and commitment was suggested as being more than sufficient to explain both Peter's refusal and Jesus' ultimatum as well as establishing a valid and challenging meaning of the text for the contemporary reader.

The conclusions followed directly, viz., that at least one meaning of the foot washing for contemporary disciples lies not in an understanding of Christian ministry in terms of self-humiliation or individual acts of menial service but as a participation in Jesus' work of transforming the sinful structures of domination operative in human society according to the model of friendship expressing itself in joyful mutual service unto death. The validity of the interpretation lies in the fact that it does justice to the text as it stands, accords well with Johannine theology, and is significant in itself for the contemporary reader.

It should now be clear how the principal difference between traditional exegesis and the interpretation suggested, that is, the integration of the appropriation process into the exegesis itself, actually functioned. In order to "make sense" of the dialogue between Jesus and Simon Peter the content of the text was placed in the context of a phenomenology of service within the structure of human relationships. The essential context for understanding the text was *contemporary experience,* not the historical-cultural situation of first-century Palestine. The latter was integrated into the interpretation as a subordinate methodological consideration where necessary. In short, the text was seen to make sense by making sense of the experience of the interpreter, not by transporting the "de-historicized" reader into the world that produced the text.

The Different Use of Traditional Methods

A subordinate question, which might further clarify the method used, concerns the way in which techniques of historical-critical exegesis were used.
Obviously they retain an important place in this type of interpretation, but
they do not dictate the questions that guide the hermeneutical process nor do
they limit, *a priori*, the type of material that can be considered relevant for
understanding.[41] They are used to clarify the original work, that is, the text,
as good lighting or art history might be used to clarify a painting. It is important to know, in other words, whether Peter said, "Lord *you* shall never wash
my feet" or simply "I'll never allow my feet to be washed." It makes a difference whether washing the feet of table guests was a cherished privilege of an
oriental host or a task too menial to be required of a slave. In other words,
philological and historical criticism helps clarify the first level of significance
of the textual elements, especially when these elements are ambiguous because
of historical, cultural, or linguistic remoteness.

In a similar way, comparison of Peter's behavior in this scene with Synoptic
material that seems to be analogous helped to indicate the direction of inquiry
into the meaning of his objection and Jesus' reply, while knowledge of the
Johannine theological perspective and Johannine literary techniques helped
indicate the insufficiency of certain seemingly obvious interpretations.

The techniques of historical-critical exegesis are called into play not to
determine methodologically the object of interpretation as the intention of
the author but to clarify whatever in the text is unclear because of historical

---

[41] A fundamental insight underlying the interdisciplinary challenge to historical-critical
exegesis considered as an exhaustive methodology is that *method determines object*. It not only
determines which aspects of a reality are to be considered and how they are to be treated but
it also declares irrelevant any elements that do not answer the questions which the method
raises. This point has been made from a theological perspective by Peter Stuhlmacher, *Historical Criticism and Theological Interpretation of Scripture: Towards a Hermeneutics of Consent*,
trans. Roy A. Harrisville (Philadelphia: Fortress, 1977); from a fundamentalist perspective by
Gerhard Maier, *The End of the Historical Critical Method* (St. Louis: Concordia, 1977); from
a psychological-sociological point of view by Walter Wink, *The Bible in Human Transformation: Toward a New Paradigm for Biblical Study* (Philadelphia: Fortress, 1973). It is also fundamental to the contributions of structuralism (see Patte, *What is Structural Exegesis?* especially
9–20), and of literary criticism. Among the representatives of the latter who have taken a special and theoretical interest in biblical interpretation is Amos Niven Wilder, particularly in his
Early Christian Rhetoric: The Language of the Gospel (Cambridge, Mass.: Harvard University
Press, 1971).

The increasing seriousness of attention to the challenge being addressed to the biblical
establishment was signaled by the presidential address to the Catholic Biblical Association by
George T. Montague, "Hermeneutics and the Teaching of Scripture," *CBQ* 41 (1979): 1–17.

distance. Historical methodology, as well as form and redaction criticism, are necessary because texts are historical artifacts and are about historical events recorded by writers according to their own purposes and for their audiences. But historical-critical methodology is neither the primary nor a sufficient methodology because the meaning of the text is not in the past to be recovered but in the present to be discovered.

Seeing and Believing
in the Glorified Jesus
(John 20:1–10)

In this chapter I wish to suggest an interpretation of the first episode in the Johannine resurrection narrative, the so-called race to the tomb of Simon Peter and the Beloved Disciple, centering the inquiry on the face veil (*soudarion*), which, according to John 20:7, the two disciples found in the tomb of Jesus on Easter morning. This verse of the Fourth Gospel has occasioned some of the most ingenious hypotheses, not to mention some of the wildest flights of fancy, in the history of Johannine scholarship. At risk of adding to one or both of these questionable categories, I would like to propose yet another interpretation, which I will summarize here by way of introduction: The face veil is best understood as a Johannine *sēmeion,* that is, as a sign (symbol) in and through which a properly disposed person can encounter the glory of God revealed in Jesus.[1]

It is difficult to treat any passage of John's Gospel without getting oneself involved in the numerous critical questions about the Fourth Gospel that remain unsolved. The position one adopts on these questions inevitably determines, to some extent, one's exegesis of the passage under consideration. This is perhaps especially true for the resurrection narrative material and particularly for the tomb account in John 20:1–10. The passage raises at least the question of sources,[2] of the necessity of resurrection material in a Gospel in which the glorification of Jesus is accomplished by his death on the cross,[3] of

---

[1] See chapter 4 on the contemporary distinction between sign and symbol and why the Johannine "signs" are actually best thought of as symbols.

[2] Raymond E. Brown, *The Gospel According to John,* 2 vols., Anchor Bible 29, 29A (Garden City, N.Y.: Doubleday, 1966, 1970), 2:975–78; Giuseppe Ghiberti, *I racconti pasquali del capitolo 20 di Giovanni,* Studi Biblici (Brescia: Paideia, 1972), 79–99.

[3] M. Jack Suggs, "The Passion and Resurrection Narratives," in *Jesus and Man's Hope,* ed. D. G. Miller and D. Y. Hadidian (Pittsburgh: Pittsburgh Theological Seminary, 1971), 325;

the identity of the Beloved Disciple and his relationship with Simon Peter,[4] of the relationship of seeing to believing,[5] and of the role of the signs in faith.[6] Obviously, it is impossible to treat all of these preliminary questions directly in a chapter of this length. But I think it important to state, without attempting to fully justify them, three critical presuppositions that govern the proposed exegesis of vv. 3–8 and the resulting interpretation of the face veil as a Johannine *sēmeion*.

PRESUPPOSITIONS

First, the Johannine tomb narrative is theologically original and cannot be interpreted in terms of Synoptic preoccupations. In all three Synoptics, the empty tomb, in and of itself, does not lead to Easter faith. Although it is quite probably historically accurate that the tomb of Jesus was found empty on Easter morning, this phenomenon remained ambiguous until it was interpreted by the angel(s), whose words were a reading back into the tomb discovery accounts of what was first revealed by the appearances of the risen Jesus. In other words, according to the Synoptics, it was only after the disciples had come to believe, on the basis of the appearances, that Jesus was risen from the dead, that the empty tomb took on theological and apologetic value as a historical trace of an eschatological event. In John, on the contrary, the Beloved Disciple came to faith (and, as I will try to show, it is genuine paschal faith) on the basis of what he saw in the tomb, prior to any appearance of Jesus and/or angelic interpretation. This constitutes a substantive reworking of the traditional empty tomb material, a reworking whose originality invites and justifies the attempt to discern characteristically Johannine theological concerns in this pericope.

Second, the two elements in the pericope that call attention to themselves

---

Christopher F. Evans, *Resurrection and the New Testament,* Studies in Biblical Theology, 2nd ser. (London: SCM, 1970), 116; Heinrich Schlier, *Über die Auferstehung Jesu Christi,* Kriterion 10 (Einsiedeln: Johannes, 1968), 25–26.

[4] William Barclay, *Introduction to John and the Acts of the Apostles* (Philadelphia: Westminster, 1976); Robert Mahoney, *Two Disciples at the Tomb: The Background and Message of John 20:1–10,* Theologie und Wirklichkeit 6 (Bern/Frankfurt-am-Main: H. Lang & P. Lang, 1974).

[5] Sandra M. Schneiders, "Symbolism and the Sacramental Principle in the Fourth Gospel," in *Segni e sacramenti nel vangelo di Giovanni,* ed. P.-R. Tragan, Studia Anselmiana 66 (Rome: Editrice Anselmiana, 1977), 227 n. 15.

[6] W. Nicol, *The Semeia in the Fourth Gospel: Tradition and Redaction,* NovTSup (Leiden: E. J. Brill, 1972).

as probable indices of the specifically Johannine theological concerns are the figure of the Beloved Disciple in relation to Simon Peter and the contents of the tomb, particularly the face veil, which leads to the reaction "he both saw and believed." The partially parallel text of Luke 24:24, "Some of those who were with us went to the tomb and found it just as the women had said; but him they did not see," bears witness to a tradition, common at least to Luke and John, that more than one disciple, probably male, went to the tomb to verify the report of the women disciples that it was empty. Although I consider Luke 24:12 (which identifies Peter as the one who went alone to the tomb) an interpolation or at least an assimilation of Luke to John, and therefore worthless as an independent witness to the identity of the male visitors to the tomb, it is certainly not unlikely that Peter was among those who went. The "other disciple" (a special Johannine character identified in John 20:2 as the "one Jesus loved") is inserted into v. 3 in exactly the same way he is inserted into John 18:15. In the tomb scene he is then played off, physically and spiritually, against Simon Peter in a way that has no parallel in the Synoptics. Apart from the doubtful text, Luke 24:12, there is no reference anywhere else in the New Testament to the contents of the tomb, and even Luke 24:12 mentions only the "cloth" and not the "face veil." Consequently, what is specific to John's tomb account is the role of the Beloved Disciple in relation to Simon Peter and the presence of the burial cloths, especially the face veil in the tomb.

Third, the pericope John 20:3–10 is intrinsic to the Johannine resurrection narrative, which is a unified whole expressing John's theological interpretation of the resurrection. Furthermore, it is an integral part of the first half of the chapter, vv. 1–18, which recounts the events at the tomb in the garden where Jesus was buried. This first half of chapter 20 is dominated by the thematic question, Where is the Lord?[7] which is answered in two stages: the Beloved Disciple discovers that the Lord is glorified with the Father, and Mary Magdalene discovers that the Lord is now present in the community of the disciples. In other words, Jesus has gone away and has come to them as he promised in John 14:28.

THE PRIORITY OF THE BELOVED DISCIPLE

Against the background of these three presuppositions, namely, that the Johannine tomb account should be interpreted in function of Johannine the-

---

[7] Paul Minear, "'We Don't Know Where . . .' John 20:2," *Int* 30 (1976): 125–39.

ological concerns; that the principal indices of these special Johannine concerns are the relationship of the Beloved Disciple to Simon Peter and the contents of the tomb; and that the Johannine tomb account is not an isolated narrative but an integral part of the Fourth Evangelist's theological interpretation of the resurrection, we can now turn to John 20:3–10 and attempt to decipher the evangelist's intent in creating this unique scene. A glance at the structure of the pericope will help to isolate the significant elements. Verses 3 and 10 constitute an *inclusio,* that is, a clear beginning and end marking off the episode: they went out to the tomb . . . they returned home. Verses 4a and 9 show us, respectively, the two disciples together physically at the beginning of the episode: "The two ran together," and together spiritually in their ignorance of the scripture at the end of the episode: "They did not yet understand the scripture that he must rise from the dead." In between, in vv. 4b–8b, the two disciples separate, first physically and then spiritually. It is, therefore, with these verses that we must concern ourselves in order to discover the point of the pericope.

Most, although not all, commentators have agreed on two fairly obvious items of interpretation: first, that the point of the pericope is contained in the words about the Beloved Disciple in v. 8b, "He both saw and believed" and therefore that his belief is somehow genuine paschal faith; second, that the clue to his spiritual superiority over Simon Peter is somehow given in the fact of his arriving first at the tomb.

To start with the second point, it is clear that the evangelist attaches importance to the fact that the Beloved Disciple *arrived* at the tomb first. The Fourth Evangelist mentions it three times: directly in v. 4b, by implication in v. 6a, and again in v. 8a. The evangelist also attaches importance to the fact that Peter *entered* the tomb first. Commentators have interpreted this in all sorts of ways, for example, that the Beloved Disciple, although swifter than Simon Peter, was acknowledging Peter's ecclesiastical preeminence,[8] or that Peter represented the priority of Jewish Christians in the order of evangelization, although not in the readiness of faith.[9] More recently Rudolf Schnackenburg (in the third volume of his commentary) and his student Robert Mahoney, in his doctoral dissertation on John 20:1–10, have suggested theological reasons for the separate performances of the two disciples.[10] According to these authors, each of the two had a different task to accomplish within

---

[8] Thus Rudolf Schnackenburg, "Der Jünger, den Jesus liebte," in *Evangelisch-Katholischer Kommentar zum Neuen Testament,* Vorarbeiten Heft 2 (Zurich: Benziger, 1970), 97–117.

[9] Rudolf Bultmann, *The Gospel of John: A Commentary,* trans. George R. Beasley-Murray (Oxford: Blackwell, 1971), 685.

[10] Mahoney, *Two Disciples,* 251–52, 259.

the pericope. Schnackenburg assigns the tasks as follows: Peter, as the leader of the Twelve, was to be the witness to the state of affairs in the tomb of Jesus, which had assumed, by the end of the first century, considerable apologetic importance; the Beloved Disciple, on the other hand, was to give the response of faith that was called for by the facts.

Mahoney further suggests that the Beloved Disciple alone has the assignment of responding in faith because the Fourth Evangelist does not want to jeopardize either the tradition that Easter faith was based on the appearance of the glorified Jesus and not on the empty tomb, or the tradition that Peter came to faith by receiving the first Easter Christophany. By having an unknown disciple respond to the contents of the tomb, the evangelist shows the reader that the tomb *should* have led to faith, but, at least in most cases, it did not.[11] Mahoney, because of what I consider his major methodological error—namely, considering John 20:1–10 as an isolated and independent unit,[12]—fails to notice that John not only does not safeguard the tradition that Peter received the first Easter Christophany, but he virtually denies it by assigning the first Christophany to Mary Magdalene.[13] Furthermore, because the Beloved Disciple, not Peter, is the authority in the Johannine community, the fact that the Beloved Disciple came to paschal faith at the sight of the contents of the tomb gives even greater weight to this belief than if Peter had come to believe. Lindars gives the most promising indication of a solution when he suggests that the reason for the disjunction in the arrival and entrance into the tomb of the Beloved Disciple is literary. The evangelist is using a delaying tactic to build up to the climax of the pericope, the Beloved Disciple's believing.[14]

My suggestion is a combination theological-literary explanation, namely, that in order to clearly identify the face veil as a genuine *sēmeion* (Johannine sign) the evangelist has to present the Beloved Disciple's experience as taking place in two steps, using Peter's experience as a foil. Verses 4b–6b are perfectly balanced: the Beloved Disciple, without entering the tomb, sees the cloths. Peter, entering the tomb, also sees the cloths. So far there is no difference in the experience of the one outside who arrived first and the one inside who arrived second. In v. 7 the difference is announced and described. Peter, who is inside, sees something that the Beloved Disciple did not see from outside,

---

[11] Ibid., 259–60.

[12] Ibid., 283.

[13] See chapter 6, pp. 110–13.

[14] Barnabas Lindars, *The Gospel of John*, New Century Bible (London: Oliphants, 1972), 600–601.

namely, the face veil arranged in a certain way. Then the Beloved Disciple enters, sees what Peter has already seen, including what he could not see from outside, namely, the face veil, and he believes.

By having the Beloved Disciple remain outside until after Peter saw both the cloths and the face veil, the evangelist accomplishes two things. First, the Fourth Evangelist makes it clear that the cause of faith is neither the absence of the body of Jesus from the tomb nor the cloths, for the Beloved Disciple sees both of these from outside without coming to faith, but rather it is the face veil, which can only be seen upon entering. Second, the evangelist makes it clear that the face veil is a genuine *sēmeion*, a perceptible reality that is, in itself, ambiguous, for Peter saw it but did not come to believe. The two-stage arrival of the Beloved Disciple allows the reader to distinguish what really constitutes the *sēmeion*, namely, the *face veil*, and to realize that the face veil is truly a *sēmeion*.

THE VEIL'S SIGNIFICANCE

Two intimately related questions remain: Of what is the face veil a sign? and What did the Beloved Disciple believe? First, of what is the face veil a sign? An enormous amount of research has been done on the word "face veil."[15] It appears only four times in the New Testament: twice in John (11:44 and 20:7) and in Luke 19:20 and Acts 19:2, where it clearly means "napkin" or "handkerchief." Every indication is that it means handkerchief, napkin, or a small piece of cloth. John uses it for the veil covering the face of Lazarus in 11:44 and for the cloth covering the face of Jesus in 20:7. It is actually a Greek transliteration of the Latin *sudarium*, meaning handkerchief. But the most interesting fact about the word is that in the Aramaic of the Targums (*Pseudo-Jonathan* and *Neofiti*), it is used to translate the Hebrew word for the veil covering the face of Moses in Exod. 34:33–35. In the Septuagint, this is translated by *kalymma*, which is the normal word for "veil." But the Hebrew word in Exod. 34:33–35 is not an ordinary Hebrew word for veil. It is a special word used only for the face veil of Moses. If John's community, which according to the most recent research was probably originally composed of Palestinian Jews,[16] was familiar with the Old Testament in Targum form,

---

[15] F.-M. Braun, *Le linceul de Turin et l'évangile de S. Jean: Etude de critique et d'exégèse* (Tournai/Paris: Casterman, 1939).

[16] Raymond E. Brown, "Johannine Ecclesiology—the Community's Origins," *Int* 31 (1977): 380–83, 385–87.

then the word "face veil" in John's account would immediately have recalled to them the face veil of Moses in a way that *kalymma* would not.

The face veil's position in the tomb, "not lying with the cloths but apart, wrapped up into one place," has been interpreted with amazing ingenuity by commentators wishing to establish and/or maximize the apologetical value of the Johannine tomb account. Some scholars have even attempted to reconstruct the scene in drawings! But it is probably not the evangelist's intent to give an eyewitness account of the details in the tomb. The point is in the perfect tense passive participle "having been wrapped up."[17] The point is that the face veil was not simply dropped or left as the cloths were, but that it was definitively wrapped up and put aside. Like Moses, who put aside the veil when he ascended to meet God in glory, Jesus, the new Moses, has put aside the veil of his flesh as he ascends into the presence of God to receive from God that glory which he had with the Father before the world was made (see 17:5). But, unlike Moses, who reassumed the veil each time he returned from God to the people, the new Moses has definitively laid aside the veil, for now he is no longer in the world, but has gone to the Father (see 17:11).

That the symbolic use of the veil of Moses to contrast the old and new covenants was not unfamiliar to the early church is clear from Paul's extended reference to it in 2 Cor. 3:7–8, where the veil is said to cover the minds of unconverted Jews until it is taken away by Christ. John's use of it to symbolize the life in the flesh of the unglorified Jesus would be perfectly consonant with his symbolic use of Old Testament realities, which, in the Fourth Gospel, take on their full meaning only when they are illuminated by the words and works of Jesus.

If it is correct that the face veil is a genuine *sēmeion*, that is, a perceptible reality that mediates the revelation of God in Jesus, then the response of the Beloved Disciple, "He both saw and believed," is the perfect response and precisely that which is evoked by the signs throughout the Fourth Gospel. Peter's failure to believe only emphasizes the *sēmeion* character of the face veil. The signs in the Fourth Gospel are, of their nature, ambiguous. They do not necessitate belief. Peter's failure to believe makes it clear to the reader that paschal faith is not *deduced* from the contents of the tomb as from a physical proof of the resurrection. The paschal believing of the Beloved Disciple is the faith response to revelation encountered in sign.

This leads to the second question: What did the Beloved Disciple believe? Verse 9 hastens to add that neither Peter nor the Beloved Disciple as yet

[17] Maximilian Zerwick, *Biblical Greek Illustrated by Examples,* trans. and adapted from the 4th Latin ed. by J. Smith (Rome: Biblical Institute Press, 1963), 96, 97.

understood the scripture that Jesus must rise from the dead. "Believe" is used in the absolute in v. 8b. The absolute use of "believe" in the Fourth Gospel usually suggests primarily an active spiritual state of personal adherence to Jesus the revealer and readiness for whatever he will do.[18] Thus, the Beloved Disciple's faith at this point is best compared to that to which Jesus calls Martha in John 11:40: "Did I not tell you that if you would believe you would see the glory of God?" Only after the raising of Lazarus does Martha understand explicitly in what the glory consists, namely, that Jesus is the resurrection and the life (see 11:25). But in order for the object of faith to become explicit, she must believe; that is, she must adhere to Jesus the revealer in open readiness for whatever he will do.

We can see something quite analogous in the Beloved Disciple at the tomb of Jesus if we bear in mind that there is a real distinction in John between the glorification of Jesus that takes place on the cross when Jesus goes to the Father and the resurrection, by which the glorified Jesus returns to his own. What the face veil reveals is the former, that Jesus, the new Moses, has ascended to God, that he has gone away. This the Beloved Disciple believes. Only with the appearances will it become clear that Jesus has also returned to his own to take up his abode in them, constituting them as his presence in the world. In this respect the Fourth Gospel does not contradict the Synoptic tradition that the resurrection was known not through the empty tomb but through the appearances of the risen Jesus. John, however, underlines both dimensions of the paschal reality, the glorification of Jesus by his return to the Father *and* his resurrection or return to his own. The Beloved Disciple's grasping of the first, that Jesus is glorified, is the beginning of the answer to Mary Magdalene's question, "Where is the Lord?": he is with God in glory. This prepares the reader for the rest of the answer, which will be given to Mary Magdalene herself in 20:11–18: he is where the disciples are gathered together. Both parts of the answer prepare for the third episode of chapter 20, Jesus' inauguration of the new covenant by pouring forth upon the community of his disciples the spirit promised in Jeremiah and Ezekiel. Thus, the episode in 20:1–10 is the first stage in the revelation of the meaning of Easter as it is perceived by the Fourth Evangelist.

The meaning of the paschal mystery as the glorification of Jesus, the return of Jesus to his own, and the constitution of the community as his new presence in the world, is actually set forth by Jesus himself in the last discourses in chapters 14–16. Chapter 20 simply uses the traditional resurrection mate-

---

[18] Lindars, *Gospel of John,* 602.

rial to involve the reader narratively in the accomplishment of that which was theologically expounded in the discourses. The face veil thus emerges, within the context of the Fourth Gospel as a whole and its highly original resurrection narrative in particular, as a genuine Johannine *sēmeion* calling forth from the Beloved Disciple, the authority and ideal disciple in the Johannine community, the response to the revelation of divine glory in perceptible realities: he both saw and believed.

13

Encountering and Proclaiming the Risen Jesus (John 20:11-18)

This chapter was originally prepared as a contribution to a symposium of Johannine scholars reading texts of John from different perspectives. Each contributor was asked to be "up front about [her or his] perspective, objective, and strategy" so that the role of the reader/interpreter in the reading offered would be clear. My perspective on the biblical text in general and the Johannine Gospel in particular is that of a believing feminist interpreter who regards the text as potentially revelatory and revelatory experience as personally transformative. I take completely seriously the original conclusion of John's Gospel in 20:30–31, which says that this text was written to enlighten and strengthen the faith of the reader in order that the believer may be transformed, that is, might have eternal life. My objective as an interpreter is to collaborate with and to serve that basic intent of the literature itself by interpreting the text in such wise that it is able to exercise its transformative power on the reader.

My strategy for achieving a transformative interpretation involves two conscious commitments. First, I aim to achieve *a* (not *the*) complete or integrated reading of the whole text rather than an exegesis of fragments, which means that my reading of the Mary Magdalene episode should make sense of that episode in itself but also in the context of the whole of the resurrection narrative in John (chap. 20) and eventually within the whole of the Gospel. This integrated reading, if it is to be a transformative one, should be both faithful to the text and creatively interactive with contemporary religious concerns. Second, I am concerned to expose patriarchal and androcentric bias in the text when such is evident and in the history of interpretation, where it is rampant, and to counteract this bias by a consciously feminist approach to the text. In actual practice, my strategy is interdisciplinary, making use of historical-critical, literary-critical, and theological methods in the service of an agenda of transformation. In other words, the overarching perspective from which I am reading the biblical text is feminist spirituality, and my methodology is essentially interdisciplinary.

PLACING THE MARY MAGDALENE EPISODE
WITHIN JOHN 20

The Mary Magdalene episode includes the two introductory verses of chapter 20 recounting Mary's discovery of the empty tomb on Easter morning and her report to Simon Peter and the other disciple (immediately identified in an obvious redactional move as the Beloved Disciple) that (the body of) the Lord had been taken away, and vv. 11–18 recounting the appearance of the glorified Jesus to Mary. This account must first be situated within chapter 20 as a whole, which is the Johannine Easter narrative. As has often been remarked by commentators, the Fourth Gospel does not "need" a resurrection narrative[1] in the same sense that the Synoptic Gospels do, because in John the death of Jesus, his lifting up on the cross, is his glorification[2] and he does not, therefore, require divine vindication after a shameful execution. In fact, as I will try to show, the primary purpose of chapter 20 is not to tell the reader what happened to Jesus after his death but to explore, through the paradigmatic and foundational experiences of the disciples, the effect on and meaning for believers of Jesus' glorification. Elsewhere I have suggested that there are two sides to the paschal event in John: *glorification* is what happens to Jesus on the cross; *resurrection* is the communication to Jesus' disciples of his paschal glory through his return to them in the Spirit.[3] When Jesus says, in 11:25, "I am the resurrection" rather than "I am the resurrected one" or "the one who will rise," he describes the role of his glorification in the life of believers, in whom he indwells, rather than something that occurred in his own life.

Chapter 20 is divided into two parts. The first, vv. 1–18, takes place in the garden of the tomb before dawn on Easter morning; the second, vv. 19–29, takes place somewhere in Jerusalem, where the community of Jesus' disciples is gathered on Easter evening and the following Sunday. The first part is gov-

---

[1] See, e.g., Christopher F. Evans, *Resurrection and the New Testament,* Studies in Biblical Theology, 2nd ser. (London: SCM, 1970), 116.

[2] See John 3:14; 8:28; 12:32, 34 on the "lifting up" and 12:16, 23, 28; 13:31–32 on the "glorification."

[3] Sandra Schneiders, *The Johannine Resurrection Narrative: An Exegetical and Theological Study of John 20 as a Synthesis of Johannine Spirituality* (Ann Arbor, Mich.: University Microfilms, 1982), 97–141.

erned by the question, *Where* is the Lord? while the second part is concerned with forming and missioning the community of the new covenant once that all-important question has been satisfactorily answered.

The theme of part 1 is announced by Mary Magdalene in v. 2. Having seen that the *stone* has been removed from the tomb, she runs to Simon Peter and his companion and announces that "the *Lord* has been removed" and that "we do not know *where*" he is (emphasis added). As Donatian Mollat pointed out many years ago, the adverbs *pou* and *hopou* ("where") have a thematic importance in John's Gospel.[4] Both occur very frequently (eighteen and thirty times respectively) and most often in theologically important contexts. The first question addressed to Jesus in John is that of the first two disciples, "Rabbi, where do you dwell?" (1:38). A principal difference between Jesus and his enemies in John is that he knows where he is from and where he is going and they do not (see 8:14). His enemies cannot go where he goes (e.g., 7:34, 36; 8:21, 22), but his true disciples and servants can (e.g., 14:3, 4; 17:24). In the last discourse(s)[5] the question of where Jesus is going becomes central (14:5). While Jesus is in the world he is the Light of the world and those who follow him walk securely knowing where they are going, but in the dark hour of the passion his disciples do not know where Jesus has gone or how to follow him (see 9:4). Mary Magdalene voices the question of all disciples caught in the pre-dawn darkness of the scandal of the cross, "Where is the Lord?" In fact, the "where" of Jesus in John is not primarily spatial or geographical location. It denotes indwelling, the communion between Jesus and God and between Jesus and his disciples. Where Jesus is, is in the bosom of the Father. He comes into the world to give the power of divine filiation to his disciples. He then departs again to resume his primordial glory in the presence of God and returns to initiate his disciples into that glory. Until the final phase, that is, until Jesus returns to his own, the darkness of the hour envelopes all.

The answer to the question Where is the Lord? is given in two stages in part 1 of chapter 20. In vv. 3–10 the Beloved Disciple, upon seeing the sign, the face cloth of the new Moses definitively rolled up and laid aside, comes to believe in the glorification. Unlike Simon Peter, who remains uncompre-

---

[4] Donatian Mollat, "La découverte du tombeau vide (Jn 20, 1–9)," *Assemblées du Seigneur* 221 (1969): 90–100.

[5] Fernando F. Segovia has made a strong case for the unity of John 13–16, which many commentators have treated as a composite of disparate discourses (Segovia, *The Farewell of the Word: The Johannine Call to Abide* [Minneapolis: Fortress, 1991]). Although I find Segovia's position persuasive I am not taking a position on the question here since it is not significant for my own argument.

hending of what he sees in the tomb, the Beloved Disciple "sees and believes" (20:8), a virtually certain linguistic indication of the presence of a *sēmeion* (a revelatory sign) in John.[6] The Beloved Disciple knows that Jesus' historical presence among them has ended in his definitive ascent into the presence of God through his glorification on the cross. The glory of Jesus is no longer veiled in his earthly humanity or in the ambiguity of his physical death. A new dispensation has begun. But neither disciple yet understands the scripture about Jesus' resurrection (see 20:9), that is, Jesus' return to his own. The first part of the answer to the question Where is the Lord? is that Jesus is in God. His glorification is his return to the Father, his repossession of the glory that he had with God before the world was made (see 17:5).

The second part of the answer, however, is that Jesus, who is glorified in God, has also returned to his own. "I go away and I come to you," he had promised in 14:28.[7] The resurrection, the return of Jesus to his own, is revealed in the encounter between Jesus and Mary Magdalene in vv. 11–18.

THE STRUCTURE OF JOHN 20:11–18
AND ITS POSITION IN THE TRADITION

Two preliminary considerations that are important for the interpretation of the Mary Magdalene scene concern the literary structure of the pericope and the place of the Johannine account in the theological tradition history of the resurrection appearances.

Structurally, the episode can be divided into three sections, each governed by a thematic participle. The first section, vv. 11–15, stands under the sign of *klaiousa*, weeping, which occurs at the very beginning of that section. Mary stands outside the tomb, weeping.[8] The second section, v. 16, is governed by *strapheisa*, "turning," which occurs exactly in the middle of the verse as the pivot between Jesus' address to Mary and her response to him. This turning, as we will see, is not a physical action but a conversion of the pre-Easter disciple away from the "things that lie behind" and toward the glorified Jesus, the only true Teacher. The third section, vv. 17–18, culminates in *angelousa*, "announcing," which occurs at the end of the scene when Mary goes to the

---

[6] See chapter 12, in which I treat the face-veil episode in detail.

[7] It is important to note that both verbs in this text are in the present: *hypagō kai erchomai pros hymas*. It could perhaps be paraphrased, "My going away (by glorification on the cross) is my coming to you (in resurrection or as the resurrection and the life)."

[8] "Wept" or "weeping" occurs four times in the five verses of this section, in v. 11 twice, in v. 13, and in v. 15.

community to proclaim that she has seen the Lord and to deliver the Easter kerygma that he has entrusted to her. We will take up each of these sections in more detail shortly.

But first it is necessary to situate this pericope theologically and ecclesiologically. Until quite recently postpatristic commentators have, virtually to a man (and I use the word designedly), treated the appearance to Mary Magdalene as a minor, private, personal, or unofficial encounter between Jesus and his (hysterical?) female follower, in which he kindly consoles her before making his official and public Easter appearances to male witnesses and commissioning them to carry on his mission in the world.[9] More recently, commentators under the influence of feminist scholarship have tended to recognize the raw sexism of this traditional interpretation, which ignores the plain content and intent of the Johannine text because patriarchal bias and the ecclesiastical power agenda blinded the interpreters to the apostolic identity of a woman witness and its potential repercussions on contemporary church order.[10]

Although I cannot mount the entire argument in this chapter, it should suffice to point out that the tradition that the first appearance of the risen Jesus was to Mary Magdalene, either alone or with women companions, is attested in Matt. 28:9–10, in the Markan appendix 16:9–10, as well as in John. It is most likely that John and Matthew, at least, represent literarily independent traditions, while Mark conflates a variety of traditions. In conjunction with the agreement of all four Gospels that women were the primary and/or exclusive witnesses of the death, burial, and empty tomb,[11] the multiply attested tradition that the first resurrection appearance was to Mary Magdalene must be judged as probably authentically historical.[12] This is

---

[9] E.g., Raymond E. Brown, *The Virginal Conception and Bodily Resurrection of Jesus* (London: Geoffrey Chapman, 1973), 101 n. 170; Xavier Léon-Dufour, *Resurrection and the Message of Easter,* trans. R. N. Wilson (New York: Holt, Rinehart & Winston, 1975); Augustin George, "Les récits d'apparitions aux onze à partir de Luc 24, 26–53," in *La Résurrection du Christ et l'exégèse moderne,* Lectio Divina (Paris: Cerf, 1969), 76.

[10] For a summary of the tradition of interpretation and an excellent marshaling of the data for reinterpretation, see Gerald O'Collins and Daniel Kendall, "Mary Magdalene as Major Witness to Jesus' Resurrection," *TS* 48 (1987): 631–46.

[11] Matt. 27:55–56, 61; 28:1–8; Mark 15:40–41, 47; 16:1–8; Luke 23:49, 55–56; 24:1–10; John 19:25–30; 20:1–2. Interestingly enough, John is the only Gospel that does not explicitly state that the burial was witnessed by the woman/women, although this is clearly implied by the fact that Mary Magdalene knows the location of the tomb on Easter morning.

[12] Raymond E. Brown, even in his early and already cited work *Virginal Conception* (p. 101 n. 170) suggests that the tradition of the appearance to Mary Magdalene, although "minor" and not the basis of apostolic witness, was very possibly historical.

especially so because the Mary Magdalene tradition rivaled the Lukan and Pauline tradition that the Easter protophany (the foundational first appearance) was to Peter and would surely have been suppressed if that had been possible. The rivalry between Peter and Mary Magdalene is vividly detailed in the extracanonical literature of the first Christian centuries such as the *Gospel of Peter,* the *Secret Gospel of Mark,* the Coptic *Gospel of Thomas,* the *Gospel of Mary,* the *Wisdom of Jesus Christ,* and others, which François Bovon reviewed in a 1984 article in *New Testament Studies.*[13] Bovon suggests that this literature was declared heterodox less because of its doctrinal content than because of the embarrassing priority among the disciples, and especially in relation to Peter, that it assigns to Mary Magdalene. In any case, it is clear from the text itself that the Fourth Gospel intends to present Mary Magdalene as the recipient of the first Easter Christophany upon which the paschal faith of the Johannine community was based just as Luke's community's faith rested on the appearance to Peter, the Gentile churches on that to Paul, and the Jerusalem community's on the appearances to James and the eleven. According to John, it is Mary Magdalene to whom the glorified Jesus entrusted the paschal kerygma in its characteristically Johannine form, whom he sent to announce that Easter message to the community of disciples, and who fulfilled successfully that apostolic commission so that the disciples in John, unlike those in Luke who dismissed the testimony of the women returning from the empty tomb (see Luke 24:11), were fully prepared to recognize and accept Jesus' appearance in their midst that evening (see John 20:20). From every point of view and according to every criterion developed in the New Testament, Mary Magdalene is, in John's Gospel, the apostolic witness upon whom the paschal faith of the community was founded.

SECTION 1: HOPELESS SUFFERING
AND SPIRITUAL BLINDNESS

Let us turn now to section 1 of the Mary Magdalene episode. This is a highly symbolic scene. It is still dark. The pre-dawn obscurity noted in v. 1 seems still to preside at least over Mary's inner landscape if not over the garden itself.[14] Only the Fourth Evangelist places the tomb of Jesus in a garden and describes Mary's ironic mistaking of Jesus for the gardener. His address to her

---

[13] François Bovon, "Le privilège pascal de marie-madeleine," *NTS* 30 (1984): 50–62.

[14] See Corina Combet-Galland, "L'Aube encore obscure: approche sémiotique de Jean 20," *Foi et vie* (September 1987) 17–25.

as "woman" and her action of "peering" through her tears into the tomb expressed by *parekypsen,* a word that occurs rarely in the New Testament[15] and, strikingly, in the Septuagint of the Canticle of Canticles 2:9 in describing the search for the beloved, alert the reader to the fact that this garden setting is intended to evoke both the creation account in Genesis, where God walks and talks with the first couple in the garden (see Gen. 2:15–17; 3:8) and promises salvation through a woman (see Gen. 3:15), and the Canticle of Canticles, which, by the time this Gospel was written, was understood to be the hymn of the covenant between Israel and Yahweh. In this garden of new creation and new covenant, Jesus, who is both the promised liberator of the new creation and the spouse of the new Israel, encounters the woman, who is, symbolically, the Johannine community, the church, the new people of God.

But Mary is distraught, overcome with hopeless sorrow. She is so fixated on the loss of the body of Jesus, which she obviously exhaustively identifies with Jesus himself, that she does not even register surprise at being addressed by angelic messengers. Like the cherubim in Exod. 25:22 and 38:7–8, who sit, one on either end of the mercy seat of the ark of the covenant, these angels in white sit "one at the head and one at the feet where the body of Jesus had lain" (v. 12). Mary is seeking Jesus, a quintessentially positive enterprise in John's Gospel, but her grief has spiritually blinded her, rendered her incapable of revelation even when Jesus himself stands before her and speaks to her. She does not recognize him. The evangelist indulges in delicious irony in having Mary identify Jesus as precisely who he is, the gardener, while completely missing the symbolic point of her own materially correct identification. Jesus challenges her weeping, trying to refocus her distraught attention from his physical body to his person with the question, "Whom [not what] do you seek?" (v. 15). But Mary remains fixated in her obsession, again interchanging "him" who is missing with the "body" which is missing as she had interchanged "the Lord" and "the stone" in reporting the body missing in v. 2. In this first section of the pericope, under the sign of *klaiousa,* that is, blinding spiritual sadness and hopelessness, the evangelist dramatically prepares the reader to accept a new mode of Jesus' presence. To do this one must surrender the obsessional fixation on the physical presence of the earthly Jesus and prepare to cross the threshold from the economy of history into that of the resurrection.

---

[15] Actually, it occurs only here and in 20:5, where it describes the Beloved Disciple looking into the tomb before the arrival of Simon Peter, and in Luke 24:12, which is a "western non-interpolation" very possibly dependent on John or on a common source.

SECTION 2: CONVERSION

Section 2 of the pericope is made up of a single verse, one of the most moving in the New Testament. The utter simplicity and symmetry of v. 16 makes
the point with lapidary eloquence. "Jesus said to her, 'Mary!' Turning
[*strapheisa*] she said to him, in Hebrew, 'Rabbouni.'" The turning, as has been
said, is obviously not physical. Already in v. 14, after Mary responded to the
angels with a repetition of her lament that "they have taken away my Lord,"
we are told, "And saying this she turned back (*estraphē eis ta opisō*) and saw
Jesus standing." Two things are to be noted. First, the phrase usually translated "around" or "back" (*eis ta opisō*) means literally "toward the things that
lie behind" or "backwards." Second, as she turns away from the angels, she
faces Jesus and speaks with him. Consequently, when Jesus speaks her name
she is already face to face with him. Her "turning" in v. 16 in response to his
address, now not qualified as "backwards" or "around" but simply as turning,
is the second member of the "turning and turning again," the "turning away"
and "turning back," the apostasy and conversion, which the word *šûb* in the
book of Jeremiah captures so well.[16]

What Mary does spiritually, by insisting that the absence of Jesus' dead
body constitutes the absence of the living person of Jesus, is to turn back, or
to turn toward what lies behind, namely, the historical dispensation, which
came to a close with the glorification of Jesus on the cross. In the historical
context of the Johannine community, it is probably also to turn back toward
the synagogue, toward religious experience governed by the coordinates of
Judaism, toward Moses as teacher of the way. When Jesus speaks her name,
as most commentators have recognized, he is calling his own by name (see
10:3). Mary did not, as some have suggested, recognize Jesus by the sound of
his voice in the ordinary sense of the word, for she had already spoken with
him, heard his physical voice, without recognizing him (see v. 15). It is being
called by name that effects the conversion. Jesus knows his own as the Father
knows him and he knows the Father (see 10:14–15). He calls his own sheep
by name, and they know his voice and they follow him (see 10:3–5). Consequently, the evangelist makes certain that the reader does not miss the significance of Mary's response, "Rabbouni." He tells us that she spoke in Hebrew

---

[16] The standard exploration of this theme is the monograph of William L. Holladay, *The
Root ŠÛBH in the Old Testament, with Particular Reference to Its Usages in Covenantal Contexts*
(Leiden: E. J. Brill, 1958). Donatian Mollat explored the relevance of this to John's Gospel
("La conversion chez saint Jean," in *L'espérance du royaume,* Parole de Vie [Tours: Mame,
1966], 55–78).

and that the word means, "Teacher." Throughout the Fourth Gospel, beginning with the Prologue, in which the reader is told proleptically that the law came through Moses but that grace and truth came through Jesus Christ (see 1:17), major questions are: Who is the true teacher of the way of salvation? Of whom are you (the reader) a disciple? Do you look to Moses or to Jesus? A choice must be made, as was dramatically presented in the story of the man born blind, who asks his Jewish questioners, "Do you also want to become his [Jesus'] disciples?" and they emphatically choose Moses while the healed man chooses Jesus (see 9:27–34) and his parents try to remain neutral (9:20–21). Here Mary, symbolic representative of the new Israel, the Johannine community and the readers, makes the salvific choice. Jesus, and Jesus alone, is the Teacher, even, according to the Fourth Gospel, for the Jews.[17]

SECTION 3: THE EASTER APOSTLE

The third section of the Mary Magdalene pericope contains the notoriously difficult v. 17, which begins with Jesus' prohibition, *mē mou haptou*, which is translated most often as "Do not hold on to me" (cf. NRSV and NIV) or "Do not cling to me," followed by the even more difficult reference to Jesus' ascension to the Father. If one puts aside, as I think we must, the temptation to interpret this text in John in the light of Matt. 28:9, in which the women clasp the feet of the risen Jesus and worship him, and stick to what the text actually says rather than imagining Mary's psychological responses, we should read, "Do not continue to touch me," or even more literally, "Not me (emphatic) continue to touch" but "Go to my brothers and sisters." The emphatic placement of the "me" at the beginning of the command and closest to the negative, which thus seems to govern the pronoun "me" rather than the verb "touch," suggests that what Jesus is forbidding is not so much the touching itself but Mary's selection of the object to touch, namely, the Jesus who stands before her as an individual. What Mary is told not to do is try to continue to touch Jesus, that is, to encounter him as if he were the earthly Jesus resuscitated. The time for that kind of relationship is over. The negative present imperative of "touch" does not really mean "cling" or "hold," for which there is a perfectly good Greek word, *krateō,* which John uses in 20:23 and Matthew in 28:9. Furthermore, "to touch" often means not simply or

---

[17] The other two papers delivered at the 1993 SBL Johannine Section, by Werner Kelber and R. Alan Culpepper, deal with the problem this Johannine perspective creates for the contemporary reader because of its anti-Jewish and potentially anti-Semitic cast.

even primarily the physical gesture of laying one's hands on a person but rather interpersonal relating such as being deeply touched by a person's kindness or touched by the Evil One as in 1 John 5:18, which is the only other place the word occurs in the Johannine corpus. In other words, I would suggest that what Jesus is really doing is redirecting Mary's desire for union with himself from his physical or earthly body (which in any case no longer exists because it is the glorified Lord who stands before her in an appearance which is temporary) to the new locus of his presence in the world, that is, the community of his brothers and sisters, the disciples.

What then are we to make of the reason Jesus seems to offer, "I am not yet ascended to my Father." If anything, this seems less a reason for not touching him than a contradiction. If Jesus is not yet ascended, that is, if he is still present in the earthly sphere, it would seem that Mary, like the pre-ascension disciples in Luke 24:29, could be invited to touch him and verify his bodily reality. But, as most commentators have pointed out, the entire mystery of Jesus' glorification takes place in the Fourth Gospel when he is lifted up on the cross. It is virtually impossible, theologically, to understand Jesus in this scene as being somewhere in between (whether ontologically, spatially, or temporally) his resurrection and his ascension. The Jesus Mary encounters in the garden is clearly the glorified Jesus. Although it would take us too far afield to develop the thesis here, I would propose to translate this part of Jesus' address to Mary not as a declarative sentence, "I am not yet ascended to my Father," as if this supplied some reason why she should not or could not touch him, but as a rhetorical question expecting a negative reply, that is, "Am I as yet (or still) not ascended?" The proper answer to the question is, "No, you are indeed ascended, that is, glorified." The grammar and syntax of the sentence allow its translation as a question,[18] and, in my opinion, that makes much better sense of the passage because Jesus' ascension to the Father, that is, his glorification, is precisely the reason Mary will now encounter him in the community of the church rather than in his physical or earthly body, which may appear to be resuscitated but is not. In brief, a paraphrastic translation of v. 17 would be the following: "It is no longer in and through my physical or earthly historical individuality that you can continue to relate to

---

[18] I am applying to this verse the theory Albert Vanhoye developed in "Interrogation johannique et exégèse de Cana (Jn 2,4)," *Biblica* 55 (1974): 157–67. Vanhoye proposed that John uses double-meaning or ironical questions whose answer is both positive and negative to lead the reader into theological reflection. In this case, Jesus *appears* to be not yet ascended because he is interacting with Mary, but what she (and the reader) must realize is that *in reality* he is now in a very different state, that is, glorified.

me. After all, am I still unascended to my Father? Rather, go to the community, the new locus of my earthly presence."

Jesus continues by commissioning Mary Magdalene to announce to the disciples what is clearly the Johannine version of the Easter kerygma. The message is not, "I have risen" or "I go before you into Galilee." The message is that all has been accomplished. The work of the Word made flesh is complete, and its fruits are available to his disciples. In the Prologue the reader was told that the Word became flesh to give the power to become children of God to those who believed in him (see 1:12–14). Now that the work of Jesus is completed by his glorification, those who believe in him have become children of God. They are Jesus' brothers and sisters; his Father to whom he ascends is now their Father. It is important to note that 20:17 is the first time in John's Gospel that the disciples of Jesus are called *adelphoi,* that is, siblings. Since it is abundantly clear in this Gospel that the circle of the disciples is not limited to males and Mary is sent not to the apostles (a term not used for Jesus' disciples in John) or to "the Twelve" (which is a term the evangelist does use, e.g., in 6:70 and 20:24) but precisely to the disciples, the plural of "brother" in this verse is evidently a collective noun in masculine form, inclusive of male and female siblings, as our English masculine collective "brethren" once was considered inclusive. We can regret the masculine form in the text, which reflects the androcentric character of the Greek language and the culture of the times, but in reading and translating it we should honor its obviously inclusive meaning.[19]

The message Jesus sends to his disciples is hauntingly reminiscent of the Old Testament. My ascension, he says, "is to my Father and your Father, my God and your God." It recalls the words by which the foreigner, the Moabite Ruth, entered into the covenant people of her mother-in-law, Naomi: "Your people will be my people and your God will be my God" (Ruth 1:16). It echoes also the prophetic promise that in the time of the new creation God will make a new covenant with a renewed people, to whom God promises, "I will be your God and you will be my people" (cf. Jer. 31:31–34). The conclusion of this scene, which takes place in a garden reminiscent of both Genesis and the Canticle of Canticles and in which Jesus, the true Gardener and the true Beloved, encounters the one who is searching for him, is the announcement that the work of Jesus is now complete. He ascends to the God he calls by right his Father. For his disciples this means that they are the first to participate in the salvation of the new creation, the first to be born not

---

[19] It is unfortunate that the NRSV and the NIV both retain the translation "brothers."

of blood, nor of the will of the flesh, nor of the desire of a man but of God (see 1:13). They are now truly his sisters and brothers, members of the new Israel, with whom God, through Jesus the new Moses, has sealed a new covenant. The gift of God in Jesus, according to John, is divine filiation, eternal life in the Spirit springing up from within the believer (see 4:10–11) and flowing forth for the life of the world (see 7:37–39 and 19:34–37).

In v. 18 Mary Magdalene, now again given her full name as in v. 1, goes to fulfill her apostolic mission. She comes "announcing" (*angelousa*). This is the third thematic participle. Mary who began this episode in the depths of spiritual darkness and sorrow, *weeping,* has been converted by *turning* away from the dispensation that lies behind to the new life offered to her in the glorified Jesus, who lives now with God and in the temple of his body (see 2:21–22) which is the community, and she now goes joyfully *announcing* that which has been revealed to her.

There is an evident redactional seam visible in this verse, which the evangelist could scarcely not have noticed and must have left for a reason. The verse says literally, "Mary Magdalene went and announced to the disciples, 'I have seen the Lord' and he said these things to her." In other words, the sentence goes from first person direct discourse to third person indirect discourse without transition or explanation. Apparently the source verse with which the evangelist was working was "Mary Magdalene went and announced to the disciples that he had said these things to her." The evangelist has opened up the sentence and inserted, in direct address, "I have seen the Lord." This is precisely the witness of the disciples to Thomas in v. 25, "We have seen the Lord," a testimony that Thomas evidently was expected to accept as the Easter kerygma. In John's Gospel, bearing witness is always based on what one has seen and heard. Jesus bore witness to what he had seen and heard with God (see 3:11). The Beloved Disciple bore witness to what was seen on Calvary (see 19:35). In other words, to claim to have seen and/or heard is to claim to be an authentic and authenticated witness. It is, quite simply, a credential formula. In the early church it seems to have been particularly the credential statement for resurrection witnesses. Paul's ultimate self-vindication as an apostle is, "Have I not seen Jesus our Lord?" (1 Cor. 9:1), which is not a reference to the earthly Jesus, whom Paul had never met, but to his experience of the risen Jesus on the road to Damascus. In other words, Mary Magdalene, contrary to what generations of condescending male commentators would have us believe, is by all accounts an official apostolic witness of the resurrection. She is the one who, in the Johannine community, takes Peter's role of confirming the brothers and sisters once she herself has been converted (cf. Luke 22:31–32). She is the only person in this Gospel to receive an individual Easter appearance and a personal and individual commission from Jesus. The meaning and particular Johannine formulation of the Easter message are given only to her, and she communicates it to the church. Jesus does not repeat it when he appears to the disciples on Easter evening (20:19–23). He presumes it, and on the basis of Mary's confirming of the disciples he commissions them to live out what he has accomplished in and for them by extending to all his work of taking away of the sin of the world (cf. 1:29 and 20:23).

CONCLUSION

I have tried to establish two points in my interpretation of the encounter between the glorified Jesus and Mary Magdalene. First, Mary Magdalene is presented by the Fourth Evangelist as the official Easter witness in and to the Johannine community. She is symbolically presented, by means of Old Testament allusions, as the beloved of the lover in the Canticle of Canticles, the spouse of the new covenant mediated by Jesus in his glorification, the representative figure of the new Israel, which emerges from the new creation. Symbolically, she is both the Johannine community encountering its glorified Savior and the official witness to that community of what God has done for it in the glorification of Jesus.

Second, the answer to the question, Where is the Lord? is that Jesus is with God, face unveiled, in the glory that he had with God before the world was made, and he is intimately present within and among his own of the first and all later generations to whom he has returned as he promised to fill them with a joy no one can take from them. By the time the first Easter ends in the Fourth Gospel, the promise made in the last discourse(s) by the departing Jesus has been fulfilled: "I will not leave you orphaned; I am coming to you. In a little while the world will no longer see me, but you will see me; because I live, you also will live. On that day you will know that I am in my Father, and you in me, and I in you" (14:18–20). And this saving revelation comes to us, as it did to the first disciples, through the word of a woman bearing witness.

14

Contemplation and Ministry
(John 21:1–14)

The interpretation of the final chapter of the Gospel of John is conditioned by the interpreter's answer to two basic questions. First, is chapter 21 an appendix added to chapters 1–20 by a later redactor who intended
to modify or even correct the theology of the evangelist? Second, is this chapter intended to be a quasi-literal account of a historical event, or is it an essentially symbolic exploration of the postresurrection experience of the
Johannine community with implications for the church of all time?

For reasons that will be discussed below, I will proceed on the assumption
that, regardless of who actually penned the chapter (i.e., the evangelist or a
later member of the Johannine community), chapter 21 is an integral part of
the Gospel in fundamental theological continuity with chapters 1–20 and
that its purpose is to bring the Gospel account to a close by transferring the
reader's attention from the experience of the first disciples with the historical
Jesus to the experience of the contemporary church with the glorified Jesus,
that is, from the story of those who "saw" to the story of those who "believe
without having seen" (see 20:29).

One's answer to the second question depends largely on how one understands the nature of the Easter appearances. I am in sympathy with an
increasing number of modern theologians who consider the events narrated
as resurrection appearances to be nondelusional (in this sense, objectively
based) religious experiences that are described in visual terms precisely
because of their symbolic character. Symbols, far from being dead or empty
"stand-ins" for something other than themselves, are perceptible realities that
mediate transcendent reality. They are usually "visual" in some sense of the
term; they convey deep and polyvalent meaning by unifying realms of significance that cannot be held together by ordinary logic; and they have transformative power because they involve the perceiver in the world of meaning

that they open to the "eye" of inner vision.[1] This inner vision, for the Christian, is faith itself. Against this background it seems to me that chapter 21 is to be understood as a narrative presentation of a faith experience that is neither imaginary nor historical in the ordinary sense of these terms but real and symbolic.

STRUCTURE OF THE PERICOPE

John 21:1–14 is a clearly delineated unit beginning with the notation that Jesus *manifested* himself *again* to the *disciples* (21:1) and ending with the notation that this was the *third* time Jesus was *manifested* to the *disciples* (21:14). The entire episode takes place at the Sea of Tiberias within the early morning hours and is divided into two parts: a narrative about the mysterious catch of fish (21:2–8) and a dialogue within the context of a mysterious meal (21:9–13).

UNIFYING THEMES OF THE PERICOPE

Two themes unify the pericope: the manifestation or revelation of Jesus to his disciples and their recognition of him; the relationship of two central roles in the community of disciples, namely, contemplation and mission, represented by the related activities of the Beloved Disciple and Simon Peter.

In the first part of the pericope the disciples have gone fishing, have caught nothing, and at the command of a stranger on the shore have cast their nets to the right side of the boat and made an enormous catch. Immediately the Beloved Disciple, who in John's Gospel is the privileged locus of and witness to God's self-revelation in Jesus, proclaims, "It is the Lord," and Simon Peter responds to this revelatory proclamation by throwing himself into the water while the other disciples come to Jesus in the boat. Peter's action has little point, narratively, but the coming to Jesus through water in response to a proclamation of his identity could easily evoke baptismal images for a Christian reader who remembered that new birth comes by water and spirit (see 3:5).

In the second part of the pericope, after the net has been brought to shore, Jesus invites the disciples to the meal he has prepared for them, and the evan-

---

[1] See chapter 4 on symbolism in the Fourth Gospel.

gelist deliberately evokes the eucharistically freighted account of 6:9–12 by saying that Jesus "*took* the bread and *gave* it to them and so with the fish" (v. 13). The one fish and one loaf here on the shore of the Sea of Tiberias are enough now for the seven disciples, as the five loaves and two fish had been for the five thousand who dined on this same shore during the life of the historical Jesus. The action of Jesus reveals his identity to the disciples, who know him in the sharing of the meal (cf. Luke 24:30–31), but, as with the disciples at Emmaus, it is a mysterious knowing that leaves room for a desire to question (see v. 12).

The second unifying theme of the pericope is developed through the relationship between Simon Peter and the Beloved Disciple. It is Peter who takes the initiative in going fishing and Peter who responds to Jesus' command to bring some of the fish they have caught by (apparently single-handedly!) dragging to shore the net (see vv. 10–11), which the disciples had been unable to haul in (see v. 6). The narrative incongruity only serves to focus the reader's attention on the obvious intention of the writer to portray Peter as the leader of the expedition.

By the time this Gospel was written the use of the image of fishing for the pastoral ministry of the church was common. In Luke 5:1–11 (see also Mark 1:17; Matt. 4:19), which is so closely related to this scene in John that they can only come from the same or a similar tradition, Jesus tells the awe-stricken Peter that henceforth he will catch living persons.

The evangelist notes that precisely 153 fish were taken. Numerous symbolic interpretations of this number have been offered in the course of history; none is entirely convincing. Whatever one makes of such interpretations, it seems fairly clear that the enormous catch, which became possible only at Jesus' command, represents the universal mission of the church carried out by those who without Jesus can do nothing (see 15:5) but who will be fruitful as long as they abide in him and obey his commands.

The net Peter hauls in remains unbroken, just as the seamless tunic of the crucified Jesus remained untorn (see 19:23–24). The unity of the church is a primary theme of the Fourth Gospel, the subject of Jesus' final prayer on the night before he died (see 17:20–21) and, by the time the Gospel was written, already a matter of some concern to the Johannine church threatened with various kinds of disunity (as is clear from the Johannine epistles). Jesus commands the disciples to bring the fish to him (see v. 10), an echo of his prayer at the Last Supper that his disciples would be with him where he is to see the glory that God had given to him as preexistent Son (see 17:21). It is Peter who responds to this command of Jesus.

Especially in light of the remainder of chapter 21, it seems clear that the evangelist (or the redactor) intends to clarify for the postresurrection community the relationship between the two constitutive activities of the church: contemplation, through which revelation is received, and ministry, through which it is mediated. The Beloved Disciple, who rested on the bosom of Jesus (13:23 and 21:20), is the Fourth Gospel's paradigmatic embodiment of contemplative openness to the revelation of Jesus, just as the Word made flesh who dwelt in the bosom of God was the incarnation of God's self-revelation to the world (see 1:1, 18).

In this pericope we are told specifically that Jesus manifested or revealed himself to the disciples, just as he had promised before his death that he would manifest himself to those who loved him and kept his word (see 14:18–23). It is the Beloved Disciple who recognizes him with perfect clarity and proclaims him authoritatively. Simon Peter's recognition of and coming to Jesus is a response to that proclamation which, in this sense, grounds his pastoral leadership. This same proclamation also illumines the ignorance of the other disciples (see v. 4), who never seem to have the same clarity or certitude that the Beloved Disciple does (see v. 12). Contemplative receptivity to the life-giving revelation in Jesus is the source of the church's proclamation, which grounds both the faith of the disciples and the church's mission to the world. In this final chapter the evangelist reaffirms the priority of love as the basis of spiritual insight that has been assigned to the Beloved Disciple throughout the Gospel but now clarifies the relationship of church leadership, recognized in Peter, to this primacy of revelatory contemplation.

THE RELATIONSHIP OF CHAPTER 21
TO THE REST OF THE GOSPEL

Many commentators, noting that the Gospel seems to end at 20:30–31, have hypothesized that chapter 21 is an appendix added by a later hand, either to complete the Gospel or to bring it into line with developments in the Great Church, in which Peter had come to enjoy a certain pastoral primacy. I would like to suggest another hypothesis, namely, that the ending in 20:30–31 is the conclusion of the account of what happened during the life and paschal mystery of Jesus and that chapter 21 is an exploration of the life of those who did not see but who believed. Thomas is presented as the last of the "seers" who proclaims Jesus Lord and God on the basis of direct experience (see 20:28).

Chapter 21 opens with a setting that both establishes continuity with the Gospel account and hints at the newness of the situation. Jesus reveals himself "again," a "third time." Three is the number of completion as well as of the new beginning. Jesus rose on the "third day." The scene takes place "just as dawn was breaking" after a night of fruitless toil. It is a new day, the day Jesus had promised, when he would come to them and manifest himself to them (see 14:20–21, 23).

The cast of characters is very interesting. It includes members of "the Twelve" (Peter, the Sons of Zebedee); the in-between disciple, the doubter-believer who is the last to believe on the basis of seeing and the first to be called to believe without seeing (Thomas the Twin); a special Johannine character who represents the new Israel, which the church is called to be (Nathanael, the Israelite without guile of 1:45–51); one who was not a member of the Twelve but who is the authoritative locus of revelation in John's community (the Beloved Disciple); and a final, unnamed disciple whose presence as a kind of "empty set" allows the reader to assume a role in the community.

The number of disciples is not twelve but seven, the symbol of fullness and perfection. This community of fishers is not exclusively the apostolic college but the complete postresurrection community of believers who obey Jesus' word and therefore "bear much fruit" and who encounter him again and again down through the centuries in the eucharistic meal that he prepares for them.

It has been suggested that the fact that Peter and the others go fishing, that is, seemingly return to their ordinary occupations, indicates that they have not yet come to faith in the resurrection. Their leaving Jerusalem and taking up their daily work seems strange in view of the joy-filled experiences recounted in chapter 20 and the apparent conclusion of 20:30–31.

No doubt the traditional source of this story is the first Galilee appearance, probably to Peter, before the appearances and their assimilation had confirmed the Easter faith of the nascent church. Yet the evangelist has deeply modified the source. The Fourth Evangelist insists that this is not the first but the third appearance. (The protophany in John is to Mary Magdalene, a fact that the church has yet to assimilate!) It is not to Peter alone, or to the Twelve, but to the community with Peter in a position of pastoral leadership relativized by his dependence on the revelatory witness of the Beloved Disciple. And it takes place precisely in the ambiguous conditions of daily life. Jesus comes to make ministerially fruitful the ordinary burdensome work of the disciples. He manifests himself to them in a simple meal offered by a stranger. Although the official witness to revelation is unambiguous in proclaiming that, "It is the Lord," the disciples themselves, though prompt in obedience and open in their recognition of the Lord, have times when they find it hard to recognize him (see v. 4) and, even in their knowing, have a desire to question him further (see v. 12).

CONCLUSION

In summary, I would suggest that this scene is neither an afterthought nor a correction but a symbolic presentation of the life of the church in the time after the resurrection. It is situated well after the cessation of the Easter appearances because Jesus foretells Peter's martyrdom (see 21:18–19) and the evangelist refers to the death of the Beloved Disciple (21:22–23). If this is not sheer clumsiness on the part of the evangelist (and this Gospel is anything but clumsy from the literary point of view!), the reader is being alerted to the fact that the episode recounted in 21:1–14 belongs to the period subsequent to the first generation of disciples.

This might suggest a reason for the apparent repetition at 21:25 of the conclusion in 20:30–31. The "first" conclusion brought to a close the account of all that Jesus did "in the presence of his disciples," both during his public life and throughout his paschal mystery. These signs, carefully selected from among the many (though finite number) that the historical Jesus did, which ended with the Easter appearances, have now been transformed into scripture for the salvation of subsequent generations who will believe in Jesus through this word.

The "second" conclusion is to the ongoing story of all the "many other things" that Jesus continues to do and which could not all be recounted even if a whole world full of books were to be written. Chapter 21 is about what is still going on: obedience to the word of Jesus resulting in fruitful ministry that must someday bring to salvation the whole world whom Jesus was sent to save (see 3:16) but who will now be drawn to Jesus by his disciples, who will do even greater works than he himself did (cf. 14:12); and ongoing sharing of life with Jesus through the contemplative experience of eucharistic community in faith. The first conclusion is definitive; the second is open-ended. This experience of the glorified Jesus will be actualized every time the proclamation resounds, "It is the Lord," and the disciples, weary from their ministerial labors, sit down to table with him.

Part 3

A Feminist Reexamination of the Authorship of the Fourth Gospel

15

"Because of the Woman's Testimony . . ."

As anyone familiar with research on the Fourth Gospel knows, one of the thorniest questions concerning this Gospel is that of its authorship. The original simple attribution of the Gospel to John the Son of Zebedee, one of the Twelve, is generally though not universally rejected by contemporary scholars.[1] Most Johannine scholars also recognize that the theological and spiritual unity, originality, and depth of this Gospel suggest that the written text itself is the work of one remarkable individual, the Fourth Evangelist, whose original document may have been edited though not substantially modified by a later hand, sometimes called, following Rudolf Bultmann, "the ecclesiastical redactor,"[2] whose emendations tend to reveal a church order agenda in some tension with the basic tendencies of the Gospel itself. But with these three tenets—that the author of the Fourth Gospel is not John the son of Zebedee, that the evangelist is a single individual, and that there was probably a final redactor who is different from the evangelist—the consensus ends.

Still subject to vigorous debate are the crucial questions of (1) whether the evangelist is to be equated with the mysterious figure called the "disciple whom Jesus loved," who appears in the second half of the Gospel as an eyewitness guarantor of the truth of the Gospel itself; (2) who the Beloved Disciple, whether or not this figure is the evangelist, actually was; (3) who the evangelist actually was; and (4) whether or not the Beloved Disciple is a real historical personage or a literary construct of the evangelist. In order to focus my attention on the piece of this puzzle I want to address I will briefly state

[1] James H. Charlesworth, *The Beloved Disciple: Whose Witness Validates the Gospel of John?* (Valley Forge, Pa.: Trinity, 1995), 197–213, gives a succinct history of the theory and its status at present.

[2] Rudolf Bultmann, *The Gospel of John: A Commentary,* trans. George R. Beasley-Murray (Oxford: Blackwell, 1971), 10–11.

the position on these questions that will function as a working frame of reference for this chapter.

First, there were at least three stages involved in the authorship of the Johannine text: the Beloved Disciple, who was an eyewitness of the Christ-event in the person and life of Jesus of Nazareth and whose testimony is the authoritative source of the content of the Gospel; the evangelist or actual writer of the text, a talented second-generation Christian who was a prominent figure in the Johannine school;[3] a later redactor who made some insertions into the text in order to make it more acceptable in the Great Church,[4] which is represented in the Johannine text by the figure of Simon Peter. Second, none of these three stages was John the Son of Zebedee. Third, when speaking of the author of the Fourth Gospel, we have to take into account both the Beloved Disciple and the Fourth Evangelist because the subject matter (due primarily to the Beloved Disciple) and its literary incarnation (due primarily to the evangelist) in the Gospel are intimately and mutually determinative.[5] However, the aspect of the question of authorship on which I want to concentrate is not that of the identity of the Fourth Evangelist, although the hypothesis may have some ramifications for that question, but the identity of the Beloved Disciple.

As Paul Minear wrote in 1977, the volume of scholarly ink already spilt on this question suggests that it requires "consummate audacity to suggest a new

[3] I basically subscribe to the thesis of R. Alan Culpepper that the Johannine community was, or included, a "school" or community of Christian scholars and/or writers who collectively interpreted the witness of the Beloved Disciple and that that interpretation is embodied in the Fourth Gospel (*The Johannine School: An Evaluation of the Johannine-School Hypothesis Based on an Investigation of the Nature of the Ancient Schools,* Society of Biblical Literature Dissertation Series [Missoula, Mont.: Scholars Press, 1975]). I will nuance slightly the issue of how the Beloved Disciple is related to the members of the school.

[4] When I use the term "Great Church," capitalized, I mean the Christian movement as it was beginning to be unified by the acceptance of Petrine primacy and a tracing of origins to the apostolate of the Twelve and their coworkers, including Paul. This movement of consolidation was under way even as the documents of the New Testament were being composed. I use the term in preference to "apostolic churches" because I believe that the claim of the community of the Fourth Gospel is precisely that it is "apostolic" in the sense of deriving its legitimacy directly from Jesus himself and holding the same faith (although understood in a superior way) as the other churches. The dispute is not over whether the Johannine community is apostolic but over who gets to define the meaning of apostolic, the Twelve alone or eyewitnesses whom Jesus legitimates through his commissioning and the gift of the Spirit.

[5] Unlike Martin Hengel (*The Johannine Question,* trans. J. Bowden [London: SCM; Philadelphia: Trinity, 1989]) and Richard Bauckham ("The Beloved Disciple as Ideal Author," *JSNT* 49 [1993]: 21–44), I do not equate the Beloved Disciple and the evangelist, whom they identify as John the Elder.

thesis for consideration."[6] This warning has not stopped such contemporary scholars as Martin Hengel in 1989, Joseph Grassi and Mark Stibbe in 1992, and James H. Charlesworth in 1995,[7] among others, from reasking the question and proposing either new hypotheses or new evidence for older ones.[8] This chapter on the subject is stimulated by the convergence of three clusters of data not yet considered in relation to each other, one arising from the literature in the field, a second from the increasing pertinence of feminist criticism to Fourth Gospel research, and a third from some miscellaneous textual and extratextual observations which seem to corroborate a new hypothesis.

FACTORS SUGGESTING RECONSIDERATION

The Literature on the Subject

A remarkable feature of the question of Johannine authorship in general and the identity of the Beloved Disciple in particular is that, despite two centuries of modern exegesis bearing on the question, not only has no consensus emerged, but no theory has become dominant except perhaps the nontheory that the answer to the conundrum is permanently unavailable.[9] Johannine scholars today are just as divided as ever over such questions as whether the Beloved Disciple was identical with or was distinct from the Fourth Evangelist;[10] whether the Beloved Disciple is a pure literary creation used as a sym-

---

[6] Paul S. Minear, "The Beloved Disciple in the Gospel of John: Some Clues and Conjectures," *NovT* 19 (1977): 123. Actually, Minear gives the best reason to continue the search: "The role of this disciple is too important to permit abandoning the search; the evidence is too baffling to permit a confident solution" (p. 105).

[7] Hengel, *Johannine Question;* Joseph A. Grassi, *The Secret Identity of the Beloved Disciple* (New York/Mahwah, N.J.: Paulist, 1992); Mark W. G. Stibbe, *John as Storyteller: Narrative Criticism and the Fourth Gospel* (Cambridge: Cambridge University Press, 1992), especially 76–82; Charlesworth, *Beloved Disciple.*

[8] Valuable sources of virtually all the historical and contemporary writing on the subject are Charlesworth, *Beloved Disciple,* especially chapters 2 and 3; and R. Alan Culpepper, *John, the Son of Zebedee: The Life of a Legend* (Columbia: University of South Carolina Press, 1994), especially chapters 3, 9, and 10.

[9] Charlesworth supplies evidence that the exegetical discussion of the identity of the Beloved Disciple and the relation of the Beloved Disciple to the evangelist goes back much further than the last two decades (*Beloved Disciple,* chapter 3). His overview of the literature on twenty-two individual or collective Johannine or extra-Johannine candidates for the role of Beloved Disciple is a real contribution.

[10] The distinction hypothesis is defended by the majority of modern commentators, but very recently Martin Hengel, followed by Richard Bauckham, has identified the two and named them as John the Elder.

bol by the Fourth Evangelist or was a real, historical person who may or may not represent some idealized role;[11] who the Beloved Disciple, if historical, was;[12] and what role the Beloved Disciple plays in the Gospel.[13]

Scholars have repeatedly tried to unravel the mystery by suggesting motives for the disguising of the Beloved Disciple's identity on the hunch that, if one could figure out why the Fourth Evangelist insisted on the importance of this figure while totally obscuring the identity, one could discern the identity. Although all kinds of motives have been suggested, from the personal humility of Jesus' favorite to the presumed knowledge of the Beloved Disciple's identity in the community, which made naming the person unnecessary, no one has come up with a motivational hypothesis that has led to the identification of the figure. I am going to suggest that such a complete and successful obscuring of the identity of the Beloved Disciple could not have been accidental. The Fourth Evangelist wanted to insist on the central importance of the Beloved Disciple while, at the same time, making it impossible to identify the figure conclusively with any particular individual in the Johannine community. The question of motive, therefore, is crucial.

Feminist Critical Considerations

The second set of factors leading me to reexamine this question arises from my feminist sensibilities. Scholars have progressively realized the surprisingly central role of women in John's Gospel.[14] The Samaritan woman in John 4 is not only the first person to hear the great *"egō eimi"* (I am) from the Revealer

---

[11] Although current research tends more toward the theory that the Beloved Disciple was a real person, even if heavily idealized in the Gospel, Rudolf Bultmann's thesis (perhaps influenced by A. Loissy) that the Beloved Disciple is a symbol of Gentile Christianity (see Bultmann, *Gospel of John,* 484) continues to attract followers.

[12] The hypothesis that the Beloved Disciple was Lazarus has emerged as a kind of "frontrunner" in recent years but, as Charlesworth has ably demonstrated, there have been at least seventeen other contenders throughout history and many are still viable candidates today (*Beloved Disciple,* 127–224).

[13] The major theories see the Beloved Disciple as the eyewitness authority behind the Gospel (e.g., Raymond Brown); a symbolic figure representing a Christianity of Gentile and non-Twelve origin rivaling Simon Peter, who symbolizes the "apostolic churches" of Jewish origin (e.g., Rudolf Bultmann and Margaret Pamment); a representative figure for the ideal disciple of Jesus (very common); or a presentation of the ideal author (e.g., Richard Bauckham).

[14] An early article calling attention to this fact was published by Raymond Brown, "Roles of Women in the Fourth Gospel," *TS* 36 (1975): 688–99, reprinted as Appendix II in *The Community of the Beloved Disciple: The Life, Loves, and Hates of an Individual Church in New Testament Times* (New York: Paulist, 1979), 183–98. See chapter 6 of this volume for my treatment of the subject.

(4:26) but also the only character in the Fourth Gospel who is presented as exercising a truly apostolic[15] role during the lifetime of the earthly Jesus, a role that the Fourth Evangelist pointedly takes away from the Twelve, who do play such a role in the Synoptics (see Matthew 10 and parallels). It is a woman, Martha, who at the tomb of Lazarus gives the full Christian profession of faith in Jesus as "the Christ, the Son of God, the one coming into the world" (11:27), that is, the fulfiller of Jewish, Gentile, and Samaritan expectations, a profession that in Matthew grounds the promise of primacy to Peter (Matt. 16:16–19). It is a woman, Mary of Bethany, who proleptically fulfills Jesus' final command, to wash the feet of those we love, and symbolically prepares Jesus for burial, thus symbolically recognizing his messianic identity and vocation, by anointing Jesus' feet and drying them with her hair (12:3–8). It is a woman, again Martha of Bethany, who serves (*diakoneō*) at the table when Jesus dines with his friends before his death (see 12:2). It is a woman, Mary Magdalene, who witnesses the death of the Lord (see 19:25), discovers the empty tomb (see 20:1–2), and receives the protophany of the risen Jesus as well as the only individual commission to announce the Easter kerygma (see 20:11–18), thus constituting her, by all the criteria of the early church, the primary and foundational apostolic figure in the Johannine community.[16] I find the recent conclusion of Robert Maccini's monograph on women witnesses in John, namely, that the evangelist simply reported female testimony because in fact females did testify but that there was no intention to highlight the gender of the witnesses, to be somewhat disingenuous[17] given the patriarchal character of the culture in which the early church devel-

---

[15] As indicated in n. 4, there is a real problem in using the word "apostolic" in relation to the Fourth Gospel. John does not use the term "apostle" for persons, preferring the term "disciple." Furthermore, there seems to be an ongoing rivalry between, on the one hand, Simon Peter and the "apostolic churches," as Raymond Brown calls those tracing their legitimacy to the Twelve, and, on the other hand, the Beloved Disciple, who is not one of the Twelve but whose authority is based on eyewitness experience of Jesus (see Brown, *Community of the Beloved Disciple*, 81–88). When I use the term "apostolic" in this chapter, I intend to denote authentic ecclesial foundations, whether stemming from the Twelve or not. I have not found a better term, since Christian legitimacy down through the centuries has been based on holding the faith that comes to us from the apostles, and restricting the term "apostolic" to the persons or communities associated with the Twelve seems to grant the premise, which I reject, that "apostles" and "the Twelve" were identical.

[16] There are actually two sets of criteria for apostleship in the New Testament: to have accompanied Jesus during his earthly life (Acts 1:21–22) and to have seen the risen Lord and been commissioned by him to preach the gospel (see Gal. 1:10–2:10; 1 Cor. 9:1–2 and 15:8–10).

[17] Robert G. Maccini, *Her Testimony Is True: Women as Witnesses According to John,* JSNTSup 125 (Sheffield: Sheffield Academic Press, 1996), especially chapter 11.

oped and the advanced state of patriarchal retrenchment in the church by the time the Fourth Gospel was written.

In short, not only are an extraordinary number of John's main characters women, but these women are assigned the very community-founding roles and functions—namely, christological confession, missionary witness, and paschal proclamation—that are assigned to Peter and the Twelve in the Synoptics, whereas the Twelve do not have these roles and functions in John. Furthermore, these female figures are delineated not only with extraordinary theological density, especially evident in the story of the Samaritan woman, but with remarkable psychological and spiritual finesse, especially evident in the Mary Magdalene Christophany.

Finally, there are two episodes in the Fourth Gospel in which the Fourth Evangelist presents Jesus as overriding, explicitly or implicitly, male objections to unusual female behavior in relation to himself and his mission. One, the objection to the foot washing/anointing, is common to all four Gospels, but only in John is it specifically Judas, the representative of the ultimate evil of unbelief in the Fourth Gospel, who is silenced by Jesus, who assigns paschal significance to Mary's action. The other episode, the consternation of the returning male disciples who discover Jesus talking with a woman of Samaria in John 4, is particular to John. The note that the disciples are shocked but do not dare to question what Jesus seeks (*zēteō*) with a woman does not in any way further the action of the narrative, which suggests that this one-verse vignette is a deliberate attempt by the Fourth Evangelist to reflect a real tension in the Johannine community over women exercising roles men consider reserved to themselves, namely, theological exploration and evangelization. If this is the case, the text presents Jesus favoring the women.

In light of the foregoing, the question arises, What man would have had so at heart the highlighting of women's roles in the community as to have assigned to women the apostolically significant roles and scenes assigned to the Twelve in the Synoptics, be so finely attuned to women's psychological and spiritual experience as to be able to create such scenes as the Samaritan woman and Mary Magdalene episodes, and be so concerned to defend women's autonomous relationship with Jesus as to have written these passages?

Miscellaneous Data

1. Textual features. A few textual features of the Gospel also raise questions about the common assumption that the Beloved Disciple is either a pure literary fiction or a single, unnamed and/or anonymous male disciple. First, there is the anomaly of the "other disciple" in the text. This mysterious figure appears four times in the Fourth Gospel: implicitly in 1:40, where we are told that one of the two disciples of John the Baptist who followed Jesus was Andrew and the second is left unnamed; in 18:15–16, where Simon Peter and an unnamed other disciple follow Jesus to the courtyard of the high priest and the other disciple gains Peter's entrance; in 20:2–10, where Mary Magdalene informs Simon Peter and the other disciple of the empty tomb and the two run to the tomb where the other disciple sees the grave clothes and face veil and believes; and in 21:2, where two unnamed disciples are among the seven who go fishing after the resurrection and are invited to breakfast by the risen Lord.

In one of these passages, 20:2, the "other disciple" is explicitly identified with the "disciple whom Jesus loved." In another passage, 21:7, there is a possible identification. There are two unnamed "other disciples" in the post-Easter fishing party, and when Jesus addresses the group from the shore "that disciple whom Jesus loved" said, "It is the Lord." Either the Beloved Disciple is one of the five named disciples in the boat or one of the two unnamed "other disciples."

Johannine scholars are as divided over the identity of the "other disciple" and the possible identification of this disciple(s) with the Beloved Disciple as they are over the identity of the latter. Part of the hypothesis I will finally offer is that the "other disciple" is the evangelist's creation of an "empty set" into which the reader, who is called to become a beloved disciple, is intended to insert him- or herself. In modern critical terminology we might say that the "other disciple" is a cipher for the implied reader.[18] This person follows Jesus when Jesus first appears and is pointed out as the Lamb of God and is invited by Jesus to "come and see," that is, to journey through the Gospel in the company of Jesus. This "other disciple" follows Jesus into the arena of the passion, sees the sign of the glorification in the empty tomb,[19] and finally is found in the company of the disciples who encounter the risen Lord. The "other disciple" is a beloved disciple, but not the historical Beloved Disciple who is the contemporary of the earthly Jesus. This historical Beloved Disciple (whose identity is still a mystery) is the model for all Jesus' followers who become loving believers in the risen Jesus. If this part of the hypothesis is well founded,

[18] See Mark Allan Powell, *What is Narrative Criticism?* Guides to Biblical Scholarship (Minneapolis: Fortress, 1990), 19, for a brief discussion of the category of "implied reader" in narrative criticism. The implied reader is distinct from any real historical reader but is a set of clues given in the text to the desired response to the text by real readers.

[19] See chapter 12 for my theory that the face veil discovered in the tomb by the Beloved Disciple constituted a sign of the glorification.

there might be some reason to question the exclusively male identity of the historical Beloved Disciple, since, obviously, the postglorification "beloved disciple," the readers of the text, includes both women and men.

A second feature of the text that calls for reexamination is the role of the Beloved Disciple at the foot of the cross in 19:25–27, two of the most exhaustively exegeted verses in the Gospel, whose full meaning continues to elude fully satisfactory interpretation. The Fourth Evangelist gives a precise list of the *dramatis personae* at the foot of the cross: the mother of Jesus, Jesus' mother's sister Mary the wife of Clopas, and Mary Magdalene. No male disciple is named, nor is there a hint that anyone else was there. Immediately after this list is given we are told "Jesus, therefore, seeing his Mother and the disciple standing by whom he loved, said . . . ." Certainly, the natural reading of this text is that the disciple whom Jesus loved as well as his mother, that is, two people standing near the cross whom the crucified Jesus could see, were both part of the group of figures named in the immediately preceding verse. The "therefore" (*oun*) connects the two verses in at least consequential, if not causal, fashion. Because these people were standing near the cross, the crucified Jesus could see them. There is no reason at all, from the text, to think that a fourth character suddenly materialized at the moment Jesus speaks.

By way of comparison, no commentator as far as I know has ever applied a similar expansionary interpretation to the very parallel passage in chapter 21. There we are told, in v. 2, that "[g]athered there together were Simon Peter, Thomas called the Twin, Nathanael of Cana in Galilee, the sons of Zebedee, and two others of his disciples." Later, in v. 7, when "that disciple whom Jesus loved said to Peter, 'It is the Lord,'" the assumption is that the Beloved Disciple was one of the seven disciples who had been previously indicated as present in the boat. No one thinks that the Beloved Disciple suddenly materialized as an eighth figure, even though no one of the previously indicated seven had been explicitly identified as the Beloved Disciple. Why, in the even more clearly and closely connected verses, 25 and 26, in the parallel scene at the foot of the cross, where the cast of characters immediately precedes the identification of the Beloved Disciple and a "therefore" connects the presence of the three women with Jesus' seeing of his addressees, do commentators assume that the Beloved Disciple was not only not one of the two women with the mother of Jesus but that the suddenly materializing fourth character was a male? This is especially curious since none of the three Synoptic accounts suggests that there were any male disciples on Calvary, something that would have been embarrassing enough for the early church that it would hardly have been let stand if it were not a fact or if appeal could have been made to the Johannine tradition to establish that at least one male disciple was faithful to the end.

The evident reply is that Jesus says to his mother, "Woman, behold your *son*" (emphasis added). This reference to the Beloved Disciple as "son" has settled for most commentators the question of the gender if not the identity of the Beloved Disciple. Must not a son be a male and therefore by definition not one of the women already indicated? I would like to suggest that this conclusion is not as evident as it might seem. First, most commentators agree that, whoever the Beloved Disciple was historically, in this scene the figure is not merely or even primarily an individual who is personally and privately united to the mother of Jesus but a representative figure[20] symbolic of some group that is to be united in a special way with her. In that case the meaning of the verse is, "Woman, behold the one who is to be to you what I (Jesus) have been." Since Jesus is Mary's son, the community represented by the Beloved Disciple becomes Mary's new "son," that is, it shares the same relationship to her as Jesus had during his earthly life. But that community, the church under some aspect no doubt, obviously includes both males and females. Consequently, the word "son" reflects the gender of the dying Jesus but not necessarily the gender of the representative figure, who, whether male or female, represents those, both female and male, who are now related to the mother of Jesus as Jesus was prior to his death.

This interpretation is well borne out by the glorified Jesus' commissioning of Mary Magdalene (20:17) to go to "my brothers" (*pros tous adelphous mou*), a group that, in John's Gospel, surely included women, with the message of his resurrection. In other words, "brothers" in 20:17 is clearly a generic masculine including female as well as male siblings. This is the first time in the Gospel that Jesus refers to his disciples as siblings. The Johannine version of the Easter kerygma is that Jesus' Father and God is now the Father and God of his disciples (cf. 20:17). In other words, the effect of the paschal mystery in the Fourth Gospel is that Jesus gives the "power to become children of God" to those who believe in him (1:12). These believers are also, through the scene at the foot of the cross, sharers in Jesus' filial relationship to his mother. And these believers, these siblings of Jesus, these beloved disciples, are of both genders.

To return now to the scene at the foot of the cross, it is striking that Jesus,

---

[20] The category of "representative figures" in John was developed by Raymond F. Collins ("The Representative Figures in the Fourth Gospel," *DRev* 94 [1976]: 26–46, 118–32) and has been generally accepted by scholars in the field.

after speaking to his Mother, does not say to the disciple, "Son, behold your mother" but simply "Behold your mother." There is no specifically masculine address to the disciple. The addressee is a disciple, *mathētēs*, a happily ambiguous term, which in Greek is female in form and generically male in meaning (since disciples in that culture, like actors or doctors in ours, are assumed to be male unless specified by an added diminutive or a feminine adjective as in "actress" or "woman doctor") and which therefore takes male articles and generates male pronouns of reference.[21] The masculine "disciple" is generic and thus tells us nothing about the actual gender of the disciple in question. We are then told that the disciple took the mother of Jesus *eis ta idia*, a neuter idiom meaning "to one's own" in the sense of *chez soi* in French. This could mean to one's own home, or into one's care, or into one's affections, or as a relative. But what is interesting is that the idiom in Greek is neuter and so gives no indication of the gender of the one receiving the mother of Jesus. It is usually translated "into his own home" because it is assumed that the disciple is male, but if that assumption is not well founded neither is the masculinizing of the neuter idiom.

The conclusion I want to draw from this exegesis is that in this one scene, which is the most crucial in the Gospel for the identification of the Beloved Disciple, it is not at all certain that the Beloved Disciple is male. In fact, were it not for the assumption throughout the centuries that all Jesus' disciples were male unless the opposite is specified, the natural reading of the text would be that the Beloved Disciple in this scene is either one of the two named women disciples who were with the mother of Jesus in the Johannine scene or the two of them together. The two women together, that is, Jesus' aunt Mary of Clopas and Mary Magdalene, as a community, could be the Beloved Disciple to whom Jesus spoke. In this case, the community represented is made up of both Jesus' natural family (represented by his mother's sister) and his disciples (represented by Mary Magdalene), composing together the family of faith. This would accord very well with the meaning of the other scene involving the mother of Jesus in John, the wedding at Cana,

---

[21] There is, of course, a female form of "disciple" in Greek, μαθήτρια (*mathētria*), but it is generally used when the only person denoted is female and/or the intention is to highlight her gender. The masculine form, μαθητής (*mathētēs*), is used both for male disciples exclusively and for groups including both men and women or when there is no particular emphasis on female gender intended. A good example of all three uses is Acts 9:36–39 where Tabitha (Dorcas) is called *mathētria* when she alone is mentioned, but the group of disciples that explicitly includes both the men (ἄνδρας [*andras*]), sent to Peter and the widows (χῆραι [*chērai*]), who were Dorcas's companions are collectively called "the disciples" (οἱ μαθηταί [*hoi mathētai*]). In other words, "disciple" is a generic masculine.

where the mother of Jesus is assimilated to those who see his glory and believe in him while she yet retains a distinctive role as the one who says, "Do whatever he tells you" (2:5). If, on the other hand, Jesus' address is to one of the two women standing with the mother of Jesus, the evident choice is Mary Magdalene. Like the Beloved Disciple, she appears in the Gospel only after the beginning of "the hour" of Jesus' glorification. She is the only figure in the Gospel who, by name, is presented as a witness of the death of Jesus, the discoverer of the empty tomb, and the recipient of the Easter protophany and of the only individual apostolic commission of the risen Jesus. If there is an eyewitness source behind the Fourth Gospel, the most clearly designated embodiment of that role in the text itself is Mary Magdalene.

2. Extratextual details. I turn now to two interesting extratextual details that seem to corroborate the suggestion that the Beloved Disciple is not necessarily exclusively male. The first is the iconographical tradition, which cannot be investigated here in even a superficial way. But I would point out that there are four distinct and fairly consistent artistic representations of "John" in the history of Christian art. The seer of Patmos who identifies himself as "John," the writer of the book of Revelation (see Rev. 1:1, 4, 9), is almost always pictured as an old man, usually with white hair and beard. The evangelist, usually accompanied by his device, the eagle, and his youthful amanuensis, Prochorus, taking dictation, is a mature man, usually bearded and balding. John the fisherman son of Zebedee, one of the Twelve, is usually pictured as a mature young man, often beardless but hardly adolescent and usually short-haired. But the Beloved Disciple, resting on the breast of the Lord at the Last Supper and standing with Mary at the foot of the cross, is strangely androgynous. This figure is virtually always beardless, often very young and delicate in appearance, and has long flowing hair and garments. In fact, his feminine appearance and his reclining in the bosom of Jesus at the supper have caused more than a little discomfort for some male commentators.[22] What I would call attention to is that it is not John, whether the seer of Patmos, the evangelist, or the son of Zebedee, who is androgynously presented in the artistic tradition but the Beloved Disciple. It is also interesting to note that the Beloved Disciple present on Calvary takes no part in the removal of Jesus' body from the cross and its entombment, which is carried

---

[22] Grassi devotes a section at the end of his book to the topic "A Note on This Close and Affectionate Male Relationship," no doubt acknowledging the discomfort of some male commentators with the scene at the supper (*Secret Identity,* 117–18).

out by two men, Joseph of Arimathea and Nicodemus. That would be very understandable if the Beloved Disciple on Calvary were female, but asks for some explanation if the disciple were male.

The second is the question already raised of why the identity of the Beloved Disciple is so carefully obscured in the Gospel text that it has been impossible, despite centuries of painstaking exegetical work, to identify this figure conclusively. It is hard to believe that if this figure is, in fact, the authority behind the Gospel the identity of this person was simply lost to memory. It is also difficult to believe that in the course of twenty-one chapters the Fourth Evangelist accidentally forgot to identify this person. In other words, the anonymity of the Beloved Disciple seems to be a deliberate, carefully executed literary strategy. The question is, strategy for what?

One possible hint of an explanation for the deliberate obscuring of the identity of the Beloved Disciple is the fact that the Gospel of John seems not to have been immediately accepted in the Great Church. Culpepper refers to the first half of the second century as the period of this Gospel's "obscurity."[23] It was not really until Irenaeus (ca. 130–200) offered his defense of the apostolic authorship of the Johannine Gospel and epistles late in the second century that the Fourth Gospel claimed its canonical place in the New Testament. There seems little doubt that part of the reason for the uncertainty of the early church about the Fourth Gospel derived from its popularity among the Gnostics, who were being labeled heretics during the second and third centuries.[24] And part of the reason for regarding the Gnostics as heretics seems to have been the very important apostolic roles and functions they assigned to women, even as the early church was retrenching from the egalitarian discipleship of the earliest Jesus movement.[25] Not only were women prominent leadership figures in the Gnostic literature, but among the women so portrayed Mary Magdalene was clearly the most important. Although Mary Magdalene plays an important role in numerous apocryphal texts, both heretical and orthodox, she is especially prominent in the Gnostic texts. It is not possible in this chapter even to begin to enter into the rapidly developing scholarly conversation about the character and role of Mary Magdalene in this literature[26] and especially about what this literature might suggest

---

[23] Culpepper, *John, the Son of Zebedee,* chapter 5, pp. 107–38.

[24] See the overview of this issue by Gerard S. Sloyan, "The Gnostic Adoption of John's Gospel and Its Canonization by the Church Catholic," *BTB* 26 (1996): 125–32.

[25] The thesis of egalitarian discipleship among the earliest Christian communities is substantiated in Elisabeth Schüssler Fiorenza, *In Memory of Her: A Feminist Theological Reconstruction of Christian Origins* (New York: Crossroad, 1983).

[26] A number of significant studies of this topic have appeared recently. See, e.g., Antti Mar-

about the apostolic identity and leadership role of the historical Mary Magdalene in the early church. However, if a composite picture of Mary Magdalene is constructed from this literature, she appears as Jesus' favorite and beloved disciple because she loves him more and better than the male disciples and is more perceptive of the deep meaning of his revelation and therefore is charged by Jesus to transmit and explain it, for which reason Simon Peter considers her a rival and tries unsuccessfully to get her demoted by Jesus. But Jesus defends her and her preeminence among the disciples as well as the superiority of her understanding of him and his message.[27] It is difficult not to recognize the features of the Johannine Beloved Disciple in this Mary Magdalene of the apocryphal literature.

If we are looking for a motive for the evangelist's deliberate obscuring of the identity of the Beloved Disciple in the Fourth Gospel, what better reason could there be than that the authoritative source of the Gospel was, or was connected in some way with, Mary Magdalene, the problematic woman protagonist in literature regarded as heretical at precisely the time that this Gospel was beginning to circulate at the beginning of the second century. The Gospel does not play down the preeminence or disguise the apostolic importance of women disciples. On the other hand, its Beloved Disciple, who is Simon Peter's rival, who rests in the bosom of Jesus and understands and believes what Peter misses, and who must mediate Jesus' secrets to Peter, is never unambiguously identified as a woman. If the Johannine community, and particularly the evangelist, was committed to assuring in the Great Church the acceptance of the Fourth Gospel through which Jesus' will that the testimony of the Beloved Disciple would "remain until Jesus comes" (cf. 21:22–23), it would be of high strategic importance that the Gospel not be identified with the agenda of the Gnostics, specifically with their promotion of women, whom the Great Church was already trying to silence by patriarchal legislation such as we find in the Pauline household codes. To me this makes better sense than the hypothesis that the Beloved Disciple remains anonymous through personal humility or by the accidental oversight of the

---

janen, *The Woman Jesus Loved: Mary Magdalene in the Nag Hammadi Library and Related Documents,* Nag Hammadi and Manichaean Studies (Leiden/New York/Cologne: E. J. Brill, 1996); Mary R. Thompson, *Mary of Magdala: Apostle and Leader* (New York/Mahwah, N.J.: Paulist, 1995), especially chapters 6 and 7; Carla Ricci, *Mary Magdalene and Many Others: Women Who Followed Jesus* (Minneapolis: Fortress Press, 1994).

[27] For a detailed treatment of Mary Magdalene in each document, see Marjanen, *The Woman Jesus Loved.* For a more synthetic treatment of the data from the apocryphal literature against the background of an understanding of female leadership in the Mediterranean world at the beginning of the Christian era, see Thompson, *Mary of Magdala.*

evangelist, much less that the community forgot who the Beloved Disciple was by the end of the first century.

THE HYPOTHESIS

Having laid out the reasons that have led me to reconsider the question of Johannine authorship, I want now to suggest a hypothesis that could open some interesting lines of research. As already stated, I regard the "author" of this Gospel to be both the authority from which the tradition stems (i.e., the Beloved Disciple) and the evangelist (a second-century Johannine Christian) mutually interacting in the production of the text. Although these figures cannot be simply identified, I think there is an overlap between them which arises from the hypothesis I will propose about the identity of the Beloved Disciple. Finally, the ecclesiastical redactor who edited the Gospel may well have further disguised that identity in order to mute the issue of gender in relation to the Beloved Disciple and thereby distance the Gospel from Gnostic texts and promote its acceptance in the Great Church.

The hypothesis I am proposing is the following: the Beloved Disciple is neither a pure literary symbol nor a single historical individual. The Beloved Disciple is a kind of textual paradigm who concretely embodies in the text the corporate authority of the Johannine school. The Beloved Disciple *in the text* is a kind of prism refracting the ideal of discipleship into a number of characters, each of whom realizes the paradigm by unfolding or acting out critical features of Johannine discipleship. The Beloved Disciple, in other words, is both a literary device (a textual paradigm) and a pluralistic historical reality (a plurality of actual disciples presented as unique and diverse incarnations of this paradigm). The Beloved Disciple is neither a pure ideal nor a single (male) historical figure but the textual presentation of the real, corporate authority of the Johannine school, which was embodied and exercised by real Johannine disciples. The textual paradigm is derived from real disciples who realize it in diverse ways. The textual figures who incarnate the Beloved Disciple paradigm are typical Johannine representative figures,[28] that is, real figures of the Johannine community and/or of the life of Jesus who have been "idealized" by the evangelist to carry some particular aspect of discipleship in a strikingly clear way. Several reasons seem to me to support this hypothesis.

---

[28] See n. 20 above.

Negative Reasons

Two negative considerations will help to clear the way for some positive ones. First, I do not think that the really crucial Beloved Disciple passages, particularly the scene at the Last Supper and the scene at the foot of the cross, absolutely require an exclusively male identification of the figure. I cannot fully substantiate that claim in a chapter of this length except to the extent that I have for the scene at the foot of the cross. Second, the Beloved Disciple, whom almost all commentators agree is intended to be the ideal disciple, is peculiarly featureless in the Gospel if taken alone.[29] If readers had to discern what discipleship means from an examination of this figure alone, they would know very little about it—and certainly not enough to pattern their own discipleship on it. The Beloved Disciple as an "individual" does not even appear until the passion, and so we have no idea how this figure responds to Jesus' words and signs during the public ministry, and we get no real insight into personal characteristics, motives, struggles, or way of following Jesus. We actually build up our understanding of the Beloved Disciple from the other characters who realize the paradigm of discipleship that the Beloved Disciple textually constellates.[30]

Positive Reasons

Several positive considerations also seem to support the hypothesis. First, excellent arguments have been given over the centuries for some of the candidates for the role of Beloved Disciple. In particular, there are very good arguments for Lazarus, whom, we are told, "Jesus loved."[31] But if the text of

---

[29] Raymond F. Collins notes that "the enigmatic Beloved Disciple plays only a minor role in the Fourth Gospel. . . . Nonetheless, the Beloved looms large in the narrative. . . . In his anonymity and stylization, the Beloved is the epitome of discipleship; he is the disciple par excellence. . . . the Beloved believes unhesitatingly that Jesus is the Lord. Virtually reduced to a single trait, the Beloved is the consummate disciple and authentic witness to the rest of the story" ("From John to the Beloved Disciple: An Essay on Johannine Characters," *Int* 49 [1995]: 367). I think Collins comes close to noting the reason the Beloved Disciple should be regarded as a textual paradigm but does not quite draw the conclusion.

[30] Although Grassi does not propose that the Beloved Disciple is a textual paradigm, he does make some interesting suggestions about others sharing this idenitity in some way (*Secret Identity*). In particular, he claims that Mary Magdalene is "almost a counterpart of the beloved disciple . . . sharing the same role from a woman's unique standpoint" (p. 90). If she and other disciples share the role, then the role is paradigmatic in the sense I am suggesting.

[31] Most recently Stibbe presents the arguments for Lazarus (*John as Storyteller*, 56–72).

John 11 is read carefully, this distinguishing note applies to Martha and Mary of Bethany as well as to Lazarus, all three of whom we are explicitly told in 11:5 "Jesus loved." Martha and Mary give us excellent vignettes of what active discipleship means in terms of believing, confessing, serving, loving, and witnessing, and Lazarus offers a more passive but important note of identification with Jesus in his persecution, which follows from sharing table [eucharistic?] fellowship with him and which promises eternal life.

Nathanael, the true Israelite in whom there is no guile, whose name, like John, means "gift of God," and who, in chapter 1, makes the proleptic confession of faith in Jesus as "the Son of God and the King of Israel" is an excellent representative of the Johannine community of disciples which was struggling to appropriate its identity as the true Israel of God in the face of exile from the synagogue. Nathanael is paralleled by Thomas the Twin, whose three appearances in the Gospel are a very effective picture of the journey of true discipleship. In 11:16 it is Thomas who says, "Let us go and die with him," when Jesus insists on returning to hostile Judea to awaken Lazarus. In 14:5–6 Thomas begs Jesus for a clear indication of the way to follow him and receives the paradigmatic answer, "I am the way, the truth, and the life," which is what every disciple finally needs to believe and live. And in 20:24–29 Thomas crosses the threshold between eyewitness faith in the earthly Jesus and paschal faith in the glorified Jesus with the confession that has been taken up by believers down through the centuries, "My Lord and my God."

The Samaritan woman, who acts out her new faith in Jesus as the Messiah by bringing her whole town to encounter him, and the man born blind, who comes to believe and accepts excommunication from Judaism rather than renounce the one who has enlightened him in the waters of the Sent One, are certainly models of the cost and the responsibilities of discipleship.

The royal official, the Gentile who believes in the life-giving word of Jesus without seeing signs, is clearly a model of Johannine faith. And Mary Magdalene, preeminently, embodies the meaning of discipleship as loving belief so powerful that it places her at the foot of the cross, brings her to the empty tomb, converts her to recognition of the Jesus she has loved in the Risen One, and makes her able to accept and fulfill his commission to announce the gospel of the resurrection.

In other words, there are a number of very well drawn portraits of disciples in the Fourth Gospel, each emphasizing different but essential aspects of the relationship to Jesus that constitutes discipleship. It takes all of them to give the reader a rounded picture of the ideal that the Beloved Disciple as textual paradigm represents. What the Beloved Disciple figure in the text does is pull all these features together into one, but without these portraits we would not know what that one actually means or involves.

A second support for this hypothesis is that it fits well with the Johannine theology of the Paraclete, who is given by Jesus to all his disciples. Unlike apostleship in the Great Church, which tends to create a hierarchical community with a few preeminent members in leadership positions, Johannine discipleship seems to create a community of equals, each of whom is called to become a beloved disciple. In John Jesus washes the feet of all his disciples and commands them to do the same for each other (see 13:1–15). All Jesus' sheep are called by name by the one and only Shepherd (see 10:1–6; 11–16).[32] All are, by equal title, branches of the true Vine of which God alone is the vinedresser (see 15:1–8). It is on the community as a whole that Jesus breathes forth the Spirit and to the community as a whole that he entrusts his own mission of taking away sins (see 20:21–23). Basically this is because all, equally, receive the gift of the Paraclete, who unites them to Jesus and the One who sent him as well as to one another.

A third factor that supports the hypothesis that the Beloved Disciple is a textual paradigm is that this hypothesis allows for affirming that the authoritative tradition behind the Fourth Gospel stems from the Johannine school without simply equating that authority with the community as a whole. The Johannine community, as the Johannine epistles seem to indicate, surely had problematic or uncommitted members. The hypothesis of the Beloved Disciple as a textual paradigm realized historically in a variety of specific individuals known in the community suggests that the tradition emerged from and is guaranteed by those who truly understood and lived the mystery of the risen Jesus, who were in fact beloved disciples. This supplies a theoretical basis for the consensus among Johannine scholars that the Beloved Disciple is both the locus of the authoritative tradition which comes to expression in the Fourth Gospel and the ideal of discipleship for those who read the Gospel down through the centuries.

Conclusion on the Beloved Disciple

Pulling these considerations together, I see three reasons for the seemingly insoluble anonymity of the Beloved Disciple in the text. First, the Beloved

---

[32] It must be noted that in John, even in 21:15–17, which may well be the work of the ecclesiastical redactor, Simon Peter is not made shepherd but is told to feed and tend *Jesus'* lambs and sheep.

Disciple cannot be specifically identified because, in fact, this figure is not one specific person but a textual paradigm realized in a plurality of textual figures who are drawn from real historical characters in the life of Jesus and/or the community.

Second, it really cannot be the case that there was or is one disciple whom Jesus loves more than all others or even to the exclusion of all others. In fact, the Gospel never tells us that "this is the disciple Jesus preferred" or "this was Jesus' favorite disciple" or this was "the only disciple Jesus loved." We are told "this is the disciple whom Jesus loved," an epithet that fits all believers who manifest certain qualifications during the lifetime of Jesus, in the time of the Johannine community, and down through the ages. The "other disciple" in John is a kind of empty set, a structured textual "space" (or implied reader) into which the reader is to insert her- or himself. This other disciple becomes a beloved disciple, or falls away, depending on what she or he does in response to the Gospel, which is written so that the reader may believe that Jesus is the Christ, the Son of God, and so have life in his name (see 20:31). To become a beloved disciple involves responding to the invitation to "come and see" and "to remain with" Jesus, to follow him even into persecution, to see and believe through the written signs even without having seen the earthly Jesus, and to do Jesus' work of bringing in the ministerial catch that Jesus initiates. These are the behaviors and roles associated with the Beloved Disciple in the text.

Third, because the Beloved Disciple in John was not exclusively or pre-eminently one of the Twelve and certainly was not beloved because of being one of the Twelve,[33] the authenticity of the Gospel arising from the tradition of this disciple would have been challengeable by the churches tracing their foundation to the Twelve or those authorized by them. If the Fourth Gospel was to be acceptable in the Great Church, it must be established that it stemmed from an authority who was an eyewitness, someone who walked with Jesus between his baptism and his final departure, saw the risen Lord, and was commissioned by him. These criteria are met, corporately, by the Beloved Disciple. But the identity of this authority, which includes both women and men, Jewish, Gentile, and Samaritan believers, must be ambiguous enough that Gnostic-fearful guardians of orthodoxy will not reject it out of hand because it includes women and yet clear enough on the preeminent role of women in the community to be true to the community's actual experience and what it really believed about the equal discipleship of men and women.

[33] The only uses of the term "the Twelve" in John are negative: 6:67–71; 20:24.

Tentative Suggestion on the Identity of the Evangelist

If the hypothesis that the Beloved Disciple is a textual paradigm realized in a plurality of Gospel figures who is both the authoritative factor in the authorship of the Fourth Gospel and the ideal of discipleship for the reader has any merit, it might throw some light on the question of the identity of the evangelist. I believe, with most commentators, that the literary, theological, and spiritual unity of the Fourth Gospel are such that the text must stem from a single religious genius, probably an outstanding figure of the Johannine school. The probable date of the writing of the Gospel, sometime between 90 and 110 C.E., suggests that the evangelist was a second-generation member of the Johannine community.

I do not think we will ever know with certainty the identity of the evangelist, because the evangelist does not want us to know it and is a good enough writer to keep us from finding it out. But of all the characters in the Gospel, the most likely candidate for the evangelist's *textual alter ego* is the Samaritan woman in chapter 4. Lacking the space to develop each point, I will list a number of factors that make me think this character might be the evangelist's literary self-portrait, whatever the historical evangelist's actual identity or gender might be. Essentially my argument is that this hypothesis would solve a number of interpretive problems in the episode of the Samaritan woman and would fit well with what we do seem able to discern about the evangelist.

The Samaritan woman in chapter 4 is certainly the most theologically sophisticated interlocutor of Jesus in the Fourth Gospel and is deliberately contrasted with the theologically obtuse "teacher in Israel," Nicodemus in chapter 3.[34] She knows both Jewish and Samaritan law and theology (e.g., about the role of the patriarchs in Samaritan theology, the appropriate place of worship, and relations between Jews and Samaritans) and requires of Jesus some reconciliation of their differences before she accepts his revelation (cf. 4:9–12, 20–24). She receives the first "*egō eimi*" (I am) revelation of Jesus' identity in the Fourth Gospel (4:26), understands that he is the messianic prophet like Moses "who will tell us all things" (4:25) awaited by the Samaritans and the "messiah" expected by the Jews, which together constitute the way that Jesus' identity is presented in the Fourth Gospel by the evangelist. And despite the fact that she obviously correctly identifies Jesus and must, therefore, believe in him since she goes off to bring her fellow townspeople to "come and see," she does not simply tell them who Jesus is but poses the ques-

---

[34] See chapter 8 on this point. See also the article by Mary Margaret Pazdan, "Nicodemus and the Samaritan Woman: Contrasting Models of Discipleship," *BTB* 17 (1987): 145–48.

tion, "Can this be the Messiah?" (4:29). This, in fact, is exactly what the evangelist does in the Gospel, that is, presents the words and works—that is, the signs—of Jesus and leaves the readers with the challenge to come and see, to decide whether to believe that this is indeed the Messiah, the Son of God, the Savior of the World, so that believing they may have life in his name (cf. 20:30–31).

The scene in chapter 4 is anomalous in several respects that might be easier to understand if the Samaritan woman is the evangelist's textual alter ego. Jesus in John, unlike in the Synoptics, does not send any of his disciples on mission during his earthly lifetime. Only the Samaritan woman, with Jesus' evident approbation (see 4:35), evangelizes, bringing many from her town to Jesus (see 4:39–41). Furthermore, they confess him to be the "Savior of the World" (4:42), hardly a possible title for the earthly Jesus, especially at the very beginning of his public ministry, but very appropriate from the postglorification Johannine community made up of Jewish, Gentile, and Samaritan Christians. My conclusion is that this episode is an account of the postglorification entrance of the Samaritans into the Johannine community, narratively read back into the lifetime of the earthly Jesus.

In this scene there is a very puzzling speech of Jesus to his returning disciples in which he tells them that in regard to the Samaritans "'[o]ne sows and another reaps.' I sent [ἀπέστειλα (apesteila), aorist tense] you to reap that for which you did not labor. Others have labored and you [i.e., presumably the Twelve and their co-workers] have entered into their labor" (4:38). Since the Twelve and their co-workers are historically the first evangelizers, who could have preceded them so that they would enter into the harvest of their predecessors? This saying would make sense if, in fact, the reference is to the Samaritan mission, evangelized (i.e., "sown") by the Johannine community, and only later acknowledged ("reaped") by the Great Church.

If this hypothesis is valid, then the Samaritan woman in the text would represent a theologically astute, second-generation Johannine Christian well able to blend Jewish and Samaritan theology into the peculiar Johannine synthesis with its "I am" God theology, anti-temple bias, high Christology, egalitarian and inclusive ecclesiology, and a sense of superiority to the churches founded by the Twelve. She is the recipient of Jesus' direct self-revelation, which constitutes her message and establishes her authority. The text subtly indicates that she, proleptically in the text but probably after the fact historically, fulfills Jesus' final prayer for not only his earthly disciples but for those who "through their word [διὰ τοῦ λόγου αὐτῶν (dia tou logou autōn)] will believe in me" (John 17:20) because many of the Samaritans believed in Jesus "because of the word of the woman bearing witness" [διὰ τὸν λόγον τῆς γυναικὸς μαρτυρούσης (dia ton logon tēs gynaikos martyrousēs)] (4:39).

If there is a Renaissance-type "signature" of the evangelist in the Gospel text, it is probably 4:27, in which the returning male disciples are shocked that Jesus is speaking with a woman but know better than to question what Jesus seeks in speaking with her. The use of the two technical Johannine revelation words, "seek" (ζητέω [*zēteō*]) and "speak" (λαλέω [*laleō*]), in this text (τί ζητεῖς ἢ τί λαλεῖς μετ' αὐτῆς [*ti zēteis ē ti laleis met' autēs*]) are very suggestive. What the male disciples see, find shocking, but know better than to question is Jesus' choice, indeed profound intention, to reveal himself to and through a woman.

SUMMARY AND CONCLUSIONS

Let me briefly summarize the conclusions I am proposing as a hypothesis worth further research in regard to the authorship of the Fourth Gospel. The authoritative tradition from which the Fourth Gospel derives is the eyewitness testimony of the Beloved Disciple, a textual paradigm realized in the leading figures in the Johannine school and refracted in the text through such characters as Nathanael, the Samaritan woman, the royal official, the man born blind, Martha and Mary and Lazarus of Bethany, Mary Magdalene, and Thomas the Twin. The most significant of these figures is certainly Mary Magdalene, who is the witness to and proclaimer of the paschal mystery. Besides the role in authorship played by the Beloved Disciple, this figure also models the Johannine ideal of discipleship, thus making the Gospel itself both a testimony to the Johannine understanding of discipleship and an invitation to the reader, the other disciple, to enter into that identity by becoming a believer and receiving eternal life.

The evangelist, the single individual who actually wrote the text, is a second-generation Johannine Christian, an outstanding representative of the Johannine school, whose identity has been permanently disguised, probably as part of the strategy to establish the legitimacy of this Gospel in the Great Church. However, the textual alter ego of the evangelist, whatever her or his actual identity and gender might have been,[35] is the figure of the Samaritan woman, which accounts for the blending of Jewish and Samaritan theology

---

[35] Elisabeth Schüssler Fiorenza attributes to me the position that John was written by a woman evangelist (*But She Said: Feminist Practices of Biblical Interpretation* [Boston: Beacon, 1992], 28). This is not quite accurate, as the foregoing argument should make clear. I think the gender as well as the specific identity of the evangelist is and will remain unavailable to us. But that means that it is no more self-evident that the evangelist was male than female, and, as I have tried to show, there are some good reasons to consider female identity.

in the Gospel, its claim to derive its authenticity directly from Jesus' revelation rather than from the evangelizing of the Twelve, and its narrative insistence on the constitutive role of women in the Johannine community.

Finally, there was probably a redactor who made minor changes in the text and perhaps added most of chapter 21 sometime after the work of the evangelist was complete (perhaps even after the latter's death) and before the Gospel began to circulate outside the community probably in the second decade of the second century. Part of the agenda of this redactor was to make the Gospel acceptable in the Great Church by softening without completely subverting the two most problematic characteristics of the Gospel: the autonomy, if not superiority, of the Beloved Disciple (i.e., the Johannine community and its witness) in relation to Simon Peter, and the preeminent role of women, especially Mary Magdalene as the foundational apostolic witness of the community. The redactor tried to assure that neither the challenge to the Great Church's understanding of Petrine primacy nor the ecclesial leadership of women, both of which had Gnostic potential, worked against the intention of Jesus that the witness of the Beloved Disciple should remain until Jesus comes (cf. 21:22) through the word of the "woman bearing witness" that is written in the Gospel text so that you, the reader, may believe and may have life in Jesus' name.

Bibliography

Aelred of Rievaulx. *Spiritual Friendship.* Translated by Mary Eugenia Laker. Washington, D.C.: Cistercian, 1974.

Anderson, Paul. *The Christology of the Fourth Gospel: Its Unity and Disunity in the Light of John 6.* Valley Forge, Pa.: Trinity, 1996.

Arendt, Hannah. *The Human Condition.* Garden City, N.Y.: Doubleday, 1959.

Ashton, John. *Understanding the Fourth Gospel.* Oxford: Clarendon, 1991.

Augustine. *On Christian Doctrine.* Translated by D. W. Robertson, Jr. New York: Macmillan, 1958.

Barclay, William. *Introduction to John and the Acts of the Apostles.* Philadelphia: Westminster, 1976.

Barnhart, Bruno. *The Good Wine: Reading John from the Center.* New York: Paulist, 1993.

Barrett, C. K. "The Dialectical Theology of St. John." In *New Testament Essays,* 49–69. London: SPCK, 1972.

———. *The Gospel According to St. John.* 2nd ed. London: SPCK, 1978.

Bauckham, Richard. "The Beloved Disciple as Ideal Author." *JSNT* 49 (1993): 21–44.

Beardslee, William A. "Recent Literary Criticism." In *The New Testament and Its Modern Interpreters,* edited by Eldon J. Epp and George W. Macrae, 175–98. Philadelphia: Fortress, 1989. Vol. 3 of *The Bible and Its Modern Interpreters,* edited by Douglas A. Knight. Society of Biblical Literature Centennial Publications.

Beck, Norman A. *Mature Christianity in the 21st Century: The Recognition and Repudiation of the Anti-Jewish Polemic of the New Testament.* Expanded and revised ed. New York: Crossroad, 1994.

Belleville, Linda. "'Born of Water and Spirit': John 3:5." *Trinity Journal* 1 (1980): 125–41.

Black, C. Clifton. "Rhetorical Criticism." In *Hearing the New Testament: Strategies for Interpretation,* edited by Joel Green, 256–77. Grand Rapids: Eerdmans, 1995.

Bligh, John. "Jesus in Samaria." *HeyJ* 3 (1962): 329–46.

Boismard, Marie-Emile. *Du baptême à Cana (Jean 1,19–2,11).* Lectio Divina. Paris: Cerf, 1956.

———. "Le lavement des pieds (Jn xiii, 1–17)." *RB* 71 (1964): 5–24.

Borg, Marcus J. *The God We Never Knew: Beyond Dogmatic Religion to a More Authentic Contemporary Faith.* New York: HarperCollins, 1997.

Bovon, François. "Le privilège pascal de marie-madeleine." *NTS* 30 (1984): 50–62.

Braun, F.-M. *Le linceul de Turin et l'évangile de S. Jean: Etude de critique et d'exégèse.* Tournai/Paris: Casterman, 1939.

Brown, Raymond E. *The Churches the Apostles Left Behind.* New York: Paulist, 1984.

———. *The Community of the Beloved Disciple: The Life, Loves, and Hates of an Individual Church in New Testament Times.* New York: Paulist, 1979.

———. *The Gospel According to John.* 2 vols. Anchor Bible 29, 29A. Garden City, N.Y.: Doubleday, 1966, 1970.

———. "Johannine Ecclesiology—the Community's Origins." *Int* 31 (1977): 379–93.

———. "The Paraclete: Spirit's Gift to the Church." Audiotape of lecture series given in 1998. Available from The Audio File, P.O. Box 93, Glenview, IL 60025.

———. *Reading the Gospels with the Church: From Christmas Through Easter.* Cincinnati, Oh.: St. Anthony Messenger Press, 1996.

———. *A Retreat with John the Evangelist: That You May Have Life.* Cincinnati: St. Anthony Messenger, 1998.

———. "Roles of Women in the Fourth Gospel." Appendix II in *The Community of the Beloved Disciple: The Life, Loves, and Hates of an Individual Church in New Testament Times,* 183–98. New York: Paulist, 1979. Originally published as "Roles of Women in the Fourth Gospel." *TS* 36 (1975): 688–99.

———. *The Virginal Conception and Bodily Resurrection of Jesus.* London: Geoffrey Chapman, 1973.

Brown, Raymond E., Karl P. Donfried, Joseph A. Fitzmyer, and John Reumann, eds. *Mary in the New Testament: A Collaborative Assessment by Protestant and Roman Catholic Scholars.* Philadelphia: Fortress, 1978.

Bultmann, Rudolf. *The Gospel of John: A Commentary.* Translated by George R. Beasley-Murray. Oxford: Blackwell, 1971.

Cadman, W. H. "The Raising of Lazarus (John 10:40–11:53)." *SE* I = *TU* 73, 423–34. Berlin: Akademie-Verlag, 1959.

Cahill, P. Joseph. "Narrative Art in John IV." *RelS Bulletin* 2 (April 1982): 44–47.

Carmichael, Calum M. "Marriage and the Samaritan Woman." *NTS* 26 (1980): 331–46.

Charlesworth, James H. *The Beloved Disciple: Whose Witness Validates the Gospel of John?* Valley Forge, Pa.: Trinity, 1995.

Collins, Raymond F. "From John to the Beloved Disciple: An Essay on Johannine Characters." *Int* 49 (1995): 359–69.

———. "Mary in the Fourth Gospel: A Decade of Johannine Studies." *LS* 3 (1970): 99–142.

———. "The Representative Figures in the Fourth Gospel." *DRev* 94 (1976): 26–46, 118–32.

Combet-Galland, Corina. "L'Aube encore obscure: Approche sémiotique de Jean 20." *Foi et Vie* (September 1987): 17–25.

Corell, Alf. *Consummatum Est: Eschatology and Church in the Gospel of St. John.* London: SPCK, 1958.

Crown, Alan D., ed. *The Samaritans.* Tübingen: J. C. B. Mohr, 1989.

Cullmann, Oscar. *The Johannine Circle.* Translated by John Bowden. Philadelphia: Westminster, 1976.

Culpepper, R. Alan. *Anatomy of the Fourth Gospel: A Study in Literary Design.* Philadelphia: Fortress, 1983.

———. *The Gospel and Letters of John.* Interpreting Biblical Texts. Nashville, Tenn.: Abingdon, 1998.

———. *The Johannine School: An Evaluation of the Johannine-School Hypothesis Based on an Investigation of the Nature of the Ancient Schools.* Society of Biblical Literature Dissertation Series. Missoula, Mont.: Scholars Press, 1975.

———. *John, the Son of Zebedee: The Life of a Legend.* Columbia: University of South Carolina Press, 1994.

———. "Reading Johannine Irony." *Exploring the Gospel of John: In Honor of D. Moody Smith,* edited by R. Alan Culpepper and C. Clifton Black, 193–207. Louisville, Ky.: Westminster John Knox, 1996.

Culpepper, R. Alan, and Fernando F. Segovia, eds. *The Fourth Gospel from a Literary Perspective, Semeia* 53. Atlanta: Scholars Press, 1991.

Dodd, C. H. "The Prophecy of Caiaphas: John XI 47–53." In *Neotestamentica et Patristica: Eine Freundesgabe, Herrn Professor Dr. Oscar Cullmann zu Seinem 60. Geburtstag,* 134–43. NovTSup. Leiden: E. J. Brill, 1962.

Donahue, John R. "Redaction Criticism: Has the *Hauptstrasse* Become a *Sackgasse?*" In *The New Literary Criticism and the New Testament,* edited by Edgar V. McKnight and Elizabeth Struthers Malbon, 27–57. Valley Forge, Pa.: Trinity, 1994.

Duke, Paul D. *Irony in the Fourth Gospel.* Atlanta: John Knox, 1985.

Dunkerley, R. "Lazarus." *NTS* 5 (1958–59): 321–27.

Dunn, James D. G. *Christology in the Making: A New Testament Inquiry into the Origins of the Doctrine of the Incarnation.* Philadelphia: Westminster, 1980.

Durand, G. *L'imagination symbolique.* Initiation Philosophique. Paris: Presses Universitaires de France, 1968.

Ellis, Peter F. *The Genius of John: A Composition-Critical Commentary on the Fourth Gospel.* Collegeville, Minn.: Liturgical Press, 1984.

Eslinger, Lyle. "The Wooing of the Woman at the Well: Jesus, the Reader and Reader-Response Criticism." *JLitTheo* 1 (1987): 167–83.

Evans, Christopher F. *Resurrection and the New Testament.* Studies in Biblical Theology, 2nd ser. London: SCM, 1970.

Fawcett, Thomas. *The Symbolic Language of Religion: An Introductory Study.* London: SCM, 1970.

Fehribach, Adeline. *The Women in the Life of the Bridegroom: A Feminist Historical-Literary Analysis of the Female Characters in the Fourth Gospel.* Collegeville, Minn.: Liturgical Press, 1998.

Flanagan, Neal. "Gospel of John as Drama." *Bible Today* 19 (July 1981): 264–70.

Ford, Josephine Massyngberde. *Redeemer—Friend and Mother: Salvation in Antiquity and in the Gospel of John.* Minneapolis: Fortress, 1997.

Forestell, J. Terence. *The Word of the Cross: Salvation as Revelation in the Fourth Gospel,* Analecta Biblica 57. Rome: Biblical Institute Press, 1974.

Fortna, Robert T. "Theological Use of Locale in the Fourth Gospel." *ATR* Supplement Series 3 (1974): 58–95.

Fowler, Robert. "Born of Water and the Spirit (Jn 3:5)." *ExpTim* 82 (1971): 159.

Freed, Edwin D. *Old Testament Quotations in the Gospel of John.* NovTSup 11. Leiden: E. J. Brill, 1965.

Gadamer, Hans-Georg. *Truth and Method.* 2nd rev. ed. Translation revised by Joel Weinsheimer and Donald G. Marshall. New York: Crossroad, 1989.

Geach, Peter, and Max Black, eds. *Translations from the Philosophical Writings of Gottlob Frege.* Oxford: Blackwell, 1970.

George, Augustin. "Les récits d'apparitions aux onze à partir de Luc 24, 26–53." In *La Résurrection du Christ et l'exégèse moderne.* Lectio Divina. Paris: Cerf, 1969.

Ghiberti, Giuseppe. *I racconti pasquali del capitolo 20 di Giovanni.* Studi Biblici. Brescia: Paideia, 1972.

Giblin, Charles H. "Suggestion, Negative Response, and Positive Action in St. John's Portrayal of Jesus (John 2.1–11; 4.46–54; 7.12–14; 11.1–44)." *NTS* 26 (1980): 197–211.

Gils, Félix. "Pierre et la foi au Christ ressuscité." *Ephemerides Theologicae Lovanienses* 38 (1962): 5–43.

Gitay, Yehoshua. "Rhetorical Criticism." In *To Each Its Own Meaning: An Introduction to Biblical Criticisms and Their Application,* edited by Stephen R. Haynes and Steven L. McKenzie, 135–49. Louisville, Ky.: Westminster/John Knox, 1993.

Grant, Robert, and David Tracy. *A Short History of the Interpretation of the Bible.* 2nd ed., revised and enlarged. Philadelphia: Fortress, 1984.

Grassi, Joseph A. *The Secret Identity of the Beloved Disciple.* New York/Mahwah, N.J.: Paulist, 1992.

Gugenbühl-Craig, Adolph. *Power in the Helping Professions.* Edited by J. Hillman. Dallas, Tex.: Spring, 1971.

Harvey, A. E. *Jesus on Trial: A Study in the Fourth Gospel.* Atlanta: John Knox, 1976.

Hengel, Martin. *The Johannine Question.* Translated by J. Bowden. London: SCM; Philadelphia: Trinity, 1989.

———. "Maria Magdalena und die Frauen als Zeugen." In *Abraham Unser Vater: Juden und Christen im Gespräch Über die Bibel,* edited by O. Betz et al., 243–56. Leiden: E. J. Brill, 1963.

Henneberry, Brian H. *The Raising of Lazarus (John 11:1–44): An Evaluation of the Hypothesis That a Written Tradition Lies Behind the Narrative.* Ann Arbor: University Microfilms, 1984.

Holladay, William L. *The Root ŠÛBH in the Old Testament, with Particular Reference to Its Usages in Covenantal Contexts.* Leiden: E. J. Brill, 1958.

Hurtado, Larry W. "Gospel (Genre)." In *Dictionary of Jesus and the Gospels,* edited by Joel B. Green and Scot McKnight, 276–82. Downers Grove, Ill.: InterVarsity, 1992.

Jones, John R. *Narrative Structures and Meaning in John 11:1–54.* Ann Arbor: University Microfilms, 1982.

Jones, Larry Paul. *The Symbol of Water in the Gospel of John.* JSNTSup 145. Sheffield: Sheffield Academic Press, 1997.

Koester, Craig R. *Symbolism in the Fourth Gospel: Meaning, Mystery, Community.* Minneapolis: Fortress, 1995.

Küng, Hans. *On Being A Christian.* New York: Doubleday, 1976.

Kysar, Robert. *The Fourth Evangelist and His Gospel: An Examination of Contemporary Scholarship.* Minneapolis: Augsburg, 1975.

———. *John.* Augsburg Commentary on the New Testament. Minneapolis: Augsburg, 1986.

———. *John: The Maverick Gospel.* Atlanta: John Knox, 1976.

Leal, J. "El simbolismo histórico del IV evangelio." *EstBib* 19 (1960): 329–48.

Lee, Dorothy A. *The Symbolic Narratives of the Fourth Gospel.* SNTS Supplement Series 95. Sheffield: JSOT Press, 1994.

Leibig, James E. "John and 'the Jews': Theological Antisemitism in the Fourth Gospel." *JES* 20 (1983): 209–34.

Léon-Dufour, Xavier. *Resurrection and the Message of Easter.* Translated by R. N. Wilson. New York: Holt, Rinehart & Winston, 1975.

Lieu, Judith M. "The Mother of the Son in the Fourth Gospel." *JBL* 117 (1998): 61–77.

Lindars, Barnabas. "The Fourth Gospel an Act of Contemplation." In *Studies in the Fourth Gospel,* edited by F. L. Cross, 23–35. London, Mowbray, 1957.

———. *The Gospel of John.* New Century Bible. London: Oliphants, 1972.

Lukken, G. M. *Original Sin in the Roman Sacramentaria and the Early Baptismal Liturgy.* Leiden: E. J. Brill, 1973.

Maccini, Robert Gordon. *Her Testimony Is True: Women as Witnesses According to John.* JSNTSup 125. Sheffield: Sheffield Academic Press, 1996.

Macdonald, John. *The Theology of the Samaritans.* Philadelphia: Westminster, 1964.

MacRae, George W. "The Fourth Gospel and Religionsgeschichte." *CBQ* 32 (1970): 13–24.

Mahoney, Robert. *Two Disciples at the Tomb: The Background and Message of John 20:1–10.* Theologie und Wirklichkeit 6. Bern/Frankfurt-am-Main: H. Lang & P. Lang, 1974.

Maier, Gerhard. *The End of the Historical Critical Method.* St. Louis: Concordia, 1977.

Marconi, Gilberto. "La vista del cieco: Struttura di Gv 9, 1-41." *Gregoriana* 79 (1998): 625–43.

Marjanen, Antti. *The Woman Jesus Loved: Mary Magdalene in the Nag Hammadi Library and Related Documents.* Nag Hammadi and Manichaean Studies. Leiden/New York/Cologne: E. J. Brill, 1996.

Marrow, Stanley B. *The Gospel of John: A Reading.* New York: Paulist, 1995.

Martin, J. P. "History and Eschatology in the Lazarus Narrative: John 11, 1–44." *SJT* 17 (1964): 332–43.

Martyn, J. Louis. *History and Theology in the Fourth Gospel.* 2nd ed. Revised and enlarged. Nashville: Abingdon, 1979.

McKnight, Edgar V. *Post-Modern Use of the Bible: The Emergence of Reader-Oriented Criticism.* Nashville: Abingdon, 1988.

————. "Reader-Response Criticism." In *To Each Its Own Meaning: An Introduction to Biblical Criticisms and Their Application,* edited by Stephen R. Haynes and Steven L. McKenzie, 198–219. Louisville, Ky.: Westminster/John Knox, 1993.

McKnight, Edgar V. and Elizabeth Struthers Malbon, eds. *The New Literary Criticism and the New Testament.* Valley Forge, Pa.: Trinity, 1994.

McNamara, M. A. *Friends and Friendship for Saint Augustine.* Staten Island, N.Y.: Alba House, 1964.

McNeil, Brian. "The Raising of Lazarus." *DRev* 92 (1974): 269–75.

Meeks, Wayne A. "The Man from Heaven in Johannine Sectarianism." *JBL* 91 (1972): 44–72.

————. *The Prophet-King: Moses Traditions and the Johannine Christology.* NovTSup. Leiden: E. J. Brill, 1967.

Michel, Marc. "Nicodème ou le non-lieu de la verité." *RevScRel* 55 (1981): 227–36.

Middleton, Deborah F. "Feminist Interpretation." In *A Dictionary of Biblical Interpretation,* edited by R. J. Coggins and J. L. Houlden, 231–34. London: SCM; Philadelphia: Trinity, 1990.

Miles, Margaret R. *Seeing and Believing: Religion and Values in the Movies.* Boston: Beacon, 1996.

Minear, Paul S. "The Beloved Disciple in the Gospel of John: Some Clues and Conjectures." *NovT* 19 (1977): 105–23.

————. "'We Don't Know Where . . .' John 20:2." *Int* 30 (1976): 125–39.

Mollat, Donatian. "La conversion chez saint Jean." In *L'espérance du royaume,* 55–78. Parole de Vie. Tours: Mame, 1966.

————. "La découverte du tombeau vide (Jn 20, 1–9)." *Assemblées du Seigneur* 221 (1969): 90–100.

Moloney, Francis J. *The Gospel of John.* Sacra Pagina Series. Collegeville, Minn.: Liturgical Press, 1998.

————. "To Teach the Text: The New Testament in a New Age." *Pacifica* 11 (1998): 159–80.

Montague, George T. "Hermeneutics and the Teaching of Scripture." *CBQ* 41 (1979): 1–17.

Moule, C. F. D. "The Meaning of 'Life' in the Gospel and Epistles of St. John: A Study in the Story of Lazarus, John 11:1–44." *Theology* 78 (1975): 114–25.

Mussner, Franz. *The Historical Jesus in the Gospel of St. John.* Translated by W. J. O'Hara. London: Burns & Oates, 1967.

Newman, Carey C. "Resurrection as Glory: Divine Presence and Christian Origins." In *The Resurrection: An Interdisciplinary Symposium on the*

Resurrection of Jesus, edited by Stephen T. Davis, Daniel Kendall, Gerald O'Collins, 59–89. New York: Oxford University Press, 1997.

Nicol, W. *The Semeia in the Fourth Gospel: Tradition and Redaction.* NovTSup. Leiden: E. J. Brill, 1972.

O'Collins, Gerald, and Daniel Kendall. "Mary Magdalene as Major Witness to Jesus' Resurrection." *TS* 48 (1987): 631–46.

O'Day, Gail R. *Revelation in the Fourth Gospel: Narrative Mode and Theological Claim.* Philadelphia: Fortress, 1986.

Origen. "On First Principles." In *Origen,* translated by Rowan A. Greer, with a preface by Hans Urs von Balthasar, 171–216. Classics of Western Spirituality. New York: Paulist, 1979.

Painter, John, R. Alan Culpepper, and Fernando F. Segovia, ed. *Word, Theology, and Community in John.* St. Louis, Mo.: Chalice Press, 2002.

Palmer, Richard E. *Hermeneutics: Interpretation Theory in Schleiermacher, Dilthey, Heidegger, and Gadamer.* Northwestern University Studies in Phenomenology and Existential Philosophy. Evanston, Ill.: Northwestern University Press, 1969.

Pamment, Margaret. "John 3:5: 'Unless One is Born of Water and the Spirit, He Cannot Enter the Kingdom of God.'" *NovT* 25 (1983): 189–90.

Patte, Daniel. *What is Structural Exegesis?* Guides to Biblical Scholarship. Philadelphia: Fortress, 1976.

Pazdan, Mary Margaret. "Nicodemus and the Samaritan Woman: Contrasting Models of Discipleship." *BTB* 17 (1987): 145–48.

Perkins, Pheme. *The Gospel According to St. John: A Theological Commentary.* Chicago: Franciscan Herald Press, 1978.

Plaskow, Judith. "Anti-Judaism in Feminist Christian Interpretation." In *Searching the Scriptures,* vol. 1, *A Feminist Introduction,* edited by Elisabeth Schüssler Fiorenza, with Shelly Matthews, 117–29. New York: Crossroad, 1993.

Pollard, T. Evan. "The Raising of Lazarus (John XI)," edited by E. A. Livingston. *SE* 6 = *TU* 112, 434–43. Berlin: Akademie Verlag, 1973.

Pontifical Biblical Commission. "Can Women Be Priests?" *Origins* 6 (1976): 92–96.

Powell, Mark Allan. *What is Narrative Criticism?* Guides to Biblical Scholarship. Minneapolis: Fortress, 1990.

Purvis, James D. "The Samaritans and Judaism." In *Early Judaism and Its Modern Interpreters,* edited by Robert Kraft and George W. E. Nickelsburg, 81–98. Atlanta: Scholars Press, 1986.

Reese, James M. "The Historical Image of Mary in the New Testament." *Marian Studies* 28 (1977): 27–44.

Reid, Barbara. *Choosing the Better Part?: Women in the Gospel of Luke*. Collegeville, Minn.: Liturgical Press, 1996.

Ricci, Carla. *Mary Magdalene and Many Others: Women Who Followed Jesus*. Minneapolis: Fortress Press, 1994.

Ricoeur, Paul. "Biblical Hermeneutics: The Metaphorical Process." *Semeia* 4 (1975): 27–148.

―――. "Creativity in Language: Word, Polysemy, Metaphor." *Philosophy Today* 17 (1973): 97–111.

―――. "Existence and Hermeneutics," translated by Kathleen McLaughlin. In *The Conflict of Interpretations: Essays in Hermeneutics*, edited by Don Ihde, 3–24. Evanston, Ill.: Northwestern University Press, 1974.

―――. "The Hermeneutical Function of Distanciation." *Philosophy Today* 17 (1973): 129–41.

―――. "Hermeneutics and the Critique of Ideology." In *Hermeneutics and the Human Sciences*, edited and translated by John B. Thompson, 63–100. Cambridge: Cambridge University Press, 1981.

―――. *Interpretation Theory: Discourse and the Surplus of Meaning*. Fort Worth: Texas Christian University Press, 1976.

―――. *The Symbolism of Evil*. Translated by Emerson Buchanan. Boston: Beacon, 1967.

Rochais, Gérard. *Les récits de résurrection des morts dans le Nouveau Testament*. SNTSMS. Cambridge: Cambridge University Press, 1981.

Ruether, Rosemary Radford. "Christology and Jewish-Christian Relations." In *To Change the World: Christology and Cultural Criticism*, 31–43. New York: Crossroad, 1981.

Russell, Letty M., ed. *Feminist Interpretation of the Bible*. Philadelphia: Westminster, 1985.

Sakenfeld, Katherine D. "Feminist Perspectives on Bible and Theology: An Introduction to Selected Issues and Literature." *Int* 42 (1988): 5–18.

―――. "Feminist Uses of Biblical Materials." In *Feminist Interpretation of the Bible*, edited by Letty M. Russell, 55–64. Philadelphia: Westminster, 1985.

Sanders, J. N. "Lazarus of Bethany." In *IDB*, 3:103.

Schlier, Heinrich. *Über die Auferstehung Jesu Christi*. Kriterion 10. Einsiedeln: Johannes-Verlag, 1968.

Schnackenburg, Rudolf. *The Gospel According to John*. Vol. 1. Translated by K. Smith. New York: Herder & Herder, 1968.

―――. "Der Jünger, den Jesus liebte." In *Evangelisch-Katholischer Kommentar zum Neuen Testament*. Vorarbeiten Heft 2, 97–117. Zurich: Benziger Verlag, 1970.

Schneiders, Sandra M. *Beyond Patching: Faith and Feminism in the Catholic Church.* Mahwah, N.J.: Paulist, 1991.

———. "Biblical Spirituality: Life, Literature, and Learning." In *Doors of Understanding: Conversations in Global Spirituality in Honor of Ewert Cousins,* edited by Steven Chase, 51–76. Quincy, Ill.: Franciscan, 1997.

———. "Faith, Hermeneutics, and the Literal Sense of Scripture." *TS* 39 (1978): 719–36.

———. "Feminist Ideology Criticism and Biblical Hermeneutics." *BTB* 19 (1989): 3–10.

———. "From Exegesis to Hermeneutics: The Problem of the Contemporary Meaning of Scripture." *Horizons* 8 (1981): 23–39.

———. *The Johannine Resurrection Narrative: An Exegetical and Theological Study of John 20 as a Synthesis of Johannine Spirituality.* Ann Arbor, Mich.: University Microfilms, 1982.

———. "Living Word or Dead(ly) Letter: The Encounter Between the New Testament and Contemporary Experience." In *The Catholic Theological Society of America: Proceedings of the Forty-Seventh Annual Convention Held in Pittsburgh 11–14 June 1992, Volume 47,* edited by Paul Crowley, 45–60. Santa Clara, Calif.: Santa Clara University, 1992.

———. "The Paschal Imagination: Objectivity and Subjectivity in New Testament Interpretation." *TS* 43 (1982): 52–68.

———. *The Revelatory Text: Interpreting the New Testament as Sacred Scripture.* 2nd ed. Collegeville, Minn.: Liturgical Press, 1999.

———. "Scripture and Spirituality." In *Christian Spirituality: Origins to the Twelfth Century,* edited by Bernard McGinn and John Meyendorff, 1–20. World Spirituality: An Encyclopedic History of the Religious Quest. New York: Crossroad, 1985.

———. "Senses of Scripture." In *The HarperCollins Encyclopedia of Catholicism,* edited by Richard P. McBrien, 1175–76. New York: HarperCollins, 1995.

Schüssler Fiorenza, Elisabeth. *But She Said: Feminist Practices of Biblical Interpretation.* Boston: Beacon, 1992.

———. "The Ethics of Biblical Interpretation: Decentering Biblical Scholarship." *JBL* 107 (1988): 3–17.

———. "A Feminist Critical Interpretation for Liberation: Martha and Mary: Lk. 10:38–42." *Religion and the Intellectual Life* 3 (1986): 21–36.

———. "The Function of Scripture in the Liberation Struggle: A Critical Feminist Hermeneutics and Liberation Theology." In *Bread Not Stone: The Challenge of Feminist Biblical Interpretation,* 43–63. Boston: Beacon, 1984.

————. *In Memory of Her: A Feminist Theological Reconstruction of Christian Origins.* New York: Crossroad, 1983.

————. "The Politics of Otherness: Biblical Interpretation as a Critical Praxis for Liberation." In *The Future of Liberation Theology: Essays in Honor of Gustavo Gutiérrez,* 311–25. Maryknoll, N.Y.: Orbis, 1989.

Scobie, Charles H. H. "The Origin and Development of Samaritan Christianity." *NTS* 19 (1972–73): 390–414.

Scott, Martin. *Sophia and the Johannine Jesus.* Sheffield: JSOT Press, 1992.

Segovia, Fernando F. *The Farewell of the Word: The Johannine Call to Abide.* Minneapolis: Fortress, 1991.

Seim, Turid Karlsen. "Roles of Women in the Gospel of John." In *Aspects on the Johannine Literature: Papers Presented at a Conference of Scandinavian New Testament Exegetes at Uppsala, June 16-19, 1986,* edited by Lars Hartman and Birger Olsson, 56–73. Coniectanea Biblica: New Testament Series 18. Uppsala: Uppsala Universitet, 1987.

Setel, T. Drorah. "Prophets and Pornography: Female Sexual Imagery in Hosea." In *Feminist Interpretation of the Bible,* edited by Letty M. Russell, 86–95. Philadelphia: Westminster, 1985.

Sloyan, Gerard S. "The Gnostic Adoption of John's Gospel and Its Canonization by the Church Catholic." *BTB* 26 (1996): 125–32.

Smalley, Beryl. *The Study of the Bible in the Middle Ages.* Notre Dame, Ind.: University of Notre Dame Press, 1964.

Smiga, George M. *Pain and Polemic: Anti-Judaism in the Gospels.* New York: Paulist, 1992.

Smith, D. Moody. *John Among the Gospels: The Relationship in Twentieth-Century Research.* Minneapolis: Fortress, 1992.

————. "John and the Synoptics in Light of the Problem of Faith and History." In *Faith and History: Essays in Honor of Paul W. Meyer,* edited by John T. Carroll, Charles H. Cosgrove, and E. Elizabeth Johnson, 74–89. Scholars Press Homage Series. Atlanta: Scholars Press, 1990.

Smith, Wilfred Cantwell. "The Study of Religion and the Study of the Bible." In *Religious Diversity,* 41–56. New York: Harper & Row, 1976.

Spriggs, D. "Meaning of 'Water' in John 3:5." *ExpTim* 85 (1974): 149–50.

Stagg, Evelyn, and Frank Stagg. *Women in the World of Jesus.* Philadelphia: Westminster, 1978.

Staley, Jeffrey Lloyd. *The Print's First Kiss: A Rhetorical Investigation of the Implied Reader in the Fourth Gospel.* SBL Dissertation Series. Atlanta: Scholars Press, 1988.

Stanley, David M. "Titles of Christ." *JBC* art. 78:22–23.

Steinmetz, David C. "The Superiority of Pre-Critical Exegesis." *Theology Today* 37 (1980): 27–38.

Stendahl, Krister. "Contemporary Biblical Theology." In *IDB*, 1:418–32.

Stibbe, Mark W. G. *John as Storyteller: Narrative Criticism and the Fourth Gospel.* Cambridge: Cambridge University Press, 1992.

———. *John.* Readings: A New Biblical Commentary. Sheffield: JSOT Press, 1993.

Stockton, E. D. "The Fourth Gospel and the Woman." *Essays in Faith and Culture* 3 (1979): 132–44.

Stuhlmacher, Peter. *Historical Criticism and Theological Interpretation of Scripture: Towards a Hermeneutics of Consent.* Translated by Roy A. Harrisville. Philadelphia: Fortress, 1977.

Suggit, J. N. "Nicodemus—the True Jew." In *The Relationship Between the Old and New Testament,* 90–110. Neotestamentica 14. Bloemfontein, South Africa: New Testament Society of South Africa, 1981.

Suggs, M. Jack. "The Passion and Resurrection Narratives." In *Jesus and Man's Hope,* edited by D. G. Miller and D. Y. Hadidian, 323–38. Pittsburgh: Pittsburgh Theological Seminary, 1971.

Talbert, Charles H. *Reading John: A Literary and Theological Commentary on the Fourth Gospel and the Johannine Epistles.* London: SPCK, 1992.

Tézé, J. M. "La gloire du sensible." *Christus* 17 (1970): 380–91.

The Gospel of John as Literature: An Anthology of Twentieth-Century Perspectives. Selected and introduced by Mark W. G. Stibbe. New Testament Tools and Studies. Leiden: E. J. Brill, 1993.

Thompson, Mary R. *Mary of Magdala: Apostle and Leader.* New York/ Mahwah, N.J.: Paulist, 1995.

Thurston, Anne. "In a New Age, Whose Story Can We Trust?" *Doctrine and Life* 48 (10, 1998): 600–604

Tite, Philip L. "A Community in Conflict: A Literary and Historical Reading of John 9." *Religious Studies and Theology* 15 (2–3, 1996): 77–100.

Tolbert, Mary Ann. *Perspectives on the Parables: An Approach to Multiple Interpretations.* Philadelphia: Fortress, 1979.

Tolbert, Mary Ann, ed. *The Bible and Feminist Hermeneutics. Semeia* 28. Chico, Calif.: Scholars Press, 1983.

Trible, Phyllis. "Feminist Hermeneutics and Biblical Studies." *Christian Century* 99 (1982): 116–18.

———. *Rhetorical Criticism: Context, Method, and the Book of Jonah.* Minneapolis: Fortress, 1994.

Trudinger, L. Paul. "The Meaning of 'Life' in St. John: Some Further Reflections." *BTB* 6 (1976): 258–63.

Van Diemen, P. "La semaine inaugurale et la semaine terminale de l'évangile de Jean: Message et structures." Doctoral diss., Rome, 1972.

Vanhoye, Albert. "Interrogation johannique et exégèse de Cana (Jn 2,4)." *Biblica* 55 (1974): 157–67.

———. "Notre foi, oeuvre divine d'après le quatrième évangile." *NRT* 86 (1964): 337–54.

Via, Dan Otto, Jr. *The Parables: Their Literary and Existential Dimension.* Philadelphia: Fortress, 1974.

Von Wahlde, Urban C. "The Johannine 'Jews': A Critical Survey." *NTS* 28 (1982): 33–60.

Wainwright, Elaine. "In Search of the Lost Coin: Toward a Feminist Biblical Hermeneutic." *Pacifica* 2 (June 1989): 135–50.

Weiss, Herold. "Foot Washing in the Johannine Community." *NovT* 21 (1979): 298–325.

Whitaker, E. C. *The Baptismal Liturgy: An Introduction to Baptism in the Western Church.* Studies in Christian Worship 5. London: Faith Press, 1965.

Wilder, Amos Niven. *The Bible and the Literary Critic.* Minneapolis: Fortress, 1991.

———. *Early Christian Rhetoric: The Language of the Gospel.* Cambridge, Mass.: Harvard University Press, 1971.

———. *Jesus' Parables and the War of Myths: Essays on Imagination in the Scriptures.* Edited by James Breech. Philadelphia: Fortress, 1982.

Wink, Walter. *The Bible in Human Transformation: Toward a New Paradigm for Biblical Study.* Philadelphia: Fortress, 1973.

Witherington, Ben, III. "The Waters of Birth: John 3.5 and 1 John 5.6–8." *NTS* 35 (1989): 155–60.

Wuellner, Wilhelm. "Where Is Rhetorical Criticism Taking Us?" *CBQ* 29 (1987): 448–63.

Yarbro Collins, Adela, ed. *Feminist Perspectives on Biblical Scholarship.* Chico, Calif.: Scholars Press, 1985.

Zerwick, Maximilian. *Biblical Greek Illustrated by Examples.* Translated and adapted from the 4th Latin ed. by J. Smith. Rome: Biblical Institute Press, 1963.

Written That You May Believe Study Guide

John C. Wronski, S.J.

This study guide is intended to be used with Bible study groups and other adult religious education programs. It assumes that all have read through the entire Gospel of John at least once before beginning the text of *Written That You May Believe*. Each part of the study guide corresponds to a chapter of *Written That You May Believe*. The study guide does not attempt to summarize or reflect *all* of the points made in the chapters of the text, but rather offers exercises that will help the individual reader or group to engage in the transformative encounter with Jesus that the author intends to serve. The author of *Written That You May Believe* clearly states,

> My perspective on the biblical text in general and the Johannine Gospel in particular is that of a believing feminist interpreter who regards the text as potentially revelatory and revelatory experience as personally transformative. I take completely seriously the original conclusion of John's Gospel in 20:30–31, which states that this text was written to enlighten and strengthen the faith of the reader in order that the believer may be transformed, that is, might have eternal life. My objective as an interpreter is to collaborate with and to serve that basic intent of the literature itself by interpreting the text in such wise that it is able to exercise its transformative power on the reader. (p. 211)

The perspective of the author as stated above is reflected in the approach of the study guide. Each part of the study guide contains statements summarizing key points of the chapter, questions that help to clarify complex content, exercises encouraging personal prayer and reflection, and activities that will assist in facilitating a group process.

269

INTRODUCTION

Summary

- This book attempts to engage the spirituality of the biblical text through critical and interdisciplinary study undertaken in the context of living faith. Its goal is to contribute to both biblical scholarship and to a transformative reading of the gospel text.

- The key to interpreting the Gospel is John 20:30–31: ". . . these are written that you may believe that Jesus is the Christ, the Son of God, and that believing you may have life in his name." Thus, the Fourth Evangelist's stated intent in writing the Gospel is that it should function for the reader as Sacred Scripture.

Clarifying Questions

1. How do you understand the relationship between critical biblical scholarship and a prayerful reading of scripture?

2. How do you understand the term "spirituality"?

Personal Reflection

1. Read the Gospel of John from beginning to end (in one sitting if possible). What surprised you? What familiar Gospel stories are missing? What is Jesus like in this Gospel?

2. Choose one character to whom you were drawn in your reading of John's Gospel. Return to the text and reread it slowly, noticing the qualities of this character and the feelings that s/he evokes in you. Journal about this character and your feelings.

Group Exercises

1. Ask each member of the group to share an element of his/her own spirituality. Discuss why these differences in spirituality emerge. (One way to do this is to ask each person to share a favorite scripture passage, a favorite devotion, type of ministry, etc.)

2. Discuss whether it is problematic or helpful to the church that each of the four Gospels has its own spirituality. What makes all four of these spiritualities *Christian*?

3. Present to the group three different reviews of the same hit movie. How are they similar? How are they different? How is the process of writing (or responding to) a movie review similar to the process of gospel writing and interpretation?

CHAPTER I:

THE FOURTH GOSPEL AS SACRED SCRIPTURE

Summary

- The Fourth Evangelist writes only of those things from the life of Jesus that are necessary for *later* disciples to come to believe through their reading of the text. The life of Jesus in first-century Palestine is the *root* of revelation, but revelation *occurs* in the faith life of *believers* in the community shaped by Jesus as encountered in the text.

- The Gospel text is meant to be read repeatedly by believers who are in an ongoing, dynamic, love relationship with Jesus. Repeated reading of the text engages and deepens this dynamic, unfolding friendship.

- According to the Fourth Gospel, Jesus is "the Messiah, the Son of God." Coming to know who Jesus is, accepting who he is in himself and for us, is the very essence of discipleship. "Knowing" in John is not merely intellectual assent to some propositional truth. Rather, it is personal affective commitment and self-donation to the Truth incarnate.

- The history of biblical interpretation includes a "pre-modern" period in which scholarship and spirituality were integrated, and a "modern" period in which a split between historical biblical scholarship and spirituality occurred. Today, interpretation strives to use the best methods of historical and literary criticism to allow the message and method of the biblical text to influence its readers in spiritually transformative ways. Today, meaning in and for the present must take precedence over, without undermining or ignoring, knowledge of the past.

Clarifying Questions

1. How is reading Sacred Scripture different from reading a history textbook about the times of Jesus?

2. Explain the difference between revelation as "static information" and revelation as "dynamic relationship." Which of these understandings of revelation does John prefer?

3. Explain how the "biblical spirituality" approach encouraged by this book compares to the pre-modern and modern methods of biblical interpretation.

4. Is it possible for a written text to mean something for us today that the original author did not foresee or intend?

5. Define and describe the four operations used in the interpretation of scripture passages in this book: (1) historical interrogation of the text, (2) literary criticism, (3) analysis of theological content, (4) appropriation of spirituality.

Personal Reflection

1. Reflect on your deepest human relationships. Do your closest friends merely reveal information *about* themselves, or are they truly *self-revealing*? How necessary is *mutuality* of self-revelation in a deep friendship?

2. Have you ever reread a treasured letter from a distant friend? Why? What happens in this process of rereading? Choose a Gospel passage that helps you to become aware of Jesus' presence. Read the passage slowly, paying attention to Jesus and the desires he elicits in you.

Group Exercises

1. Discuss what happens in the group when a member reveals a personal feeling or experience. Is this sharing merely a matter of passing on *information*, or is it a matter of *formation* of the group? What happens to a group that is engaged in *self-revelation*, rather than mere communication of information?

2. If your group has been together for a while, do you often reminisce about past times experienced together? What happens when these "same old stories" are recalled and relived by the group? Relate this group dynamic to John's intention that the Gospel text be read repeatedly by believers.

3. The author states, "While scholarly historical-critical work is crucial for the church's understanding of the background of the sacred text, it is primarily in the literary experience of reading (or hearing), of allowing ourselves to get caught up in the Jesus story that is being told, that we are drawn into the salvific revelation dynamic." (p.11)

Choose a passage from John's passion account (e.g., 18:28–40, Jesus before Pilate). Prayerfully read the passage to the group. After allowing some time for silence, ask the group to share their experience of "getting caught up in the Jesus story." Why (or why not) was this experience salvific for the members of the group?

4. Discuss the experience of hearing the scriptures proclaimed in different contexts: during liturgy, on a retreat, at a protest or peace rally, at the end of an ordinary day.

CHAPTER 2: THE FOURTH GOSPEL AS TEXT

Summary

- The Gospel of John is structured as a narrative drama consisting of a prologue (1:1–18), a body (1:19–20:31), and an epilogue (21). The body is commonly divided into a "book of signs" (chaps. 1–12) and a "book of glory" (chaps. 13–20). John's "simple" language and vocabulary are deeply rich in meaning. John also uses literary devices such as cyclical development, repetition, double meaning, literal misunderstandings, irony, parallelism, paradox, dialectic, and symbolism to draw the reader into the mystery of divine union.

- The Johannine Jesus almost always deals with individuals (rather than crowds), who are well-rounded figures (Martha, Judas, the Samaritan woman, etc.). These "representative" figures are developed by both using and transcending their historical identity. One trait of the character's identity is stressed to turn the character into a symbolic carrier of a particular feature of relationship with Jesus.

- John's Gospel does not merely contain symbols; it is itself symbolic. Jesus is the great symbol of God, the Word made flesh. The Gospel is the literary symbol of Jesus, that is, the "place" of our encounter with him and through him with God, just as his humanity and earthly activity were the place of encounter with God for his first disciples. All disciples are, then, "first generation Christians."

- The Beloved Disciple, an eyewitness of the life of Jesus, was probably the source of the special tradition lived in the Johannine community. The actual evangelist was probably a second generation Christian who wrote sometime shortly before the death of the Beloved Disciple. Later, the text was revised to smooth some of the discrepancies between the Fourth Gospel and the practice of the "Great Church."

- The Johannine community had a sect-like character, yet contained some members who were "closet Christians," afraid to openly confess Jesus as the Messiah or too attached to their Jewish roots. In this highly egalitarian community the Spirit was given to all members, male and female, Jewish, Samaritan, and Gentile. Discipleship and communion, rather than office and institution, were central values.

Clarifying Questions

1. Why is it absurd to understand the term "the Jews" as a literal application to *all* the Jews of Jesus' time and of later centuries? Explain why this is a good example of the importance of critical historical scholarship in doing biblical interpretation.

2. "A symbol does not stand for an absent reality; it is a way of being present of something that cannot otherwise be expressed." Explain why an exit sign is *not* a symbol in the Johannine sense. Why is it proper to say that our bodies are symbols of ourselves?

3. How did scholars arrive at the conclusion that John's Gospel was written between 90 and 110 C.E.?

Personal Reflection

1. Prayerfully read John 1:35–51. Do you identify with any of the first disciples in this passage? How do you respond to Jesus' questions?

2. How would you explain John's use of the term "the Jews" in a homily or other pastoral setting?

3. Pray with the following verses from John's Gospel: 14:1, 14:6, 15:4, 15:12. Reflect on the richness of these "simple" words: *believe, life, abide,* and *love.*

Group Exercises

1. Read John 9:1–41 (the man born blind). What detail from this story is a reference to members of the Johannine community who might be considered "closet Christians?"

2. With your group, role play a member of the Johannine community (Samaritan, Gentile, diaspora Jew, etc.). From your unique perspective, dialogue with the group about the tensions with the Jewish authorities before the split with the synagogue, *or* dialogue about the discrepancies with the "Great Church" at the time of the revision of the Gospel text.

3. With your group, first read John 4:1–15 (Samaritan woman) and then read John 6:25–34 (bread from heaven). Discuss how these passages are an example of John's use of "cyclical repetition."

4. Is your Christian community characterized primarily by discipleship and communion or office and institution?

CHAPTER 3: THE THEOLOGY AND
SPIRITUALITY OF THE FOURTH GOSPEL

Summary

• *Revelation* is the central category that governs the theology and spirituality of John's Gospel. Revelation connotes a mutual relationship in which self revelation is always an invitation to another to enter intimately into one's life, to participate in one's self-hood. The shared life that results is called friendship, another important Johannine category.

• The ever-deepening relationship between Jesus and his disciples can be captured in the terms *witness* (divine self-gift), *believing* (the human response), *life-light-love* (the dynamic of shared life), and *discipleship* (the living of the vocation to divine life).

• John weaves together a theology of the resurrection, a theology of the Holy Spirit, and a theology of Christian community into a seamless whole that is essentially mystical and immediate rather than ritual or institutional.

• In John's Gospel, Jesus is glorified in and by his death on the cross. His lifting up on the cross is his exaltation and enthronement, his return to the Father in glory. The resurrection narrative in John is about what happened to Jesus' disciples after the crucifixion, namely, that Jesus has returned to them. The community, filled with the Holy Spirit, has become the risen body of the glorified Jesus, which testifies to the world by means of the Gospel for all who will believe. The task of the community is to be, through love, Jesus' bodily presence, and thus the giver of his Spirit to all who will come to believe down through the ages.

Clarifying Questions

1. How is John's notion of salvation (by revelation) different from expiatory sacrifice or substitutionary suffering?

2. "It was a particular lived experience of union with God in the risen Jesus through his gift of the Spirit/Paraclete within the believing community (spirituality) that gave rise gradually to a particular articulated understanding of Christian faith (theology)" (p. 48). Explain in your own words the relationship between spirituality and theology.

3. What are the stages of "believing into" Jesus? Read John 1:35–51 and identify these stages. Why is it important to notice that John always uses the verbal form of believe, rather than the nouns "faith" or "belief"?

Personal Reflection

1. "Wise people do not engage in indiscriminate self-revelation" (p. 49). Reflect on a personal experience of self-revelation. What are the risks and rewards involved in self-revelation?

2. Prayerfully read John 4:46–54 (the royal official). Reflect on the openness of the royal official to divine initiative. Do you feel open to God's initiative? If not, what do you think is keeping you from this openness?

3. "Revelation is never complete" (p. 49). Create a timeline of your relationship with God, starting with childhood. How has God's self-revelation unfolded in your life? How is it unfolding now?

Group Exercises

1. "Revelation achieves its consummate expression and full efficacy in Jesus' ultimate witness, through his laying down of his life for those he loves, to who he is and the active acceptance of and entrance into that life by the representative disciples at the foot of the cross" (p. 53).

   Prayerfully imagine yourselves together at the foot of the cross with the Beloved Disciple.

   One group member should read aloud John 19:17–30. After some prayerful silence, discuss this experience of "accepting and entering" into the life of Jesus.

2. "Because salvation in John is accomplished through revelation, the relationship between Jesus and those who believe in him is most appropriately
   one of discipleship, which fructifies in friendship" (p. 55). Discuss the
   relationship between revelation, salvation, discipleship, friendship and the
   death of Jesus.

3. Discuss the group's lived experience of being the risen body of Jesus. Does
   the "living water of the Spirit" continue to flow from the Christian
   community as it flowed from the side of Jesus on the cross? Give some
   examples.

CHAPTER 4: SYMBOLISM IN THE FOURTH GOSPEL

Summary

- The Gospel of John, which mediates the encounter between Jesus and the
  contemporary believer, is not simply a historical work that includes the
  occasional freestanding "symbol," but it is an essentially symbolic text in
  which the historical material itself functions symbolically. Taking this fact
  into account in the interpretation of the Fourth Gospel is not an optional
  exercise, but a condition of validity.

- Symbol can be defined as (1) a sensible reality (2) which renders present to
  and (3) involves a person subjectively in (4) a transforming experience
  (5) of transcendent mystery.

- In the incarnation, the Word of God, Holy Wisdom, became flesh. That
  symbol, Jesus of Nazareth, constituted the sensible locus of relationship
  with God. In turn, the disciple of Jesus individually and the community of
  believers as a body become the real symbolic presence of the glorified Jesus
  in the world.

- John intended what he wrote to have the same revelatory function for his
  readers that the symbolic activity of the earthly Jesus had for the first disciples. This is the key to the relation between history and symbol in the
  written gospel. The Gospel is the resymbolization of Jesus for successive
  generations.

- The "representative figures" of John's Gospel are well drawn, engaging individuals who appear in intense interaction with Jesus. Each has a particular
  character trait historically associated with a real, historical person. The

reader of the text identifies with these figures, engaging the symbol, and thus enters into the process of revelation.

Clarifying Questions

1. Explain why it is often assumed that a story which is "factual" or "historical" carries more "truth" than a mythical or symbolic story. Do you agree with this assumption? Would John agree with this assumption?

2. Explain: "John's Gospel does not copy the historical Jesus. Rather, the Gospel is *another* symbol of the Word of God" (p. 71).

3. Compare John's Gospel to a portrait by an impressionist painter. Why are painted portraits (and other artistic symbols) often more revelatory than the actual physical face itself?

4. Reread the distinction between "sign" and "symbol" at the beginning of the chapter. Why is it incorrect to ask the question, "*What does this symbol stand for?*" Give one example of a *sign* and one example of a *symbol*.

Personal Reflection

1. Reflect on your relationship with God through Jesus. Through whom have you come to know Jesus? How is this *symbolic* relationship *transforming* you into a child of God, born from above into eternal life?

2. Do you ever think of yourself as a symbol of Jesus, that is, Jesus' way of being present in the world, here and now?

Group Exercises

1. Discuss the unintended negative effect of the collective symbolic personality of "the Jews" in John's Gospel.

2. Discuss the group's immediate, affective reaction to this statement: "There are in John's theology, no second-generation Christians. All are, as were the original disciples, in direct relationship with Jesus, who is present and active in the community" (p. 77).

3. Pray together with John 15 (the vine and branches). Together as a group, create an artistic or bodily representation of this prayer experience. Then discuss the symbolic nature of this artistic expression.

CHAPTER 5: COMMITMENT
IN THE FOURTH GOSPEL

Summary

- Following the destruction of the temple in 70 C.E., the Jewish authorities attempted to consolidate Judaism in terms of belief and practice. Christian belief in Jesus as divine Messiah thus became a threat to Jewish monotheism. These Jewish Christians, faced with excommunication from the synagogue, therefore faced a choice between their membership in Judaism and their commitment to Jesus of Nazareth as the Christ and Son of God.

- Idolatrous attachment to their own interpretation of the Law rendered some of the officials of first-century Judaism incapable of responding to divine revelation in Jesus. Paradoxically, then, for John's community, fidelity to the meaning of the original commitment to the Law and Prophets entailed abandoning it because of the changed historical situation. To remain a true Israelite, the first-century Christian had to abandon institutional Judaism.

- According to John, "unbelief" is the great impediment to salvation. Unbelief is a deep perversion of the spirit that makes a person incapable of accepting the truth because of an idolatrous commitment ("seeking one's own glory") to something other than God.

- The true meaning of Christian commitment is to believe unreservedly in Jesus. For John, the verb "to believe" denotes a fundamental disposition of openness to the truth, which makes the person capable of seeing the glory of God whenever and wherever it is revealed. To believe in Jesus is to accept him, to identify with him, to follow him, to grow in discipleship.

Clarifying Questions

1. Why was the problem of Christian commitment so urgent for the Johannine community?

2. Explain in your own words: "The Jewish authorities had become committed to their commitment rather than to God" (p. 82).

Personal Reflection

1. Reflect on the way modern Western society influences your ability to maintain fidelity in your interpersonal relationships. Where do you find support when fidelity becomes difficult? What role does the loving fidelity of God play in your struggle?

2. Reflect on how the quality of your life is determined by the type of relationships you establish. What, for you, is the sole final arbiter in the case of conflicting commitments?

3. "Only the person who truly seeks the glory of God can be open to the totally unexpected, even to that which calls into question one's understanding of sacred traditions and institutions and relativizes the laws and practices that have seemed absolute" (p. 86). Have you ever questioned or rejected a sacred institution because the glory of God had drawn you into a new and unexpected experience that didn't fit the status quo?

Group Exercises

1. Discuss why the Jewish officials of Jesus' time were incapable of seeing the truth in the signs and words of Jesus.

2. Together, prayerfully read the story of the man born blind in chapter 9 of John's Gospel. Each group member should then role play one of the characters in the story (the man, the parents of the man, the Jewish officials, Jesus) reflecting back on the experience and describing in hindsight whose glory they were seeking. How does this seeking of glory bear upon the commitments of each of these characters?

3. Discuss your immediate affective reaction to the following statement: "Believing is the fundamental openness of heart, the basic readiness to see and hear what is really there, the fidelity to one's experience no matter how frightening or costly it appears to be, the devotion to being that refuses to tamper with reality in order to preserve a situation with which one is familiar" (p. 88).

4. Pray together as a group with John 6:60–71. As the passage is read aloud, imagine yourselves gathered around Jesus. What are some of the challenging choices faced by the followers of Jesus in the Johannine community? What are some of the choices faced by members of your study group in your following of Jesus today? Discuss this passage and prayer experience in terms of "believing" and "commitment."

CHAPTER 6: WOMEN IN THE FOURTH GOSPEL

Summary

- The New Testament is not an answer book supplying prescriptions for the solution of problems not even envisioned by its authors. Rather, our engagement with the biblical text is meant to form in us the mind of Christ, so that we can confront the issues of our own time in the spirit of Jesus, who is for all Christians throughout the ages the way, the truth, and the life.

- John, unlike the Synoptic Gospels, does not present women in tandem with men and subordinate in comparison with them but in stark contrast to men, with the women appearing in the more positive light. No woman is shown as failing to believe, deserting Jesus, or betraying him. The roles they play in the text, showing initiative and decisive action, are unconventional for first-century women.

- It seems more than likely that real women, actually engaged in theological discussion, competently proclaiming the Gospel, publicly confessing their faith, and serving at the table of the Lord, stand behind these Johannine characters.

- John's Gospel relates two examples of male objections to the activity of women (the disciples in Samaria and Judas at Bethany), both of which were effectively suppressed by Jesus, and two examples of the acceptance of the effective testimony of women (the Samaritans and the disciples after the glorification).

- In John's Gospel, women are the recipients of three of Jesus' most important self-revelations. Women are the two most important witnesses to Jesus both during his public life and during his "hour." Women officially represent the community in the expression of its faith, its acceptance of salvation, and its role as witness to the gospel.

Clarifying Questions

1. Explain in your own words, and give an example of this statement: "The Gospel is normative of Christian life. But this does not mean that whatever was done in the first-century Christian communities must be done by all subsequent communities nor that anything that was not done in the first century can never be done" (p. 94).

2. How can the New Testament function as revelatory text in a community living in circumstances and with a historical experience vastly different from those of the communities which produced this text?

Personal Reflection

1. Journal about your feelings and reactions to this chapter. Be sure to describe *all* of your feelings: anger, joy, frustration, excitement, etc. Why did this chapter evoke these feelings? Did this chapter surprise you in any way?

2. Has this chapter brought you into deeper intimacy with Jesus? Why or why not?

3. Choose one of the women discussed in this chapter. Prayerfully read the passage from John's Gospel. How is the experience of praying with this passage different after reading the interpretations in this chapter?

4. Reflect on women in your own community who are like the Samaritan woman, Martha, Mary of Bethany, or Mary Magdalene. Describe the qualities they share with these Johannine characters.

Group Exercises

1. Discuss the situation of women in the church and world today. What light does this chapter shed on the experience of women today? What kind of world and church do these texts invite the reader to inhabit and build?

2. Have each member of the group role play one of the women in this chapter. Each woman character should share with the group something about the personal relationship and commitment to Jesus that empowered her to take on unconventional roles in a patriarchal society. What were the greatest obstacles? What was most liberating and energizing? How did their roles influence the men and the larger community of Jesus' followers?

3. Is this chapter liberating for both women *and* men? Role play a conversation among the male disciples that might have followed the scene with Jesus and the Samaritan woman (John:4:27–38).

CHAPTER 7: BORN ANEW (JOHN 3:1–15)

Summary

- The Nicodemus text engages the reader to the point that she or he partic-ipates in building up the multilayered meaning and, at the same time, comes to the decisions that involve him or her in the community of believ-ers that the evangelist is trying to create. The locus of *meaning* and *revela-tion* of the text is thus the *text as it stands* in interaction with the reader. The irony, symbolism, double meanings and metaphors of the text engage the reader just as the works and words of Jesus engaged his first disciples with the newness of ongoing revelation.

- The textual Nicodemus is actually a type of the true Israelite, who pro-gresses in faith from seeing the signs, to doing the truth according to the scriptures, to finally confessing Jesus openly as the one in whom the Old Testament finds its fulfillment.

- The reader is meant to identify with Nicodemus who is enslaved by the theological assumptions of the religious establishment, and thus not pre-pared to hear what is really new in the revelation of Jesus. A "feminist sus-picion" alerts the interpreter of this passage to the ignoring, neutralizing, distorting and suppressing of women's experience.

Clarifying Questions

1. Explain why the Nicodemus text is a good example of the following state-ment: "The text remains a fountain of meaning whose waters can be end-lessly gathered but never exhausted" (p. 124).

2. What does it mean to say that the primary meaning of the text lies not "behind it in history but in it as text" (p. 123)?

Personal Reflection

1. Read John 3:1–21. What are your initial feelings toward Jesus as you read this passage?
   What are your feelings toward Nicodemus? Are these feelings the same after several readings of the passage?

2. Nicodemus comes to Jesus "at night." When you pray with this passage, what effect does this detail of the story have on you?

3. Have you ever come to know Jesus more deeply by "*doing* the truth?" Describe this experience.

Group Exercises

1. Read John 7:50–52 and John 19:39–42. Discuss how these later passages about Nicodemus relate to the dialogue in John 3.

2. Reread John 3:1–15 together as a group. Identify the many examples of the evangelist's use of irony. Discuss how this literary technique engages the reader, thus contributing to the meaning of the passage. How does the use of irony engage the reader in the quest for meaning, and lead the reader to automatically sympathize with Nicodemus?

3. Discuss the image of God as *mother* in John 3.

CHAPTER 8: INCLUSIVE DISCIPLESHIP
(JOHN 4:1–42)

Summary

- The transformational hermeneutic of feminism aims not only at the liberation of the oppressed through the transformation of society but at the liberation of the biblical text from its own participation in the oppression of women and the transformation of the church that continues to model, underwrite, and legitimate the oppression of women in family and society.

- The interpreters of the biblical text never have been, and are not now, objective. Everyone interprets from a perspective that is controlled to some extent by her or his own social location.

- Feminist critical strategies include (1) translation, (2) focusing on texts with liberating potential, (3) raising women to visibility, (4) revealing the text's "secrets," (5) rescuing the text from misinterpretation.

- The hermeneutical approach of this chapter is aimed at allowing the world of Christian discipleship as it is projected by this Gospel text to emerge and invite the transformative participation of the reader. The chapter describes the identity and role of the Samaritan woman as "Christian disciple-apostle."

Clarifying Questions

1. What is the connection between the story in John 4 and the postresurrection experience of the presence of Samaritan converts in the Johannine community?

2. What kind of "type story" is this, and what is its relation to the "Cana to Cana" literary development of John 2–4?

3. Explain why it can be said that the dialogue between Jesus and the woman is really not about her private moral life.

Personal Reflection

1. What was your initial reaction to this *interpretation* of the *text*? Did the interpretation process itself have a transforming effect on you? How is this similar to the effect *Jesus* had on his first disciples?

2. Describe the living water for which *you* thirst.

3. Jesus meets the woman at noon, the brightest time of the day. What effect does this detail of the story have on you when you pray with the passage?

Group Exercises

1. Discuss how this text is usually approached by preachers. Why is it so easy to simply focus on the woman's sinfulness? As a group, propose some ways that a feminist interpretation of John 4 can be used in preaching. Each group member should then prepare a homily based on the insights gained from group discussion and prayer.

2. As a group, role play the town's reaction to the woman's message about Jesus. What are some of the changes in the town that might have been initiated during Jesus' two-day stay there?

3. Discuss how Jesus' dialogue with the Samaritan woman differs from his dialogue with Nicodemus in John 3.

4. What kind of world, and what kind of church, does the text of John 4 project and invite you to inhabit? Why would a feminist reader also experience the "not yet" quality of this new world? What concrete things can

you do as a group that will lead to the transformation of this world into the world of discipleship that the text projects?

CHAPTER 9: TO SEE OR NOT TO SEE
(JOHN 9:1–41)

Summary

- The man born blind is "everychristian" in John's community who came into the world incapable of seeing the reign of God but who, through washing in the "Sent One," is enlightened and enlivened by God, and is able to respond as an *alter Christus* to questions posed by friends or challenges posed by enemies.

- John 9 is a long trial scene in which witnesses are called and interrogated by "the Jews" who assert their authority over the man's revelatory experience. The man, like Jesus throughout the Gospel, refuses to testify to anything except what he has seen and heard. His capacity for salvific revelation lies in his openness and fidelity to reality and his own experience of it.

- Seeking one's own glory seems to be the root of the incapacity of some people to believe. God alone is the source and norm of all reality. To "seek one's own glory" is to ascribe to oneself what belongs to God, to make oneself the measure of what God can do in the world and in one's own life. It is to be impervious to *revelation,* which is the inbreaking of what is truly new, beyond human power and imagination.

Clarifying Questions

1. Why can it be assumed that the original *Sitz-im-Leben* for this story was the sacramental initiation of believers in the Johannine community?

2. Explain the connection between the story of the man born blind (John 9), the story of the paralyzed man (John 5:1–18), and the story of the raising of Lazarus (John 11:1–57).

3. Explain the difference between being "congenitally sinful" and "congenitally blind." What is the remedy for congenital blindness according to John 9? Does John have a theology of original sin?

Personal Reflection

1. In his healing of the Blind Man, Jesus reveals himself as the Light of the world (9:3–5). Pray with this image of Jesus as "the Light."

2. Read the story of the paralyzed man (John 5:1–8). Do you identify more with the paralyzed man or the man born blind (John 9)? Why?

3. The man born blind could not deny his experience of being healed by Jesus. Has fidelity to your own *experience* of reality (especially experience opposed to authority or the religious status quo) ever led you to "see" more clearly God's action in your life?

Group Exercises

1. Together, create an artistic/visual representation of Jesus as the Light of the world.

2. Discuss the risks involved in being faithful to your personal *experience* of Jesus. Why is it so difficult to let go of "seeking your own glory" and live instead for God's glory? What is it about Jesus that compels some people to take these risks?

3. Prayerfully read John's account of the trial of Jesus (John 18:12–19:16). Do you find yourself standing with Jesus, or with Pilate? With whom do you desire to stand? What are the risks involved? How is the blind man's "trial" in John 9 similar to Jesus' trial?

4. Look through several newspapers to find examples of people in positions of authority who resort to raw power in the face of truth coming from an "inferior." How would John describe their "blindness?"

CHAPTER 10: THE COMMUNITY
OF ETERNAL LIFE (JOHN 11:1–53)

Summary

• John 11 integrates the history, theology and spirituality of the Gospel. While history lies *behind* the text and theology is expressed *in* the text, spirituality is *called forth* by the text as it engages the reader. In John 11 the story of Jesus and that of the Johannine community are fused in a narrative that engages the experience of any Christian who has ever lived through the death of a loved one.

- John 11 answers questions of the Johannine community about how the death of believers is to be understood. Human death, though real, is not victorious because, though caused at one level by natural and human factors, it finally serves the purpose of God, which is to bring all believers into union with God in Jesus.

- The raising of Lazarus is not a private favor, but Jesus' culminating self-revelation on the eve of the passion. Just as Jesus gave physical sight to reveal himself as Light of the world and physical bread to reveal himself as bread from heaven, so he here raises Lazarus to physical life to reveal himself as the resurrection and life.

- Through the characters of Martha and Mary the reader participates in the symbolic appropriation of Johannine faith as the horizon of Christian existence. Christian spirituality is neither escape from real life nor denial of its pain but a way of living that is transfigured, even now, by the resurrection and the life which is Jesus.

Clarifying Questions

1. Explain why the death of believers was such a conundrum for the Johannine community.

2. Explain how Jesus' physical separation from those he loves is not to be understood as complete absence.

3. How does the understanding of death and life change within the horizon of Jesus' resurrected presence in the world and those who believe?

Personal Reflection

1. What is your experience of "eternal life" here and now?

2. Pray with John 11:17–27. Listen carefully to Jesus asking you this question: "Do *you* believe this?" Is Jesus looking for theological/doctrinal assent or a personal spiritual transformation, a declaration of love and total commitment?

3. Were you surprised by the strong leadership role of Martha, a woman, in this presentation of the life of the Johannine community? Was this interpretation of the text transforming for you?

Group Exercises

1. Prayerfully read John 11:28–37. After some silent reflection, discuss how this scene captures the painful reality of suffering, death, and loss, even in the midst of the presence of the risen Jesus and the experience of eternal life in the here and now.

2. Pray together as a group for loved ones who have died. Open and conclude the prayer service with a reading of John 11:25–27.

CHAPTER 11: A COMMUNITY OF FRIENDS
(JOHN 13:1–20)

Summary

- In the foot washing Jesus is presented as servant and symbolically characterizes his impending suffering and death as a work of service. Peter takes a stance opposed to Jesus' salvific mission, the laying down of his life for his friends, because the equality that Jesus' action represents challenges Peter's own desire for power and authority.

- Friendship is the one human relationship based on full equality. It may be heroic to die for another, but it is only genuine service if the other is truly another self, a friend. To die that a friend might live is to live in a transcendent way. Jesus' self-gift was an act of friendship. By sharing divine life with his disciples Jesus overcame by love the inequality that existed by nature between himself and those whom he had chosen as friends. He symbolized this equality by washing their feet.

- In the Johannine perspective what definitively distinguishes the community that Jesus calls into existence from the power structures so universal in human society is the love of friendship expressing itself in joyful mutual service for which rank is irrelevant.

- At least one meaning of the foot washing for Christians today lies not in an understanding of Christian ministry in terms of self-humiliation or individual acts of menial service but as a participation in Jesus' work of transforming the sinful structures of domination operative in human society according to the model of friendship expressing itself in joyful mutual service unto death.

Clarifying Questions

1. The first part of this chapter is a helpful review of hermeneutical presuppositions described elsewhere in the book. In light of the five presuppositions provided by the author, explain why we are concerned primarily with the meaning of the *text itself*, not with the author's meaning.

2. The last part of the chapter reviews how the hermeneutical approach to this text was carried out. Explain how this process necessarily involved the context of contemporary experience as primary and the use of the traditional tools of historical exegesis as secondary and supportive.

Personal Reflection

1. Reflect on a friend in your life for whom you would be willing to die. Describe the feelings and desires that surface.

2. Prayerfully read John 13:1–8. Can you identify with Peter's resistance to Jesus' expression of friendship? What are the risks involved in being washed by Jesus?

3. How does friendship with Jesus influence or change your relationship with other friends of Jesus—poor, outcast and marginalized people?

Group Exercises

1. Design and conduct a foot washing prayer service that reflects the understanding of service and friendship explored in this interpretation of the text.

2. As a group, volunteer to serve dinner at a soup kitchen or homeless shelter. How will this interpretation of the text influence the way you relate to the people there?

3. Describe the world and church proposed by this text. Does your participation in this world through the interpretation process lead you to envision steps you can take to transform the sinful structures of domination

operative in our church and our society? What are some of these structures? What are some of these concrete steps?

4. Do some research on the social teachings of the church. Each group member should present a document that promotes the kind of society encouraged by this contemporary reading of John 13.

CHAPTER 12: SEEING AND BELIEVING
IN THE GLORIFIED JESUS (JOHN 20:1–10)

Summary

- The face veil is best understood as a Johannine "sign" in and through which a properly disposed person can encounter the glory of God revealed in Jesus. The paschal believing of the Beloved Disciple at the tomb is the faith response to revelation encountered in this sign of the face veil.

- By having the Beloved Disciple remain outside the tomb until after Peter saw both the cloths and the face veil, John makes clear that the cause of faith is neither the absence of the body of Jesus from the tomb nor the cloths, but rather it is the face veil, which can only be seen upon entering the tomb.

- The word "face veil" in John's account recalls the veil of Moses who puts the veil aside when he ascends to meet God in glory. Jesus, the new Moses, has definitively put aside the veil of his flesh and has ascended into the presence of God. This the Beloved Disciple believes, but he has not yet understood the reality of Jesus' resurrection, which is Jesus' return to his own, the community of disciples.

Clarifying Questions

1. How is John 20:3–10 considered intrinsic to the Johannine resurrection narrative?

2. How has ideologically motivated concentration on the comparison between Simon Peter and the Beloved Disciple impeded recognition of the sign in this episode?

Personal Reflection

1. Peter's failure to believe makes it clear that paschal faith is not deduced from the contents of the tomb as from a physical proof of the resurrection. The paschal believing of the Beloved Disciple is the faith response to revelation encountered in sign (the face veil). What "signs" have led to your own faith response to revelation?

2. Do you think that some contemporary Christians, like the disciples, find it easy to affirm that Jesus is personally glorified but not to believe that he is truly risen, that is, that he has returned to his disciples, that he is alive with us today?

Group Exercises

1. Read John 14:28. Discuss how John 20 uses the traditional resurrection material to involve the reader narratively in the accomplishment of that which was theologically set forth in the discourses.

2. Discuss your reaction to the process of interpretation in this chapter. What questions guided the process?

CHAPTER 13: ENCOUNTERING AND PROCLAIMING
THE RISEN JESUS (JOHN 20:11–18)

Summary

- The primary purpose of John 20 is not to tell the reader what happened to Jesus after his death, but to explore, through the paradigmatic and foundational experiences of the disciples, the effect on and meaning for believers of Jesus' glorification.

- There are two sides to the paschal event in John: *glorification* is what happens to Jesus on the cross; *resurrection* is the communication to Jesus' disciples of his paschal glory through his return to them in the Spirit.

- The Fourth Gospel intends to present Mary Magdalene as the recipient of the first Easter Christophany upon which the paschal faith of the Johannine community was based. She is symbolically presented, by means of

Old Testament allusions, as the beloved of the lover in the Canticle of Canticles, the spouse of the new covenant mediated by Jesus in his glorification. Symbolically she is both the Johannine community encountering its glorified Savior and the official witness to that community of what God has done for it in the glorification of Jesus.

Clarifying Questions

1. How does feminist spirituality inform this reading of the text? Describe the interdisciplinary methodology of this interpretation of John 20.

2. Why does the Fourth Gospel not *need* a resurrection narrative in the way the Synoptic Gospels do?

3. Describe the structure of John 20 in terms of the three themes: *weeping, turning,* and *announcing.*

Personal Reflection

1. Prayerfully read John 20:11–13. Note that "it was still dark" when Mary went to the tomb (John 20:1). Reflect on a time in your life when darkness, uncertainty, or suffering led you to ask, "Where is the Lord?"

2. Reflect on the leadership role played by a woman, Mary Magdalene, in this scene. Is this interpretation of the text transforming for you?

3. Prayerfully read John 20:14–18. Listen to the risen Jesus *call you by name* as he called Mary Magdalene. What is your response?

Group Exercises

1. Prayerfully read the Canticle of Canticles (sometimes called Song of Solomon or Song of Songs) to get a sense of the tradition that colors the Mary Magdalene scene in John 20.

2. Discuss the implications of this feminist interpretation of John 20, especially the apostolic role of Mary Magdalene.

3. Role play a possible reaction/conversation of the disciples following Mary Magdalene's delivery of the Easter kerygma.

4. Read John 10:3–5. Discuss how this discourse about the Good Shepherd is similar to John 20:14–16. Who is the true shepherd, the true teacher, the new Moses?

CHAPTER 14: CONTEMPLATION AND MINISTRY
(JOHN 21:1–14)

Summary

- Chapter 21 is an integral part of the Gospel in theological continuity with chapters 1–20. It brings the Gospel to a close by transferring the reader's attention from the experience of the first disciples with the historical Jesus to the experience of the contemporary church with the glorified Jesus.

- Two themes unify the passage: (1) the manifestation or revelation of Jesus to his disciples and their recognition of him, (2) the relationship of two central roles in the community of disciples, namely, contemplation and mission, represented by the related activities of the Beloved Disciple and Simon Peter.

- Contemplative receptivity to the life-giving revelation in Jesus is the source of the church's proclamation, which grounds both the faith of the disciples and the church's mission to the world.

- The community of fishers is not exclusively the apostolic college but the complete postresurrection community of believers who obey Jesus' word and therefore "bear much fruit" and who encounter him again and again down through the centuries in the eucharistic meal that he prepares for them.

Clarifying Questions

1. Explain how the evangelist stresses the primacy of revelatory contemplation in this passage, while not diminishing the relative importance of church leadership and office.

2. Explain the significance of Jesus' threefold question, "Do you love me?" to Simon Peter.

Personal Reflection

1. As you read John 21, do you identify more with Peter or the Beloved Disciple? Why?

2. What is your experience of encountering Jesus in the eucharistic meal? Is it ever difficult to recognize Jesus in the breaking of the bread?

3. Pray with John 21:9–13. Has Jesus ever "multiplied" *your* catch of fish so that it could feed a multitude?

4. In your personal prayer, sit near the charcoal fire with Jesus and speak some word of love and commitment to him.

Group Exercises

1. Discuss the consequences of ministering or leading without a solid grounding in a contemplative relationship with Jesus.

2. Discuss how Jesus makes fruitful the ordinary, burdensome work of your daily life. If your group had a fishing net, with what would it be filled?

3. Who in your group is often the first to recognize Jesus' presence in the course of your conversations and activities? That is, who is the first to say "It is the Lord!" (John 21:7)? Who are the "contemplatives" in your larger Christian community, and what role do they play in relation to those in official leadership positions?

CHAPTER 15:

BECAUSE OF THE WOMAN S TESTIMONY . . .

Summary

- The authoritative tradition from which the Fourth Gospel derives is the eyewitness testimony of the historic Beloved Disciple (possibly Mary Magdalene). The Beloved Disciple of the Gospel text, however, is a *textual paradigm* realized in the leading figures in the Johannine school and refracted in the text through characters (both men and women) who realize this ideal discipleship in diverse ways.

- The evangelist, the single individual who actually wrote the text, was probably a second-generation Johannine Christian whose identity has been permanently disguised, perhaps as part of the strategy to establish the legitimacy of this Gospel in the "Great Church." The textual alter ego of the evangelist is the figure of the Samaritan woman.

- There was probably a redactor of the text whose agenda was to make the Gospel acceptable in the Great Church by softening without completely subverting the autonomy of the Beloved Disciple in relation to Simon

Peter, and the preeminent role of women, especially Mary Magdalene as the foundational apostolic witness of the community.

Clarifying Questions

1. Explain how the "other disciple" (mentioned four times throughout the Gospel) functions in drawing the reader into the text and thus into the process of coming to believe.

2. Explain why the ambiguous gender of the Beloved Disciple is significant for the inclusive, egalitarian purpose of the Gospel: ". . . written that you may believe" (John 20:31).

Personal Reflection

1. Reflect on your prayerful reading of the Fourth Gospel. Which of the disciples in the text is your favorite model of *beloved discipleship*?

2. Have you become reacquainted with Mary Magdalene through your study of John's Gospel? What words does she speak to you?

Group Exercises

1. Discuss your immediate emotional reaction to the possibility that the Beloved Disciple (historically and textually) is a woman. Is participation in the world projected by this interpretation of the text a transforming experience for you? How does this experience of interpretation engage your mind, heart, and hands?

2. Discuss how the particular questions and issues of a contemporary feminist interpreter led to this theory about the identity of the Beloved Disciple and the authorship of John's Gospel. Could the same conclusions have been reached without this feminist perspective?

3. Discuss how the group's study of John's Gospel corresponds with the following quote:

To become a beloved disciple involves responding to the invitation to "come and see" and "to remain with" Jesus, to follow him even into persecution, to see and believe through the written signs even without having seen the earthly Jesus, and to do Jesus' work of bringing in the ministerial catch that Jesus initiates. (p. 250)

Index of Ancient Sources

Index of Names and Subjects